Doing Things with Texts

ESSAYS IN CRITICISM
AND CRITICAL THEORY

Doing Things with Texts

ESSAYS IN CRITICISM
AND CRITICAL THEORY

M. H. ABRAMS

Edited and with a Foreword by Michael Fischer

W · W · Norton & Company

NEW YORK   LONDON

First published as a Norton paperback 1991

The text of this book is composed in Baskerville, with display type set in Deepdene Italic. Composition and manufacturing by The Maple-Vail Book Manufacturing Group.

Library of Congress Cataloging-in-publication Data
Abrams, M. H. (Meyer Howard). 1912–
    Doing things with texts : essays in criticism and critical theory, / by M. H. Abrams; edited and with a foreword by Michael Fischer.—1st ed.
    p. cm.
1. Criticism.   2. Literature—History and criticism—Theory, etc.
PN85.A27   1989
801′.95—dc19

ISBN 0-393-30747-6

W. W. Norton & Company, Inc., 500 Fifth Avenue, New York, N.Y. 10110
W. W. Norton & Company Ltd, 10 Coptic Street, London WC1A 1PU

2 3 4 5 6 7 8 9 0

Contents

IV. Doing Things with Texts: Theories of Newreading

Foreword

In contemporary literary study, many prominent critical theorists have also been students of Romantic poetry. I have in mind not only Northrop Frye, who claimed to find the keys to poetic thought in Blake, but also E. D. Hirsch, Hazard Adams, Harold Bloom, Geoffrey Hartman, Paul de Man, and M. H. Abrams (among others). Listing Abrams here may come as a surprise. He has not written a book specifically on his theory of criticism, and he says very little about his own method and theoretical assumptions in his best-known works, *The Mirror and the Lamp* (1953) and *Natural Supernaturalism* (1971). But he has expressed his view of theory in numerous influential articles and reviews, collected here for the first time.

Spanning three decades, these essays touch on many of the most important developments in contemporary criticism, including the New Criticism of Cleanth Brooks, John Crowe Ransom, and W. K. Wimsatt; the "Newer Criticism" of Northrop Frye and Philip Wheelwright; the "Newreading" championed by J. Hillis Miller, Harold Bloom, Stanley Fish, and Jacques Derrida; and the New Historicism practiced by Jerome J. McGann and Marjorie Levinson. In addition, one essay ("Types and Orientations of Critical Theories") offers an extraordinary overview of the history of criticism from Plato and Aristotle to Derrida and Paul de Man. Two essays ("Art-as-Such: The Sociology of Modern Aesthetics" and "From Addison to Kant: Modern Aesthetics and the Exemplary Art") discuss in detail the emergence—as well as the powers and limitations—of the remarkably influential modern view that a work in any of what we now call "the fine arts" is an autonomous object (or, in an alternative metaphor, a world of its own), to be contemplated disinterestedly and for its own sake.

Some of these essays respond to specific occasions: requests to review books (Frye's *Anatomy of Criticism* and Wheelwright's *The Burning Fountain*); invitations to lecture on topics ranging from the role of ethical, political, and religious beliefs in interpreting works of literature to the significance of various theories of "Newreading"; and opportunities to address someone else's treatment of his work, for instance Wayne C. Booth's sympathetic discussion of Abrams's pluralism and Morse Peckham's critique of Abrams's commitment to Romanticism.

Although the essays in this volume thus address diverse issues and take on various tasks, we can isolate several recurring emphases and assumptions:

1. An interest in classifying literary theories according to their primary orientation and dominant metaphors. Long before attention to figurative language in discursive writing became fashionable, Abrams proposed (in *The Mirror and the Lamp*) that we take metaphors "no less seriously when they occur in criticism than when they occur in poetry." Far from compromising the rigor of critical writing, Abrams argued, figurative language provides the theorist "serviceable analogues" for dealing with literature. In *The Mirror and the Lamp* he went on to categorize diverse theories according to the "constitutive metaphors" each typically employs—a project extended and brought up-to-date in "Types and Orientations of Critical Theories," reprinted here.

2. A commitment to the utility—in fact, indispensability—of theory to critical practice. As early as 1972 (in "What's the Use of Theorizing about the Arts?"), before the dependency of facts on interpretive strategies became a commonplace in contemporary criticism, Abrams was emphasizing the fluidity of critical discourse, or its com-

plex deployment of the (often tacit) premises, uncodified rules, and value-laden assumptions that inform the very "facts" that the critic relies on for support. Even rudimentary critical observations about a work turn out to rely on assumptions and categories that are largely inherited from the rich history of theoretical speculation about the arts. For Abrams, the critic's reliance on one among alternative theories, as well as the fluidity of critical discourse, makes criticism neither strictly scientific nor rigorously certain, despite the claims of Frye and others. Any good criticism is nonetheless rational and evidentiary by virtue of its power to yield valid knowledge about literary works. The norms of good critical discourse are precisely adapted to deal with the complexities and varieties of the literary and human matters that criticism addresses.

3. An uneasiness with "the confrontation model of criticism" (see "A Note on Wittgenstein and Literary Criticism"). This model, often associated with the New Criticism, conceives the paradigmatic critical situation to be an isolated person confronting a single, autonomous work of art and detecting features that are already there, without reference to such "external" relations as the interests of the perceiver or the truth, usefulness, or morality of the work. According to Abrams, attending to the actual discourse of good critics reveals that they bring to the critical transaction particular assumptions, categories, and modes of reasoning. Literary works, moreover, make a constant, if sometimes implicit, call on cognitive beliefs, moral sentiments, and political sympathies. A "partial circularity" thus characterizes our dealings with literature: a literary work or an interpretation can succeed only if readers have something in common with the writer even before they begin to read (see "Rationality and Imagination in Cultural History").

4. A readiness to place both literature and criticism in their larger cultural context. In accounting for the abrupt appearance and rapid development of critical interest in art-as-such, for example, Abrams draws attention to

important social changes in the eighteenth century, and especially to the appearance of a variety of new arrangements and institutions, including the commercialization of literature and the inauguration of public concerts and public museums. Though widely thought to formulate universal truths about the essential nature of the arts, the theory of art-as-such is thus seen to define the fine arts on the basis of a widely shared, though newly acquired, social function; it is also seen to have developed in response to circumstances and needs specific to the eighteenth century and to our own era as well. In addition to exploring the social origins of art-as-such, Abrams has considered the social consequences of deconstruction and other recent theories. According to him, assessing deconstruction is partly a matter of "cultural cost-accounting," of weighing what we gain from Newreading against what we lose, by reference to political and ethical as well as literary considerations.

5. An insistence that a comprehensive view conceives literature as a human product, addressed to human readers, and dealing with matters of human concern; hence that literary criticism, if it is to be adequate to its task, cannot limit itself to formal or structural considerations. Abrams returns to this point in considering a wide range of theories, from art-as-such and the New Criticism to deconstruction. While appreciating the formal complexity of literary works, Abrams emphasizes that they are by, for, and about human beings.

These five constants in Abrams's work not only contribute to its consistency, they also bring out its originality. If contemporary literary theorists share any one aim, it is the desire to advance beyond New Critical formalism by contesting the independence of the isolated literary work and questioning the disinterestedness of the supposedly objective reader. Judging by the essays gathered here, I think Abrams ought to be valued as a pioneer in this effort, even as a critic ahead of his time.

I make this judgment well aware that Abrams is often denigrated or praised in accordance with his own description of himself—in which one detects a touch of Socratic irony—as a "traditionalist" and an "Oldreader," relying on nothing more than inherited standards and common sense to ward off the nihilism of deconstruction and the radicalism of the New Historicism. His critique of these recent developments, however, is much more complex and is qualified by a recognition of their positive contributions. He appreciates the vulnerability of literary works to the diverse things Newreaders do with them. From his point of view, literary criticism is not governed by clear-cut facts, absolutely certain truths, and unquestionably authoritative rules. Instead, it is a cultural practice—what Wittgenstein would call a form of life—that we acquire by learning how to put into play complicated, fluid, and uncodified "consensual regularities," or norms. When Newreaders like Derrida, Fish, and Bloom assert that a passage means something radically different from what it is ordinarily taken to mean, we consequently lack the support of unimpeachable criteria; "in the last analysis, we can only appeal to our linguistic tact, as supported by readers who share that tact" (from "How to Do Things with Texts").

For Abrams, however, this shared expertise and tact are sufficient to provide not the absolute certainty that Derrida demands, and whose possibility he rightly denies, but a "warranted assurance" that we can claim to understand an author's intended meaning. Our assurance (that the sentences composing a text mean what we understand them to mean) is warranted by the assent of competent readers engaged with us in what Abrams calls the "evolving give-and-take of dialogue" (from "A Note on Wittgenstein and Literary Criticism"). When Abrams objects to the empirical incorrigibility of Frye's archetypal criticism, the unverifiability of Bloom's work on literary influence, the predetermined results of deconstructive criticism, and the ideological fixity of the New Historicism, I think he is encouraging every kind of critical approach (his own included) to open itself to criticism from other points of view. At best, the response to a critical commentary on a work of literature will consist of a cautious "Yes, but": *yes*, there is something to what you say, *but* there is more to say. The inevitability of something more to say motivates Abrams's pluralism—his view that only the convergence of

diverse perspectives approaches (without ever finally achieving) the vision-in-depth that constitutes humanistic truth.

Abrams's pluralism reaches its limits when he confronts a
theory like deconstruction that seems to undermine the
decidability of meaning and the possibility of the critical dialogue that he favors. Even here, however, he tries to take the
same steps as the writer he is criticizing: by summarizing what
he thinks the author has said, by quoting him at length
(Abrams's way of letting the author speak for himself), and
by giving credit where he thinks credit is due. These are not
little concessions, made so Abrams can take great advantages
(to paraphrase Blake's complaint about Sir Joshua Reynolds's tactics in the *Discourses*). They result from Abrams's
effort to bring out the strengths as well as the limitations of
every critic that he discusses.

Abrams encourages us to read him as he reads others. His
balanced assessment of Frye exemplifies the sympathetic, yet
critical, approach I have been describing. After questioning
the scientific claims Frye makes for the *Anatomy*, Abrams goes
on to praise the book as an example of the wit and creativity
that Frye rightly values in literature. The book fails as a science of criticism (a science of criticism being for Abrams an
impossible dream), only to succeed in a more important way.
Although, as Abrams puts it, the search for humanistic truths
may have no ending, in an astute review like this one it is well
under way.

Notes appear at the back of the book. Heading each set are
the details of each essay's original publication, along with brief
summaries of the essays to which, in a few instances, Abrams
is specifically responding. Each essay is reprinted as originally published, except for corrections of misprints or other
errors and a revision of the references in the footnotes to
make them consistent in form with Abrams's recent *The Correspondent Breeze: Essays on English Romanticism,* edited by Jack
Stillinger (W. W. Norton, 1984).

Author and editor wish to express their gratitude to Professor Jack Stillinger, the University of Illinois, for his advice
on preparing the present volume; to Professor Robert Calk-
ins, Cornell University, for help in finding the illustration on

the dust-jacket; to Dianne Ferriss, Cornell University, for her patient expertise in helping to prepare the text for publication; and to John Benedict, of W. W. Norton and Company, for his advice and unfailing encouragement. They wish also to thank the copyright holders for their generous permission to reprint the essays in this volume.

Michael Fischer

I. Types and Uses of Critical Theories

Types and Orientations of Critical Theories

THERE IS NO uniquely valid way to classify theories of poetry; that classification is best which best serves the purpose in hand. The division of theories presented here is adopted because it is relatively simple; because it stresses the notable extent to which later approaches to poetry were expansions—although under the influence of many new philosophical concepts and poetic examples—of Greek and Roman prototypes; and because it defines in a provisional way certain large-scale shifts of focus during 2,500 years of Western speculation about the identity of poetry, its kinds and their relative status, the parts, qualities, and ordonnance of a single poem, and the kinds of criteria by which poems are to be evaluated. But like all general schemes, this one must be supplemented and qualified in many ways before it can do justice to the diversity of individual ways of treating poetry.

Most theories take into account that poetry is a fabricated thing, not found in nature, and therefore contingent on a number of factors. A *poem* is produced by a *poet*, is related in its subject matter to the *universe* of human beings, things, and events, and is addressed to, or made available to, an *audience* of hearers or readers. But although these four elements play some part in all inclusive accounts of poetry, they do not play an equal part. Commonly a critic takes one of these elements or relations as cardinal, and refers the poem to the external world, or to the audience, or to the poet as preponderantly "the source, and end, and test of art"; or alternatively, he considers the poem as a self-sufficient entity, best to be analyzed in theoretical isolation from the causal factors in the universe from which the poem derives its materials, or the tastes, convictions, and responses of the audience to which it appeals, or the character, intentions, thoughts, and feelings of the poet who brings it into being. These varied orientations give us, in a preliminary way, four broad types of poetic theory, which may be labeled mimetic, pragmatic, expressive, and objective.

MIMETIC THEORIES

In Plato's *Republic* 10, Socrates said that poetry is mimesis, or "imitation," and illustrated its relation to the universe by a mirror that, turned round and round, can produce an appearance of all sensible things. Plato thus bequeathed to later theorists a preoccupation with the relation of poetry to that which it imitates, and also the persistent analogy of the reflector as defining the nature of that relation. But in the cosmic structure underlying Plato's dialectic, the sensible universe is itself an imitation, or appearance, of the eternal Ideas which are the locus of all value, while all other human knowledge and products are also modes of imitation. A poem therefore turns out to be the rival of the work of the artisan, the statesman, the moralist, and the philosopher, but under the inescapable disadvantage of being an imitation of an imitation, "thrice removed from the truth," and composed not by art and knowledge but by inspiration, at a time when the poet is not in his right mind *(Ion)*. Plato thus forced many later critical theorists into a posture of defense, in a context in which poetry necessarily competes with all other human enterprises, and is to be judged by universal criteria of truth, beauty, and goodness.

In Aristotle's *Poetics* the various kinds of poetry are also defined as "modes of imitation" of human actions. Aristotle attributes the origin of poetry to our natural instinct to imitate and to take pleasure in imitations, and grounds in large part on the kinds of subjects that are imitated such essential concepts as the different species of poetry, the unity of a poem (since an imitation "must represent one action, a complete whole"), and the primacy of plot in tragedy (for "tragedy is essentially an imitation not of persons but of action and life"). But Aristotle's use of the term *imitation* sharply differentiates his theory of poetry from that of Plato. In Aristotle's scheme, the forms of things do not exist in an otherworldly realm, but are inherent in the things themselves, so that it is in no way derogatory to point out that poetry imitates models in the world of sense. On the contrary, poetry is more philosophic than history, because it imitates the form of things and so achieves statements in the mode of "universals, whereas those of history are singulars." Furthermore *imitation* in Aristotle is a term specific to the arts, distinguishing poems from all other activities and products as a class of objects having their own criteria of value and reason for being. And by exploiting systematically such distinctions as the kinds of objects imitated, the media and manner of imitation, and the variety of emotional effects on an audience, Aristotle implements his consideration of poetry as poetry by providing means for distinguishing among the poetic kinds—for example, tragedy, comedy, epic—and for discriminating the particular parts, internal relations, power of giving a specific kind of pleasure, and standards of evaluation proper to each type of poem.

Later the eclectic Cicero *(Ad M. Brutum Orator 2)* and Plotinus *(Enneads 5.8)* demonstrated that it was possible to assume a world-scheme that includes Platonic Ideas, yet to allow the artist to short-circuit the objects of sense so as to imitate, in Plotinus's phrase, "the Ideas from which Nature itself derives." In accordance with this strategy, later critics used building blocks from Plato's cosmos to construct aesthetic theories which could raise poetry from Plato's inferior position to the highest among human endeavors. The claim that poetry imitates the eternal Forms was developed by Italian Neoplatonists in the sixteenth century, occasionally echoed by neoclassic critics (including, in England, Dennis, Hurd, and Reynolds) and played a prominent part in the writings of German Romantic philosophers such as Schelling and Novalis. Diverse cognitive claims for poetry as approximating verities beyond sense-experience are also found in the English Romantic critics Blake, Coleridge, and Carlyle. Shelley, in his eloquent *Defence of Poetry,* demonstrates the reductive tendency of an uncompromising Neoplatonic theory. Since all good poems imitate the same Forms, and since these Forms, as the residence of all values, are the models for all other human activities and products as well, Shelley's essay all but annuls any essential differences between poem and poem, between poetic kind and poetic kind, between poems written in various times and in various places, and between poems written in words and the poetry of all other men who "express this indestructible order," including institutors of laws, founders of civil society, inventors of the arts of life, and teachers of religion. In our own day a formal parallel to such critical monism is to be found among the critics who, after Jung, maintain that great poems, like myths, dreams, visions, and other products of the collective unconscious—or else of the generic imagination compelled by enduring human needs and desires—all reproduce a limited set of archetypal paradigms, and ultimately the whole or part of that archetype of archetypes, the cycle of the seasons and of death and rebirth. (See, for example, the reviews of Philip Wheelwright and Northrop Frye below on pages 217–33.)

Among mimetic theorists proper, however, the concept that art reproduces aspects of the sensible world has been much more common than the Neoplatonic or transcendental variant. The doctrine that poetry and the arts are essentially imitations of this world, in a variety of systematic applications, flourished through the Renaissance and well into the eighteenth century. In *Les Beaux Arts réduits à un même principe* (1747), Charles Batteux found in the principle of imitation the "clear and distinct idea" from which he undertook to deduce the nature and the rules of the various arts. The Englishman Richard Hurd declared that "all poetry, to speak with Aristotle and the Greek critics (if for so plain a point authorities be thought wanting) is, properly, *imitation . . .* having all creation for its object" ("Discourse on Poetical Imitation," 1751). And Lessing's classic *Laokoon* (1766), although it set out to substitute an inductive method for the blatantly deductive theories of Batteux and other contemporaries, still discovered the "essence" of poetry and painting to be imitation, and derived the bounds of the subjects that each art is competent to imitate from the differences in their media.

Since the eighteenth century the mimetic doctrine has been more narrowly employed by proponents of artistic realism, or in theories limited to the more realistic literary genres. In the Renaissance there had been many echoes of the saying Donatus had attributed to Cicero that dramatic comedy is peculiarly "a copy of life, a mirror of custom, a reflection of truth." In the early nineteenth century, when prose fiction had superseded comedy as the primary vehicle of realism, Stendhal put the mimetic mirror on wheels: "a novel," he said, "is a mirror riding along a highway." Since that time representational theories have been voiced mainly by exponents of naturalistic fiction and imagist poetry, as well as by Marxist critics who claim that great literature "reflects" (or at least ought to reflect) the "objective" reality of our bourgeois era.

The mimetic approach to literature, accordingly, has been used to justify artistic procedures ranging from the most refined idealism to the rawest realism. What the various theories have in common is the tendency to look to the nature of the given universe as the clue to the nature of poetry, and to assign to the subject matter that is represented—or that ought to be represented—the primary role in determining the aims, kinds, constitution, and criteria of poems. The key word in mimetic definitions of poetry, if not *imitation,* is another predicate that aligns the poem in the same direction: the poem is an *image, reflection, feigning, counterfeiting, copy,* or *representation.* The underlying parallel for a poem, which often comes to the surface as an express comparison, is Plato's mirror, or "a speaking picture," or a photographic plate. The focus of attention is thus on the relation between the imitable and the imitation, and the primary aesthetic criterion is "truth to nature," or "truth to reality." In purely representational theories, the patent discrepancies between the world as it is and the world as it is represented in poems tend to be explained not by reference to the psychology of the poet or the reader, or to the conventions and internal requirements of a work of art, but by reference to the kinds or aspects of reality to be imitated. Transcendental theorists maintain that poetry represents the poet's intuitions of models existing in their own supramundane space. This-worldly theorists claim that poetry represents, or should represent, a composite of the beautiful and moral aspects of things, or "la belle nature," or the statistical average of a biological form, or the universal, typical, and generically human, or the quotidian, the particular, the unique, and "the characteristic," or the conditions of bourgeois reality. In all these instances, however opposed, the objects or qualities are conceived to be inherent in the constitution of the universe, and the genius of the poet is explained primarily by his acuity of observation, enabling him to discover aspects of reality hitherto unregarded, and by his artistic ingenuity, enabling him to select and arrange even the more familiar elements into novel combinations which, nevertheless, surprise us by their truth.

PRAGMATIC THEORIES

The pragmatic scheme sets a poem in a means-end relationship, regarding the matter and manner of imitation as instrumental toward achieving certain effects in the reader. "Poesy therefore," declared Sir Philip Sidney in a typical formulation which assimilates mimesis to a pragmatic orientation, "is an art of imitation . . . a speaking picture: with this end, to teach and delight." Ancient rhetorical theory provided the conceptual frame and many of the terms for this approach to poetry, for it was held that the aim of rhetoric is to effect persuasion, and there was wide agreement (for example Cicero, *De Oratore* 2.28) that this end is best achieved by informing, winning, and moving the auditor. But the great prototype for the pragmatic view of poetry was Horace's *Ars Poetica,* with its persistent emphasis that the aim of the poet, and the measure of poetic success, is the pleasure and approval of the contemporary Roman audience and of posterity as well.

Aristotle has been more often quoted, but Horace has in fact been the most influential critical exemplar in the Western world. For the pragmatic orientation, exploiting the mode of reasoning and many of the concepts and topics presented in Horace's short epistle, dominated literary criticism through the Renaissance and most of the eighteenth century and has made frequent reappearances ever since.

"Aut prodesse volunt, aut delectare poetae," Horace declared—"Poets wish either to instruct or to please"— although pleasure turns out to be the ultimate end, with instruction requisite only because the graver readers will not be pleased without moral matter. Later critics added from rhetoric a third term, *movere,* to sum up under the three headings of instruction, emotion, and pleasure the effects of poetry on its audience. Most Renaissance humanists, like Sidney, made moral profit the ultimate aim of poetry; but from Dryden through the eighteenth century it became increasingly common to subordinate instruction and emotion to the delight of the reader, as the defining end of a poetic composition. Samuel Johnson, however, continued to insist that "the end of poetry is to instruct by pleasing," and that "it is always a writer's duty to make the world better" *(Preface to Shakespeare).* In the nineteenth century the influential reviewer Francis Jeffrey deliberately justified writing in such a way as to please the least common denominator of public taste, and in this procedure he has been followed by later peddlers of formulae for achieving popular success. Neoclassic pragmatists, however, justified the sophisticated preferences of the classically trained connoisseurs of their own day by the claim that these accorded with the literary qualities of works whose long survival prove their adaptation to the aesthetic proclivities of man in general (Johnson's "common reader"), and that works written in accordance with these principles have the best chance to endure. The renowned masters, John Dennis said, wrote not to please only their countrymen; "they wrote to their fellow-citizens of the universe, to all countries, and to all ages."

We recognize pragmatic critics of poetry, whatever their many divergences, by their tendency to regard a poem as a made object, the product of an art or craft, which (after due allowance for the play of natural talent, inspired moments, and felicities beyond the reach of art) is still, for the most part, deliberately designed to achieve foreknown ends; we recognize them also by their tendency to derive the rationale, the chief determinants of elements and forms, and the norms of poetry from the legitimate requirements and springs of pleasure in the readers for whom it is written. Thus the *ars poetica* looms large in this theory, and for centuries was often codified as a system of prescriptions and "rules." "Having thus shown that imitation pleases," as Dryden summarized the common line of reasoning, "it follows, that some rules of imitation are necessary to obtain the end; for without rules there can be no art" *(Parallel of Poetry and Painting)*. These rules were justified inductively as essential properties abstracted from works that have appealed to the natural preferences of mankind over the centuries; in the eighteenth century, especially in such systematic theorists as Beattie, Hurd, and Kames, they were also warranted by a confident appeal to the generic psychological laws governing the responses of the reader. Through the neoclassic period, most critics assumed that the rules were specific for each of the fixed genres, or kinds, but these poetic kinds in turn were usually discriminated and ranked, from epic and tragedy at the top down to the "lesser lyric" and other trifles at the bottom, by the special moral and pleasurable effects each kind is most competent to achieve. Poetic deviations from the truth of fact, which in strictly mimetic theories are justified by their conformity to objects, forms, and tendencies in the constitution of the universe, are warranted pragmatically by the reader's moral requirements, and even more emphatically by his native inclination to take delight only in a selected, patterned, heightened, and "ornamented" reality.

In 1651 Davenant *(Preface to Gondibert)* attacked the traditional use of pagan machinery and supernatural materials on the mimetic assumption that the poet undertakes to "represent the world's true image"; a point of view Hobbes at once abetted by proscribing all poetic materials that go "beyond the conceived possibility of nature" *(Answer to Davenant)*. To this mimetic interpretation of poetic probability as correspondence to the empirical constitution and order of events, pragmatic critics responded by shifting the emphasis from the nature of the world to the nature of man, and by redefining poetic probability as anything that succeeds in evoking the pleasurable responsiveness of the reader. "The end of poetry is to please," Beattie wrote in his *Essays on Poetry and Music* (1776), and "greater pleasure is . . . to be expected from it, because we grant it superior indulgence, in regard to fiction," than if it were "according to real nature." Later Thomas Twining justified for poetry "not only impossibilities, but even absurdities, where that end [of yielding pleasure] appears to be better answered with them, than it would have been without them" (Preface to *Aristotle's Treatise on Poetry*, 1789).

EXPRESSIVE THEORIES

The mimetic poet is the agent who holds the mirror up to nature; the pragmatic poet is considered mainly in terms of the inherent powers ("nature") and acquired knowledge and skills ("art") he must possess to construct a poetic object intricately adapted, in its parts and as a whole, to its complex aims. In the expressive orientation, the poet moves into the center of the scheme and himself becomes the prime generator of the subject matter, attributes, and values of a poem. The chief historical source for this point of view was the treatise *On the Sublime* attributed to Longinus. In this treatise the stylistic quality of sublimity is defined by its effect of *ekstasis*, or transport, and is traced to five sources in the powers of the author. Of these sources, three have to do with expression, and are amenable to art; but the two primary sources are largely innate and instinctive, and are constituted by the author's greatness of conception and, most important of all, by his "vehement and inspired passion." Referring the major excellence of a work to its genesis in the author's mind, Longinus finds it a reflection of its author: "Sublimity is the echo of a great soul."

The influence of Longinus's essay, after it became generally known in the third quarter of the seventeenth century, was immense, and its emphasis on thought and passion, originally used to explain a single stylistic quality, was expanded and applied to poetry as a whole. The effect on poetic theory was supplemented by primitivistic concepts of the natural origins of language and poetry in emotional exclamations and effusions, as well as by the rise to high estate of "the greater lyric," or Pindaric ode, which critics (following the lead of Cowley) treated in Longinian terms. By 1725 the boldly speculative Giambattista Vico combined Longinian doctrines, the Lucretian theory of linguistic origins, and travelers' reports about the poetry of culturally primitive peoples into his major thesis that the first language after the flood was dominated by sense, passion, and imagination, and was therefore at once emotional, concrete, mythical, and poetic. In Vico is to be found the root concept of the common expressive origins and nature of poetry, myth, and religion which was later exploited by such influential theorists as Herder, Croce, and Cassirer; this mode of speculation is still recognizable in the recent theories of Suzanne Langer and Philip Wheelwright, among many others.

In the course of the eighteenth century there was a growing tendency to treat poetry, although still within a generally pragmatic frame, as primarily an emotional, in contrast to a rational, use of language, especially among such Longinian enthusiasts as John Dennis, Robert Lowth, and Joseph Warton (see, for example, Warton's *Essay . . . on Pope,* 1750–82). By the latter part of the century, unqualifiedly expressive theories of poetry as grounded in the faculties and feelings of the poet are to be found in Sir William Jones's "Essay on the Arts Called Imitative" (1772), J. G. Sulzer's *Allgemeine Theorie der schönen Künste* (1771–74), and Hugh Blair's "Nature of Poetry" (*Lectures on Rhetoric and Belles Lettres,* 1783). German Romantic theorists such as the Schlegels, Schleiermacher, and Tieck formulated the expressive view in the terminology of post-Kantian idealism; Novalis, for example, said that "poetry is representation of the spirit, of the inner world in its totality" *(Die Fragmente).* In France Mme. de Staël announced the new outlook on poetry in *De L'Allemagne* (1813), and in Italy it manifested itself, later on, in some of Leopardi's speculations on lyrical poetry.

Wordsworth's "Preface" to *Lyrical Ballads* is the heir to a century of developments in this mode of thinking, and became the single most important pronouncement of the emotive theory of poetry. His key formulation, twice uttered, is that poetry "is the spontaneous overflow of powerful feelings." The metaphor "overflow," like the equivalent terms in the definitions of Wordsworth's contemporaries—"expression," "uttering forth," "projection"—faces in an opposite direction from "imitation," and indicates that the source of the poem is no longer the external world, but the poet himself; and the elements which, externalized, become the subject matter of the poem are, expressly, the poet's "feelings." The word *overflow* also exemplifies the water-language in which feelings are usually discussed, and suggests that the dynamics of the poetic process consists in the pressure of fluid feelings; later John Keble converted the water to steam, and described the poetic process as a release, a "safety valve," for pent-up feelings and desires. The poetic process, therefore, as Wordsworth says, is not calculated, but "spontaneous." Wordsworth still allows for the element of "art" by regarding the success of spontaneous composition to be attendant upon prior thought and practice, and takes the audience into account by insisting that "poets do not write for poets alone, but for men." But in the more radical followers and successors of Wordsworth, including Keble, Mill, and Carlyle, the art of affecting an audience, which had been the defining attribute of poetry in pragmatic theory, becomes precisely the quality that invalidates a poem. "Poetry," wrote John Stuart Mill, "is feeling, confessing itself to itself in moments of solitude." And when the utterance "is not itself the end, but a means to an end . . . of making an impression upon another mind, then it ceases to be poetry, and becomes eloquence" ("What is Poetry?" 1833). Later writers adapted the concept of poetry as emotive expression to a communicative, or pragmatic, frame of reference. That poetry is emotional communication is the basic principle of Tolstoy's "infection theory" of art (*What is Art?* 1898), as well as of the earlier writings of I. A. Richards, who claimed that emotive language is "used for the sake of the effects in emotion and attitude produced by the reference it occasions," and that poetry "is the supreme form of emotive language" (*Principles of Literary Criticism*, 1924).

Feelings overflow into words, so that it is characteristic of Wordsworth and later emotive theorists through the school of I. A. Richards, to give to the nature and standards of poetic diction, or "language," the systematic priority that earlier critics had given to plot, character, and considerations of form. In earlier discussions of poetry as an imitation of human actions, the chief instances of poetry had been narrative and dramatic forms, and the usual antithesis to poetry had been history, or the narration of events that have actually happened. But Wordsworth, Hazlitt, Mill, and many of their contemporaries, conceiving poetry as the language of feeling, thought of the lyrical poem, instead of epic or tragedy, as the exemplary form, and replaced history as the logical opposite of poetry by what Wordsworth called "matter of fact, or science." This Romantic innovation, positing poetry as an antithesis to "science," has become a common theoretical gambit in the twentieth century; and, as we shall see, both Continental Formalists and American New Critics tend to establish the essential nature of poetry by detailed opposition to the features attributed to the language of science.

Among expressive theorists of the nineteenth century, the old criterion of truth to objective or ideal nature was often reinterpreted as truth to a nature already suffused with the poet's feelings, or reshaped by the dynamics of desire. More commonly still, the criterion was turned around, in the demand that poetry be "sincere"; it was in this period that "sincerity" became a cardinal requirement of poetic excellence. "The excellence of Burns," as Carlyle said, clearly revealing the reversal of the standard of "truth," "is . . . his *sincerity,* his indisputable air of truth. . . . The passion that is traced before us has glowed in a living heart." Or as J. S. Mill asserted, in a phrasing anticipating the theory of later Symbolists and Expressionists, poetry embodies "itself in symbols which are the nearest possible representations of the feeling in the exact shape in which it exists in the poet's mind." The mirror held up to nature becomes a mirror held up to the poet, or else it is rendered transparent: Shakespeare's works, according to Carlyle, "are so many windows, through which we see a glimpse of the world that was in him." Correspondingly, the elements constituting a poem become in large part qualities it shares with its author: feelings, imagination, spirit, and (in Matthew Arnold, for example) such traits of character as largeness, freedom, benignity, and high seriousness.

As Carlyle shrewdly observed so early as 1827, the grand question asked by the best contemporary critics is "to be answered by discovering and delineating the peculiar nature of the poet from his poetry." Essays on Shakespeare, Milton, Dante, Homer became to a singular degree essays on the temperament and moral nature of the poet as manifested in his work. The most thorough exponent of poetry as self-expression was John Keble in his *Lectures on Poetry* (1832–41), whose thesis was that any good poem is a disguised form of wish-fulfillment—"the indirect expression," as he said in a review of Lockhart's *Scott,* "of some overpowering emotion, or ruling taste, or feeling, the direct indulgence whereof is somehow repressed"—and who specified and applied a complex set of techniques for reversing the process and reconstructing the temperament of the poet from its distorted projection in his poems. In both critical premises and practice, Keble has hardly been exceeded even by critics in the age of Freud who, like Edmund Wilson, hold that "the real elements, of course, of any work of fiction, are the elements of the author's personality: his imagination embodies in the images of characters, situations, and scenes the fundamental conflicts of his nature" (*Axel's Castle,* 1936). Another recent development is that of the Geneva School of "phenomenological criticism," or "critics of consciousness." These critics conceive a literary work, in its elements and form, to be an objectified embodiment of the unique mode of consciousness of its author, and propose that the chief aim of the reader should be to re-experience this immanent consciousness. As Georges Poulet wrote, in "Phenomenology of Reading" (1969): "When I read as I ought . . . my consciousness behaves as though it were the consciousness of another." As early as 1778, J. G. Herder had declared: "This *living reading,* this divination into the soul of the author, is the *sole* mode of reading, and the most profound means of self-development." The quotation reveals the extent to which consciousness-criticism, although employing phenomenological concepts derived from the philosopher Husserl, is rooted in the Romantic conception that a work of literature is the expression of a unique self.

The principal alternative in nineteenth-century expressive theory to the view that poetry is the expression of feelings, or unrealized desires, of an individual personality, was Coleridge's view that "poetry" (the superlative passages that occur both in poems and other forms of discourse) is the product of "that synthetic and magical power, to which we have exclusively appropriated the name of imagination" (*Biographia Literaria*, 1817). The creative imagination of the poet, like God the Creator, is endowed with an inner source of motion, and its creative activity, generated by the tension of contraries seeking resolution in a new whole, parallels the dynamic principle underlying the created universe. Following the lead of post-Kantian German theorists, especially Schelling and A. W. Schlegel, Coleridge opposes the organic imaginative process to the mechanical operation of the fancy; that is, he deals with it, in terms that are literal for a growing plant and metaphoric for imagination, as a self-organizing process, assimilating disparate materials by an inherent lawfulness into an organic unity revealed "in the balance or reconciliation of opposite or discordant qualities." Coleridge thus inaugurated the organic theory of poetry in England, as well as the aesthetic principle of inclusiveness, or the "reconciliation of opposite or discordant qualities," which became both the basic conception of poetic unity and the prime criterion of poetic excellence in I. A. Richards and many of the New Critics.

One other variant of the expressive theory deserves mention. Longinus had attributed the sublime quality especially to the stunning image, or to brief passages characterized by "speed, power, and intensity," comparable in effect "to a thunder-bolt or flash of lightning," and recognizable by the transport or "spell that it throws over us." Many expressive theorists, assuming the lyric to be the paradigm of poetry, depart from the Neoclassic emphasis on distinct and hierarchically ordered poetic kinds by minimizing other genres except as the occasion for the sporadic expression of lyrical feeling, as well as by applying to all poems qualitative and evaluative terms independent of their generic differences.

Joseph Warton and other eighteenth-century Longinians had gone still farther, by isolating the transporting short poem, or the intense image or fragment in a longer poem, and identifying it as "pure poetry," "poetry as such," or the "poetry of a poem." In the nineteenth century, there emerged the explicit theory that the essentially poetic is to be found only in the incandescent and unsustainable short poem or passage, originating in the soul, unachievable by art, and unanalyzable by critics, but characterized by the supreme aesthetic virtue of "intensity." This mode of thinking is to be found in Hazlitt's treatment of "gusto"; in Keats's concept that "the excellence of every art is its *intensity*"; in Poe's doctrine (picked up by Baudelaire) that "a poem is such, only inasmuch as it intensely excites, by elevating, the soul; and all intense excitements are, through a psychal necessity, brief" ("The Philosophy of Composition," 1846); in Arnold's use of fragmentary touchstones for detecting "the very highest poetical quality"; in the Abbé Bremond's theory of "la poésie pure"; and, more recently and explicitly still, in A. E. Housman's *The Name and Nature of Poetry* (1933).

OBJECTIVE THEORIES

Aristotle, after defining tragedy as an imitation of a certain kind of action with certain characteristic "powers," or effects, showed the way to the further consideration of the tragic poem as an entity in itself, subject to internal requirements (such as unity, probability, progression from beginning through complication to catastrophe) which determine the selection, treatment, and ordering of the parts into an artistic whole. Despite their persistent appeal to Aristotle as exemplar, however, most later critics in effect assimilated Aristotle to the Horatian theoretical frame, aligning the poem to its audience. In the eighteenth century, however, a radical shift occurred in the approach to poetry, as to the other arts. Ever since classical times the theoretical framework had been a construction paradigm, in which the enterprise was to establish the "art" of poetry, or what Ben Jonson had called "the craft of making" a good poem, which would also serve to inform critics how to judge whether a poem was good, or well made. In the eighteenth century this often gave way to a perceptual paradigm, in which a perceiver confronts a completed poem, however it got made, and analyzes the features it presents to his attention and "taste," or sensibility. Addison's *Spectator* papers on "The Pleasures of the Imagination" (1712) is an innovative document in the theory of art, above all because, by adopting the general stance of Locke's epistemology, it substitutes for the old view of the *poeta* as a "maker" and the *poema* as a "made thing" the stance of a perceiver to the poem as a given object. Within this altered paradigm, or theoretical stance, two critical models for the nature of a poem were exploited during the eighteenth century until they effected a shift, among philosophers of art, from the earlier mimetic or pragmatic theories to an objective theory of poetry-as-such. (For a discussion of the nature, social causes, and conceptual origins of this shift, see the essays below, "Art-as-Such: The Sociology of Modern Aesthetics" and "From Addison to Kant: Modern Aesthetics and the Exemplary Art.") One of these is the heterocosmic model, in which each work constitutes a unique, coherent, and autonomous world. The other is the contemplation model, in which each work is a self-sufficient object that is contemplated disinterestedly for its own sake.

The figurative model of a poem as its own created world had been inaugurated by thinkers of the Italian Renaissance—Cristoforo Landino, Tasso, Scaliger—who proposed that the poet does not imitate God's world but, like the God of Genesis, creates his own world; and, it was sometimes suggested, *ex nihilo,* "out of nothing." Such high claims, however, served at first merely as a passing topic of praise within an overall pragmatic view of poetry, used in order to counter the derogation of poets and the charge that their fictions are lies. With this aim Sidney, for example, glorified poetry above all other human achievements by claiming that the poet alone, "lifted up with the vigor of his own invention, doth grow in effect into another nature," when "with the force of a divine breath he bringeth things forth far surpassing her doings"; he at once turns, however, to his basic formulation that poetry

is an "art of imitation" that is designed "to teach and delight."
The revolutionary possibilities of the concept that the poet is
the creator of a new world began to be exploited only when
it became necessary to justify poetry against the claim by writers
in the age of the "new philosophy" that (as Hobbes put it in
Answer to Davenant) since poetry is "an imitation of human
life," the poet may not go "beyond the conceived possibility
of nature." Addison's counter-claim, in defending "the fairy
way of writing" in *Spectator* 419, is that in such products of
the poet's "invention" and "imagination" we "are led, as it
were, into a new creation," and that in its nonrealistic components, poetry "makes new worlds of its own, shows us persons who are not to be found in being." The young German
philosopher Alexander Baumgarten, in *Philosophical Reflections on Poetry* (1735), developed this concept that some kinds
of poetry are a new creation by translating into poetics the
cosmogony of Leibniz, according to which God, in creating
this "best of all possible worlds," chose from an indefinite
number of "possible worlds," each constituted by "compossible" (mutually coherent) elements and each ordered by its
unique internal laws. In Baumgarten's poetics, the nonrealistic elements in a poem, which he calls "heterocosmic fictions," are justifiable in that they are capable of co-existing in
another "possible" world; he also, in an important theoretical
move, extends the heterocosmic analogue to account for the
"interconnection" of elements in all poems whatever: "The
poet is like a maker or creator. So the poem ought to be like
a world"; hence each poetic world, since it is governed by its
own system of laws, manifests a "poetic" truth that is not of
correspondence to the real world but of internal coherence.
The adaptation to poetry of Leibniz's philosophy of divine
creation effected similar conclusions in the Swiss-German
critics Bodmer and Breitinger. As Breitinger summarized this
view in his *Critische Dichtkunst* (1740), the poetic imagination
finds its originals "not in the actual world, but in some other
possible world-structure. Every single well-invented poem is
therefore to be regarded in no other way than as the history
of an other possible world. In this respect the poet alone
deserves the name of *poietes;* that is, of a creator." The consequence, as Bodmer put it, is that "poetic truth," within the

distinctive world of a poem, differs from "rational truth" in that its probability consists not in correspondence to the existing world but "in its coherence with itself" (*Von dem Wunderbaren*, 1740). In England critics who adopted Addison's metaphor of a poem as a new creation achieved parallel results, though in less detail and without the underpinning of Leibnizian cosmogony. In explicit refutation of Hobbes, for example, Richard Hurd (*Letters on Chivalry and Romance*, 1762) affirmed that "poetical truth" is independent of "philosophical or historical truth," on the grounds that "the poet has a world of his own, where experience has less to do, than consistent imagination."

The alternative model—the concept that a poem, like other works of art, is a self-bounded object that is to be contemplated disinterestedly and for its own sake—also had a theological origin, but one quite different from that of the poem as an alternative to God's creation. The historical roots of this concept are in Plato's assertion, in the *Symposium*, that the highest good of life consists in the "contemplation of beauty absolute" (that is, of the Idea of Ideas), as seen "with the eye of the mind"; also in Plotinus's derivative claims, in the *Enneads*, that the Absolute, or One, is "wholly self-sufficing," "self-closed," and "autonomous," and that the ultimate aim of the human soul, impelled by "love," is to "contemplate Absolute Beauty in its essential integrity" and thus to achieve a peace without "movement," "passion," or "outlooking desire." In the early Christian centuries various Church Fathers conflated the self-sufficient Absolute of Plato and Plotinus, however incongruously, with the personal God of the Bible. St. Augustine, more than any other, fixed these ideas in Christian thought, in his reiterated claims that all the good and beautiful things in this world of sense are to be loved only for their "use," but that God alone, as "the Supreme Beauty," and thus self-sufficient, is to be loved not for use but for pure "enjoyment," as His own end and *non propter aliud*, for His own sake (*propter se ipsam*), and *gratis* (free of profit to the self). And in this life, Augustine says, the highest manifestation of love is an "enjoyment" of God which is a *visio*, or contemplation by the mind's eye, of God in His supreme beauty. It was the third Earl of Shaftesbury, in his *Characteristics* (1711), who introduced the theological terms *contemplation* and *disinterested* into the context of a discussion of the way we apprehend beautiful earthly objects, including works of art; but Shaftesbury dealt with such sensible beauties only as ancillary to his Neoplatonic ethical and religious philosophy, which permitted no essential distinction among religious, moral, and aesthetic "contemplation." It remained for Shaftesbury's philosophical successors in Germany, where he enjoyed an enormous vogue, to secularize and specialize the terms *contemplation, disinterested,* and *for its own sake,* by transferring their application from God to works of art, and by using these terms specifically to differentiate aesthetic experience from religious and moral, as well as from practical and utilitarian, experience.

The young German thinker Karl Philipp Moritz was the first to propound an unqualifiedly objective theory of art and poetry as such, and in doing so he deployed both the contemplation model and the heterocosmic model of art, in a way that evidenced the degree to which the two were in fact conducive to similar artistic concepts and criteria. In an "Essay on the Unification of All the Fine Arts" (1785), Moritz attacks the reigning views that the arts aim at an "imitation of nature" with the "end" of giving pleasure to an audience. Only the mechanical, useful arts, Moritz asserts, have an "*outer* end." "In the contemplation of the beautiful object [of art], however . . . I contemplate it as something which is *completed . . . in its own self,* which therefore constitutes a whole in itself, and affords me pleasure *for its own sake*" (Moritz's italics). Three years later, in his essay "On the Formative Imitation of the Beautiful," Moritz buttresses these views by adverting to the heterocosmic model of a work of art as its own creation: the "formative power" of the artist dissolves reality in order "to form and create" what nature has left unrealized "into a self-governing, self-sufficient whole." In this way the artist's power "creates its own world, in which . . . every thing is, in its own way, a self-sufficient whole" that has "its entire value, and the end of its existence, in itself."

It is evident that when, only a few years later, Kant published his epochal *Critique of Aesthetic Judgment* (1790), he assumed the perceiver's, instead of the maker's, stance to a work of art; also that he adopted, but greatly subtilized, the contemplation model and the distinctive philosophical vocabulary, descended from the Neoplatonists and Augustine, that we have traced in Moritz. According to Kant the "pure judgment of taste" (that is, the normative aesthetic perception) "combines delight or aversion immediately with the mere *contemplation* of the object, irrespective of its use or any end"; it is "the one and only disinterested and *free* delight," in that it is "purely contemplative," "without desire," and free of reference to the "external" ends of use or moral good; and it "pleases for its own sake (*für sich selbst gefällt*)." Like Moritz, Kant also conjoins the contemplative to the heterocosmic model: "The [productive] imagination is a powerful agent for the creation, as it were, of a second nature out of the material supplied to it by actual nature," in which, "following, no doubt, laws that are based on analogy," the materials are worked up into "what surpasses nature."

Various of these Moritzian and Kantian concepts of art-as-such were assimilated by Schiller, the Schlegels, Schopenhauer, and others, and became elements in the mainstream of professional aesthetics. In the mid-nineteenth century similar views emerged among practicing poets and critics, when the concept that a poem, as a sufficient and autonomous object, is to be contemplated disinterestedly for its own sake became a common tenet among French proponents of *l'art pour l'art*. One source of this view was, through Baudelaire as intermediary, Poe's laudation in "The Poetic Principle" (1848–49) of the "poem *per se*—this poem which is a poem and nothing more—this poem written solely for the poem's sake" and offering a "pure" pleasure "from the contemplation of the Beautiful." Another important source was a popularized version of Kant's aesthetic ideas in Victor Cousin's lectures on *The True, the Beautiful, and the Good*, available in numerous editions after their first publication, twenty years after they had been delivered in 1817–18. "The mere imitation of nature," as Gautier wrote in 1847, "cannot be the end of the artist." The purpose of the modern school of *l'art pour l'art* is "to seek beauty for its own sake with complete impartiality, perfect disinterestedness." This concept of disinterested contemplation, as in the latter eighteenth century, was often merged with that of a literary work as its own created world. To Flaubert, for example, the relation of an author to his second creation should be like that of God to his original creation, both immanent and transcendent: "An author in his book must be like God in the universe, present everywhere and visible nowhere. Art being a second Nature, the creator of that Nature must behave similarly"—a view that Joyce's Stephen Dedalus echoed, in *A Portrait of the Artist as a Young Man,* in asserting that "the artist, like the God of the creation, remains within or behind or beyond or above his handiwork, invisible, refined out of existence, indifferent, paring his fingernails."

In his essay "Poetry for Poetry's Sake" (1901), A. C. Bradley undertook, he said, to salvage the basic truths within the exaggerated claims of art for art's sake. The experience of poetry, he declared, "is an end in itself," and "*poetic* value" is "this intrinsic worth alone," independent of a poem's "ulterior worth" as means to ends outside itself; for a poem is not "a part, nor yet a copy of the real world," but "a world by itself, independent, complete, autonomous," and the reader must "conform to its laws." Poetry and reality "are parallel developments which nowhere meet . . . they are analogues." And the reciprocal of this concept, from the standpoint of the reader, is that the poetic otherworld exists for our disinterested contemplation; as Bradley puts it, the poem "makes no direct appeal to those feelings, desires, and purposes [of our life in this world], but speaks only to contemplative imagination."

The objective conception of poetry-as-such, expressed in one or another idiom, became the dominant mode of thinking for many literary theorists and critics, as well as for many major authors, in the half-century or so beginning in the 1920s. The "Russian Formalists" set up a fundamental opposition between literary (or poetical) language and ordinary "practical," "referential," or "scientific" language. Whereas ordinary language communicates by references to the outer world, literary language is self-focused, exploiting various devices in order to "foreground" the utterance itself, to "estrange" it from ordinary discourse, and to draw attention from outer relations to its own "formal" features, the interrelationships among the linguistic signs themselves. The loose-boundaried critical movement of French Structuralism, beginning in the 1950s, absorbed some Formalist concepts, but viewed a literary work as primarily a second-order signifying system; that is, it uses language, the first-order system, as its medium, and is itself to be analyzed on the model of the linguistic theory propounded by Ferdinand de Saussure in his *Course in General Linguistics* (1915). Structuralism opposes the views that literature imitates reality, or expresses the subjectivity of an author, or is a mode of communication between author and reader. Instead it regards a work (whether a novel or a poem) as a mode of writing *(écriture)* that, like the linguistic system that precipitates it, is a self-determining structure of interrelations constituted by a play of specifically literary conventions and "codes." The general aim of Structuralist critics, as Jonathan Culler put it in *Structuralist Poetics* (1975), is to "construct a poetics which stands to literature as linguistics stands to language"—that is, as the general laws of a *langue* stand to a specific utterance or *parole*.

Among American literary theorists between 1930 and 1960, the most widely accepted formulations were that a literary work is "autotelic," and that we must consider poetry "primarily as poetry and not another thing" (T. S. Eliot); or that the first law of criticism is to "cite the nature of the object" and to recognize "the autonomy of the work itself as existing for its own sake" (J. C. Ransom); or that the essential task of the critic is the "intrinsic," not the "extrinsic," study of literature (Wellek and Warren). The "Chicago Critics," while acknowledging the usefulness of an "integral criticism" that considers poetry, in an inclusive context, as sharing essential features with other human products, themselves advocate and pursue a "differential criticism" that deals with a poem as such, in its distinctive internal characteristics. This they do by expanding upon a procedure they attribute to Aristotle: they view each poem as an artistic whole that is formally constructed to achieve a particular "working or power"; the elements, interrelations, and structure of the poem are systematically analyzed as internal causes of that power—causes that are theoretically separable from extra-artistic causes of a poem in the nature of an individual author, in the audience addressed, or in the state of the language that the author inherits ("Introduction," *Critics and Criticism,* ed. R. S. Crane).

The most widespread and commonly applied theory of poetry in the quarter-century between the mid-1930s and 1960 was that named by John Crowe Ransom in 1941 "the New Criticism"; it became the reigning point of view in American colleges and schools especially after the publication in 1938 by Cleanth Brooks and Robert Penn Warren of the widely used textbook *Understanding Poetry.* These critics differ in the details of their theory, but share the concept that poetry in the large (with little or no attention to diverse poetic genres) is to be considered as a special mode of language, which is defined by positing for poetry features that are systematically contrary to the abstract, literal, and conceptual nature, the empirical claims, and the referential and practical purposes attributed to the language of "science." A poem thus becomes its own world—a distinctive universe of discourse—which is set against representations of the ordinary world of things, people, and events; and the integrity and boundaries of this world, or poetic "object," are carefully guarded by prohibitions against the "personal heresy," "the heresy of paraphrase" (Cleanth Brooks), and what W. K. Wimsatt and Monroe Beardsley called the "intentional fallacy" (reference to the purpose and state of mind of the author) and the "affective fallacy" (reference to the responses of the reader). The sole end of a poem is the poem itself as a self-sufficient "structure of meanings." The New Critics developed a formidable apparatus for their most innovative and distinctive procedure, the detailed "explication," or "close reading," of individual poems as a totality of "logical structure" and "local texture" (Ransom), or an equilibrium of multiple "tensions" (Allen Tate), or an "organic unity" of ironies, ambiguities, paradoxes, and image-patterns (Brooks). The attempt was often made to reconnect the poem-as-such to the ordinary world by positing as its organizing principle a "theme," which is embodied and dramatized in the poem's evolving imagery and "symbolic action," and is to be judged by such tests as "seriousness," "maturity," "profundity," and the subtlety of the "moral awareness" that the poem manifests. (See Brooks's "Irony as a Principle of Structure"; also, the highly influential writings of the English critic F. R. Leavis, which are in parallel with many of the assumptions and practices of his American contemporaries.) But as W. K. Wimsatt stresses in *The Verbal Icon,* such reassertions of the thematic and moral aspects of a poem are to be understood not in an expressive or pragmatic, but in an objective, orientation: "Neither the qualities of the author's mind nor the effects of a poem upon a reader's mind should be confused with the moral quality expressed by the poem itself." Similarly with the assertions of Ransom and other New Critics—in opposition to the positivist's claim that valid knowledge is the sole prerogative of science—that poetry is "cognitive" and provides, as Tate says, a "special, unique, and complete knowledge" ("The Present Function of Criticism"). It turns out that the knowledge yielded by a poem is not that of correspondence to the world, but that of the concrete and bounded world of the poem itself: "It is sufficient," as Tate puts it, "that here, in the poem, we get knowledge of a whole object." And as in the earlier applications of the heterocosmic concept, the mimetic truth of correspondence is replaced by a truth of coherence that is coterminous with the poem. As W. K. Wimsatt puts this view in *The Verbal Icon,* a poem does not mirror the world but, by the multiplicity of its internal relationships, becomes an object that is itself densely physical, hence isomorphic with the world, to which it stands in the relation of an "icon" or (in the term earlier used by A. C. Bradley) an analogue: "The dimension of coherence is . . . greatly enhanced and thus generates an extra dimension of correspondence to reality, the symbolic or analogical."

Resistant, in this century, to the theories of poetry-as-such have been Freudian critics who, whatever the refinements they introduce, continue to treat poetry as primarily a product, under a variety of cunning disguises, of the poet's unconscious desires. Another counter-theory is that of Marxist critics who in recent decades have produced complex and subtle versions of the basic view that literature both expresses and reflects an ideology that, in the final analysis, derives from the structure and conflict of classes attendant upon the distinctive means of economic production in any given era; the special emphasis is on the literary "reflection," in the modern bourgeois era, of the class conflicts, contradictions, crippling intellectual conditions, and human alienation under capitalism. A major new challenge to reigning views was mounted by Northrop Frye's archetypal theory, announced in his *Anatomy of Criticism* (1957) and elaborated in a number of later writings. Frye substitutes for the autonomous single work of the New Critics an all-inclusive autonomous realm, the "self-contained literary universe," which has over the ages been bodied forth by the generically human imagination so as to humanize an inhuman reality by incorporating it into persisting mythical forms that serve to satisfy enduring human needs and concerns. The four radical *mythoi* (structural principles) are the primary genres of comedy, romance, tragedy, and satire; but within each genre, individual works inevitably play variations upon many other archetypes, or inherited imaginative forms, that literature shares not only with other "discursive verbal structures" and with myths, but also with ritualized forms of social activities.

RECENT DEVELOPMENTS

Since the mid-1960s, all traditional theories of poetry have been thrown into considerable disarray by a number of intellectual movements which, whatever their radical divergences, coincide in focusing on the way in which we read, and in the conclusion that there are "no right readings" of any poetic or literary writing, hence that, since the meanings of a text are radically indeterminate, a critic is liberated from his traditional subordinacy to the work he comments on, and in fact achieves the production of meaning—the function of "creativity"—that earlier critics had mistakenly attributed to the author of a work. (These recent developments are discussed at greater length in part 4, below.) In *The Anxiety of Influence* (1973) and a number of later books, Harold Bloom proposes that a poet as reader experiences some poem, or poems, of a precursor as an intolerable threat to his own imaginative uniqueness and autonomy. This anxiety brings into inevitable play a variety of psychic defenses that distort

drastically the precursor-poem even as it is re-embodied in
the poet's own "belated" poem, and so gives this latter the
precarious illusion of being "prior" to its poetic predecessor
and model, both in psychological time and in imaginative
originality. But readings of the later poem, whether by poets
or by critics of poetry, are in their turn bound to be "defensive," hence inescapably distortive "misreadings." In essays
written during the 1970s, collected in *Is There a Text in This
Class?* (1980), Stanley Fish established himself as the most
radical exemplar of the international movement of Reader-
response Criticism. Fish proposes, in what he calls his "affective criticism," that the text of a poem is simply a set of blank
signs, an empty stimulus, in response to which a reader,
deploying one or another "interpretive strategy," in effect
"writes" the text in its formal features, and does not discover
but "creates" all its meanings, as well as its postulated author
and his presumed intentions in writing the text. In his later
writings Fish stresses the concept of "interpretive communities"; in each such community its members, since they share
interpretive presuppositions and habits of reading, are able
to agree, approximately at least, in the meanings they find;
but the number of possible strategies and communities is
indefinitely large, and since each produces its own reading
of a text, the result is an indefinite number of incompatible
yet undecidable interpretations.

Most prominent in the 1980s has been Deconstructive
Criticism, based primarily on the writings, beginning in the
latter 1960s, of the Poststructuralist French thinker Jacques
Derrida. Derrida views poetry and literature as instances of
writing, *écriture,* which, like all Western writing, are "logocentric," in that they presuppose a "logos" or "presence"—an
absolute "ground," or a "transcendental signified"—that exists
outside of, and is unmediated by, language, and that functions to organize a language system and to warrant the deter-
minability of any utterance or writing in that language. In
the inevitable absence of such a ground, Derrida claims, all
writing inevitably deconstructs itself by "disseminating" without limit into an "undecidable" suspension of significations
that involve "aporias"—that is, conflicting or contradictory
meanings. American deconstructionist critics, such as Paul

de Man and J. Hillis Miller, have adapted Derrida's views of writing, as well as his standard practice of the deconstructive reading of selected textual passages, to the close reading of individual poems and other literary works, or of passages from such works, in the attempt to show that, by the internal rhetorical, figurative, and counter-logical economy of their textuality, these works are ultimately allegories about their own language, and inevitably disseminate into self-conflicting aporias of undecidable meanings. As Hillis Miller describes the enterprise ("Stevens' Rock and Criticism as Cure, II"): "The deconstructive critic seeks to find . . . the element in the system studied which is illogical, the thread in the text in question which will unravel it all. . . . Deconstruction is . . . a demonstration that [the text] has already dismantled itself." It should be noted that neither Fish's type of Reader-response viewpoint nor Deconstructive Criticism is a theory specifically of poetry or literature, but a theory of reading and writing in general. Deconstructive critics, however, favor, or "privilege," literary texts in their critical analyses on the ground that they show more self-awareness—in de Man's term, they are less "mystified"—about their own fictional and illusionary textual tactics.

The multiplicity, and what seem the unresolvable contradictions, among competing theories of poetry has led to repeated attacks against the validity or utility of such theorizing. Some analytic philosophers, for example, have attacked all such theories as illegitimately grounded on "essentialist" definitions of art or poetry, and as manifesting a variety of logical and linguistic errors and confusions; to them, the only valid criticism consists of verifiable statements about the properties of individual poems or other works of art. (See, for example, *Aesthetics and Language,* ed. William Elton, 1954.) Such "meta-criticism," however, mistakes the historical function of theory in the practice of criticism. A profitable theory, although in its own way empirical (by beginning and ending with an appeal to the features of poems), is not a science like physics but an enterprise of discovery—what Coleridge called "a speculative instrument." The definitions of poetry or art from which most theories set out, for example, may or may not have been intended by their proponents to be assertions of the essence or ultimate nature of poetry; in practice, however, they have often served as an indispensable heuristic device for blocking out an area of investigation and establishing a point of vantage over that area; they have functioned also as the principles of reasoning about poetry, and the grounds for developing a coherent set of categories and distinctions to be used in classifying, analyzing, and appraising particular poems. (On the justification for critical theories, see the following essay in this volume.) The diverse theories described in this article—however contradictory an excerpted statement from one may seem when matched against an isolated statement from another—may in fact serve as alternative and complementary procedures for doing the critic's job, with each theory, from its elected vantage, yielding distinctive insights into the properties and relations of poems. Criticism without some theoretical understructure—whether this theory, as in Aristotle or Coleridge, is prior and explicit, or, as in Johnson and Arnold, is adverted to only as occasion demands—is largely made up of desultory impressions and of unsystematic concepts that are supposedly given by "common sense," but turn out to have been inherited from earlier critics, in whose writings they were implicated in a theoretical structure. And the history of criticism at the hands of its masters, from Aristotle through Johnson, Goethe, and Coleridge to the present, testifies that the applied, or practical, criticism applauded by impressionists and philosophical analysts alike has been neither purely impressionistic nor ad hoc, but most telling when grounded on the principles, distinctions, and coherent reasoning that constitute precisely what we mean by a theory of poetry.

What's the Use of Theorizing about the Arts?

THE DEROGATION or dismissal of theory in the criticism of art has a long history and has been manifested even by writers who have themselves engaged in both criticism and theory. In the last two or three decades, however, a number of philosophers have mounted an attack against critical theory, whether applied to a particular genre or to art in general, on grounds that, if they can survive scrutiny, are wholly devastating. For the claim is that, although the criticism of particular works of art is a valid activity, a valid critical or aesthetic theory is a logical impossibility.

These inquirers write in the philosophical climate of linguistic analysis that has been pervasive in England and America since the major writings of Bertrand Russell and G. E. Moore, and they deploy especially concepts derived from the later thought of Ludwig Wittgenstein, as represented in his *Philosophical Investigations* (1953). A number of earlier essays in this mode have been collected in *Aesthetics and Language*, edited by William Elton;[1] others have appeared at intervals in philosophic and aesthetic journals; but this approach to the problems and procedures of critics and theorists of art has been most persistently sustained, and most fully developed, by Morris Weitz, first in a series of essays and then in a substantial book, *Hamlet and the Philosophy of Literary Criticism* (1964).

These philosophers treat criticism exclusively as a mode of language, and their analysis of criticism consists in identifying and describing the use of the distinctive terms, and in validating or invalidating the distinctive arguments, in critical discourse. In this aspect analytic metacriticism (the criticism of criticism) participates in the reigning intellectual tendency of our age, in and out of philosophy, to reduce all modes and subjects of inquiry to linguistic terms. The analytic approach to the language of criticism, however, takes its cues primarily from Wittgenstein's subtle exploration of his guiding concept that to determine the meaning of a word or expression we must look not to the things it names or refers to but to its use; naming is only one kind of use of some kinds of words in some contexts. The uses of a word or expression (or of the concept that it verbalizes) are the roles or functions that it performs or is capable of performing in actual utterances, and in performing these roles, it is governed by unstated rules that are observed by persons who know how to use the language. Discourse, then, is describable, metaphorically, as a diversity of language-games, and its rules of usage (thoughAnya: implicit and flexible) are comparable to the rules (though these are explicit and rigid) that govern the possible moves of a piece in a game of chess. The conventions that constitute the role or function of an expression in accordance with its implicit rules Wittgenstein calls its "grammar," or sometimes its "logical grammar," or "logical syntax." Unwittingly to violate the logical grammar of the way expressions function in everyday language is to run the risk of philosophical muddle, paradox, and error.

Applying such insights to critical discourse about the arts, a number of philosophical analysts discriminate a variety of typical linguistic usages, each with its distinctive logical form. As Morris Weitz puts the enterprise, a problem of "the philosophy of art" is "the description of the actual functioning of the basic terms and kinds of argument of criticism"; in other words, "to get clear about the logic of critical talk about art."[2] All critics, and most philosophers, he claims, assume that the questions raised in criticism are of a single logical type, "namely, factual ones . . . to which true (or false) answers can be given," by reference to objectively existing facts in the work of art, or in the world. Weitz instead specifies four distinct procedures in critical discourse which, since they "function differently," "do different critical jobs," "play different roles," are logically "irreducible."[3] Three of these logical enterprises (description, explanation or interpretation, and evaluation) are legitimate, but a fourth (poetics or theory) is not. Though other analysts are not so systematic or detailed in their inventory, what they say indicates similar distinctions and paradigms of use, and a similar opposition between criticism and critical theory. Thus:

(1) Descriptions consist of true or false assertions about a work (for example, assertions about the words in the text, about the characters and their actions, or about the sequence of events in the plot), which are, in principle, verifiable by reference to "données," or "facts," about which there can be no doubt or reasonable dispute. If assertions of this type remain doubtfully true or false, that is because, though they are verifiable in principle, the available evidence is inadequate to resolve the doubt.[4]

(2) Explanation and interpretation undertake to clarify a work by answering such questions as why a character acts as he does, what the proper meaning is of a passage or of the work as a whole, which of the elements in a work are central or primary, how the details of a work relate to each other. Interpretations cannot be proved to be true, but they can be "supported" by "reasons." C. L. Stevenson conceives an interpretation to be ultimately normative, or quasi-imperative, and claims that the reasons are not logically related to an interpretative judgment, but serve only to "guide" a critic's decision, as well as the decision of the reader to whom the critic addresses himself, by causal (that is, psychological) influence.[5] Morris Weitz, however, views interpretations as functioning "logically," in that they are explanatory "hypotheses" which can be "confirmed" by reasons that appeal to the factual elements, and the order of these elements, in the work that is being interpreted. As a hypothesis, however, an interpretation cannot be confirmed in the sense of being

proved true, or uniquely correct, since counterhypotheses remain logically possible. An interpretation can be confirmed only by showing it to be "adequate," to the extent that it is clear, self-consistent, and serves to account for the data of a text without obvious omissions or distortions.[6]

(3) When a critic says that a work is good or bad, great or trivial, he does not assert or describe a property of the work; instead, he utters a judgment, or verdict, or assessment, which he supports by reasons, some of which are good reasons. Reasons for an evaluation involve criteria of value, or "criterion-characters," which are shown to be realized in the properties of the work of art.[7] Since the criteria of artistic merit depend on the kind of work being discussed, and also differ from age to age, from artistic school to school, and from critic to critic, disagreements about criteria (hence disagreements in evaluation) are perennial, and cannot be finally resolved. All a critic can do, when his criteria of value are challenged, is to justify them by further reasons, which may win assent but cannot be probative. Weitz, unlike other analysts, puts forward at this point the claim that some reasons for an evaluation are good reasons because they employ criteria of value—examples are "subtlety," "integration," and "freshness"—which are unchallengeable; that is, "the question, 'But what have these to do with . . . greatness?' cannot be intelligibly asked since no answer to it can be given."[8]

(4) Theory (or "poetics," "aesthetics") is a fourth, logically distinct linguistic activity which is engaged in by traditional philosophers and aestheticians, and also by practicing critics in a philosophical humor. Theory is defined as the attempt to answer, and to support the answers to, questions taking the form, "What is X?": "What is tragedy?" "What is poetry?" "What is art?" But unlike the questions about particular works raised by practicing critics, these are bogus questions, and the answers to them are fallacies. Criticism (description, interpretation, evaluation) is a legitimate linguistic activity, but critical theorizing is not.

Analysts of critical discourse share Wittgenstein's distrust of what he calls "our craving for generality" which "is the resultant of a number of tendencies connected with particular philosophical confusions," and their critique of theory rests heavily upon his associated remarks about "family resemblances": Don't assume, for example, that the many proceedings we call "games" must have one thing in common, else they would not be called "games"; instead, *"look and see."* And when we look, we see nothing that is common to all things so called, but only "a complicated network of similarities overlapping and criss-crossing," like "the various resemblances between members of a family: build, features, colour of eyes. . . . And I shall say: 'games' form a family."[9]

This remarkably seminal analogy, which Wittgenstein used to show that we use some terms for things that share no single property, has been worked by some analytic philosophers into the view that a valid critical and aesthetic theory is a logical impossibility. Their claim is that such theory consists solely, or at least primarily, in the assertion and the systematic attempt to prove or support a true and essential definition of art, or of some type of art. "Traditional aesthetics," says William E. Kennick, "searches for the nature of Art or Beauty and finds it by definition," on the assumption that "all works of art must possess some common nature . . . a set of necessary and sufficient conditions for their being works of art at all."[10] The "main avowed concern" of aesthetic theory, according to Morris Weitz, is "the determination of the nature of art which can be formulated into a definition of it. It construes definition as the statement of the necessary and sufficient properties of what is being defined, where the statement purports to be a true or false claim about the essence of art." Similarly, the narrower theory called "poetics" consists of the attempt to answer a question about the nature of "one or other of the arts, or species of them" such as literature, painting, music, poetry, drama, or tragedy. "To each question, a poetics is a purportedly true answer in the form of a theory of the essential, defining, or necessary and sufficient, properties of the art in question."[11]

The characteristic procedure is then to show that this undertaking exemplifies the "essentialist fallacy," or the false assumption of *"unum nomen; unum nominatum,"* hence "radically misconstrues the logic of the concept of art." For these general terms in fact have a great diversity of uses in ordinary and critical language, in which they are applied to works that possess no common property, but at most a varying pattern of family resemblances, among which none can qualify as a set of either necessary or sufficient conditions for the correct use of the term.[12] To this widespread argument Weitz adds another. Terms such as *art, painting, tragedy* are "open concepts," in that historical usage has assigned to them the task of allowing for application to new and unforeseen cases. Thus "the very expansive, adventurous character of art, its ever-present changes and novel creations, makes it logically impossible to ensure any set of defining properties," for to close the open concept by specifying the necessary and sufficient conditions for its application "is to foreclose upon the use of the concept which is, at least in part, to accommodate itself to these new conditions."[13]

The conclusion is that aesthetic and poetic theory, as Kennick says, "rests on a mistake"; or as Weitz puts it, "aesthetic theory—all of it—is wrong in principle," "logically misbegotten," "logically impossible"; similarly, "poetics, unlike description, explanation, and evaluation, is an illegitimate procedure of criticism in that it tries to define what is indefinable."[14] Oddly, however, such apparently disabling pronouncements are often conjoined, by aesthetic analysts, with the acknowledgment that aesthetic theory has made valuable*Anya:* contributions—Weitz says "supremely valuable" contributions—to our understanding of particular works of art. For, mistakenly thinking that he is defining artistic essence, the theorist has inadvertently accomplished something else that is useful. Weitz explains this anomaly by adapting Charles Stevenson's concept of "persuasive definitions." "Every theory of art, like every poetics, is neither true nor false, but an honorific redefinition of 'art.' " For the terms *art, poetry, tragedy* in critical discourse convey an element of praise, and what are presented as definitions of the necessary and sufficient conditions for the use of such terms in fact function as a disguised, and thereby all the more effective, way of recommending these conditions as criteria of excellence in particular works of art, and thus serve to direct our attention to features of a work that may hitherto have been overlooked or distorted. Aesthetic theory, as definition, is "logically doomed to failure," but if looked upon as the use of "the definitional form, almost epigrammatically, to pin-point a crucial recommendation" that we concentrate "on certain criteria of excellence," it serves to teach us "what to look for and how to look at it in art." Or, as Kennick puts a similar point of view: "The mistake of the aestheticians can be turned to advantage." "The quest for essences" has "a by-product," in which the definition performs real work—not, however, "the work which the philosophers assign it, but a work of teaching people a new way of looking at pictures."[15]

1. SOME USES OF DEFINITIONS IN THEORY

Even a stripped-down précis indicates the capacities of this metacriticism and its great advantages over its immediate predecessor in analytic philosophy. Logical positivism had tended to apportion all uses of language into one of two cat-egories: verifiable or falsifiable empirical assertions (syste-matized according to the rules of logic) and nonverifiable expressions, scientific language and emotive language, knowledge and pseudo-knowledge, sense and nonsense. One great advance of this current analysis is that it recognizes a*Anya:* variety of linguistic procedures in criticism, in addi-tion to verifiable descriptions of fact, which, while not demonstrably and exclusively true, are nonetheless in their diverse ways rational, valid, and profitable human pursuits.

Still, some aspects and results of this procedure seem on the face of it questionable, and especially the easy way in which it disposes of all critical theory. The claim is that, for more than two thousand years, beginning with Aristotle, some of the most acute minds on record, in theorizing about the arts, have committed the same grammatico-logical blunders in stubborn pursuit of the same logically impossible goal—*enfin Wittgenstein vint.* The further claim is that the admittedly valuable consequences of critical theory are an unintended by-product, a spinoff from an inevitably abortive undertak-ing. Now, there is nothing inherently impossible in these assertions, and the advances in some areas of knowledge provide examples of long-standing errors that seem in some ways comparable. Nonetheless, before we accept this paradox of private errors-public benefits, it seems prudent to inquire whether the fault may lie, in at least some instances, not in the critical theories that are analyzed but in the analysis itself.

I should like to pursue such an inquiry, and to do so in accordance with what seem to me to be some important implications of Wittgenstein's own procedures in elucidating the uses of language. Wittgenstein's later writings are often cryptic, and like the insights of all philosophers of genius, they may be applied in opposite ways, one inhibiting and the other liberating. One of Wittgenstein's liberating insights is that the validity of language consists in the way it is in fact used to some purpose, rather than in its accordance with logical models of how it should be used; and another is his view that meanings do not consist in what expressions name and describe but in how they are used. The uses of language, he points out, are very many, and operate consonantly to a great diversity of implicit rules or conventions; to discover the actual use of language, we must be careful not to stop at the isolated expression or sentence, and not to insist that each stage of a discourse must be a picture corresponding to the facts. Instead, we must look to the "surroundings" of each expression, and these surroundings involve not only the immediate verbal context, and not simply a consideration of that particular one of many possible language-games the speaker or writer is playing. Also (and ultimately) we must look to the "form of life" of which each language-game is inherently a part— including the kind of human purposes, interests, and values that a particular language-game has evolved to realize. This is the liberating aspect of Wittgenstein's thought because it affirms that the role of philosophy is not to proscribe or limit, but to clarify and authenticate the powers that language, in its long development as part of man's "natural history," has shown that it in fact possesses in effecting man's needs.[16]

What, in fact, have critical and aesthetic theorists been up to? In answering this question, it behooves us to follow Wittgenstein's excellent advice: Don't say they *must* have done one thing or another, but "*look and see.* . . . Don't think, but look!"[17]

It soon appears, however, that what we find when we look depends upon what theorist we look at, where in his writings we look, and with what expectations, categories, and aims.

The analysts I have been discussing cite, with striking unanimity, Clive Bell's theory as representative of aesthetic theory in general. If we look at Bell's influential little book we find that he sets out, as the title informs us, to answer the question *What Is Art?* He says that his answer will be an attempt at "a complete theory of visual art," and assumes that "either all works of visual art have some common quality, or when we speak of 'works of art' we gibber." He claims that to the question, What quality is common to all works of visual art? "only one answer seems possible—significant form," hence that although "the representative element in a work of art may not be harmful, always it is irrelevant." He then applies this discovery to the discussion both of Postimpressionist and of earlier examples of visual art.[18] It does not seem unduly omissive nor distortive to say about Bell's theory, as the analysts do, that it consists of the proposal, elucidation, and attempted proof of a definition of visual art that purports to specify the necessary and sufficient conditions for the correct use of the term, that this attempt failed, but that in its failure it achieved something of great value to our appreciation of the arts. It achieved this end because, at a time (1914) when Edwardian amateurs were preoccupied with the representational elements of painting, Bell's theory taught them—by its actual function as persuasive rhetoric under the logical disguise of essential definition—how to look at the new nonrepresentational painting, and also how to discriminate and enjoy features in earlier representational painting that connoisseurs had hitherto minimized or overlooked.

But is Bell's little book in fact paradigmatic? Do all theories of art consist solely or primarily of the attempt to posit and prove an essential definition of art, or of a type of art? And does the validity of the overall theoretical enterprise depend on the logical possibility of an essential definition of these general terms?

In this respect it is instructive to note that the philosophical critics of critical theory, although united in their rejection of the validity of general statements about what art is, do not themselves hesitate to make unqualified assertions about "art," "painting," "criticism," "aesthetics," "aesthetic theory." And sometimes they use these general terms as the subjects of sentences that look very much like definitions.

Take for example the major book of Morris Weitz, the most thorough, and in many ways the most illuminating, of the metacritical analysts. His *Hamlet and the Philosophy of Literary Criticism* begins with the following paragraph:

> Criticism is a form of studied discourse about works of art. It is a use of language primarily designed to facilitate and enrich the understanding of art. Involved in its practice are highly developed sets of vocabularies, various sorts of procedures and arguments, broad assumptions, and a vast diversity of specific goals and purposes.

This is surely a statement that, in logical as well as ordinary grammatical discourse, we would call a "definition of criticism." Its first sentence has the "X is a b c" form, in which "X" is the term to be defined and "a b c" specifies the meaning of X in the classical manner, *per genus et differentiam*, employing terms that the succeeding sentences go on to specify and expand. Weitz also asserts later that "the question, What is criticism?" is "the major concern of this book" (p. 133); so that one has grounds to claim, if one is inclined to be contentious, that Weitz's book, no less than Bell's, is a theory, in that the whole is designed to pose, elucidate, and prove a definition of the general term that names his subject, with the difference that the subject of Bell's theory is "art" and the subject of Weitz's is "criticism."

But is the "logical function" of Weitz's *definiens* to specify the essential, or the necessary and sufficient, conditions for the use of the word *criticism?* Weitz himself claims that it is not, for on the page following this definition he rejects "the persistent logical motivation of traditional philosophy of criticism that a definitive and univocal answer is forthcoming to the question, What is criticism?" But such evidence for the function of his own definition is immediately undermined by his salutary advice, in the next sentence, that "we actually 'look and see' (to borrow a phrase from Wittgenstein), i.e.,

[that] we examine what critics do in their essays of criticism instead of what they *say* they do" (p. viii).

If what Weitz says that he is doing isn't adequate evidence, then how are we to find out what is the actual role (hence, "logic") of his opening definition? No amount of looking at the isolated definition—considered as a fixed and self-identifying logical form, outside its verbal surroundings—will serve to settle the matter. The role of this definition can be determined only by examining what it in fact does when it is put to work in the rest of the book. Only after we have done this are we able to say with assurance that Weitz's initial statement does not function as an essential definition—that is, as a closed concept of "criticism" whose claim at complete generality is made plausible only by ignoring or steam-rollering over counterevidence. Instead we find that it is used not as a ruling definition but as a working definition: it serves, in a preliminary way, to block out the area of his inquiry, and also to introduce some categories that he will use to organize his inquiry into that area. For example, by delimiting his use of "criticism" to "studied discourse," Weitz rules out of his cognizance the use of "criticism" for what Anatole France called the narration of "the adventures of [the critic's] soul among masterpieces," and by delimiting it to discourse about "works of art," he rules out a large part of the area covered by the term in such a standard work as Matthew Arnold's "The Function of Criticism at the Present Time." Furthermore, by predicating that criticism is "a use of language" involving a variety of "procedures and arguments" adapted to "a vast diversity of specific goals," Weitz posits the main exploratory categories—as against the many alternative categories used by other metacritics—that are characteristic of the current philosophy of linguistic analysis, and that in his book demonstrate their usefulness by producing the profitable, if not entirely satisfactory, discoveries I have already outlined.

In short, Weitz does what any inquirer must do, whatever his subject and however he eschews *a priorism* and the craving for generalization: he indicates what he proposes to talk about, and how and to what end he undertakes to talk about it. And the more diverse the family of objects to which a general term is applied in common discourse, the more important it becomes, if we are to talk to some effect, that we specify and limit our own use of the term. For this purpose a formal definition is not indispensable (some inquirers, including a number of philosophical analysts, prefer to leave the what and how of their inquiry to be inferred from their practical and piecemeal operations), but it is certainly a very handy, economical, and widely used linguistic device, whether it is presented, as Weitz and most other writers present it, at or near the beginning of their work, or whether it is allowed to emerge by a seeming induction in the middle, or even at the end.

The question, then, is not whether critical theorists define art, or even whether they claim the definition to be an essential one, but whether all of them in fact use the definition in the way that Weitz and other philosophical analysts say they do, rather than in the way that Weitz uses his definition of criticism. The only way to find out is to look and see, and then only on condition that we adopt an inquiring rather than a contentious posture and set ourselves to see what is going on, rather than what we are certain in advance must be going on, and only if we avoid the analysts' mistake of stopping too soon at the isolated definition, instead of observing how it functions in its total surroundings. We are also more apt to be enlightened if, instead of looking at the theory of a polemicist like Clive Bell (who was the effective champion of an important revolution in taste, but a bit short on philosophical acumen), we look at the work of nonprogrammatic theorists who, by wide consent, have made the most important contributions to our knowledge. A good example of this sort is the writer whose treatise made "poetics" a standard term for the theory of an art.

Aristotle's *De Poetica*, after a brief announcement of its main topics, begins:

> Epic poetry and tragedy, as also Comedy, Dithyrambic poetry, and most flute-playing and lyre-playing, are all, viewed as a whole, modes of imitation. But at the same time they differ from one another in three ways, either by a difference of kind in their means, or by differences in the objects, or in the manner of their imitations.

In his *Topics*, 1. 5, Aristotle declared that "a 'definition' is a phrase signifying a thing's essence." Now let us assume, although he doesn't say so, that he offers the sentences I have quoted from the *Poetics* as a definition of the essence of the arts (including, as he soon makes clear, painting and dancing, as well as poetry and music), and let us assume also that he would consent to the maneuver whereby philosophical analysts equate an essential definition with a statement of necessary and sufficient conditions. Still, what matters is the actual role that his definition plays in his overall inquiry, and this role, it soon becomes evident, is not legislative but exploratory, and in a very enlightening way.

Take the key predicate, *imitation*. Aristotle adopted the word *mimesis* from ordinary language, but instead of feeling committed to its ordinary usages, he specialized it to suit the purposes of his inquiry—no less legitimately than physicists in later centuries specialized the ordinary meanings of words like *mass, acceleration, energy* for their own, very different purposes. Plato, for example, had employed *mimesis* to include the work of the artisan, the statesman, and the moralist, as well as the poet and artist. That usage suited the purpose of his inquiry, in which the prime issue, as he says in his discussion of poetry in the *Republic*, is "whether a man is to be good or bad"; and the basic terms of his theory are devised to make it impossible to consider poetry otherwise than in rivalry with all other human products and institutions, although at a farther remove from the ultimate criterion of all reality and value, the realm of Ideas. Thus as Plato's lawmaker, in politely rejecting poets from his state, explains: "Our whole state is an imitation of the best and noblest life. . . . You are poets and we are poets . . . rivals and antagonists in the noblest of dramas."[19] Aristotle, as the course of the *Poetics* makes clear, establishes for *mimesis* a very different role, as a term specific to both rudimentary and developed forms of poetry and the arts as distinct from all other human activities and products, and he thereby sets up a new language-game. For this game, by severing poetry from rivalry with other human pursuits, makes it possible to consider poetry as poetry and not another thing, according to its distinctive criteria and artistic reasons for being.

By employing his supplementary distinctions between the objects of human experience that are imitated, the artistic medium of the imitation, and the manner (such as narrative or dramatic) in which the imitation is rendered, Aristotle is also able to differentiate poetry from the other arts, and then to establish classes of poems, such as epic, comedy, and tragedy, each with its distinctive features and appropriate criteria. Focusing his attention on tragedy, he defines this genre in its turn as an imitation of an action that is serious and complete, in appropriate language and in the dramatic manner, then adds an identification of its distinctive emotional power: "arousing pity and fear, wherewith to accomplish its catharsis of such emotions." Applying the total theoretical tools now available, Aristotle goes on to discriminate within a tragedy such elements as plot, characters, diction, thought, and to consider both the relative importance and the interrelations of these elements. He then analyzes the features and construction of each element, from the point of view of what best serves the artistic purpose of tragedy by maximizing the distinctively "tragic pleasure," or "tragic fear and pity." Hence, for example, his criteria for the most effective tragic plots: the need for a unified plot, representing a single action that constitutes a complete whole; the need to reshape any materials provided by history into a plot by substituting artistic determinants for historical contingency; the effectiveness of the use of peripety and discovery to mark the shift from complication to dénouement, in the turning point at which the hero of the tragedy, greater and nobler than the normal person, through his tragic error falls from happiness to misery; and so on, through all the diverse observations of this terse and original little treatise.

Some observations are in order about what Aristotle does, as against what a number of analysts assume that, as a critical theorist, he must be doing:

(1) The whole of the *Poetics,* according to the criteria of the analysts, counts as theory and not as applied criticism, for its basic statements are all generalizations about the arts, or about a class of art such as poetry, or about a species of poetry such as tragedy and its typical elements, organization, and effects; Aristotle refers to particular works only to exemplify or clar-

ify such general statements. Of this theory, however, definitions certainly do not constitute a major part, but are used only briefly and passingly, as a way of introducing one or another area of investigation. And the body of the theory does not consist of an attempt—whether vain or successful— to support and "prove" the definition. It consists instead of putting to work the terms, distinctions, and categories proposed in the initial definition (which are supplemented, in a way consistent with this definition, as the need arises) in the analysis of the distinctive elements, organization, and characteristic powers of various kinds of poetic art.

(2) This theory makes a valid contribution to knowledge. It provides, among other things, knowledge of how to experience and enjoy works of art—not only tragedies as a class but also a particular tragedy—by providing terms and analytic devices that enable us to experience them in a discriminating rather than a crude way, through directing our attention to their important features and the ways these features are ordered according to distinctively artistic reasons for order. This contribution to our ability to see works of art with new eyes is not an inadvertent by-product of Aristotle's attempt at a logical impossibility; it is the result of his deliberate undertaking, as he asserts in his opening statement, "to speak not only of the art [of poetry] in general but also of its species and their respective capacities; of the structure of plot required for a good poem; of the number and nature of the constituent parts of a poem; and likewise of any other matters in the same line of inquiry." The degree to which we are indebted to Aristotle's theory for concepts that make possible a discriminating and organized appreciation of literary art is obscured by the extent to which his terms and distinctions long ago became the common vocabulary of discourse about works of narrative and dramatic literature.

This is the primary service of a good critical theory, for in bringing us, with new insights and powers of discrimination, to individual works of art in their immediacy, it enhances our appreciation of the only places where artistic values are in fact realized. But as inquisitive beings we are interested not only in knowing *how* to enhance our direct experience of these values, but also in knowing *about* the works in which such values have their residence, including their relations to each other and to other human pursuits. In a number of brief but pregnant passages Aristotle also contributes to our knowledge about art as it is diversely related to, yet distinguishable from, other human activities and achievements such as history, philosophy, and politics—and here, too, in a systematic and coherent way that follows from the extended application of his initial definition and analytic categories.

(3) Although Aristotle's theory is grounded, inescapably, on the Greek dramas then available to his inquiry, there is nothing in the logical nature of the theory itself to make it function as a closed definition that forecloses the possibility of encompassing dramatic creativity and novelty. It is true that a number of later critics, especially in the Renaissance, used the *Poetics* as though it were a legislative and regulative rather than an open and empirical theory, with the result that they condemned innovative forms of serious drama, or else distorted their features by describing them in forced accordance with Aristotle's commentary. But if employed in his own spirit of inquiry, Aristotle's method and distinctions enable us to recognize, and to specify the novel characteristics of, non-Aristotelian forms of tragic drama and tragic plots. For example, Shakespeare's *Macbeth* and Arthur Miller's *Death of a Salesman,* different as they are from Sophocles' *Oedipus* and from each other, both "imitate" actions that have seriousness, dimension, integrity, and end in a catastrophe for the protagonist, so that we may, with good reason, decide to extend to these plays the term "tragedy." But the very distinctions introduced in the *Poetics* enable us to identify those important differences in the protagonists, plot, language, and effects that distinguish these tragedies from Aristotelian tragedy and from each other as well. Furthermore, Aristotle's general method for differentiating literary types and for establishing their distinctive criteria by the systematic investigation of their multiple "causes" (in other words, of their diverse artistic reasons) is itself an open method, which can be adapted to the analysis of any literary form, including those, such as the novel or cinema, that were not invented until long after the *Poetics* had been written.[20]

2. THE USES OF DIVERSITY

We are faced with the fact, however, that Aristotle is only one of many theorists, and that in the predicates of their definitions of art other theorists replace Aristotle's operative term, *imitation,* by terms and expressions with patently different meanings: a work of art is a means to the end of teaching, or pleasing, or both; or an expression of feelings; or a product of the creative imagination; or a distinctive form of communication; or a world of its own autonomous kind; or a variant form of an archetypal myth; and so on. Philosophical analysts have used such discrepant assertions to add plausibility to their claim that an essential definition of a work of art is logically impossible; for if it were possible, how do we explain that no one has yet located a common feature of objects denoted by the general term *art* that will satisfy more than a fraction of people who profess to be experts on the subject?

Some theorists, like Clive Bell, have indeed claimed to have discovered the essence of art, and many more have felt that, in order to justify their own definitions, they had to attack the definitions of other theorists. Yet upon investigation we find that all those who, in the course of time, emerge with the reputation of major theorists of art have in fact contributed important new knowledge—both knowledge about how to look at and appreciate art, and knowledge about art in its diverse circumstances and relations—and they have succeeded in doing so not despite their basic discrepancies, but as a direct result of these discrepancies.

The actual use of an expression can only be determined (in Wittgenstein's term) within its surroundings. If now we enlarge our view from the surroundings of a definition within a particular theory to its surroundings in all the other definitions that it was intended to counter or qualify or supplant, I think we can make out a use, and accordingly, a "logical character," both of a definition and of the total theory within which the definition occurs, that we have hitherto overlooked; for this is a use that is relative to alternative manners of proceeding. It now appears that to propose a definition of art, or of a form of art, though it is couched in a grammatical form indistinguishable from that of a universal assertion, is much like taking a stand. The theorist takes his stand on that one of many possible vantage points that will provide what strikes him as the most revealing perspective on the area of his interest. Or, to use a different visual analogy adopted from Coleridge (who was critic, theorist, and metacritic, and especially interested in the role of alternative theories in observation), the use of a critical theory is not to reflect the given artistic facts, but to serve as a "speculative instrument" that will arm one's critical vision. As Coleridge put it, observation is to meditation (by which he means theory) only "as eyes, for which [meditation] has pre-determined their field of vision, and to which, as to *its* organ, it communicates a microscopic power." And again: "The razor's edge becomes a saw to the armed vision."[21] Whatever analogue we adopt needs to bring out the fact that critical definitions and theories may be discrepant without conflict, and mutually supplementary instead of mutually exclusive, since each delimits and structures its field in its own way. The test of the validity of a theory is what it proves capable of doing when it is put to work. And each good (that is, serviceable) theory, as the history of critical theory amply demonstrates, is capable of providing insights into hitherto overlooked or neglected features and structural relations of works of art, of grouping works of art in new and interesting ways, and also of revealing new distinctions and relations between things that (from its special point of view) are art and things that are not art. One way to estimate their diverse contributions is to imagine the impoverishment to criticism if we did not possess the theoretical writings of, say, Aristotle, Horace, Longinus, Kant, Coleridge, Eliot—or Clive Bell. No theory is adequate to tell the whole story, for each one has limits correlative with its powers. As a speculative instrument, it has its particular angle and focus of vision, and what for one speculative instrument is an indistinct or blank area requires an alternative speculative instrument if it is to be brought into sharp focus for inspection.

Better to bring out one other point, let me return from optical metaphors to Wittgenstein's favorite analogue of a game. Each critical theorist, it can be said, pursuing his particular interests and purposes, selects and specializes his operative and categorical terms, and in consequence sets up a distinctive language-game whose playing field overlaps but doesn't coincide with that of other critical language-games and which is played according to grammatico-logical rules in some degree special to itself. The aims, fields, and rules of various critical language-games are sufficiently similar, however, so that some of their assertions are conflicting rather than alternative; but to determine which assertions these are, and how to decide the conflict between them, is a difficult exercise in the comparative grammar of language-games.

To lend plausibility to these sweeping claims beyond that provided by the prior experience of each reader, I have space for only a single example; so I shall choose Coleridge, both because his critical theory is as different as it could be from that of Aristotle and because it represents a type that is treated with particular severity by philosophical analysts. As Morris Weitz remarks:

> Throughout [Coleridge's] writings there is a steady concern for philosophy, for essences, and fundamental principles, and a pervasive conviction that philosophy, psychology, art, and criticism are interrelated. Indeed, Coleridge's most ostensible characteristic, even as a practicing critic, is this recurrent reference to fundamental principles. . . .
> It would be a fascinating task, even if devastating to Coleridge, I believe, to subject his doctrines to a more adequate philosophical scrutiny than he would have tolerated.[22]

Coleridge as critic dismays the analyst not simply because he is an inveterate theorist, but because his type of theory violates so many current caveats. Under the compulsion to be inclusive and coherent in his thinking, Coleridge derives his generalizations about art from metaphysical generalizations about the total universe. He insists that the only criticism that is "fair and philosophical" is one based on "principles, which [the critic] holds for the foundation of poetry in general," and he chooses to base his own criticism on "the component faculties of the human mind itself, and their comparative dignity and importance." As a consequence his operative terms and categories are hopelessly "mentalistic," and also are deliberately contrived to conflate description and evaluation, for "according to the faculty . . . from which the pleasure given by any poem or passage was derived, I estimated [its] merit."[23] Unembarrassedly setting himself the question, "What is poetry?" Coleridge proceeds to answer it in terms of the nature of the "poetic genius itself," which involves above all the activity of "that synthetic and magical power, to which we have exclusively appropriated the name of imagination," and which "reveals itself in the balance or reconciliation of opposite or discordant qualities."[24] And he defines the imagination, in turn, as a creative power that operates as an organic process to effect an organic product. The resulting theory would seem to be a hopeless tangle of categorical confusions. On the one hand, Coleridge finds imagination manifested not only in poetry but also in many nonartistic human processes and products. And on the other hand, he represents imaginative creativity as analogous to all modes of creativity—that is, to all processes of the bringing-into-being of anything really new, including the universe itself; and he often describes such creative process and its products in organic terms—that is, in terms that are literal for a growing plant, but metaphorical for artistic invention and a work of art. For example: "Could a rule be given from *without,* poetry would cease to be poetry, and sink into a mechanical art. . . . The *rules* of IMAGINATION are themselves the very powers of growth and production." As opposed to "mechanic" form, "organic form," such as we find manifested in Shakespeare's plays, "is innate; it shapes as it develops itself from within, and the fullness of its development is one and the same with the perfection of its outer form."[25]

Weitz, citing this and other passages, remarks in understatement that Coleridge's doctrine of poetic drama "implies a metaphysical theory about nature that is certainly disputable." Oddly, however, although he finds Coleridge's critical principles untenable and his arguments "inconsistent," Weitz gives Coleridge's applied criticism the very highest marks. His criticism "is magnificent in its fullness and concreteness," his apologia for Shakespeare "stands in evaluative criticism as a model," and his analysis of the opening scene in *Hamlet*

is "one of the great examples of descriptive criticism any-
where," "a marvel of pointed reading such that one can never
read or see that first scene except through his eyes."[26]

Are we to take it, then, that Coleridge's criticism is a happy
escape from his unfortunate metaphysical theory, or achieved
in spite of it? If we look and see, all the indications are otherwise. The major insights of Coleridge's critical analyses,
interpretations, and evaluations, including the passages on
Shakespeare that Weitz most praises, are integral with his
metaphysical and critical theory, in that they put to work the
terms and categories developed within the theory. For
example, Coleridge declared that in Shakespeare we find
"*growth* as in a plant. No ready cut and dried [structure]."
"All is growth, evolution, *genesis*—each line, each work almost,
begets the following."[27] The reigning Neoclassic theory had
viewed art as artisanry: the artist selects parts and puts them
together according to the rules of "decorum," or fittingness,
to achieve a preconceived design and appropriate effects. A
cardinal aspect of both Coleridge's metaphysics and his aesthetic theory is the replacement of the model of the artisan
by that of the genesis and growth of a plant, and such resulting critical concepts as generation from a seed-idea or element, evolution according to inherent principles or "laws,"
and the assimilation of disparates into an organic unity in
which the elements alter their identities as parts in an organized whole are what enabled him to discriminate features
and relations of literary works that had been inconceivable
to earlier critics, in the literal sense that they lacked the general concepts through which to see them.

If we accept the view that the meaning and justification of
a way of speaking is the purpose it serves in its surroundings,
we ought also to accept the difficult conclusion that once a
concept or assertion is adopted as the basis of a critical theory, its origin and truth-claim, whether empirical or metaphysical, cease to matter, for its validity in this context is to
be determined by its power of illumination when brought to
bear in the scrutiny of works of art. An organic theory of art
served Coleridge as a primary, although not exclusive, speculative instrument, and the value of the discoveries it made
possible is attested not only by the virtues of his own criti-

cism, but also by the extent to which the use of organic language in applied criticism has, in various ways, been adopted by other critics ever since it was established and developed in the theories of Coleridge and his German contemporaries. But of course it is difficult to measure the contribution of innovative terms whose very success has brought them into the public domain of aesthetic discourse.

3. LOGICAL GRAMMAR AND FLUID CRITICAL DISCOURSE

I want to return briefly to the practice of Weitz and other philosophical analysts of distinguishing the procedures of critics into diverse logical types, because it seems to me that the way they apply these distinctions has concealed the pervasive and varied role of theory in applied criticism. The formulation of logical models is validly based on inherent demands or necessities in the ways we use critical concepts and support critical judgments—necessities that we all sense, but that traditional logic leaves largely out of account—and such paradigms can be used to clarify the implicit structure of aesthetic reasoning. We want to be sure, however, that they are applied only in a way that is appropriate to the language-game as it is in fact played. The models, for example, are fixed, delimited in their sphere of operation, and explicit in their rules. But when we look at the actual goings-on in this or that critical essay, we find everything quite otherwise: the discourse is fluid, the concepts and associated modes of reasoning are complex and mixed, and the inherent demands, or "rules," of usage are implicit, variable, tenuous, and elusive. Only in his own paradigms of artifice are Weitz's four modes of critical usage, as he claims, "irreducible." In the fluid movement of a sustained critical discourse they are indistinct, inter-involved, and, in a quasi-systematic fashion, interdependent. Wittgenstein asks us "to compare the multiplicity of the tools in language and of the ways they are used . . . with what logicians have said about the structure of language. (Including the author of the *Tractatus Logico-Philoso-*

phicus.)"[28] In applying Wittgenstein's own comments on logical grammar in order to enlarge the number of logical formulas, we must beware the risk of distorting and hampering the flow of profitable discourse by a reductive logical "calculus" that is merely a different form of the calculus that Wittgenstein had undertaken to develop in his *Tractatus,* and against which his later philosophy is a sustained warning, through the presentation of counterexamples.

Take, as an instance, the logical form that Weitz in his analysis of *Hamlet* criticism calls "description," which he identifies as true-or-false assertions of "data or *données* that cannot be denied." The critical questions capable of answers that approximate this ideal are very limited; for example: How many words are there in a particular speech, or in the whole play? Which speeches are in verse and which in prose? Does Hamlet in his soliloquy utter the speech-sounds "too, too solid flesh" or "too, too sullied flesh"? But when we move from words to the meanings of a speech or passage, we are in another realm, for meanings need to be construed, and whatever is construed in a work of literature tends to depart from the logical paradigm. Weitz lists as an example the question, Is Hamlet "athletic, fearless, vulnerable, dilatory, adoring of his father . . . mad . . . ambitious . . . melancholic"? Questions of this order do not meet Weitz's own criteria of being capable of answers that are "true or false, verifiable and logically independent of explanation and evaluation."[29] For the answers require interpretation, and in accordance not only with linguistic but also with *artistic* criteria, in that the interpretation of Hamlet's character is interinvolved with the interpretation of the play in which he plays a central role. Such answers are, therefore, rationally contestable and have in fact been persistently contested.

And what critical utterances fit the logical paradigm by which "interpretations," in their turn, are strictly divided from "evaluations"? Among Weitz's examples of pure interpretation we find the statements that a work is "poignant," "vivacious," "serene," "profound."[30] That such predications involve—give us to know—not only how a critic sees or interprets features of a work, but also that he sees these features as invested with value, becomes clear if we imagine what it would be like if a critic, after asserting that a work is serene and profound, should go on to the verdict that it is valueless, or a bad work of art. Such a sequence would not constitute a logical fallacy, but it would be a linguistic surprise, because the implicit rules for the ordinary critical use of such terms lead us to assume the critic's approval and esteem. A critic would need in some way to establish a special context of usage in order to be able to say that he finds a work serene and profound, yet artistically worthless, without giving the effect of incoherence or indecisiveness. In most criticism, in fact, evaluation is continuously effected in the process of describing and interpreting, through the use of the hundreds of available expressions such as subtlety, vividness, economy, precision, coherence, sincerity, maturity, unified sensibility, tightly organized, complexly ironic. ... When we find an assertion that matches Weitz's evaluative paradigm, "X is good, great, excellent, mediocre," or "X is good ... because P," it is apt to be in a polemical context, or to be used to assess a work for the buying public, or to clinch a case already implicitly made, or to enhance the persuasiveness of a critique by a show of intellectual rigor.

My main caveat against a rigid use of logical models, however, is that they take no account of the obvious character of any instance of sustained critical discourse—not only that it is fluid, but that it has a source, that (despite eddies and side runnels) it is flowing somewhere, and that it flows in response to forces that are to some extent inherent in the kind of critical discourse it is. Let me drop this hydrodynamic analogue at the point where it becomes an inconvenience. The potential facts, or features, of a work of art or literature—whether long like *Hamlet,* or of middle length like "Lycidas," or short like "A Spirit Did My Slumber Seal"—are numberless, and some of them only come into view from a particular theoretical perspective. For many of what count as artistic or literary facts are in part constructed, and they are constructed by the act of being construed. As Coleridge, who was interested in this as in all aspects of the role of theory, put it: "Facts, you know, are not truths; they are not conclusions; they are not even premisses, but in the nature and parts of premisses."[31] The theoretical principles, categories, distinctions, and manner of proceeding built into a critic's elected mode of discourse—his language-game—cooperate with whatever constitutes the *données* of a work so as both to shape the facts and to identify which are the significant facts, and also to foster the kinds of hypotheses the critic will bring to the interpretation of particular passages and of the work as a whole, as well as the kinds of criteria that enable him both to discover and to assess the values in the work. These activities are performed not separately or sequentially, but in a continuous and interdependent process, in a discourse that is kept coherent and directional toward the ends in view by the pervasive but often implicit influence of the critic's theoretical premises and orientation.

Sometimes a shift in the theoretical vantage effects a spectacular transformation in the description as well as the interpretation and evaluation of works of art. As an example: for centuries it was entirely obvious to all critics of Shakespeare, however divergent their perspectives, that the salient features of his plays were the kind that Aristotle had identified—that is, characters who perform the actions and speak the language constituting the text. Then, less than a half-century ago, a number of able critics took the theoretical stand that a poetic drama, like all genuine literature, is essentially a mode of language that is antithetical to the language of science; hence that, since the language of science is literal, simple in its reference, logical in its method, and has verifiable truth as its aim, the antithetic language of poetry is inherently figurative or symbolic, ambiguous in its meaning, ironic, paradoxical, and in other ways "counterlogical" in its method, and organized so as to explore a "theme" rather than to assert a truth. In the criticism of writers such as Wilson Knight, Philip Wheelwright, Cleanth Brooks, and Robert Heilman, the salient features of Shakespeare's plays, when examined from this perspective, were not characters, but patterns of words and images, and the central action turned out to be an ironic and paradoxical "symbolic action," of which the dynamic element is an evolving theme. The evaluation of Shakespeare from this point of view equaled the earlier high estimation of his artistic standing, although on very different grounds and criteria. The same perspective, however, when applied to writers such as Donne, Blake, Wordsworth, Shelley, or Tennyson, resulted in a drastic reordering of their traditional rankings in the hierarchy of the English poets. And though he may himself prefer to take his stand on the premise that literature is primarily about people rather than constituted by patterns of thematic imagery, the candid reader will not deny the value of some of the insights made possible by a criticism based on the alternative possibility.

4. DOES CRITICISM PRESUPPOSE THEORY?

But a number of philosophical analysts claim that some criticism is entirely theory-free and carries on its proper work of analysis and assessment unimpeded by general presuppositions. William Kennick, for example, says that a second mistake of traditional aesthetics, coordinate with the mistake of thinking that a theory of art is logically possible, is the "assumption: Criticism presupposes Aesthetic Theory"—an assumption he translates as "the view that responsible criticism is impossible without standards or criteria universally applicable to all works of art." "Criticism," according to Morris Weitz, "need not state, imply, or presuppose a true poetics . . . or an aesthetics of art in order to render intelligible or to justify its utterances" about a particular work. Stuart Hampshire is even more insistent: "Neither an artist nor a critical spectator unavoidably needs an aesthetic; and when in Aesthetics one moves from the particular to the general, one is travelling in the wrong direction." There is here a craving for aesthetic particularity no less extreme than the traditional craving for generality against which Hampshire is reacting. The critic, he asserts, "is a mere spectator: . . . it is only required that he should see the object exactly as it is," and as a "unique object . . . individual and unrepeatable." "The peculiar features of particular objects, with their own originality of arrangement, remain constant and unaffected by the spectator's choices and priorities."[32]

Hampshire's comments suggest a conceptual model of the

critical encounter which, I think, lurks also behind the insistence by other analysts that the ultimate use of criticism, and the by-product which makes even bogus definitions inadvertently profitable, is to demonstrate by example "what to look for and how to look at it in art." The ideal is one in which an intelligent and sensitive observer, undistracted by any theoretical presuppositions about the nature of art or of a kind of art, engages with a unique work, which comes endowed with aesthetic features that are simply (though more or less obviously or obscurely) there, and proceeds to register those features that he is acute enough to discover. This model of a pure critical confrontation, of course, does not even remotely approximate the conditions of our actual dealings with a work of art. Should that anomaly, a cultivated and intelligent man whose mind was unviolated by general aesthetic preconceptions, encounter a work of art, he would have nothing to say that we should account artistic criticism.

Does all criticism presuppose theory? Not if by *presuppose* we mean a logical relation, such that a given theory strictly entails a particular critique, or that from a given critique we can infer its precise theoretical antecedents. The interrelated elements of an explicit theory—including definitions, categories, distinctions, criteria, and method of proceeding—are not related to their specific application to a particular work, or class of works, in this strictly logical way, nor merely in a simple causal way, as the conditions that effect particular aesthetic judgments. Instead, they are related in the curious way, compounded of quasi-logical and causal relations, that we indicate by terms such as "foster," "generate," "suggest," "bring out," or even "control" and "inform."

Granted the use of *presuppose* to include relations of this sort, we can say with assurance that yes, all criticism presupposes theory, and in at least two ways. First, any discourse about works of art that is sufficiently sustained and ordered to count as criticism has attributes—for example, the kinds of features in the work it discriminates or ignores, the kinds of terms it uses or fails to use, the relations it specifies, the literal or analogical mode of reasoning it exhibits—that serve as indices of the type of theoretical perspective to which the critic is committed, whether explicitly or implicitly, and whether deliberately or as a matter of habit. Second, any sustained critical discourse is likely to use some terms that have been invented for their own purposes by earlier aesthetic theorists, and will inescapably use other terms taken from ordinary language, but applied in accordance with specialized rules of usage which, historical investigation shows, have been developed by earlier aesthetic theorists. These terms and modes of usage have become part of the linguistic and cultural tradition that all educated people inherit, so that the discourse of any individual critic presupposes theory, in the sense that at least some elements in the language-game he elects to play, although open to modification, have in the first instance come to him ready-made from the history of critical theory.

Here is a simple example from Matthew Arnold, whom I choose because, more than almost all major critics, he seems to approach Hampshire's ideal—that the critic "should see the object exactly as it is"—by deliberately undertaking to eschew general theory and, in his words, "to see the object as in itself it really is." In "The Study of Poetry," Arnold briefly surveys important English poets in the endeavor to detect in each

> the degree in which a high poetic quality is present or wanting there. Critics give themselves great labour to draw out what in the abstract constitutes the character of a high quality of poetry. It is much better simply to have recourse to concrete examples . . . and to say: The characters of a high quality of poetry are what is expressed *there.*

Coming to Chaucer, he cites two passages spoken by the Prioress in *The Canterbury Tales,* then comments that, great though Chaucer's poetry is, it falls short in an essential aspect of the poetic quality of the greatest writers such as Homer, Dante, and Shakespeare: "The substance of Chaucer's poetry, his view of things and his criticism of life, has largeness, freedom, shrewdness, benignity; but it has not this high seriousness."[33]

From evidences in this one sentence we can infer some important presuppositions which, had Arnold been an inveterate theorizer like Coleridge, he might have asserted in an express theory of poetry. For example, since he employs terms such as "freedom," "benignity," "high seriousness" as criteria for high poetic quality, and since the use of such terms involves a moral aspect, we know that Arnold did not, like some of his contemporaries, view poetry from the vantage of art for art's sake, but instead was committed to an alternative theoretical position, that poetic qualities and values are not exclusive of, nor even discriminable from, moral qualities and values. Furthermore, Arnold's terms for poetic qualities are of a special kind: they signify, literally, aspects of human character that involve a man's general attitudes to life. Undertaking to look directly at Chaucer's poetry and to describe simply what he finds there, Arnold discovers its most prominent and important features to be qualities of character that many critics of Chaucer do not mention and others expressly reject as an instance of the "personal heresy," hence aesthetically irrelevant.

It is clear that Arnold's discovery of these features presupposes the view that there is a detectable authorial presence behind all the fictitious characters in a narrative poem like *The Canterbury Tales,* and that the moral aspects and attitudes manifested by that presence are the primary features of a work which determine both the kind and excellence of its poetic quality. Arnold was able to presuppose that view because it was an element in the diverse critical languages that he had inherited—an element that had in the first instance been the product of a specific theory. We find it in Aristotle—not in his *Poetics* but in his *Rhetoric*—in the claim that a public speaker inescapably projects an ethos, a personal character which may be different from his actual self but serves as an important means of persuading the audience to give credence to him and his arguments. The Greek critic Longinus expanded the use of this concept from rhetoric to literature, by asserting that the supreme stylistic quality he calls "the sublime" reflects the character of its author: "Sublimity is the echo of a great soul." This way of dealing with literature, by the time it was inherited by Arnold, had been greatly extended and subtilized, especially by those Romantic critics who based their criticism on the theoretical premise that literature is the expression

of its author's character and feelings. And though, during
the three or four decades that have just passed, the predom-
inance of the New Criticism, based on the alternative premise that a poem is an autonomous object, blocked out as
poetically irrelevant "the personal heresy" or "the biographical fallacy," current critics are adopting a stance from which,
with some excitement, they are rediscovering characterolog-
ical features that are "objective" properties of a work of art—
although they now attach these properties to a projected and
pervasive presence in a work that they call not "ethos," nor
"Chaucer," but "voice."

5. DOES METACRITICISM PRESUPPOSE THEORY?

Are those philosophical analysts who deny the logical possibility of aesthetic theory themselves theory-free? As soon as
we examine what these philosophers, in analyzing critical discourse, find it relevant or irrelevant to talk about and how
they elect to talk about it—as soon as we do meta-metacriti-
cism—it becomes clear that they have privately known all along
the extension of the general term *art,* and the criteria by which
this extension is at least loosely specified. Their claim of ignorance about the proper meaning of *art* has in fact functioned
as a pretense, like Socrates' guise of ignorance, in the service
of pursuing a special kind of philosophical inquiry in a special way. Furthermore, this meaning does not coincide with
any use of the term in "ordinary language." Instead, the criteria of *art* presupposed by the analysts are highly specialized, are employed exclusively by a class of intellectuals who
share a current climate of opinion, and are a heritage from
quite recent developments in aesthetic theory.

Sometimes the evidences for these prepossessions are quite
explicit. Stuart Hampshire raises the possibility that "perhaps there is no subject-matter" of aesthetics, and, as we know,
he regards any movement in criticism from the particular to
the general as retrograde. Yet he hangs his argument on the
assertion that "a work of art is gratuitous"—not some works,

or some class of works, but "a work of art" in the universal sense. "The canons of . . . perfection and imperfection," he says, are thus "internal to the work itself." On this ground Hampshire differentiates sharply between "aesthetic judgments" and moral judgments, and forbids any intrusion into criticism of the "common vocabulary" which, since it was "created for practical purposes, obstructs any disinterested perception of things." For "in so far as the perfection of the work is assessed by some external criterion, it is not being assessed as a work of art." "Nothing but holding an object still in attention, by itself and for its own sake, would count as having an aesthetic interest in it."[34] Kennick agrees with Hampshire that "a work of art is gratuitous," and generalizes that "art has no function or purpose . . . and this is an insight to be gained from the 'art for art's sake' position." Paul Ziff, although equally suspicious of aesthetic generalization, asserts: "Nothing can be a reason why [a] painting is good unless it is a reason why the painting is worth contemplating. (One can add: for its own sake, but that is redundant.)"[35]

In Morris Weitz the indications are less direct, but point to a similar preconception about what is and is not aesthetic. Evaluations of works of art, he says, apply criteria that are supported by reasons, and the good reasons are unchallengeable reasons. Criteria such as "truthful" or "moral" cannot be supported by good or convincing reasons "since it is always possible to dissociate artistic greatness from truth or morality"; indeed, all criteria are challengeable that have to do with "the *effects* of art," as well as with "the *relation* between art and the world." But the case is entirely different for such statements as "X is great because it is subtle, integrated, fresh." Criteria such as these are "aesthetic, where by aesthetic I mean some criterion which cannot be challenged," for to ask what such criteria have to do with artistic greatness "makes no sense," because nothing can possibly serve as an answer.[36] Now, by "unchallengeable" Weitz cannot mean that such criteria have not been challenged, for they certainly have been. "Freshness," for example: "You praise a thing for being 'fresh,' " T. E. Hulme remarked, implying that "it is good because it is fresh. Now this is certainly wrong, there is nothing particularly desirable about freshness *per se*. Works of art aren't eggs."[37] By an "unchallengeable," hence an "aesthetic" criterion, Weitz means that, unlike criteria of artistic greatness that involve moral or veridical or psychological claims, it does not relate the work to something outside itself, but terminates in the work *qua* work. "In aesthetic validation," he declares, "this is where we must all stop for there is no further place to go."

Note that the claim that a work of art is "gratuitous"—serving no purpose beyond the work itself—does not accord with the claims of the artists who made these works, until about a hundred or so years ago. Dante declared to Can Grande that the purpose of his *Divine Comedy* was "to remove those living in this life from a state of misery and to lead them to a state of happiness"; Milton wrote *Paradise Lost* "to justify the ways of God to men"; Wordsworth said that each of his poems "has a worthy *purpose,*" and that he wished "either to be considered as a Teacher, or as nothing"; while for many Christian centuries painters undertook to represent and enforce religious truths and musicians composed for the greater glory of God. Also, for fifteen hundred years and more it occurred to no critic to use the terms of the modern analysts, in assertions that the criteria of a work of art are "internal to itself," or that the proper perception of a work is "disinterested," a mode of contemplation "for its own sake," or that aesthetic judgments are to be sharply distinguished from moral and practical judgments, in that they assess the work of art "as a work of art"—that is, as the locus and terminus of aesthetic qualities and values, without reference to "external" relationships.

This critical vocabulary had its specific origins in the eighteenth century, in a particular social and intellectual milieu, and as part of a newly emerging mode of life.* In western Europe, at a time of expanding wealth and a rapidly growing middle class, there was an immense spread of a leisure-time pursuit hitherto confined to the life style of some members of the aristocracy. This pursuit was connoisseurship, the

---

*For expanded discussions of the development of this theory of art in the eighteenth century, see "Art-as-Such: The Sociology of Modern Aesthetics" and "From Addison to Kant: Modern Aesthetics and the Exemplary Art," in this volume.

development of "taste" in a variety of experiences that were pursued primarily for pleasure. The market for poetry and "belles-lettres" expanded; there developed great public collections of paintings and sculpture; the audiences for theater, concerts, opera grew apace; tours were organized to visit and admire architectural monuments, including the great private mansions and their landscaped settings. A consequence of this social phenomenon was the natural assumption that these objects—literature, painting, sculpture, music, landscape gardening, architecture—despite their patent differences in media and other features, have something in common that makes them eligible for the common experience of connoisseurship.[38] Another consequence was a theoretical interest in a mode of activity that was patently not moral or utilitarian, since it was an escape, a holiday from everyday moral and utilitarian concerns; with this was often associated a demand for practical guidance in developing a "good taste" that would serve not only to enhance the pleasures of connoisseurship but also as a sign of social status. All these concerns are writ large in the essays of Joseph Addison, whose acute *Spectator* papers on such subjects, especially the group on "The Pleasures of the Imagination," served to found an amateur's science of aesthetics, which Alexander Baumgarten later in the century named, professionalized, and elevated to philosophical respectability.

The new aesthetic theory developed in two separate but parallel modes, both adumbrated in Addison, Shaftesbury, and other amateur theorists before they were adopted and elaborated by professional philosophers, and both (it is of interest to note) reliant on the importation into the field of art of terms and concepts that had earlier been developed in metaphysics and theology. In one line of thought, the root concept was that the artist possesses a creative faculty called the "imagination," that his act of bringing-into-being a work of art is like that of God in creating the universe, and that his artistic product is therefore a "second nature," or "second world," different from the natural world, whose sole responsibility is to its own internal laws and whose sole end is simply to exist. Viewing the poet's creative act on the model of Leibniz's cosmogony—according to which God's creation of the world necessarily accorded with the laws of noncontradiction and "compossibility"—Baumgarten, inventor of the term *aesthetics,* effected the artistic theory that, because it is produced by a poet who is "like a maker or a creator . . . , the poem ought to be a sort of world." But since the poetic world is "heterocosmic," it is not subject to the criterion of truth to the world we live in, but only to the criterion of "heterocosmic truth"—that is, self-consistency and internal coherence. The "aesthetic end" thus has no reference to ordinary morality and ordinary truth, but is simply "the perfection of sensuous cognition . . . that is, beauty." Or, as Karl Philipp Moritz wrote in 1788, a work of art is its own microcosm whose beauty "has no need to be useful." For beauty "needs no end, no purpose for its presence outside itself, but has its entire value, and the end of its existence in itself. . . . [The energy of the artist] creates for itself its own world, in which nothing isolated has a place, but everything is after its own fashion a self-sufficient whole."[39]

The other line of thought took as its starting point the experience not of the maker but of the connoisseur of the arts, and defined the common element in such experience as a special attitude and a special kind of judgment. The basic concept was, in this instance, imported from theological and ethical views of the attitude appropriate to God's moral perfection. Combating post-Hobbesian theories of egoistic ethics and a utilitarian religion, Shaftesbury had defined as the proper religious attitude "the disinterested love of God" for his own sake, because of "the excellence of the object," as against the service of God "for interest merely." In Shaftesbury and various followers, the disinterested concern with God for His internal rather than instrumental excellence became the model for describing both the "moral sense" and the artistic "taste"—that is, both the cultivated man's attitude to moral virtue or moral beauty and the connoisseur's attitude to artistic virtue or sensuous beauty. Later, however, "disinterestedness" came to be used to differentiate specifically aesthetic attitudes and judgments from moral as well as practical and utilitarian concerns.[40] By 1790, when Kant formulated the classic definition of aesthetic perception and judgment, it had come to a conclusion parallel with the definition of art by reference to aesthetic creation and the mode of being of a work of art. "Taste," according to Kant, is the faculty of judging "by means of a delight or aversion *apart from any interest.* The object of such delight is called *beautiful";* and the judgment of beauty is differentiated from judgments of truth and of moral goodness in that it is "simply *contemplative,"* "disinterested," indifferent to the reality of the object, and free of "utility" or reference to any end "external" to the perfection of the object itself.[41]

The basic aesthetic terms and concepts in a number of analytic metacritics, it is apparent, emerged only some two centuries ago, were imported from metaphysical, theological, and ethical doctrines, and were developed by the very thinkers who established the field of art as a separate philosophical discipline, for which they coined the name *aesthetics* and within which they undertook to frame a theory of the utmost generality in a vocabulary that would enable them to talk about all the arts at once. The question arises, Why should some analytic philosophers think that just these presuppositions about the nature of art and aesthetic experience are so obviously true as to require no defense, and so free of theory, essential definitions, and aesthetic generalizations that they can serve as the ground of arguments against the validity of all such theory, definitions, and generalizations?

There are, I think, two plausible reasons for this anomaly. For one thing, to assert about the work of art that it is gratuitous, to be enjoyed as an end in itself, and to be appraised by criteria internal to itself, is to generalize in terms of function, purpose, attitudes, in a way that might seem to be free of the *"unum nomen; unum nominatum"* fallacy and the family-resemblance mistake—though only on the naive view that, taking Wittgenstein's behest to "look and see" entirely literally, assumes that nothing is to be accounted a common element if it is not a visible feature of the objects denoted by a general term.[42] More important, however, is the fact that the success of these terms in dealing with certain problems of the arts have made them in the course of the last century the current coin of aesthetic interchange. The expressions, with their implicit rules of specialized use, have become so much a part of the common language of both literate amateurs and professional philosophers of art—or what comes to the same thing, they have become so much a part of the modern intellectual climate—that they seem to be simply given in common experience, and so serve as what Aristotle in his *Rhetoric* called "commonplaces": concepts from which we argue, but for which we feel no need to argue.

Is the theory of art employing these commonplaces as primary categories a valid theory? Surely it is, for it has served as the great enabling act of modern criticism in that it has made it possible for us to talk about art for what it distinctively is, in differentiation from all other human products and all moral and practical activities—to talk about art as art, a poem as a poem, and an individual work of art as a unique entity, to be described and judged by criteria most appropriate to itself and not another kind of thing. It is not the sole language that has been developed for such a purpose: Aristotle's theory, as we saw earlier, provided quite different terms which nonetheless enabled him to talk about some artistic products in a way appropriate to their own distinctive features, causes, modes of organization, and criteria; but our eighteenth-century heritage of the view of art-as-such, and especially its new emphasis on the experience of the connoisseur, has better suited modern interests and proclivities. But is this theory in itself adequate to deal with all the important human concerns with art? We need only to bring ourselves down from the high and radically simplifying vantage point of current aesthetic discourse into the clutter and tangle of the total "surroundings" of an actual encounter with *King Lear,* or the "St. Matthew's Passion," or *Guernica,* to see how inadequate such a theory is to account for the way these works engage our total consciousness and call insistently upon our sympathies and antipathies, our range of knowledge, our common humanity, our sense of what life and the world are really like and how people really act, our deep moral convictions and even religious beliefs (or lack of them).

But how are we to do theoretical justice to the full range of our experience of a work of art? Only by dropping the useful but limited way of talking about art *qua* art and developing an alternative language, or much more likely, by adapting one of the existing languages, such as Plato's, or

Johnson's, or Arnold's, or Lionel Trilling's, which were developed to deal with a work of art in some of the many ways in which it is deeply involved with other human activities, values, and concerns. But can't we devise a single critical language that will do all of these useful and valuable things? I believe not, for no one set of premises and coherent mode of discourse suffices to say everything important, but only the kind of things, relative to selected human purposes, toward which that discourse is oriented.

If I am right in asserting that what we account as critical theory is diverse in its composition and function and inescapable in extended critical discourse, and also that a diversity of theories are valid, in the variety of their usefulness for a comprehensive understanding and appreciation of art, then we are in a position to judge the assertion by some philosophical analysts with which we began. The claim was that all critical and aesthetic theory consists solely, or primarily, in the assertion and attempted proof of an essential definition of art and thus is an extended logical mistake. About this claim we can now say that (1) it is itself the attempt to assert and prove an essential definition of the term "critical theory"; (2) it is a mistake that forecloses investigation of what able theorists have in fact done; and (3) it actually functions as a persuasive redefinition of "critical theory," in that it delimits the common uses of the term by setting up a preferred criterion for its application that serves to discredit what it purports to define.

6. CERTAINTY, RATIONALITY, AND CRITICAL KNOWLEDGE

The inadequacy of their views of the role of critical theory has not prevented these philosophers from saying many important things about criticism itself. An especially important service, I earlier remarked, has been their insistence that a variety of critical arguments are rational even though they can achieve certainty only in the limited area in which the arguments concern artistic facts. I have argued, indeed, that even this in some ways claims too much—that the analytic paradigms for each type of critical argument are often inapplicable to fluid critical discourse, and that not only interpretations and evaluations but even what count as significant artistic facts are to some extent relative to a theoretical frame of discourse which has been elected by the individual critic. And this raises a crucial question: Is no certainty possible in critical discourse? And if not, how can we claim that critical discourse yields valid knowledge?

Put in this way, the question is, I think, misleading, because "certainty" is a loaded term: it gives the impression that it is a universal criterion for knowledge, yet tends in philosophical discourse to be tied to certain highly specialized models of reasoning. In the seventeenth century, when the model for achieving certainty (outside of divine revelation) was logic, defenders of the emerging "new science" tried to validate its claim to certain knowledge by concepts, such as the "principle of sufficient reason," that seemed to bridge the gap between the necessary truths of logic and assertions of empirical facts and laws. Later, when the physical sciences had triumphantly established their own claim to cognitive validity, the methods of scientific verification tended to assume a status, on a peer with that of logic, as the sole model for achieving knowledge in all empirical inquiries. Such was the assumption, in the nineteenth century, of the philosophy of positivism, and, in the twentieth, of the philosophy of logical positivism. And even in our post-positivist climate many of us still feel uneasy about claiming validity for knowledge that cannot be certified by some plausible simulacrum of the model of formal logic, or of "scientific method," or of both together. But we will get clear about what we are really doing in artistic criticism, and in various related areas of inquiry, only if we face up to the full consequences of the realization that these pursuits are neither logic nor science, but their own kinds of discourse, adapted to their own kinds of problems, having their own criteria of rationality, and yielding their own kinds of knowledge, to which the term *certainty* does not apply. But if this knowledge is not "certain," neither is it, strictly speaking, "uncertain"; both terms, insofar as they are tied to alien models of discourse, are misleading.

In this respect, one must be wary about the attempt by E. D. Hirsch, in "Value and Knowledge in the Humanities," to renew our confidence "in the scientific side" of criticism and related studies by claiming that they share with the sciences a "universal logic of inquiry" which results in a body of knowledge that "is scientific in precisely the same sense that geology or physics is scientific," differing only in degree of "exactitude." Hirsch identifies the logic of inquiry common to criticism and the physical sciences as that described by Karl Popper and other philosophers of science: it is the method of positing, testing, and falsifying alternative hypotheses by the principle of "evidence and logic" with the result of achieving an ever higher degree of tenability for the hypothesis that survives the ordeal.[43]

I concur with the general tenor of Hirsch's argument for the rationality of literary study and am dismayed, as he is, by the irrationality and irresponsibility of much that passes for criticism. And one can, like Hirsch in his various writings, refer to the hypothetico-deductive model in order to say enlightening things about the procedures, such as interpretation, that are involved in literary and aesthetic criticism. But to look at the procedures of a physical scientist and of a critic in their overall surroundings is to see how radical are the differences in problems, aims, and activities that are obscured by asserting that both enterprises accord with a single logical model.

For example: the physicist tacitly shares with other physicists a perspective that sharply limits what shall count as facts; he poses questions that rule out all normative or evaluative terms; he tries to formulate hypotheses that are capable of being indubitably falsified by specific experimental observations; and his overall aim, by a drastic exclusion of individual differences, is to achieve an ever greater generality in knowledge, in a procedure so controlled by rigid rules as to approximate certainty (in the sense of universal agreement by other competent observers) at every step of the way. In dealing with complex literary texts, on the other hand, a critic employs one of many available perspectives to conduct a fluid and largely uncodified discourse, in which some facts have the property of being altered by the hypothesis that appeals

to them for support; his questions typically involve normative and evaluative elements; there is no clear line at which
his interpretative hypothesis is falsified; a central aim, at the
extreme from maximum generality, is to establish the knowledge of individual objects in their distinctive, concrete, and
value-full particularity; and although he may claim that his
interpretation is uniquely true, he is not really surprised to
find that other intelligent and able critics disagree. E. D. Hirsch
does well to remind us that the progressiveness of literary
studies depends on its status as a collaborative enterprise in
which diverse practitioners consent to the criteria of rationality. We must remember, however, that this progress consists in part in the accumulation of alternative and
complementary critical theories and procedures, in a fashion
very different from the progress of the science of physics
toward ever greater generality. The difference is indicated
in Whitehead's dictum that a science that hesitates to forget
its founders is lost. A humane study that forgets its founders
is impoverished; a great critic is subject to correction and
supplementation, but is never entirely outmoded; and progress in fact depends on our maintaining the perspectives and
the insights of the past as live options, lest we fall into a contemporary narrowness of view, or be doomed to repeat old
errors and laboriously to rediscover ancient insights.

Rather than to exaggerate the commonality of method in
science and criticism, it would be more profitable to say that
while criticism involves the use of logic and scientific method,
it must go far beyond their capacities if it is to do its proper
job. Though responsible to the formal rules of reasoning,
and though in its own way empirical, criticism must initiate
its chief functions in an area where these simplified calculi
stop, for the models of logic and of scientific method achieve
their extraordinary efficacy and their diverse modes of certainty by the device of systematically excluding just those features of experience that, humanly speaking, matter most.
Inevitably, therefore, when critical discourse engages with its
objects, it is controlled in considerable part by norms that we
call good sense, sagacity, tact, sensibility, taste. These are terms
by which we indicate that, though we are operating in a region
where the rules are uncodified and elusive and there is room

for the play of irreducible temperamental differences, yet decisions and judgments are not arbitrary, but are subject to broad criteria such as coherent-incoherent, adequate-omissive, penetrating-silly, just-distorting, revealing-obfuscatory, disinterested-partisan, better-worse. Although such a mode of discourse is rarely capable of rigidly conclusive arguments, it possesses just the kind of rationality it needs to achieve its own purposes; and although its knowledge is not, judged by an alien criterion, certain, it must satisfy an equivalent criterion in its own realm of discourse, for which, in lieu of a specialized term, we use a word like *valid,* or *sound.*

A pertinent comment is that of Wittgenstein, in discussing the difference between mathematical and other modes of certainty: "We remain unconscious of the prodigious diversity of all the everyday language-games," and "the kind of certainty is the kind of language-game." He goes on to remind us also that in these matters language is not the ultimate reference, for "what has to be accepted, the given, is—so one could say—*forms of life.*"[44] Let us imagine a critical language-game, and the form of life that it inescapably involves, that would in fact achieve the goal of certainty that one is tempted to hold up as the ideal of all rational discourse. There would be only one permissible theoretical stance, all the descriptive and normative terms would have fixed criteria of use, and reasoning would proceed entirely in accordance with established logical calculi. Such a language, if applied to a work of literature by any intelligent and practiced critic, could indeed be expected to yield certainty, in the sense that the resulting interpretation and evaluation would be conclusive and would enforce the consent of all critics who follow the rules of that critical game. If, however, instead of holding up such certainty as an abstract ideal, we realize in imagination the form of life in which such critical discourse would be standard, we find it inhuman and repulsive; for it is an ideal that could be achieved only in a form of political, social, and artistic life like that which Aldous Huxley direly foreboded in *Brave New World* or George Orwell in *1984.*

Writing in the spirit of Wittgenstein, J. L. Austin remarked that our language is not an ideal form, but is designed for use "in the human predicament."[45] One way to describe criticism and related modes of inquiry is to say that they are a language-game—or a family of language-games—designed to cope in a rational way with those aspects of the human predicament in which valid knowledge and understanding are essential, but certainty is impossible. This is of course an extremely difficult undertaking, but as Wittgenstein remarks, what cannot be gainsaid is, "This language-game is played;"[46] and what its great exponents have achieved shows how well and profitably the game can in fact be played. The name of this game is the humanities.

A Note on Wittgenstein and Literary Criticism

Two years ago I published an essay "What's the Use of Theorizing about the Arts?" directed against certain tendencies in the recent philosophy of aesthetic criticism, and especially against the rejection of all critical theory on the ground that it is a logical fallacy, since its impossible aim is to prove an essential definition of art. Some of my claims in that essay have been queried by a number of commentators, both in reviews and in colloquia on the philosophy of literary criticism. In response to these objections, I want to expand and justify what I said in the essay about the bearings of Wittgenstein's later philosophy on literary criticism, and then to consider briefly questions that have been raised about the implication of my views with respect to truth and subjectivity in aesthetic criticism.

1

We know, from the account by G. E. Moore and from recently published notes by several students, that Wittgenstein discussed aesthetic and critical topics in his lectures of 1930–33 and again in the summer of 1938.[1] The *Brown Book* that Wittgenstein dictated in 1934–35, as well as the *Philosophical Investigations* that he wrote between 1945 and 1949, include a number of passing comments about music, pictures, novels, and poems. In addition, a variety of Wittgenstein's more general philosophic concepts and procedures have been applied to aesthetics, sometimes in greatly expanded form, by a number of critics and writers about criticism. Chief among these are Wittgenstein's family-resemblance view, of course; what he says about the linguistic expression of feelings and of states of mind; his insistence that the use of a language involves "a form of life"; and, most extensively, his discussions of "seeing as" and of the relation between the physical properties and the perceived "aspects" of a visual object.

My present concern, however, is not with Wittgenstein's particular aesthetic or philosophical concepts. I want instead to raise the question of the overall tenor of Wittgenstein's language-philosophy, and of its broad bearing on the characteristic uses of language and processes of reasoning that we find in critics of literature and the other arts. A number of philosophers about criticism who have been influenced by Wittgenstein have, on logical grounds, denied the validity of some standard critical practices and the aesthetic pertinence of some others. My essay in effect proposed that these philosophers—for convenience of reference I call them "metacritical analysts"—are mistaken in much of what they deny; that they are mistaken, however, not because they are Wittgensteinian, but because they are not Wittgensteinian enough.

In his account of the lectures, G. E. Moore stressed Wittgenstein's repeated insistence that his discussions of language were not intended to be comprehensive, but were directed only to those misunderstandings about the way language works that have led to important philosophical "errors" or "troubles" (Moore, 257, 324). This clearly remained Wittgenstein's orientation throughout his later lectures and writings. He undertook, that is, to expose the typical mistakes of traditional philosophy (including the mistakes in his own earlier *Tractatus*) by showing that they are vain attempts to solve "a muddle felt as a problem," or the results of inappropriate pictures, misused analogies, and "a misinterpretation of our forms of language,"[2] or efforts to solve what seem to be problems about matters of fact but are actually expressions of "deep disquietudes" and inner torments. All such undertakings, Wittgenstein says, constitute a "disease of thinking," for which his demonstrations of the way language works are intended to serve as "therapies" that will cure us of the compulsion to pose the pseudo-questions (*Brown Book* 143; *PI* III, 133, 593). Given this corrective orientation of Wittgenstein's discussions of language, it is understandable that his early effect on philosophers was mainly to stimulate a demolition project against philosophical errors in various linguistic enterprises, including traditional aesthetics and literary criticism.

Wittgenstein warns us many times about the danger of analogy; at the same time, he is himself an inveterate deviser of striking analogues. He says, for example, that his kind of philosophy reveals the "bumps that the understanding has got by running its head up against the limits of language" (*PI* 119). Now this figure might suggest that language is an invisible cage which impedes our quest for knowledge but from which, unfortunately, there is no escape. But no simile, Coleridge remarked, "runs on all fours," and as Wittgenstein said, the danger in the use of any analogy is that it "irresistibly drags us on." One of Wittgenstein's ways of avoiding dragging in irrelevant features of any one of his similes for the uses and abuses of language is to supplement it with a variety of others, and a number of his alternatives emphasize not the limitations but the resources of language. One of his most revealing similes is this one: "The confusions which occupy us arise when language is like an engine idling, not when it is doing work" (*PI* 132; cf.88). This figure is aligned with Wittgenstein's many comparisons of the component words of a language to "tools," to "instruments characterized by their use" (e.g., *Blue Book* 67; *PI* II, 569). The distinction between language when it is idling and when it is doing work comports also with Wittgenstein's repeated assertions that diverse forms of expressions are simply different ways of putting something, and that any manner of speaking is acceptable so long as we "understand its working, its grammar," and therefore is "all right so long as it doesn't mislead us when we are philosophizing" (*Blue Book* 7, 41). "I am at liberty to choose between many uses, that is, between many different kinds of analogy" (*Blue Book* 62)—provided I don't make the mistake of translating the form of any particular way of talking into a picture of the facts. "Does it matter which we say, so long as we avoid misunderstandings in any particular case?" (*PI* 48). He insists also on the requisiteness of many concepts "with blurred edges," for "isn't the indistinct [concept] often exactly what we need?"—and this is especially the case, he goes on to say, for "our concepts in aesthetics or ethics" (*PI* 71, 77; cf. 88).

In many observations like these, Wittgenstein indicates the powers rather than the limits of language; he also suggests the indispensability, in many areas of human concern, of fluidity and variability in our ways of speaking. The view that the justification for a linguistic procedure is not what forms of expression it uses, but whether it is really "doing work," is neither inhibitive nor prohibitive, but liberative. And such a view may be taken to confirm—not in details, but overall—the very diverse ways that our best literary critics have in fact used language in order to achieve their profitable discoveries and conclusions, as against what some recent analysts claim that the critics have done, or should instead have done.

2

Now I can restate what I had in mind in saying that some recent philosophers of aesthetics who follow Wittgenstein's lead are not Wittgensteinian enough. Instead of emulating Wittgenstein's openness about accrediting the diverse ways of speaking that have demonstrated their capacity to do profitable work in the criticism of the arts, they codify certain of Wittgenstein's concepts and set up paradigms of the "logical grammar" of fixed classes of critical expressions. In other words, they tend to establish for criticism rules of procedure that Wittgenstein called "calculi." Such calculi are modeled on the "ideal" languages (formal logic, mathematics, the exact sciences) which have been constructed to achieve highly specialized and limited purposes; but, Wittgenstein warns us, they apply only rarely to the loose and informal "grammar" that characterizes other forms of language.

Years ago I was struck by the fact that some of my young philosophical friends, in arguing a question, persistently referred to what they were doing as "moves." When one put forward an assertion, he called it a "move," and he tended to anticipate—often correctly—a philosopher's response as a "counter-move." It dawned on me that these philosophers had been "dragged on," as Wittgenstein put it, by his carefully delimited analogy between using language and playing chess, to the degree that their own philosophizing followed the model of the game of chess, with its rules that strictly define all possible moves and its single purpose—which, in their instance, was to win the game by checkmating an opponent's philosophical king. These philosophers were not following Wittgenstein's flexible and resourceful example, but instead were playing a new philosophical game—a *Wittgenspiel.*

Such early abuses of the innovations of a great and original philosopher are to be expected, and are not in the long run dangerous because they are easily detected. Much more difficult to detect are the subtler distortions of Wittgenstein's procedure that we find in philosophers of criticism who have much to say that is important and enlightening. In my essay I sketched some of the ways in which philosophical metacritics seem to me to have hardened Wittgenstein's concepts into calculi. For example, they convert Wittgenstein's family-resemblance concept—a striking way of showing, by analogy, how some words in ordinary use refer to a great variety of things which may, or may not, have shared features—into a Geiger counter for detecting the fallacy of "essentialism" in order to reject, as logically abortive, procedures that many of the best critics and theorists have employed in pursuit of their profitable undertakings. They succumb also to the temptation that Wittgenstein calls "a tendency to sublime the logic of our language" (*PI* 38), by imposing simplified logical models on the complex ways in which critics actually talk. All the intricate goings-on of the myriad expressions and sentences in critical discourse—fluid, multiform, inter-involved, in which the component parts exhibit a continuum of subtle differences in ever shifting and interchanging logical roles—are thereby forced into a few fixed classes of "irreducible" logical grammars, such as "description," "interpretation," "evaluation," and "theory." There is, I would agree, an indispensable use for such class-terms in discussing what happens in criticism; to be serviceable rather than inhibitive, however, such terms need to be kept open, adaptive, and overlapping instead of being treated as rigid, mutually exclusive, comprehensive of all logical roles in critical language, and applicable to a given expression outside its use in a particular context. Expressions with bounded and codifiable logical roles are not frequent in fluid critical discourse, nor can they be if a critic is to do his proper job.

3

In my essay I pointed to another bias in our thinking against which Wittgenstein warns us: the tendency in describing something, and in setting up norms for dealing with it, to replace the complex facts and their variable circumstances by a simplified and invariable picture or model. The use of such a picture can be the servant of understanding, so long as we remain aware that we are using it and for what purpose; but if its presence and its influence on our thinking are hidden, it readily gets out of hand and becomes, in Wittgenstein's metaphor, a picture that holds us captive (*PI* 114–15).

At the present time a widely prevalent explanatory picture is one that we can call the confrontation model of aesthetic criticism. This hidden picture lurks behind such assertions (cited in my essay) as that *the* function of criticism is to teach us "what to look for and how to look at it in art," or that the critic "is a mere spectator . . . it is only required that he should see the object exactly as it is"—an object whose "peculiar features . . . remain constant and unaffected by the spectator's choices and priorities." The model represents the paradigmatic critical situation as an isolated person confronting a single work of art; this work is almost always, explicitly or implicitly, a painting which, hanging there on the wall, is fixed in the present moment and is consistently cut off from its surroundings by a frame. In terms of the implicit model, therefore, a critical eye is fixed on a given object and proceeds to detect and communicate the particular features that are already, although more or less patently, there.

Such a picture has, in recent aesthetic history, proved itself a fruitful one for fostering concepts that serve limited critical purposes; but if it is not to prevent us from discovering matters relevant to other and equally important critical purposes, we must remain ready to put the simplified model of critical activity back into its complex and variable surroundings. When we do so, we find that the most important thing the model leaves out is the role played in the transaction by language—both by the general system of language and by the characteristic language of the individual critic. In terms of the model, language comes into play only insofar as the critic, having made his aesthetic discoveries, proceeds to render his visual perceptions in words. What a purely visual experience of a painting might be like I can't imagine; but that isn't the present issue. What concerns us is that the critic has thought about art before he looks, and also thinks while he looks; that what he says to himself is essential to both what he thinks and what he sees; and that the result of this process doesn't become criticism until he tidies up the syntax of what he says to himself, elaborates and organizes it, and makes it public in the mode of a sustained utterance.

Consideration of the part played by the critic's language breaks down the seeming isolation both of the critic and of the painting by putting them into a variety of contexts. For example, the general language that the critic uses belongs to a system that he inherits, and is subject to the loose and elusive, yet effective, control of rules or criteria that he may alter, but not evade, if what he says is to be intelligible and coherent. His language, furthermore, includes groups of expressions—subsets of ordinary language—which have in the course of time become more or less specialized to the critical enterprise. Most expressions in these specialized subsets, as I tried briefly to show in my essay, have been introduced into the available critical vocabulary by those aesthetic theorists who

are given short logical shrift by analytic philosophers, and
many of the expressions had an indubitably metaphysical, or
even theological, source; but without recourse to such
expressions, with their built-in valencies, a critic would be
able to say little or nothing that we would count as criticism.
(By its "valency" I mean not only the appraisive weight of a
term, but also its tendency to consort with certain terms and
to clash with or exclude others.) It is also worth noting that
many of these critical terms had a moral provenience in ordinary language, and that they maintain a moral valency when
used to bring out an aspect of a work of art. Some good critics try to eschew such quasi-moral terms; for others, no less
high in the widely accepted critical hierarchy (including Dr.
Johnson, Arnold, Leavis, Trilling), they are central and pervasive components in the critical lexicon.

The individual also brings to the critical transaction an
immense amount of applicable information. He does not,
usually, see simply a painting, but an identifiable painting—
let's say, he knows that it is the Arnolfini marriage portrait,
painted in the 1430s by Jan van Eyck. His knowledge of the
repertory of conventions and devices current in that time and
place, as well as the repertory specific to van Eyck himself,
brings out aspects of the painting of which he would otherwise remain unaware. When he looks at the Arnolfini painting, for example, what he would otherwise see simply as
carefully rendered realistic objects in formal relationships—
a burning candle, a little terrier, a casually discarded pair of
white pattens, the carved figure of a saint on the back of an
armchair standing next to the nuptial bed—he now sees as
invested also with rich and subtle symbolic significances. Furthermore, he sees the material and symbolic objects as related
to an overall subject which only his historical information about
Flemish marital customs of that era enables him to identify
not as a newly married couple but as a couple in the very act
of marrying themselves before the eyes of the artist as a legal
witness, who accordingly inscribes the painting "Johannes de
Eyck fuit hic. 1434."

No less important is the context of the total essay or book
in which we ordinarily find the critic's analysis of a particular
painting. In that larger context, the types of expressions the

critic habitually uses and the kinds of things he says (as well as the many alternative types of expressions he doesn't use and the kinds of things he doesn't say) manifest his critical perspective and guiding principles—no less effective when they are implicit than when they are expressed in the theoretical mode of definitions and systematic generalizations—which, by fostering certain types of critical expressions, bring out, in a critical confrontation, those aspects and values of the painting that he detects, interrelates, and communicates.

The limitations of the confrontation model become even plainer if we bring to mind the act of criticizing not a painting but a work of literature. When the medium of art is words, and the apprehension of a work of art extends over a long period of time, the claim that the critic "is a mere spectator" who "should see the object exactly as it is" becomes a very distant metaphor. Consider, for example, what you in fact do when what you are told to "look for" and "look at" in a novel is a character trait, a type of plot, a specified style, a mode of irony, or a distinctive authorial voice.

I have saved for last a prime inadequacy of the confrontation picture of the critical act, and that is that only a very small fraction of actual criticism corresponds to the normative model, according to which the critic limits himself to assertions about particular features of a single work of art. Random leafing through the pages of any critic whose writings we find illuminating will reveal how large a part of what he says involves, by various linguistic means, classifying features of the work in hand with those of a shifting variety of other works—works written by the same author, or written by other authors in the same period, or else types of works produced over many periods. The conspicuous tendency in the last fifty years or so, fostered especially by the New Criticism, to focus on single works or passages for close critical commentary is in this respect misleading. For what the close reader typically does is to bring to bear on the particular item diverse classes of other items which, by their similarities or oppositions, serve in concert to bring out aspects of the work that seem, after their discovery, to have been there in all their particularity all the time. The physical features of the work do not change; but it is only when we compare one critical analysis with an analysis of the same work by another critic, equally rewarding in his discriminations, that we recognize how much the evocation of particular aesthetic aspects is the result of a critic's deployment of linguistic devices for classifying and cross-classifying things in any number of distinctive, unpredictable, and illuminating ways.

I have emphasized what many will probably agree is the obvious; but my point is that circumstances that are obvious on any particular occasion are apt to drop out of view when we deal with the general terms "the work of art" and "aesthetic criticism"; for these terms, by being inclusive, are radically omissive, and invite us to suppose that a simple normative model is adequate to account for the transactions between them. It seems evident, furthermore, that certain elements in my description of critical encounters with a work of art will evoke objections from some analytic philosophers of criticism, and we can anticipate, from typical assertions in their writings, what they might say. "But some uses of language that you describe are irrelevant to criticism—the application of terms that have a moral source and significance, for example, or the assertion of critical judgments that depend on extraneous information about the individual artist or about the historical and social circumstances at the time the work of art was made. Criticism precludes the use of nonaesthetic terms and the reference to external circumstances, for criticism is disinterested and concerns itself solely with what is distinctively art, with the qualities of art *qua* art, which are given in the work and are to be judged by criteria internal to the work." This is an interesting and involuted logical maneuver. It sets a narrow boundary around the application of the term *art*—a boundary that certainly does not coincide with the wide range of historical and current uses of that family-term; then it refers to the term so bounded in order to draw another boundary, equally at variance with the range of common uses, around the term *criticism*.

To philosophers so alert to symptoms of the essentialist fallacy, the temptation is to retort, "Aha! Essentialism!" In my essay I succumbed to this debater's temptation to turn the tables. But in fact, I see no fallacy in setting up definitional boundaries of artifice in this way, or even in the seemingly logical eddy of positing an arbitrary boundary for one term in order to establish a boundary for one's use of a correlative term. Some such stratagem, indeed, seems indispensable if we are to talk to any purpose about matters signified by terms*Anya:* so vague and diverse as *art* and *criticism.* The provisos are that we had best be aware of what we're doing and why; and above all that we use the bounds we stipulate for these terms not as ruling definitions but as working definitions, to block out in a preliminary way what we undertake to talk about and how we propose to talk about it. Or, in Wittgenstein's metaphor, the crucial issue is whether the way we use a seemingly essential definition is language idling or language doing work.

4

My debater's stance in opposition to some of the procedures and claims of analytic philosophers disguises the extent to which I concur with their general approach to critical language and with many of their particular discoveries. These philosophers have taken a decisive step by rejecting the narrow logical-positivist views of rationality—based on formal logic and on empirical reasoning in the physical sciences—and have directed our attention from such highly specialized models to what able critics in fact do, in pursuing their indispensable cultural enterprise. To the discursive processes by which critics achieve their illuminating judgments, relate them to a variety of general assertions, and support them by pertinent reasons, it is absurd to deny rationality. The rational thing is instead to enlarge the criteria of rationality so as to encompass the diverse procedures that have again and again demonstrated their power to achieve valuable results. Wittgenstein's later thinking has helped recent philosophers to recognize and to explore the consequences of this approach to the uses of language in various humanistic pursuits, including literary criticism. My demurral is simply that they have stopped too soon and, by imposing premature logical limits, have denied rationality to a number of profitable critical procedures. Coleridge once warned us not to pass an act of uniformity against poets; no more should we against critics.

I shall close by considering briefly a recurrent objection to this point of view; that is, that by my broad conception of what constitutes valid rational procedures in criticism, I have eliminated the possibility of any general criteria for distinguishing between true and false critical assertions and between good and bad critical procedures. I have done so, it is claimed, by making all important critical judgments relative to the individual critic, and in two different ways: a critic's judgments (1) are conceptually relative to his elected theoretical frame or perspective; and (2) are "subjective," in the sense that they are relative to his own temperament and taste.

(1) With respect to the charge of conceptual relativity, I was struck by some things that Mr. Bambrough said in his essay on "Literature and Philosophy." It is, he said, a mistake to assume (prior to investigation) that, in philosophy or in discussions of literature, a generalization necessarily disqualifies a conflicting, or even a seemingly contradictory, generalization. In such areas there is no one totally satisfactory way of putting something in words; different ways of putting it may in fact constitute alternative perspectives on the matter in hand; and only the superposition of views from diverse vantage points will yield what Bambrough strikingly describes as a "vision in depth" or "multi-dimensional description." To guard against the seeming suggestion of a skeptical relativism, Bambrough also reminds us "that what a thing is like from this point of view and from that point of view is all part of what the thing *is* like, and that if that is what we want to know we are not at liberty to choose part of it and represent it as being the whole." These remarks apply precisely to the function I attributed to the diversity of profitable critical theories: each of the theories serves as a critical perspective which does not conflict with but supplements the alternative perspectives. The use of such diverse but complementary conceptual vantages seems to me to be not only rationally justifiable but necessary to the understanding of art, and indeed of any subject of humanistic inquiry; and I would say that the resulting vision in depth is a characteristic feature of

humanistic truth, as distinguished from mathematical or scientific truths.

(2) Mr. Bambrough himself, however, has in a recent letter raised a different but related issue, and one in which other commentators on my essay have concurred. The claim is that what I say implies that critical judgments are "subjective," in that they are relative to inherent differences in the temperament of individual critics, so that there are no objective criteria for deciding between conflicting judgments.

Now, I do say a number of things that might be taken to suggest some such view. I say, for example, that once an assertion is adopted as the premise of a critical theory, "its origin and truth-claim cease to matter," for its validity is to be measured by its demonstrated power to yield valuable critical insights; that the particular theoretical perspective employed by a critic not only selects but in some fashion alters the features of a work of art (in Wittgenstein's terms, the perspective affects both what he is apt to see and what he sees it *as*); that some range of disagreement in literary interpretations and judgments of value is endemic to criticism; that the ultimate standards of valid critical judgments are not sharp-focus but soft-focus standards which we signify by terms such as *sensibility, good sense, sagacity, tact, insight,* and that the application of such standards allows "room for the play of irreducible temperamental differences"; and also that the term *certainty* does not without special qualification apply to most critical conclusions about a work of art. It may seem that as a consequence I am committed to the view that all aesthetic judgments are equally sound, that there's no disputing about taste, and that one should leave one's critical language alone.

This is a matter of concern to me, especially since much that passes for criticism in the present age strikes me as uncommonly irresponsible, so that we can ill afford to minimize the availability of standards for discriminating between sound and unsound procedures in critical reasoning. I don't, however, hold the relativistic opinions I have just described, nor do I think that they are entailed by anything I have said. I in fact believe that we possess valid criteria for judging when criticism is good and when it is bad, and that we are able to disqualify many aesthetic judgments out of hand. But I also think that it is a mistake to assume, and self-defeating to pretend, that these criteria are simple and obvious, or that they are similar to the criteria for distinguishing between a right and wrong answer to a mathematical problem or to a question of empirical fact.

Misunderstanding on this issue is in some part a result of what my essay undertook to do; if it had set out to expose what's wrong in bad criticism, rather than to justify what's right in good criticism, its emphases would have been quite different. But in large part the risk of misunderstanding is inherent in the nature of critical problems and of the language we have evolved for dealing with them. Wittgenstein, in the closing pages of *Philosophical Investigations* (227–28), made some remarks that are very much to that point. He is discussing the reasons why we get general agreement in "judgments of colours" but fail to get such agreement in answer to the question of whether someone's "expression of feeling is genuine or not." He points out that we may reasonably argue about whether the expression of feeling is or is not genuine, but "we cannot prove anything"; that, on the whole, better judgments will be made by those who are expert, but that this expertise is not acquired through a course of systematic instruction but only "through 'experience,' " and can only be described by a vague expression such as having a "better knowledge of mankind"; that such knowledge can be taught, yet not as "a technique," but only by giving someone "the right *tip*"; that "there are also rules, but they do not form a system," so that "unlike calculation rules," only "experienced people can apply them right"; and finally that, while "it is certainly possible to be convinced by evidence," the term " 'evidence' here includes 'imponderable' evidence," and "what does imponderable evidence *accomplish?*" And Wittgenstein exclaims, poignantly: "What is most difficult here is to put this indefiniteness, correctly and unfalsified, into words."

I think that the important critical questions are not like the question, "What color is it?" but much more like the question, "Is this expression of grief genuine?" A persistent dilemma for the philosopher of criticism is how to give due recognition to the indefiniteness of the evidence for an answer, yet not be taken to deny that there are sound, and often convincing, reasons that support one answer rather than another. Because of this difficulty in putting the matter "correctly and unfalsified into words," a monologue is not a very satisfactory way of conducting a philosophical inquiry into aesthetic criticism. To get progressively clearer as to the multiple and interdependent discriminations involved requires the evolving give-and-take of dialogue. Mr. Bambrough applies to such dialogue the ancient philosophical term *dialectic*, and says (citing F. R. Leavis) that the most to be expected is that when a proponent says, "This is so, isn't it?" his interlocutor will reply, "Yes, but . . ." That is in the nature of all humanistic discourse, and a reason why the search for humanistic truth has no ending.

Belief and the Suspension of Disbelief

Nominally the current preoccupation with the role of belief in literature goes back only some thirty-five years, to the issue as raised by I. A. Richards and debated by T. S. Eliot, Middleton Murry, and the many other critics and philosophers who took up the challenge. In fact, however, Richards's theory is a late stage in a perennial concern about the clash between what poets say and what their readers believe to be true. The problem of belief, in one or another formulation, is no less ancient than criticism, and it has always been argued in terms of "knowledge," "truth," and "reality," which are the cruxes of all philosophical disagreement. After twenty-five centuries, there seems greater weight than comfort in T. S. Eliot's weary conclusion that "the problem of belief is very complicated and probably quite insoluble."[1] But a review of the conditions of this endless debate may itself offer some possibility of headway. We have inherited from the past not only the problem but the largely unvoiced aims and assumptions that control the way it is posed and answered, and to know how we got where we are may help us to decide where we are to go from here.

It all began, of course, with Plato. Plato's cosmos is the frame for the play of his dialectic, and cosmos and dialectic cooperate to force the consideration of poetry as a rival of philosophy for access to the true and the good, but under conditions—since poetry is an imitation of an imitation of the criterion Ideas—in which it is hopelessly out of the running. And how remarkably acquiescent the interlocutor in *The Republic* is to this management of the question! "Yes," "Quite true," "Just so," "That follows," "I agree." But suppose he had interjected: "Now look here, Socrates. I see your game. You've got me trapped in a set of premises by which the end is foreordained. But I refuse to consider poetry in a context in which it must aim to do what philosophy can do better. I propose instead that when we consider poetry, we consider it as poetry and not another thing."

Had the interlocutor delivered himself thus, the history of criticism might well have been radically different. It seems quite plain now that Aristotle's *Poetics* transferred the discussion to precisely these new grounds, but silently, so that over the centuries Aristotle has been interpreted as refuting or correcting Plato's theory on its own terms. As a consequence literary criticism has been maneuvered into a defensive stance from which it has never entirely recovered. Alone among the major disciplines the theory of literature has been mainly a branch of apologetics; and we shall mistake the emphases of many major critical documents, whether or not they are labeled a Defense of Poetry, if we fail to recognize the degree to which they have constituted the rebuttal in a persistent debate. The positions most strongly defended have shifted, to meet the threat from one or another enterprise claiming exclusive access to the kind of truth poetry was supposed to pretend to: philosophy, history, Christian theology and morals, and then, in the seventeenth century, the New Philosophy. But in every age the seemingly positive principles of criticism have been designed for the defense of poetry, and usually, as in the Platonic dialogues, on a terrain selected by the opposition.

Since the eighteenth century the situation has stabilized, for the great and portentous claimant to truth has become, and has remained, science. Consonantly, attempts to save the credit of poetry have been directed mainly against the pretensions to universal application of scientific standards of language, and against scientific criteria for judging the validity of all claims to knowledge and value. And quite early the pressure of a scientific culture gave their characteristic shape to two types of poetic theory which set the conditions under which we still for the most part undertake to deal with the problem of belief in literature. The first theory conceives poetry to be a special language whose function is to express and evoke feelings, and which is therefore immune from the criteria of valid reference, as well as from the claims on our belief, appropriate to the language of science. The second theory conceives a poem to be an autonomous world all its own, and therefore immune from the requirement that it correspond to our knowledge and beliefs about the world revealed by science.

Early in the nineteenth century Jeremy Bentham, heir to the traditional English semantics of scientific language, charged that by the standards of "logical truth" poetic statements are false. "All poetry is misrepresentation." "Indeed, between poetry and truth there is a natural opposition: false morals, fictitious nature."[2] John Stuart Mill, a disciple of Bentham who became an ardent defender of poetry, although in terms controlled by the semantics of positivism, defined poetry as "the expression or uttering forth of feeling" and therefore what he called the "logical opposite" of "matter of fact or science." Accordingly, while science "addresses itself to belief" by "presenting a proposition to the understanding," poetry acts by "offering interesting objects of contemplation to the sensibilities"; so that the reader can accept it, without belief, for the sake of its emotional effects. Poetic illusion, he wrote, "consists in extracting from a conception known not to be true . . . the same benefit to the feelings which would be derived from it if it were a reality."[3]

By Matthew Arnold's time religion had become codefendant with poetry against the attack of positivism; and Arnold, accepting as inevitable the demise of dogmatic religion because it "has attached its emotion to the fact, and now the fact is failing it," transferred its function to poetry because (like Mill) he regarded it as emotively efficacious independently of its truth or the reader's belief. For "poetry attaches its emotion to the idea; the idea *is* the fact." And I. A. Richards, who used this pronouncement from "The Study of Poetry" as the epigraph to his *Science and Poetry,* expanded upon it in terms of a more developed form of the positivist semantics he shared

with Hobbes, Bentham, and Mill. All language divides into
two kinds. On the one side is "scientific statement," whose
truth is ultimately a matter of correspondence "with the fact
to which it points." On the other side is "emotive utterance,"
including poetry, which is composed of "pseudo-statements"
whose function is not to assert truths but to organize our
feelings and attitudes. And since we have learned to free the
emotional efficacy of poetry from belief, poetry must take
over the function of ordering our emotional life hitherto
performed by the pseudo-statements of religion.[4]

In our age, dominated by the odd assumption that all discourse which is not science must be of a single kind, many
opponents of positivism fall in with the tendency to conflate
religion with poetry in a common opposition to science. But
this tactic will not do, whether we hold, with the positivists,
that poetry will replace religion because it works without belief,
or, with the antipositivists, that poetry and religion share access
to a special kind of nonscientific truth beyond logic and the
law of excluded middle. On this distinguished panel I stand
as an infidel *in partibus fidelium,* but I will venture the opinion
that it is equally unjust to religion to poetize it and to poetry
to sanctify it. Religion is patently not science, but no more is
it poetry; and it can survive only if granted its own function
and processes and claims upon belief. As for poetry, I shall
soon maintain that it depends for its efficacy upon evoking a
great number of beliefs. Besides, it must inevitably paralyze
our responsiveness and ready delight to approach a poem as
a way to salvation—in Richards's words, as "capable of saving
us."[5]

To the view that poetry is an emotive use of language, the
most common alternative is the view that poetry is a world
sui generis, to be experienced and valued on its own terms,
independently of its correspondence to reality or of its emotive and moral effects on the reader. This concept also originated as a defensive tactic, this time against the demand that
the materials of poetry be limited to the objects and possibilities of the empirical world revealed by the new science. In
rebuttal eighteenth-century proponents of the mythical and
marvelous in poetry developed the possibilities of the old
Renaissance analogy—the most influential new concept in

postclassical criticism—between the poet and the Creator. The poet, it was said, emulates God by creating a "second world" which is not an imitation of the real world, but a world of its own kind, subject only to its own laws, and exhibiting not the truth of correspondence, but only the truth of coherence, or purely internal consistency. "Poetic truth," as Richard Hurd said in 1762, is not the truth to "the known and experienced course of affairs in this world" demanded by Hobbes. For "the poet has a world of his own, where experience has less to do than consistent imagination."[6]

The radical implications of the concept of a poem as an *alter mundus* were exploited most fully in Germany, especially after Baumgarten for the first time set out to construct a philosophy of the fine arts in general, for which he coined the term *aesthetics*. In Baumgarten's formulation, the end of a work of art is not to reflect reality, nor to foster morality or yield pleasure; "the aesthetic end is the perfection of sensuous cognition . . . that is, beauty." Produced by a poet who is "like a maker or a creator . . . the poem ought to be a sort of world," related to the real world "by analogy." Poetic fiction is "heterocosmic," consisting of things possible in another world than the one we live in, and subject therefore not to the criterion of strict philosophic truth, but only to the criterion of "heterocosmic truth"; that is, self-consistency and the maximum internal coherence.[7] In his *Critique of Judgment* Kant added the corollary ideas that a beautiful work of art is experienced as an end in itself, by an act purely contemplative, disinterested, and free from any reference to desire, will, or the reality and utility of the object.

Now that these discoveries have become so commonplace that they seem the intuitions of common sense, it is easy to derogate the attempts of aesthetic philosophers to talk about all the arts at once. But the achievement of eighteenth-century aestheticians was immensely important: they made current a set of premises enabling the defenders of poetry to meet the charges of Plato and his successors, not on grounds that poetry can compete successfully with the philosopher, the scientist, and the moralist, but on grounds that poetry is entirely its own kind of thing, with its own laws, its own reason for being, and its particular mode of excellence. No won-

der, then, that in the nineteenth century these ideas were
enthusiastically seized upon and deployed (at first mainly on
hearsay) by French and English theorists of art for art's sake
in their strenuous counterattack against the demands for truth,
morality, and utility in art by philosophical positivists, literary conservatives, and a society of Philistines. In his inaugu-
ral lecture at Oxford, "Poetry for Poetry's Sake," A. C. Bradley
stripped this theory of its curious theological and ethical
adjuncts about art as a religion and life as a work of art, and
gave it a classic statement. The experience of poetry, he says,
"is an end in itself," and "its *poetic* value is this intrinsic worth
alone." For the nature of poetry

> is to be not a part, nor yet a copy, of the real world . . . but to
> be a world by itself, independent, complete, autonomous; and
> to possess it fully you must enter that world, conform to its
> laws, and ignore for the time the beliefs, aims, and particular
> conditions which belong to you in the other world of reality.

And since this poetic world is an indissoluble unity of content
and form, he decries in criticism "the heresy of the separable
substance."[8]

For a lecture delivered more than a half-century ago, this
sounds remarkably up-to-date. It should indeed, for its primary assumptions continue to be the grounds of the most
familiar contemporary criticism. We assent heartily to Eliot's
dictum that poetry is "autotelic" and to be considered "as
poetry and not another thing."[9] We affirm with Ransom "the
autonomy of the work itself as existing for its own sake,"[10]
and conceive the poem to be a self-sustaining entity—variously described as "an object in itself" or an "independent
poetic structure" (Brooks) or an "icon" (Wimsatt) or "a kind
of world or cosmos" (Austin Warren)— although, in accordance with the modern *furor semanticus,* we tend to think of
the poetic other-world as a universe of discourse rather than
a universe of creatures, setting, and events. And by a tactic
reminiscent of A. C. Bradley's "heresy of the separable substance," and of "the heresy of the didactic" exposed by a still
earlier proponent of art for art, Edgar Allan Poe, we severely
proscribe a variety of heresies and fallacies which threaten to

violate the independence and integrity of the sovereign poem.

This austere dedication to the poem *per se* has produced an unprecedented and enlightening body of verbal explication. But it threatens also to commit us to the concept of a poem as a language game, or as a floating Laputa, insulated from life and essential human concerns in a way that accords poorly with our experience in reading a great work of literature. Hence, I think, the persistent struggle in recent criticism to save the autonomy of a poem, yet to anchor it again to the world beyond itself and to re-engage it with the moral consciousness of the reader. One example is the frequent insistence that a poem is cognitive and yields valid knowledge, although in the final analysis the knowledge a poem yields usually turns out to be coterminous with the poem itself. The poem's value, as Allen Tate puts it, "is a cognitive one; it is sufficient that here, in the poem, we get knowledge of a whole object."[11] By a procedure that has been a constant corollary of the view that a poem is a world in itself ever since it was expounded by Baumgarten and his contemporaries, the truth of a poem is interpreted to be a truth of inner coherence, and the relation of the poetic world to the real world is conceived to be a relation not of correspondence but of analogy. Just as A. C. Bradley declared at the beginning of this century that poetry and life "are parallel developments that nowhere meet . . . they are analogues," so John Crowe Ransom's cognitive claim for poetry comes down to the proposal that the structure and texture of a poem are an analogical reminder that the world's body is "denser and more refractory" than the "docile and virtuous" world represented by poetry's great opposite, science.[12] And if I read him correctly, W. K. Wimsatt's point about literature as "a form of knowledge" is that poetic truth is inner coherence and the relation of a poem to the world is one of analogy. In his words, "the dimension of coherence is by various techniques of implication greatly enhanced and thus generates an extra dimension of correspondence to reality, the symbolic or analogical."[13]

We are particularly uneasy today about the pressure of the doctrine of poetic autonomy toward the conclusion of art for art; with a candor that is rare in contemporary discussion of this issue, Allen Tate affirms "that poetry finds its true use-fulness in its perfect inutility."[14] The attempt to break out of the sealed verbal world of the poem-as-such is, I think, one cardinal motive for the current insistence that, in all poems that are more than trivially agreeable, the structure of symbols, images, and meanings is governed by a "theme." In practice this theme frequently turns out to be a moral or philosophical commonplace which bears a startling likeness to the "moral," or governing proposition, once postulated by the didactic theorists of the Renaissance and Neoclassic ages. Homer, declared Dryden in his Preface to *Troilus and Cressida*, undertook to "insinuate into the people" the moral "that union preserves a commonwealth and discord destroys it; Sophocles, in his *Oedipus*, that no man is to be accounted happy before his death. 'Tis the moral that directs the whole action of a play to one center." The difference is that, according to the modern critic, the theme subsists only in the concrete embodiment of the poem, as an ownerless, unasserted, non-referential, uncredited, and thoroughly insulated something which serves nevertheless to inform the meanings of a poem both with their unity and their moral "seriousness," "maturity," and "relevance." This existential oddity has been engendered by the opposing conditions of poetic autonomy and poetic relevance under which modern critics typically conduct their inquiry into the relations between poetry and life. As W. K. Wimsatt describes the conditions governing his essay on "Poetry and Morals": "We inquire . . . about the work so far as it can be considered by itself as a body of meaning. Neither the qualities of the author's mind nor the effects of a poem upon a reader's mind should be confused with the moral quality of the meaning expressed by the poem itself."[15]

I confess that my own view of the matter involves something like this divided premise, with its attendant difficulties. It seems to me that our experience in reading serious literature, when uninhibited by theoretical prepossessions, engages the whole mind, including the complex of common sense and moral beliefs and values deriving from our experience in this world. Yet I also think it essential to save the basic insight of aesthetic theory since the eighteenth century: that a poem is a self-sufficient whole which is to be read for its own sake, independently of the truths it may communicate or the moral and social effects it may exert, and that its intrinsic value constitutes its reason for existing as a poem and not as something else. I am also uncomfortably aware that this looks very much like an attempt to have art for art's sake and eat it too.

I would suggest that the apparent antinomy comes from relying too implicitly on aesthetic ideas inherited from a polemical past. The persistently defensive position of criticism, and its standard procedure of combating charges against poetry by asserting their contraries, has forced it into an either-or, all-or-none choice that breeds dilemmas: either language is scientific or it is purely emotive; either a poem corresponds to this world or it is a world entirely its own; either poetry has a moral aim or it is totally beyond judgment of good or evil; either all our beliefs are relevant to reading poetry or all beliefs must be suspended. What we obviously need is the ability to make more distinctions and finer discriminations; and perhaps these will follow if we substitute for concepts developed mainly as polemical weapons a positive view designed specifically for poetic inquiry and analysis.

Suppose, then, that we set out from the observation that a poem is about people. Or a bit more elaborately, that a poem presents one or more persons recognizably like those in this world, but imposes its artistic differences by rendering the characters and their perceptions, thought, and actions so as to enhance their inherent interest and whatever effects the poem undertakes to achieve. This statement is not to be understood as contradicting the statements that a poem is an emotive use of language, or that a poem constitutes a verbal universe. It is offered merely as an alternative point of critical departure for inquiry into such questions as the role of belief in the appreciation of poetry. Furthermore, this viewpoint is as old as Aristotle's *Poetics*, and will produce no radical novelties. But I think the issue of morality and belief in poetry has been made to seem unnecessarily recondite because of the common tendency to define a poem as a special kind of language, or a special structure of words and meanings, and then to slip in characters and actions quietly through a back door.

I propose also not to begin with universal statements about

"all poetry" or "all art," but to proceed inductively, beginning with single poetic passages and using these, in Wittgenstein's parlance, as "paradigm cases" on which to base only such generalizations as they promise to support. Convenient instances to hand are the few examples of poetic statements that have been mooted again and again in discussions of belief, although with little heed to their differences in kind and usually as illustrations for a foregone conclusion. The examples are: "Beauty is truth"; "Ripeness is all"; "In His will is our peace"; and "Thou best philosopher . . . Mighty Prophet! Seer blest!"

1

"Beauty is truth, truth beauty" is not asserted by Keats, either as a statement or as a pseudo-statement. The Grecian Urn, after remaining obdurately mute under a hail of questions, unexpectedly gives voice to this proposition near the end of the poem. In discussions of the problem of belief the significance of this obvious fact is often overlooked or minimized. Middleton Murry, for example, although he observes that the speaker is the Urn, goes on immediately to reconstruct the biographical occasion Keats himself had for such a comment, and then (like so many other critics) evolves an elaborate aesthetico-ontological theory to demonstrate that the statement is philosophically valid, and merits assent.[16] For his part, I. A. Richards describes "Beauty is truth" as "the expression of a certain blend of feelings," and asks us to accept such emotive expressions without belief; and T. S. Eliot replies that he would be glad to do so, except that "the statement of Keats" seems to him so obtrusively meaningless that he finds the undertaking impossible.[17]

There is also a second and more important speaker in the poem. The whole of the *Ode on a Grecian Urn*, in fact, consists of the utterance of this unnamed character, whose situation and actions we follow as he attends first to the whole, then to the sculptured parts, and again to the whole of the Urn; and who expresses in the process not only his perceptions but his thoughts and feelings, and thereby discovers to us a determinate temperament. By a standard poetic device we accept without disbelief, he attributes to the Urn a statement about beauty and truth which is actually a thought that the Urn evokes in him. How we are to take the statement, therefore, depends not only on its status as an utterance, in that place, by the particular Urn, but beyond that as the penultimate stage, dramatically rendered, in the meditation of the lyric speaker himself.

Obviously the earlier part of the *Ode* by no means gives the Urn a character that would warrant either its profundity or its reliability as a moral philosopher. In the mixed attitudes of the lyric speaker toward the Urn the playfulness and the pity, which are no less evident than the envy and the admiration, imply a position of superior understanding:

> Bold lover, never, never canst thou kiss,
> Though winning near the goal—yet, do not grieve;
> She cannot fade, though thou hast not thy bliss. . . .

The perfection represented on the Urn is the perdurability of the specious present, which escapes the "woe" of our mutable world only by surrendering any possibility of consummation and by trading grieving flesh for marble. The Urn, then, speaks from the limited perspective of a work of Grecian art; and it is from the larger viewpoint of this life, with its possibilities and its sorrows, that the lyric speaker has the last word, addressed to the figures on the Urn:

> That is all
> Ye know on earth, and all ye need to know.

The Urn has said, "Only the beautiful exists, and all that exists is beautiful"—but not, the speaker replies, in life, only in that sculptured Grecian world of noble simplicity where much that humanly matters is sacrificed for an enduring Now.[18]

I entirely agree, then, with Professor Brooks in his explication of the *Ode*, that "Beauty is truth" is not meant "to compete with . . . scientific and philosophical generalizations," but is to be considered as a speech "in character" and "dramatically appropriate" to the Urn. I am uneasy, however, about his final reference to "the world-view, or 'philosophy,' or 'truth' of the *poem as a whole*."[19] For the poem as a whole is equally an utterance by a dramatically presented speaker, and none of its statements is proffered for our endorsement as a philosophical generalization of unlimited scope. They are all, therefore, to be apprehended as histrionic elements which are "in character" and "dramatically appropriate," for their inherent interest as stages in the evolution of an artistically ordered, hence all the more emotionally effective, experience of a credible human being.

Is an appreciation of the *Ode*, then, entirely independent of the reader's beliefs? Surely not. As it evolves, the poem makes constant call on a complex of beliefs which are the product of ordinary human experiences with life, people, love, mutability, age, and art. These subsist less in propositional form than in the form of unverbalized attitudes, propensities, sentiments, and dispositions; but they stand ready to precipitate into assertions the moment they are radically challenged, whether in the ordinary course of living or in that part of living we call reading poetry. Kant's claims, as I have said, seem valid, that the apprehension of a work of art, as opposed to our ordinary cognitive and practical concerns, is properly contemplative, disinterested, and free from will and desire, and that the function of presentative art is not to persuade us to beliefs or actions, but to be a terminal good. But here is where we need to make an essential discrimination. These observations are valid in so far as we are concerned to make a broad initial distinction between poetic and nonpoetic experience, and to separate specifically poetic values from effects outside the experience of the poem itself. But when applied to our apprehension, of what goes on *inside* a poem, they seem to me, as often interpreted, to be not merely misleading, but directly contrary to aesthetic experience. If the poem works, our appreciation of the matters it presents is not aloofly contemplative, but actively engaged. We are not disinterested, but deeply concerned with the characters and what they say and do, and we are interested in a fashion that brings into play our entire moral economy and expresses itself continuously in attitudes of approval or disapproval, sympathy or antipathy. And though the poet is not concerned to persuade us to take up positions outside the poem, it is his constant concern to persuade us to concur with the common-sense and moral positions presupposed by the poem, to take the serious seriously and the comic comically, and to acquiesce in the probability of the thoughts, choices, and actions that are represented to follow from a given character. All these results, however distinguishable from our responses in practical life, depend in great part on beliefs and dispositions that we bring to the poem from life; and these operate not as antagonists to our aesthetic responses, but as the indispensable conditions for them, and therefore as constitutive elements in our appreciation of the poem as a poem. The skillful poet contrives which of our beliefs will be called into play, to what degree, and with what emotional effect. Given a truly impassive reader, all his beliefs suspended or anesthetized, he would be as helpless, in his attempt to endow his work with interest and power, as though he had to write for an audience from Mars.

So with Keats's *Ode*. We accept without disbelief the given situation of the speaker confronting and talking to an Urn, and we attend delightedly to the rich texture and music of his speech. But if what follows is to be more than superficially effective, we must take the lyric speaker's emotional problem seriously, as possessing dignity and importance according to the criteria of ordinary experience. By the same criteria, we must find the speaker himself credible and winning—sensitive, intelligent, warm, yet (unlike many of the profoundly solemn commentators on his utterance) able to meditate the woes of this life and the limitations of art with philosophic lucidity and a very lively sense of the irony of the human situation, and even of the humor of his dialogue with an Urn. Above all, we must so recognize ourselves and our lot in him as to consent imaginatively to his experience until it is resolved, in both artistic and human terms, in a way that is formally complete, hence beautiful, and intellectually and emotionally satisfying.

2

Whatever the case may be with the lyric, it had always seemed obvious that the words of a drama constitute speeches by determinate characters until several decades ago, when by a notable stratagem we critics succeeded in dehumanizing even Shakespeare's tragedies by converting them into patterns of thematic imagery. But I am bound by my critical premise to take "Ripeness is all" in the old-fashioned way, as a statement by a person in a given situation rather than as a moment in the dialectic of a vegetational symbol.

The statement is Edgar's, and it is not uttered in philosophical humor as a summary philosophy of life, but with sharp impatience, for an urgently practical purpose, at a desperate moment in the action. The battle has been lost, Lear and Cordelia captured, and Edgar must rally his blind father from a recurrence of his suicidal impulse, in the hopeless decision to bide and be captured:

EDGAR: Give me thy hand! Come on!
GLOUCESTER: No further, sir. A man may rot even here.
EDGAR: What, in ill thoughts again? Men must endure
      Their going hence, even as their coming hither;
      Ripeness is all. Come on.

The question of our giving or withholding assent to this statement, taken as a universal philosophic predication, has arisen only because it has been pulled out of Shakespeare's context and put in the artificial context of our own discussions of the problem of belief. In its original place we respond to the speech, in the curt perfection of its phrasing, as following from Edgar's character, appropriate both to the bitter events preceding and to the exigency of the moment, and also, it should be noted, as an element in the action of people whose fortunes we strongly favor.

A popular opinion about Shakespeare's objectivity seems to place his characters completely outside the purview of our moral beliefs and judgments. It derives ultimately from Kant's concept of disinterested aesthetic contemplation, came to

England by way of Coleridge and Hazlitt, and received its best-known formulation in Keats's comment on Shakespeare's "negative capability" and his claim that the poetical character "has as much delight in conceiving an Iago as an Imogen. What shocks the virtuous philosopher delights the camelion poet," for whom all ends "in speculation."[20] Rightly understood, the concept is true and important. We apprehend Shakespeare's villains with a purity and fullness of appreciation possible only in art, where we see the characters from within, and independently of the practical effects on us of their being what they are. But the aesthetic attitude, though different from the practical attitude, is not so different as all that. In Dr. Johnson's phrase, the attitude is one of "tranquillity without indifference"; our aesthetic judgments, while not those of a participant, remain those of a partisan. We may take as great delight in Shakespeare's villain as in his hero, but we are constantly aware that the villain is a villain and the hero a hero. I. A. Richards has said in *Science and Poetry* that we must have no beliefs if we are to read *King Lear*. But *King Lear* presents a conflict of characters in which the author must make us take sides; and he is able to do so only by presupposing that we bring to the work deep-rooted moral beliefs and values which will cause us instinctively to attach our good will to some characters and ill will to others, and therefore to respond appropriately to their changing fortunes with hope and disappointment, delight and sadness, pity and terror.

Like all the greatest poets Shakespeare pays the human race the compliment of assuming that it is, in its central moral consciousness, sound. So from the opening words of the play we are invited to accept without disbelief the existence of King Lear and his three daughters, but to believe, and never for a moment to doubt—however the violence of circumstance may shake the assurance of this or that character in the play— that a king, while regal, ought to possess human understanding, moral penetration, and a modicum of humility, and that daughters should be loyal, kindly, and truthful, not treacherous, sadistic, and murderous. Shakespeare does not lay out Dante's geometrical distinctions between the utterly damnable and the merely damnable, but he does presuppose that we find good to be admirable and evil abhorrent, in the nuance of their manifestations in concrete behavior. We relish a villain like Edmund, skillfully rendered by the poet in all his unillusioned intelligence, self-insight, and vitality. But if, through some lapse in the author or some obtuseness or obliquity in ourselves, we remain indifferent, paring our fingernails, or so lose our moral bearings as to attach our sympathies to Edmund and the pelican daughters instead of to Lear and Gloucester (however flawed) and to Cordelia, Edgar, and Kent, then the play collapses into an amorphous mass without catastrophe or catharsis.

3

Far from Dante himself asserting that "In His will is our peace," he portrays Piccarda making the assertion to him, in smiling commiseration for the narrowness and pettiness of his earthly mind, and in a tone as near reproof as is possible for a spirit in felicity. For Dante has just inquired whether Piccarda is not dissatisfied with her place on the lowest of the heavenly spheres, and she replies that God draws all wills to what he wills, so that "In His will is our peace; it is that sea to which all moves." And Dante is enlightened and convinced: "Clear was it then to me how every where in heaven is Paradise."

This statement, then, like our earlier examples, is uttered in a dramatic context. There are, however, important differences in its literary conditions. The poem is not lyric or dramatic, but narrative in form; the author himself plays a role both as narrator and as one of his own characters; the total assertion this time involves a theological subproposition ("God exists"); and the passage occurs in a work of which the aim is not presentative, but didactic.

So Dante himself insists in his *Letter to Can Grande*. His work, he says there, is allegorical; its purpose "is to remove those living in this life" from misery to happiness; and its genus is ethical, "for the whole and the part are devised not for the sake of speculation but of possible action" (§§7–16). The *Divine*

Comedy, then, like *Paradise Lost, Prometheus Unbound, A Doll's House,* and *Lady Chatterley's Lover,* is a work of literature specifically designed to dramatize and empower a set of beliefs. In it Piccarda's statement about God's will (in Dante's words) is one of the many things "that have great utility and delight" which are asked from the blessed souls in heaven "who see all the truth" (§33). The function of this statement is not, like that of "Ripeness is all," merely to instance character and advance the action, but to render in a dramatic, and therefore in the most efficacious possible way—as a truth achieved through error—a universal doctrine which is one aspect of the total theological truth propagated by the poem. For the first time in our discussion, accordingly, it becomes relevant to consider the relation of the reader's beliefs to his apprehension of an isolated poetic statement, offered for his assent. And the testimony of innumerable readers demonstrates that the passage can certainly be appreciated, and appreciated profoundly, independently of assent to its propositional truth. It touches sufficiently on universal experience—since all of us, whether Catholic, Protestant, or agnostic, know the heavy burden of individual decision—to enable us all to realize in imagination the relief that might come from saying to an infallible Providence, "Not my will, but Thine be done." This ability to take an assertion hypothetically, as a ground for imaginative experience, is one we in fact possess, and the business of critical theory is to recognize and confirm our reading skills, not to inhibit them by arguments from inadequate premises.

The *Divine Comedy,* however, raises other questions about the role of belief that are specific to thesis narratives. What Dante undertakes, as a poet, is so to realize his abstract theological scheme as to transform our intellectual assent, which he largely takes for granted, into emotional consent and practical action. This task sets him extraordinarily difficult artistic problems. To take one striking example, he must persuade us, against all our natural inclinations, that the Inferno, with its savage, repulsive, and exquisitely ingenious tortures protracted in perpetuity, is not only required by God's justice but (as the Gate of Hell announces) is entailed by God's "Primal Love." And the more credible and terrifying Dante, in his one function as moral monitor, makes the exemplary sufferings of the damned, the more difficult he makes his other task of winning our emotional consent to the thesis that God is Love, and Hell follows.

To this end Dante inserts himself, a mortal like us, into the poem as the experiential center through whose eyes and sensibility we invariably view Hell, as well as Purgatory and Heaven. And he exhibits with entire credibility the terror, the anguish, the incomprehension, the divided mind and emotions of the finite and temporal intelligence which is forced to look upon the universe under the aspect of eternity. He repeatedly misapplies his sympathy, feels an irrepressible admiration for the strength and dignity of some of the sinners in their ultimate adversity, weeps with such an abandon of fellow feeling that Virgil must sternly reprimand him, and when he hears Francesca's tender story, faints with pity.

Dante's invention of himself is the supreme artistic achievement of the *Divine Comedy*. For Dante is a poet, though a didactic poet, and like any poet must endow his work with emotional power by engaging the sympathies and feelings of his readers with the matters he presents. To do so he appeals not merely to our theological beliefs (which we can yield or deny him) but also to beliefs and attitudes that are broader than any particular creed, and almost irresistibly compelling; for all of us, whatever our doctrinal differences, share the humanity of his central character and so follow and consent to his entirely human experiences, whether of the inhuman horrors of the doomed in Hell or the inhuman felicity of the Saints in Heaven.

Since he is, however, though a poet, a didactic poet, Dante relies on our prior beliefs and sentiments to involve us with the matters he shows forth, not as an end in itself, but as a means toward retroacting upon and reforming our beliefs and sentiments. If we circumvent him by stopping at the appreciation of what he shows forth, he would no doubt consider his great undertaking a failure. But for most of us the enjoyment of his didactic poem as, simply, a poem must perforce be enough.

4

In our final example the question of belief is raised by the author himself, and in a form that makes it especially pertinent to contemporary literature. Wordsworth told Isabella Fenwick in 1843 that his *Ode: Intimations of Immortality* was based on experiences of his own childhood which he regarded "in the poem . . . as presumptive evidence of a prior state of existence." But he did not, he affirms, mean "to inculcate such a belief." "I took hold of the notion of preexistence as having sufficient foundation in humanity for authorizing me to make for my purpose the best use of it I could as a poet."[21]

With Wordsworth we impinge on our own age of self-consciousness about multiple choices in beliefs when, as T. S. Eliot declared, it is impossible to say how far some poets "write their poetry because of what they believe, and how far they believe a thing merely because they see that they can make poetry out of it"[22] William Blake had already created his own mythical system lest he "be enslaved by another man's," and thereby set the example for the spirits who came to give Yeats "metaphors for poetry."[23] So Wordsworth tells us that he did not mean to assert Platonic metempsychosis, but utilized it as an available poetic premise, an as-if ground for a metaphorical structure by which to manage what he called "the world of his own mind."

In this comment Wordsworth probably remembered what Coleridge had said about the *Ode* in the *Biographia Literaria* some twenty-six years earlier. There Coleridge described poetic illusion as "that *negative* faith, which simply permits the images presented to work by their own force, without either denial or affirmation of their real existence by the judgment." In the same chapter he went on to justify Wordsworth's use of Platonic preexistence as an uncredited poetic postulate, necessary in order to deal with "modes of inmost being, to which . . . the attributes of time and space are inapplicable and alien, but which yet can not be conveyed save in symbols of time and space." But Coleridge refused equal immunity from disbelief to those lines in the *Ode* hailing a six-year-old child as "Thou best philosopher . . . Mighty

Prophet! Seer blest!" "In what sense," he demands, "can the magnificent attributes . . . be appropriated to a *child*, which would not make them equally suitable to a *bee*, or a *dog*, or a *field of corn?*" For "the child is equally unconscious of it as they."[24]

In his *Coleridge on Imagination*, I. A. Richards took Coleridge severely to task for this limitation on the principle of suspended disbelief. For "we may," he said, "if we wish, take all the alleged attributes of Wordsworth's child," and even their applicability to a field of corn, "as fictions, as part of the myth."[25] But again, I think, we need to make distinctions. While it is true that the poet may educe from the myth of preexistence the conclusion that a child is the best philosopher, the myth by no means enforces this conclusion, as Plato's original use of it amply demonstrates. We must remember that Wordsworth's *Ode,* as he himself said, is not primarily about the myth; rather, the myth is auxiliary to the poetic management of events in this life to which every one, "if he would look back, could bear testimony." The lyric, we can say, presents the meditation of a man like ourselves, confronted abruptly by the need to adapt himself to a discovery which, in one or another form, is universally human: the discovery that in losing his youth he has lost the possibility of experiences on which he places the highest value. The postulate of the preexistence of the soul, realized in the great image of the rising and westering sun, affords him the spatial and temporal metaphors he needs in order to objectify, dignify, and resolve what Coleridge called "a fact of mind." Ultimately the resolution depends on a shift in the point of view. From the vantage of the "imperial palace" of our origin, the earth is a "prison-house" and the process of aging a cumulative loss. But from the alternate vantage of this earth and this life—with its acquisitions of strength, sympathy, faith, and the philosophic mind, which spring from the very experience of human suffering—maturity is seen to have compensatory rewards; so that the metaphoric sun of the initial myth, which has risen "trailing clouds of glory," sets as the material sun we know in this world, yet takes another, if more sober, coloring from an eye "That hath kept watch o'er man's mortality."

What Coleridge queries is the credibility, in a poem that bears on our ordinary experience, and after Wordsworth has already described a very realistic six-year-old at his childish games, of the sudden apostrophe:

> Thou best Philosopher, who yet dost keep
> Thy heritage, thou Eye among the blind,
> That, deaf and silent, read'st the eternal deep,
>
> .   .   .   .
>
> Mighty Prophet! Seer blest!

This is grandly said, but I understand and think I share Coleridge's sensation that, in its place and circumstances, it arouses counterbeliefs about real urchins which enforce an impression of what Coleridge called "mental bombast." If a child is a philosopher only in the sense that a field of corn is one, why the passionate and superlative encomium?

But this is a delicate decision, and I would not insist on it against contrary judgments by Richards, Brooks, and other expert readers. I want to insist, however, on the validity of Coleridge's implicit principle. A poet is entitled to his initial predication, or myth, or *donnée,* whether or not he is prepared to assert it outside the poem, and especially if, as Wordsworth said, it has "sufficient foundation in humanity" for his purpose "as a poet." But the inference is not justified that, from then on, anything goes. The poet must still win our imaginative consent to the aspects of human experience he presents, and to do so he cannot evade his responsibility to the beliefs and prepossessions of our common experience, common sense, and common moral consciousness. Even a phantasy such as the *Ancient Mariner,* Coleridge noted, requires a protagonist endowed with "a human interest and a semblance of truth sufficient to procure . . . that willing suspension of disbelief for the moment, which constitutes poetic faith";[26] and in a more recent literary nightmare, Kafka put at the center of *The Trial* the matter-of-fact character K., to whose extraordinary experiences we acquiesce because his responses are so entirely ordinary.

The artistic cost of failure in this essential respect is demonstrated by the writings of accomplished craftsmen in which the substance is too inadequately human to engage our continuing interest, or which require our consent to positions so illiberal, or eccentric, or perverse that they incite counterbeliefs which inhibit the ungrudging "yes" that we grant to masterpieces. Blake's prophetic poems, for instance, lack what the *Divine Comedy* possesses—a human center of reference on which the imagination can rest; so that, fine isolated passages apart, and when we have exhausted their interest as symbolic puzzles, they become not a little tedious. Swinburne solicits our sympathy for modes of feeling so *outré* that a number of his lyrics remain brilliant items of literary *curiosa*, teetering on the edge of self-parody. In *The Counterfeiters* André Gide lavishes his intricate art to beguile us into taking seriously a resolution in which a nephew cohabits with his uncle, but the inherent risibility of an anomaly which is multiplied so ingeniously makes the resolution precarious. The difficulty is not in the literary material as such. Vladimir Nabokov's *Lolita,* which treats a somewhat parallel and even more scabrous matter, seems to me humanly right in inviting an attitude of horrified hilarity toward Humbert Humbert, on whom outrageous nature has forced the grotesque role of parent and paramour to a bobby-soxer. Ernest Hemingway's *The Short Happy Life of Francis Macomber* is a triumph of spare artistry. The discovery, however, that all depends on the street-corner assumption that a man's physical courage, his sexual virility, and his dominance over his wife are mutually implicative, provokes a skepticism which makes the triumph a somewhat hollow one. We have been assured that D. H. Lawrence is one of the few English novelists in the Great Tradition; yet, for all the power of the individual scenes, perhaps other readers share my imperfect accord with many of his protagonists: the Aaron of *Aaron's Rod,* for example, who deserts his wife and children to give unfettered scope to his ego, only to end by delivering his will over to the writer Lilly, that peculiarly Laurentian version of the God-given Great Man.

Here we reach the twilight zone between reasoned discussion of a critical problem and the expression of idiosyncrasy, and it is important not to let disagreement about particular applications obscure the issue in question. The implicit but constant requisition of a serious literary work upon our pre-dispositions and beliefs is not an end in itself, but a necessary means to engage our interest and feelings, in order to move them toward a resolution. Furthermore, the great writer does not merely play upon the beliefs and propensities we bring to literature from life, but sensitizes, enlarges, and even transforms them. But in order to get sufficient purchase on our moral sensibility to accommodate it to the matters he presents, any writer must first take that sensibility as he finds it. There is no escaping the circumstance that a poet must submit to the conditions of human nature in order to be their master.

II. Cultural History
and the History
of Criticism

Rationality and Imagination in Cultural History

WAYNE BOOTH is quite right: for all my interest in the methods of literary criticism, I say nothing about method in my two historical books, *The Mirror and the Lamp* and *Natural Supernaturalism*. The reason for my silence on this issue is simple: these books were not written with any method in mind. Instead they were conceived, researched, worked out, put together, pulled apart, and put back together not according to a theory of valid procedures in such undertakings but by intuition. I relied, that is, on my sense of rightness and wrongness, of doubt and assurance, of deficiencies and superfluities, of what is appropriate and what is inappropriate. I should like to think that these intuitions were the kind that Coleridge describes, which follow from

> such a knowledge of the facts, material and spiritual, that most appertain to [the writer's] art, as, if it have been governed and applied by *good sense,* and rendered instinctive by habit, becomes the representative and reward of our past conscious reasonings, insights, and conclusions, and acquires the name of TASTE.[1]

We must distinguish between ignorant intuitions and those which are the reward of prior experience, reading, and thinking; the play of this latter class of intuitions is what we mean by expertise.

In retrospect, I think I was right to compose *Natural Supernaturalism* (let us, following Booth, focus our discussion on this book) by relying on taste, tact, and intuition rather than on a controlling method. A book of this kind, which deals with the history of human intellection, feeling, and imagination, employs special vocabularies, procedures, and modes of demonstration which, over many centuries of development, have shown their profitability when applied to matters of this sort. I agree with Booth that these procedures, when valid, are in a broad sense rational, and subject to analysis and some degree of definition. But the rules underlying such a discourse are complex, elusive, unsystematic, and subject to innovative modification; they manifest themselves in the intuitive expertise of the historian; and the specification of these rules should not precede, but follow, practice.

The risk of premature codification is that the code will inhibit the free play of our procedures of demonstration and fail to do justice to our intuitions that something sound, useful, and illuminating has in fact been accomplished. In particular the risk is that the codes that have already been worked out for valid demonstration in mathematics, formal logic, and the physical sciences will intrude as models for our dealings with quite disparate intellectual enterprises, each of which has its own kind of subject matter, aims, and ways of proceeding. The result is a foregone conclusion: it will be a more or less elaborated and qualified, but still recognizable variant of the result of Hume's test for all methods of inquiry:

> If we take in our hand any volume . . . let us ask, *Does it contain any abstract reasoning concerning quantity or number?* No. *Does it contain any experimental reasoning concerning matter of fact and existence?* No. Commit it then to the flames: for it can contain nothing but sophistry and illusion.[2]

By this strict test *Natural Supernaturalism* would of course be committed to the flames, and by any softened version of such a test, most of its procedures would be gravely suspect. But to all such tests, the proper retort is Booth's question (p. 175), which might be restated in this way: After reading certain books that violate calculi modeled on logic and the exact sciences, which would do more violence to my sense of what is rational and my intuition that I have learned new truths—to decide that these books don't yield knowledge, or to decide that the calculi are inappropriate to the procedures of discovery and demonstration that their authors have in fact employed?

After the fact, nevertheless, a book like *Natural Supernaturalism* is subject to close critical inquiry about its methods and rationale. I am grateful to Booth for opening up such an inquiry, and for doing so in a way that is not only disarming, but seems to me to be the most promising of useful results. That is, instead of adopting a prosecutorial stance, demanding: "Justify the rationality and probative force of what you have done; it looks damned suspicious to me," he has adopted the friendly tactic of saying: "Your book, in my experience of it, has yielded discoveries that I want to call knowledge, by methods, however deviant from standard rubrics of valid reasoning, that it seems irrational to call nonrational. Let's set out to clarify what these methods are, and to see what grounds we can find for the claim that they provide warranted knowledge."

1

I confess that I was taken aback to discover, in Booth's just analysis, what a strange book *Natural Supernaturalism* is, and how extraordinary are the claims it presumes to make on its readers. It involves, explicitly or implicitly, a wide range of propositional truth-claims, of which only a fraction assert literal causation. Other propositions are assertions about an epoch, "Romanticism," and its special importance to us, and about the validity of the contention of some Romantic writers that they are "prophets" or "seers"; others assert not only facts, but values—the great values in the poems of certain

Romantic authors, especially Wordsworth, and the high moral
values that constitute the general Romantic "ethos"; still other
implicit propositions even undertake to offer justifiable, if
partial, answers to such questions as who we now are, where
we are, where we came from, and what all this means. The
basic mode of "proof" employed for this mixed bag of assertions is their incorporation into a story—more specifically,
into a story made up of many stories, in which we can distinguish, within the overarching narrative, a number of middle-
sized "novellas" and a great many "short stories"; and the
book as a whole requires that the reader enter into its "narrative world" and be convinced that "*all of this happened*—this
story is *true*," as a necessary condition for being persuaded of
the soundness of the truth-claims and value-claims that the
narrative implicates.

   And what a very odd thing this story itself turns out to be!
Its chief elements, or protagonists, are neither integral literary documents nor A. O. Lovejoy's unit ideas, but a fusion of
ideas, structural shapes, and values. The connections asserted
among these elements range from temporal and causal relations, through analogical relations (sometimes stated in terms
that suggest a Platonic belief in timeless forms in which particulars "participate"), to a great diversity of other connectives which are left out of account in standard inventories of
rational relationships. And as Booth points out, the temporal
order is again and again "scrambled," for the diverse narratives move bewilderingly back and forth in time between the
Romantic present, its ancestral past, and its portended future
up to the time in which the book was written. In candor I
must add to Booth's list another oddity, which some reviewers have in part noted but which Booth, perhaps out of kind-
ness, chose to leave out of his account: the book as a whole
has a structure that is deliberately iconic of the spiral form
which many Romantic thinkers considered the necessary shape
of all intellection, and in which many Romantic writers ordered
their philosophies, their histories, and their fictional writings
in verse and prose. That is, each of the component sections
of *Natural Supernaturalism* constitutes a circle of exposition
and narrative out of and back to a passage in Wordsworth's
Prospectus to *The Recluse*; while the book as a whole ends

where it began, with the opening passage of the Prospectus, but on a level of understanding that, the author presumes, will incorporate the results of the narrative exposition that has intervened.

About this strange performance Booth has raised a number of searching questions, which play variations on one central question: how to justify the claim that this complex story and its inherent propositional claims not only are convincing, but *ought* to be convincing, and on rational grounds, rather than merely by their rhetorical, emotional, and imaginative appeal? He also, and insistently, poses to the author a second-order question: if I believe this history of what happened in the Romantic era to be, by and large, true, how can I justify my pluralist claim that alternative and conflicting histories of the same era may also be true?

All of Booth's questions I find entirely warranted, but also very puzzling; I feel confident that I will continue to wrestle with them for some time to come. For many of them I can't at this point conceive any better answers than Booth has himself formulated for me. But let me at least offer interim comments about a few of the issues that Booth has raised, both in his questions and in his answers.

2

One source of confusion about what I tried to do lies in my use of that pesky word *Romantic* (and *Romanticism*), which is one of those terms historians can neither do with nor make do without. I am not on this issue, as Booth suggests (p. 146), a "Platonist," but am instead, like R. S. Crane and A. O. Lovejoy, a "nominalist." That is, I don't believe that there exists an abstract entity, named *Romanticism,* whose essential features are definable; or, to put it in another way, that we can set the necessary and sufficient conditions for the correct use of the term *Romanticism.* Instead, I use the word as an expository convenience to specify, as I say on the opening pages, "some of the striking parallels, in authorial stance and persona, subject matter, ideas, values, imagery, forms of

thought and imagination, and design of plot or structure"
that are manifested in a great many important English and
German writers, in a great variety of literary, philosophical,
and historical forms, during those three or four decades after
the outbreak of the French Revolution which, following common historical usage, I call the Romantic era (*Natural Super-*
naturalism, pp. 11–12). How inescapable is the use of such
period terms for summary reference, both Crane and Lovejoy show in their actual practice; for Crane wrote an essay
called "English Neoclassical Criticism," and Lovejoy, after all
his warnings about the advisability of eliminating the term
Romanticism, or at least of using it only in the plural form,
wrote a chapter called "Romanticism and the Principle of
Plenitude."[3]

But having stipulated my nominalist choice for the reference of the term *Romantic,* I go on in the course of the book
to refer to such things as "the Romantic *Bildungsgeschichte,"*
"the Romantic spiral pattern," "the Romantic ethos," without
reiterating each time the warning that I mean the term
Romantic to apply only to my stipulated set of writers and
documents. As a result, some reviewers have been misled into
claiming that I undertook a complete "typology of Romanticism," or a "grand synthesis of Romanticism," or a "definitive" study of Romanticism; and some have happily announced
that I had once and for all demolished Lovejoy's claim that
there is no single entity called Romanticism. But the same
misunderstanding of what I set out to do opened to other
reviewers the opportunity to assert that my conspectus of
Romanticism is radically omissive, or else that it distorts the
true nature of the Romantic achievement. In either case, the
discussion has shifted from questions of the sort: "Did the
distinctive complex of literary and cultural phenomena I chose
to discuss really take place in the period conventionally called
Romantic? Was it central enough to be worth such extended
treatment? Is the analysis of this complex and its interrelations accurate and adequate?" to another type of question:
"What is the proper, or correct, or central, or primary meaning of the term *Romanticism?*" That is, "Romanticism" has
shifted over from being a nominal convenience for the literary and cultural historian, who stipulates what he uses it to

denote, to a status in which, like "justice," "democracy," and "a Christian life," it is what W. B. Gallie calls an "essentially contested concept."[4] I don't know, short of the use of intolerable circumlocutions, how to avoid such slippage, to which all of us are extremely vulnerable; for if we go against the grain of usage and substitute a different term for *Romanticism*, it will soon be reified in its turn, and so re-inaugurate the old debates about its proper meaning.

It is instructive to list some of the things various reviewers have proposed that *Natural Supernaturalism,* as a survey of "Romanticism," ought properly to have treated. The missing topics include "the impact of Oriental cultures"; the " 'Catholic' tradition of Romantic religious experience"; Romantic irony and the ironic perspective in general; the actual political events of the day, and not merely the effect of these events on thought and imagination; the Romantic mode of "anti-redemptive, anti-explanatory, explanation"; "the literature of sentiment [and] the Gothic strain in poetry and fiction"; and "necrophily . . . diabolism, masochism, and suicide." Among the authors whom, it is said, I should have, or at least might well have, treated are Byron, the Pre-Raphaelites, Whitman, and Hardy; Scott and other novelists; Von Baader, Franz Molitor, Schleiermacher, S. Maimon, Kleist, E. T. A. Hoffmann, Richter, Heine; de Vigny, Gobineau, Hugo, Zola, Michelet, Amiel, Nerval, Balzac, Stendhal, Constant, Gautier; Leopardi, Manzoni; Lermontov, Pushkin. . . . Now, all these topics and writers are entirely eligible for treatment in books on Romanticism, and they have in fact been so treated; so that an initial but only partial answer to Booth's question about historical pluralism is to say that diverse historians have the right to focus their attention on different areas of historical concern. I claim no more than that the interrelated topics I have elected to treat, and the writings in which these topics are instantiated, were very important in their own time and continue to be of great interest to us today; that to tell this chosen story with any adequacy is quite enough for one book to try to do; and that if I have done my job properly, both the historical importance and continuing human interest of these selected topics are confirmed and expanded in the course of their historical exposition.[5]

3

Reviewers have greatly exaggerated the degree to which I rely on parallels, consonances, and analogues to establish the connections between the elements in the various stories I tell. Even Wayne Booth, after pointing out that I in fact employ many "literal" connections such as "cause," "influence," "source"—and despite his consent to the view that a historian must deploy a great diversity of relationships to match the tangled complexity of intellectual and cultural history—suggests that I may be committed to a "Platonic" belief in "some permanent human interest or eternal idea" to explain parallels or analogues between two works "that cannot have been literally caused in temporal history" (pp. 155–56; see also pp. 165–66).[6]

I didn't intend, however, to posit eternal ideas or universal traits of human nature to explain the relations between the various themes and structures that I identify and trace through time. I took care, in fact, to assert early on that the history I undertook to tell is strictly culture-bound. That is, it is a history limited to Western European thought and imagination; and one of my major assertions is that this has long been, and to a certain extent now remains, "essentially, although in derivative rather than direct manifestations, a biblical culture," in which we "readily mistake our hereditary ways of organizing experience for the conditions of reality and the universal forms of thought"; I suggest also that we can't escape "religious formulas which, since they are woven into the fabric of our language, control the articulation of our thinking" (*Natural Supernaturalism*, pp. 65–66). The evidence for such a sweeping historical claim, and for supplementary assertions of the way that biblical schemes assimilated elements from classical philosophy, is cumulative as the narrative progresses; and when I do point to parallels and analogues, they are meant to be explicable, in part, by the persistent and subtle play of literal causes, or inter-influences, within this pervasive linguistic and cultural context.

But even within this overall context of a biblical culture, it seems to me that there are relatively few instances in which I do no more than present similarities and analogues between important items in the stories I narrate. Take, for example, a central motif of the book, that of the changing conceptual design of the past, present, and future of human history. The assimilation of the right-angled biblical pattern of Paradise–Fall–Redemption–Paradise Regained into the postbiblical circular pattern of Unity–Multiplicity–Unity Regained is not simply asserted by analogy but shown to be the product of explicit interpretations of biblical history, by exegetes who had clear access, direct or indirect, to the Neoplatonic circular scheme of emanation and return. And the Romantic adaptation of this pattern of history—from a supernatural to a natural frame of reference as the self-education of the human race, and into the characteristic Romantic design of man's educational journey as a spiral progress from Unity to Disintegration and Alienation to the higher Unity of Reintegration—is shown, in its early instances, to be the product of philosophers and writers of *Universalgeschichte* who, entirely explicitly, set out to translate the truth within the myth-and-picture thinking of the Bible into the higher truth of a purely conceptual formulation. Such a reinterpretation of biblical history, as numerous quotations demonstrate, was the deliberate and specifically formulated enterprise of (among others) Lessing, Herder, Schiller, Schelling, Fichte, Hegel, and surprisingly, even Kant (e.g., *Natural Supernaturalism,* pp. 67–68, 178–92, 199–225). A similar secularization of the biblical design is unmistakably implied by Wordsworth (in his programmatic statements in the Prospectus and elsewhere) as well as, among other writers, by Hölderlin, Novalis, Blake, Shelley, Keats (who undertook to sketch "a system of Salvation which does not affront our reason and humanity"), and Carlyle (who, in "The Mythus of the Christian Religion," set out to satisfy the great need of the age "to embody the divine Spirit of that Religion in a new Mythus"). (See *Natural Supernaturalism,* pp. 67–69, and passim for the authors mentioned.)

My basic claim, in other words, is that the secular design of human history, Y, is connected to the earlier religious design,

X, by the relationship of continuity-in-change; and my evidence for this claim is not simply to show that X and Y possess similarities-in-difference, but to show that many of the chief authors in the history I narrate have expressly asserted, while others have clearly implied, that they offered Y as an interpretation of X—an interpretation intended to save the essential truth embodied in the mythical vehicle of X, while translating that truth into the higher-order conceptual terms acceptable to their own rational era. Such evidence isn't "causal" in any strictly scientific sense, but it seems to me the strongest possible evidence for the kind of relationship I assert within that distinctive area of investigation we call cultural history. It is furthermore supported by other kinds of evidence, such as the remarkable retention, in many manifestations of the secular design of history, of the central terms and imagery in the biblical design of history—terms such as "fall" and "redemption," and imagery such as "a new heaven and new earth," or the marriage of separated beings that gets used to signalize the achievement of self-integration after self-division. These mixed kinds of evidence are cumulative, and conjoin with other evidence to add probative weight to further assertions about the secular continuity-in-change of concepts that were originally religious—a probative weight that we can't precisely measure, yet rightly intuit to add up to a sound demonstration of the general claim.

A historian can't go on asserting and reasserting these diverse modes of evidence without making his book unreadable, so he does the best he can by citing such proofs only at strategic points in his exposition, in the hope that the reader will note and remember their relevance to everything that precedes and follows; even while, as an experienced historian, he knows full well that such a procedure places on the reader a responsibility for close reading and total recall which he can't realistically expect the reader to fulfill. That's a central problem in all expositions of a complicated history of ideas, imaginative patterns, feelings, and values; it's a problem I confess that I don't know how satisfactorily to resolve.

4

In the final analysis, of course, the evidence for all of the diverse claims I make comes down to the meaning of the texts to which I refer, and this brings up the subject of the way I use what Booth describes as my "thousands of allusions and quotations" (p. 154). On this as on other matters, in a way that any author learns to expect, the judgments of reviewers are divided. They range the spectrum from the opinion that there is "too great a reliance on summary and paraphrase," to the admission that, to the reviewer's taste, there is "a superfluity of instantiation and quotation," to the sweeping claim that there is little point in leaving authors to be "understood in their own words," because "a quotation proves nothing. It merely exemplifies an interpretation already given or provides the occasion for an interpretation."[7]

William James remarked that he had "to forge every sentence" of his *Principles of Psychology* "in the teeth of irreducible and stubborn facts." In the history I undertook to relate, the ultimate "facts" that it organizes and explains are what the authors it deals with actually said. It seems an unconvincing tactic simply to *tell* what these authors said (leaving it to each reader's vague memories of relevant texts to check the accuracy and adequacy of what is being said), instead of backing up the telling by *showing* the relevant passages to the reader, so that he can make his own judgment on them. The scope of the subjects I deal with enforced a considerable amount of "summary and paraphrase"; but when I made a large historical generalization, I felt that it called for a good deal of instantiation to back it up; and in these instances, it seemed only fair to let the authors speak for themselves, up to what I judged to be the limits of the publisher's cost accounting and of my readers' patience and ability to keep track of the story I was telling. Incidentally, I also hoped that some readers would share my own pleasure in reading a variety of passages from splendid writers for their inherent interest and cogency, apart from their function as evidence for an historical assertion.

One repeated objection to this procedure is the claim that

I violated the formal integrity of individual texts, and especially of poems, by pulling out excerpts for isolated attention
and analysis. To this objection my reply is that which Booth
has sketched—what I undertook to do necessitated such a
procedure, and no one book can try to do everything in general without failing to do anything in particular. Poets, no
less than philosophers, have ideas which they write into their
poems, and although they use ideas in distinctively poetic ways,
and for distinctively poetic ends, these differences are not so
absolute but that we may excerpt the ideas they shared with
their contemporaries, for consideration in a story whose scope
requires the inclusion of poetry and novels, as well as books
of philosophy, theology, and "universal history." And after
all, as Booth points out, I allow the poets to speak, as poets,
in copious quotations.

Even Booth, however, fails to specify one recurrent tactic
in *Natural Supernaturalism:* it consists not only of generalizations, explanations, and stories-within-a-story, but includes a
number of what we may call "vignettes," in which the history
pauses to render an account of a particular text in its subject
matter, structure, organizing principle, and formal artistry.
I introduced these explications in instances in which the
importance and literary value of a document seemed to warrant consideration of its distinctive particularities, as confirming a historical generalization, while serving at the same
time as a useful reminder of how diverse may be the particular embodiments of the general feature. Among such
vignettes are the treatments of Hegel's *Phenomenology,* Coleridge's *Ancient Mariner* and *France: An Ode,* Shelley's *Prometheus Unbound,* the Induction to Keats's *Fall of Hyperion,*
Carlyle's *Sartor Resartus,* Hölderlin's *Hyperion,* Schiller's *Der
Spaziergang,* and above all, Wordsworth's *Prelude.* My discussions of *The Prelude* add up to a length greater than many
published critiques of that poem; and I judge that they constitute a fairly full treatment of *The Prelude* in its poetic integrity. What obscures this fact is that the treatment is not
consecutive, but is scattered through various parts of the book.
Not only, then, is the temporal order of my history "scrambled," but also a number of the poems it comments on are
fragmented; so that it can be charged that the book fre-

quently presents *disjecta membra poetae*. I can only reply that the complexity of the overall story I undertook to tell required a number of substories, and I simply lacked the wit that would enable me to tell these stories without scrambling the temporal order of events and without dissevering for separate consideration various components or aspects of the major documents that these multiple stories were about.

Another and much more crucial indictment brings into question the validity of the entire book, for it asserts that the "facts" on which I rely as evidence are not facts at all, but my unwarranted interpretations of the passages I cite. This indictment is brought by J. Hillis Miller, who (I agree with Booth) wrote an especially thoughtful and interesting review of *Natural Supernaturalism*. Miller asserts that I commonly "illustrate some straightforward point with a quotation which is not 'interpreted,' in the sense of being teased for multiple meanings or implications," nor explicated, "in the sense of unfold, unravel, or unweave." My interpretive fallacy is the standard one, that a text "has a single unequivocal meaning 'corresponding' to the various entities it 'represents.' " But what Nietzsche and his followers, Derrida and the other modern "deconstructionists," have demonstrated, is that there is no single or "objective" interpretation. Miller sums up the basic truths about interpretation in a series of passages that he quotes from Nietzsche: "The same text authorizes innumerable interpretations: there is no 'correct' interpretation." "Ultimately, man finds in things nothing but what he himself has imported into them." "In fact interpretation is itself a means of becoming master of something," by an exertion of one's will to power. As Miller summarizes Nietzsche's views, "reading is never the objective identifying of a sense but the importation of meaning into a text which has no meaning 'in itself.' " He concludes, in considerable understatement, that "from the point of view of such a theory of interpretation all of Abrams' readings can be put in question."[8]

My view of interpretation is not quite so simple as Miller makes out. I in fact hold that all complex passages are to some degree ambiguous, and that some passages are radically and insolubly ambiguous. Furthermore I have myself, when writing critiques of poems, engaged in the critical game of teasing a passage for multiple meanings and of unraveling its ambiguities and implications. I do, however, approach the passages I quote in *Natural Supernaturalism* with certain interpretive assumptions, which I think I share with all historians who rely on texts for their basic data. These assumptions are: the authors cited wrote not in order to present a verbal stimulus (in Roland Barthes's term, *un vide*) to the play of the reader's interpretive ingenuity, but in order to be understood. To do so, they had to obey the communal norms of their language so as to turn them to their own innovative uses. The sequences of sentences these authors wrote were designed to have a core of determinate meanings; and though the sentences allow a certain degree of interpretive freedom, and though they evoke vibrations of significance which differ according to the distinctive temperament and experience of each reader, the central core of what they undertook to communicate can usually be understood by a competent reader who knows how to apply the norms of the language and literary form employed by the writer. The reader has various ways to test whether his understanding is an "objective" one; but the chief way is to make his interpretation public, and so permit it to be confirmed or falsified by the interpretations of other competent readers who subscribe to the .same assumptions about the possibility of determinable communication.

Booth's reply to Miller's deconstructionist claims about meaning is first, to challenge him to produce a deconstructionist history that will meet "the standards by which [such an account] is to be tested," and second, to assert that every effort at such interpretation "is plainly and simply parasitic on the work of people like Abrams," who put forward the obvious or univocal reading which the "free" interpreter undertakes to deconstruct (pp. 169, 170). I would add to these a more radical reply. If one takes seriously Miller's deconstructionist principles of interpretation, any history that relies on written texts becomes an impossibility. If a production is to be accounted a history, it must be a history of something determinate and determinable; and the elementary assumption that a cultural historian must make is that he is able to understand, in the sense that he is at least able to approximate, the core of meanings that certain writers at certain times expressed in their writings. A narrative about texts by a historian who genuinely proceeds on the belief (in Miller's non-deconstructionist interpretation of Nietzsche) that his procedure need be nothing more than "the importation of meaning into a text which has no meaning 'in itself,' " will turn out to be a history only of what it itself expresses—a history, that is, of the historian's will to power, as manifested through that one of the many possible deconstructionist codes of interpretation that he has elected to press into the service of this will to power.

5

Well, that at least sets one limit to what, according to my pluralist views, I would accept as a sound alternative history to my own: I would not accept a history genuinely written according to radically deconstructionist principles of interpretation. But within that rather broad limit, I am willing to go farther than Wayne Booth supposes. He says, for example, that "we can expect [that Abrams] will *not* go all the way, will reject any history arguing, say, that Wordsworth was *not* representative and his poems *not* great . . ." (p. 164). On the contrary: I can readily imagine a sound and enlightening history of Romantic literature that will deal with many of the same authors I deal with, and even some of the same passages, but will argue precisely these claims about Wordsworth. In fact, knowing the prevailing currents of literary and critical interests, and the kinds of commentary that have already been applied to single Romantic authors, I would be willing to gamble that such a history will soon be written, and even to predict some lines that its arguments will take.

    This imaginary history will focus on what several reviewers chided me for omitting, the ironic perspective in general and the theory and practice of "Romantic irony" in particular. It will claim, rightly, that the very concept of Romantic irony was developed by German writers of that era, and also that the theory and practice of the ironic mode is not only a primary Romantic achievement, but the most important and forward-looking one, since it anticipated what is most characteristic in our present temper and established the basic models which are being exploited by the best and most representative writers of our own era. The history will bring to the forefront German writers such as Friedrich Schlegel, whom I hardly mention, as well as others, such as Tieck, Richter, Heine, and Büchner (the author of *Woyzeck*), whom I did not mention at all. In this plot, the hero among the English Romantics will be Byron, a poet I immensely admire but deliberately left out because I did not want to complicate my already complex history with a poet who, as I said, "in his greatest work . . . speaks with an ironic counter-voice and deliberately opens a satirical perspective on the vatic stance of his Romantic contemporaries" (*Natural Supernaturalism*, p. 13).* Keats will rank high; and Blake, Shelley, and even Coleridge, despite their vatic pretensions, will readily be shown to sing an ironic counterpoint to their own visionary claims. But Wordsworth, because he is "the egotistical sublime"—self-absorbed, complacent, and inflexibly solemn and unironic in his pronouncements—will inevitably drop to the bottom of the scale as the weakest and least representative of the prominent poets in this central mode of the Romantic imagination and achievement.

I can imagine such an account of "Romanticism" which would be well enough organized, argued, documented, and written to pass Wayne Booth's tests for a sound history; in fact, I can almost imagine writing such a history myself. I would ungrudgingly accept such a book as a valid alternative history to my own. Does that make me a relativist?

*Byron unerringly identifies and shows us, from the hindside, not only the prophetic stance of his contemporaries, but also its basis in a secular version of Christianity:

> Sir Walter reign'd before me; Moore and Campbell
> Before and after: but now grown more holy
> The muses upon Sion's hill must ramble
> With poets almost clergymen, or wholly.

It is an index to the discrepancy between our rigid categories for discussing these matters and the lability and resilience of the human sensibility, to note that a historian can delight in Byron's irreverent gibe and still write a long book which treats the butts of Byron's irony with seriousness and respect.

Not, I think, in any dismaying sense of that word, for it does not obviate the claim that both books tell a story that is true. Their judgments about Wordsworth seem "contradictory," but they are not so in the logical sense of that word, which assumes that the clashing assertions meet on the same plane of discourse. The disparate judgments about the representative quality and greatness of Wordsworth's poetry, however, follow from different controlling categories which effect a different selection and ordering of the historical facts and implicate a different set of criteria by which to assess what is representative and great. The insights and assessments of each book, in other words, are relative to the vantage point chosen by its author, and each tries to make us see selected goings-on in the Romantic era in a certain way; but these diverse goings-on are there to be seen in that way. Each, that is, tells only a *part* of the truth, but it is a part of the *truth*.

All sound attempts to add to our humanistic understanding are written from some one of various possible perspectives or points of view (the recourse to optical metaphors is almost inevitable in discussing such matters), and the convergence of diverse perspectives is needed to yield what the philosopher J. R. Bambrough calls a "vision in depth"[9] in place of the two-dimensional vision that we get from any one vantage point. Only such a vision in depth approximates the full humanistic truth about any matter of our deep concern. That is why, as Wayne Booth puts it, "it is not just that we should tolerate a plurality of histories, we should demand them" (p. 168). But there are an indefinite number of revealing perspectives, and each age will no doubt continue to generate new ones that accord with its interests and intellectual climate. And that is why, as I said in the passage that Booth quotes (p. 143), the search for humanistic truth has no ending.

6

Booth makes it plain that what he found most novel in *Natural Supernaturalism*—and also most surprising, because it violated his critical presuppositions—is that it functions as what he calls "epideictic history, a history designed to show forth the greatness of the phenomena it explains" (p. 163). What surprised him is that, although an investigation of the sources and influence of Romantic poems can discover only facts that are "extrinsic" to the poems, these discoveries somehow served in the book to "demonstrate" the high literary values in the poems themselves, and especially the high literary values in the poems of Wordsworth.

I must admit that when I decided to use Wordsworth's Prospectus as a recurrent point of departure in my exposition, I had no intention of making Wordsworth the hero of my story, nor of writing a kind of work that would prove "a poem's greatness by discovering what kind of historical account you can give of it—both of what went into it and of what came out" (p. 161). I simply took Wordsworth's greatness as a poet for granted, and chose his Prospectus as a persistent reference mainly because it—together with *The Prelude,* whose subject and role the Prospectus announced in lines 93–99— so strikingly and tersely embodied the Romantic themes and concepts and manner of proceeding that I wanted to deal with. My conspectus of Wordsworth's contemporaries was designed less to prove how "representative" Wordsworth was than to show the many important features that were shared by a great diversity of major Romantic writings. And I chose an exegesis that was historical (that is, retrospective and prospective as well as conspective) because I believed that the only way to understand the particulars of my humanistic investigation—the only way fully to realize what they are— involves knowing where they came from, what changes were made in them, and what those changes portended for what they were to become. I suppose that what Booth has in mind when he says of the resulting book that it "in a sense provides a conspectus on the whole of Western civilization" (p. 145) is not only that it ranges in time from the Bible to Allen Ginsberg, but also that the Romantic themes it elucidates turn out to be altered versions of the persistent forms of imagination by which our great religious visionaries and philosophers had tried to make sense of themselves, their past and anticipated future, and their place in the world, and in which they had found a sanction for their values and moral norms. As the most clear-sighted of the Romantic writers saw, these forms of imagination, or "myths," constitute the fabric of Western civilization, and they believed that, despite their own drastically altered circumstances, these myths must not be rejected, but reconstructed on new conceptual foundations, if that cultural fabric was to endure.

Even though I set out to deepen understanding rather than to demonstrate literary values, I nonetheless found as I went along, just as Booth did, that the values of certain Romantic poems were enhanced as my awareness of the complex tradition that they embodied continued to grow. That an increase in knowledge alters our sense of poetic values is a matter of common experience; it seems mysterious to us only because we are taken in by our own critical metaphors. It is useful, for some analytic purposes, to distinguish extrinsic from intrinsic, external from internal, criticism, and to regard historical knowledge as something external to a poem. But the inside of a poem is not like the inside of a house where, except for a zone of dubiety at the threshold, the boundary between what is inside and what is outside is sharp and stable. The full significance of a poem depends on what we bring to our interpretation of its determinable meanings, and as our knowledge of the importance of a tradition enlarges, so does the significance of a poem which represents that tradition. We don't think first of the poem and then of the tradition outside the poem. Instead, we experience its traditionality as a dimension of the poem's meaning, as a resonance within the poem itself. And when we recognize in a poem a powerful but altered restatement of a great theme in our Western culture, uttered with an art and in a voice that endures comparison with the greatest art and voices of its ancestral past, that attribute becomes a measure of the poem's greatness. If our aesthetic theory disqualifies such a measure as extrinsic, hence irrelevant to poetic value, our experience in reading the poem discredits the theory and not the value. This is apparently what T. S. Eliot had in mind when he said that whether something is literature or not can be determined only by literary standards, but its greatness as literature cannot be determined solely by literary standards.

7

We come finally to my discussion of "the Romantic ethos" and of "the Romantic positives." A book of humanistic inquiry is written not only from a particular conceptual perspective, but also from within the temporal perspective, the climate of values and opinions, of the age in which it is composed. Rather than to try ineffectually to extricate myself from this perspective in order to achieve a viewpoint *sub specie aeternitatis*, I decided to end *Natural Supernaturalism* by identifying, in my chosen authors, those Romantic positives that deliberately reaffirmed the elementary values of the Western past, and to present these values in a way directly addressed to our own age of anxiety and of incipient despair of our inherited civilization. I was well aware that this section set itself against the prevailing way of reading the Romantics, and—moved perhaps by a touch of perversity—opened it by listing their chief positives as baldly and challengingly as possible: "life, love, liberty, hope, and joy" (*Natural Supernaturalism*, p. 431). After this provocative beginning, however, I tried to show, by extensive analysis and quotation, that these traditional positives were radically reinterpreted, interrelated, and managed with great subtlety of discrimination; and that in their literary contexts, they are powerfully and convincingly stated. I tried also to show that the right to make these affirmations was fairly earned, by authors profoundly aware of the negative conclusions that seemed pressed upon them by human history and their own experience; and that the reason for their insistence is that they saw their era as we see our own—as a crisis of civilization and consciousness. In Wordsworth's description (the passage has many analogues in his contemporaries) his poetry is specifically addressed to counter

> these times of fear,
> This melancholy waste of hopes o'erthrown,
> . . . mid indifference and apathy
> And wicked exultation . . .
>   this time
> Of dereliction and dismay.
>
> (*The Prelude*, 1805, 2:448–57)

My claim was that, in the face of life's clamorous counter-evidence, the Romantic writers, in those works in which they assumed the traditional persona of the poet-prophet—to put it in another way, in which they undertook to speak with an authoritative public voice—deliberately adopted their affirmative stance. As Coleridge and others said, a man has to choose between despair and hope, and the choice is a moral choice, because despair is self-confirming but hope releases the human powers in which lie the only possibility of remedy. If this is optimism, it is so only in the radically qualified sense that Shelley gave the word, in a passage I quoted in which he expresses his secular version of the traditional theodicy:

> Let us believe in a kind of optimism in which we are our own gods. . . . It is best that we should think all this for the best even though it be not, because Hope, as Coleridge says, is a solemn duty which we owe alike to ourselves & to the world—a worship to the spirit of good within, which requires before it sends that inspiration forth, which impresses its likeness upon all that it creates, devoted & disinterested homage.
> (*Natural Supernaturalism*, p. 447).

I was not greatly surprised, though a bit chagrined nonetheless, to find that, despite all the skill I could muster to communicate the nuance and shadow in the great passages of Romantic affirmation, this section of *Natural Supernaturalism* was described by some critics as a product of the author's own optimism, which found a matching optimism in the Romantic poets only by selecting the evidence and ignoring the dark undertones in the passages selected.

The failure to achieve a general meeting of minds on this issue leads me to a final observation on method: a cultural history requires from the historian something no less important than a sound method of demonstration, and that is, an effort of the sympathetic imagination. In a famous statement John Stuart Mill said that Bentham looked at ancient or received opinions from the viewpoint of his own convictions and asked, "Is it true?" Coleridge on the other hand asked, "What is the meaning of it?" and to answer this question, he "looked at it from within, and endeavoured to see it with the eyes of a believer in it; to discover by what apparent facts it was at first suggested, and by what appearances it has ever since been rendered continually credible."[10] This way of looking at the past is a Romantic discovery, and it seems to me to be a necessary condition for any full understanding of the past. In *Natural Supernaturalism* I tried, by an effort of imagination, to understand a great Romantic enterprise by looking at it from within. In the process of coming to understand this segment of our past I also discovered, and tried at the end to communicate the discovery, that to know who and what and where we were then helps us to understand who and what and where we are now. I tried in addition to communicate my sense that this Romantic past is a usable past, in that it presents a stance toward ourselves and the world that affirms human dignity and the grounds for a qualified hope, and thus shows us what was possible for men who were no less sagacious and unillusioned than we are now.

Wayne Booth says that he was convinced and moved by what I found moving and convincing in the history I tried to tell. But Booth also says, and I entirely agree, that his response of being persuaded "is an experience that many sincere and competent readers will for various reasons not discover" (p. 150). A humanistic demonstration, unlike a scientific demonstration, is rarely such as to enforce the consent of all qualified observers. For it to carry the reader through its exposition to its conclusions requires some grounds for imaginative consent, some comparative ordering of values, some readiness of emotional response to the matters shown forth, which the reader must share with the author even before he begins to read; and these common grounds are no doubt in part temperamental, hence variable from reader to reader.[11] If this assertion constitutes relativism, then we simply have to live with the relativism it asserts, for it is an aspect of the human predicament that the languages and complex strategies of proof in humanistic inquiries are designed to cope with, but can never entirely overcome.

Art-as-Such: The Sociology of Modern Aesthetics

For the last two centuries the professional philosophy of art, and more recently the practical criticism of the various arts, has been grounded on a theory that, for easy reference, I shall call "art-as-such." This theory uses a very distinctive terminology to make the following claims:

(1) "Art" is used as a term interchangeable with "the fine arts," which consist primarily of five arts: poetry (or literature), painting, sculpture, music, and architecture. The consideration of these essentially related products constitutes an area of inquiry which is *sui generis*.

(2) What defines a work of art is its status as an object to be "contemplated," and contemplated "disinterestedly"—that is, attended to "as such," for its own sake, without regard to the personal interests or the possessiveness or the desires of the perceiver, and without reference to its truth or its utility or its morality. A work of art may or may not be true to the world or serve practical ends or have moral effects, but such considerations are held to be supervenient upon (or, in some views, destructive of) the defining experience—that is, the absorbed and disinterested contemplation of the product for itself, simply as a work of art.

(3) A work of art is accordingly described as an object that is self-sufficient, autonomous, independent. It is asserted to be an end in itself, not a means to an external end, and its artistic value is said to be intrinsic, not extrinsic, to its own being. The work, in other words, is conceived as an entity that exists simply in order to be looked at or read or listened to with an absorbed, exclusive, and disinterested attention.

One can illustrate such theories by two terse but comprehensive statements. One is by T. E. Hulme, whose views had an important formative influence on T. S. Eliot and the American New Criticism that began about 1930. "Contemplation," Hulme says, is "a detached interest."

> The object of aesthetic contemplation is something framed apart by itself and regarded without memory or expectation, simply as being itself, as end not means, as individual not universal.[1]

The other is a felicitous summation by Iris Murdoch (a practicing novelist as well as a philosopher) in her Romanes Lecture on art in 1976:

> Good art [provides the] clearest *experience* of something grasped as separate and precious and beneficial and held quietly and unpossessively in the attention.[2]

Such formulations are usually presented by aesthetic philosophers and critics as universal and timeless truths about works of art, and we tend to think of the history of art theory as a sustained movement toward the triumphant discovery of these truths, sidetracked and delayed by various false leads. The historical facts, however, make this view a dubious one. For more than two thousand years after the philosophical consideration of one or another of the arts was inaugurated by Plato and Aristotle, theorists and critics did not even class together the diverse products that we now identify as "the fine arts." Instead, they grouped one or another of these arts with mathematics or with the natural sciences or with a practical art such as agriculture or shoemaking. They proposed no terms for specifying a distinctive or essential artistic property, nor for talking about works of art in a way that undertook to be distinctive for that class and exclusive of all other human artifacts. Instead, they discussed one of the arts at a time; and when they paralleled that art to another of what we now call "the fine arts"—especially poetry to painting—it was for limited comparative purposes, and with reference only to selected features. And during those two millennia, it occurred to no thinker to assert that a product of even one of the human arts exists in order to be contemplated disinterestedly, for its own sake, without reference to things, events, human beings, purposes, or effects outside its sufficient and autonomous self.

The historical fact is that the theory and vocabulary of art-as-such was introduced, quite abruptly, only some two or three centuries ago into what had hitherto been a relatively continuous development of the traditional views and terminology that philosophers and critics had inherited from Greek and Roman antiquity. And in retrospect, it becomes clear that the revolution effected in the theory of art involved a replacement of the implicit understructure of traditional theory by a radically different understructure.

Theorists of the various arts, from classical Greece through most of the eighteenth century, whatever their divergencies, had assumed the maker's stance toward a work of art, and had analyzed its attributes in terms of a construction model. That is, they posited a poem or any other work of art to be an *opus*, a thing that is made according to a *techne* or *ars*, that is, a craft, each with its requisite skills for selecting materials and shaping them into a work designed to effect certain external ends, such as achieving pleasure or instruction or emotional effects on an audience, as well as for adapting the work to a particular social occasion or function. It is clear that from the viewpoint of this construction model, the patent differences between the materials and practical skills of a poet, a painter, a sculptor, a musician, or an architect would keep these diverse occupations and products from being classified together in any systematic fashion, and for other than limited purposes. The critical undertaking, consequently, was to deal with a single art—most often, in classical times, poetry or a subclass such as tragedy; and the critical treatises were designed at least as much to guide a poet in writing a particular kind of good poem as to help a reader to judge whether, and in what ways, the poem is good or bad. In this orientation to the making of a poem, Aristotle's *Poetics*, whatever its important differences, is congruent with the views of Horace,[3] whose enormously influential *Ars Poetica* is explicitly a how-to document; that is, it is a verse-letter addressed to a novice instructing him how to write poems that will appeal most widely and enduringly to a discriminating readership. In this aspect of their treatises, both these writers are at one with the rhetoricians and with Longinus; and all of these thinkers together established the basic mode and operative terms for dealing with the verbal, and later the plastic and musical, arts that persisted, without radical innovations, through the seventeenth century.

In sharp contrast, theories of art-as-such tacitly presuppose not the maker's stance to his work in process but the perceiver's stance to the finished product; and they formulate their discussion not on a construction model but on a contemplation model. That is, they assume that the paradigmatic situation, in defining and analyzing art, is that in which a lone perceiver confronts an isolated work, however it happened to get made, and simply attends to the features that it manifests to his exclusive attention.

What I want to do is to sketch the emergence of the point of view and operative vocabulary of art-as-such, and then to investigate some of the attendant conditions, both social and intellectual, that may explain why, after so many centuries of speculation, this radical innovation appeared suddenly just when it did and why it developed rapidly in just the way it took.

1

The perceiver's stance and the contemplation model were products not of late-nineteenth-century aestheticism but of the eighteenth century. More precisely, they appeared at the end of the first decade of the eighteenth century, in the writings of Joseph Addison and of the third Earl of Shaftesbury; only eighty years later, in 1790, they had developed into the full modern formulation of art-as-such in Immanuel Kant's *Critique of Aesthetic Judgment.*

Let me stress what, for our enterprise, are salient features of Kant's theory. Despite its epoch-making importance for the philosophy of art, there is hardly a single observation about the nature and experience of an aesthetic object that Kant did not find in his eighteenth-century precursors, English and German, beginning with Addison and Shaftesbury. In fact, Kant does not even argue for, but simply accepts, certain concepts, already current, and devotes himself to grounding and systematizing these concepts by showing how the uniquely distinctive aesthetic experience (what he calls "the pure judgment of taste") is possible, as he puts it, *a priori—* that is, how it can be accounted for by reference to the faculties and their operations that the mind brings to all its experience. And his theory relies squarely and exclusively on the perceiver's stance and the contemplation model. As Kant posits the situation that he assumes to be paradigmatic for the philosophy of aesthetics: a pure judgment of taste "combines delight or aversion immediately [i.e., without the intervention of "concepts"] with the bare contemplation [*Betrachtung*] of the object irrespective of its use or of any end."[4] Only after he has established this frame of reference does Kant go on, in the second book of his *Critique,* to discuss what he calls *die schönen Künste,* or fine arts; his list of the major arts is the one that had recently become, and still remains, the standard one of poetry, painting, sculpture, architecture, and music—to which he adds the other arts, prominent in his time, of eloquence and landscape gardening. In this second section of his treatise, Kant also introduces the topic of the production of a work of art. His aim, however, is precisely opposed to traditional constructive theories, which undertook to establish the principles by which an artist deliberately selects and orders his materials in order to effect preconceived ends. Kant's enterprise, on the contrary, is to explain how the producing artist, despite such concepts and intentions, nonetheless manages, however unintentionally, to achieve a product that meets the criteria already established by reference to the concept-free and end-independent encounter between a percipient and a ready-made aesthetic work.

In discussing the nature of the normative aesthetic encounter, Kant encompasses all the key concepts and terms that constitute the theory of art-as-such in our own time. Crucially, the percipient's aesthetic judgment is, he says, "disinterested" or "a pure disinterested delight," in the sense that it is "purely contemplative" [*bloss kontemplativ*], hence "impartial"—that is, it is free of any reference to the interests or acquisitiveness or desires of the perceiver, and is indifferent even to the reality of the thing that is represented in the mode of art. The object contemplated, Kant says, "pleases for its own sake" [*für sich selbst*], in strict independence from what he calls the "external" ends of utility or of morality. A "fine art," accordingly, is "intrinsically final, devoid of an [extrinsic] end."[5] In Kant's overall view, a human work of art, no less than a natural object, is to be regarded as having no end other than simply to exist, to be just what it is for our disinterested aesthetic contemplation.

Aspects of Kant's theory were quickly adopted and developed by a number of German metaphysicians, including Schiller, Schelling, Hegel, and Schopenhauer, and so entered the mainstream of aesthetic philosophy. What needs to be stressed is the rapidity and completeness of this Copernican revolution in the theory of art. In the course of a single century a great variety of human products, from poetry to architecture, conspicuously diverse in their media and required skills, as well as in the occasion and social function of individual works within each art—products of arts that hitherto had been grouped with diverse human crafts, or even sciences—came to constitute a system of "the fine arts";[6] that is, a single, essentially related, and unique class of products. The construction model, which had treated each of the arts as a procedure for selecting and adapting its distinctive elements to preconceived ends and uses, was replaced by the contemplation model, which treated the products of all the fine arts as ready-made things existing simply as objects of rapt attention. And the essential feature predicated for the fine arts, setting them off from all cognitive, practical, and moral pursuits, was that each work is to be experienced disinterestedly, for its own sake, unalloyed by reference to the world, or to human life or concerns, or to any relations, ends, or values outside its all-sufficing self.

A conceptual revolution so sudden and drastic cannot be plausibly explained as an evolution of the traditional ideas about the arts; the orientation and operative terms of art-as-such, as I have pointed out, were entirely alien to that tradition. To account for the revolution we must, I think, turn to external factors which enforced, or at least fostered, the new way of thinking. Let us pose this question: Was there, just preceding and during the eighteenth century, a radical alteration in the social conditions and social uses of the diverse products that came during that period to be grouped as the fine arts—changes both concurrent and correlative with the conceptual changes I have outlined? This is, broadly speaking, a question concerning the sociology of art; but whereas altering social conditions have often been used to explain changes in the subject matter, forms, and styles of practicing artists, I shall instead advert to social conditions in order to explain a drastic change in the general *theory* of art—that is, in the focal concepts by which the arts were identified, classified, and systematically analyzed.

2

A conspicuous phenomenon in the seventeenth and eighteenth centuries was the rapid spread of a mode of life, hitherto limited to a privileged few, that I shall label "connoisseurship." By this term I mean the devotion of part of one's leisure to the study and enjoyment of the products of an art for the interest and pleasure they afford. Since the attitude and theory of art-as-such emerged in England and was developed in Germany, I shall focus on the social phenomenon of the spread of connoisseurship in those two countries.

We can begin in the seventeenth century with the introduction of two new terms from the Italian into the English critical lexicon. The first term was *gusto,* translated as "taste," and applied in the metaphorical sense of a capacity to respond to the beauty or harmonious order of objects, whether natural or artificial. This responsiveness was considered to be an innate sensibility, inherited by individuals in various degrees, yet capable of being trained so as to constitute a socially desirable "good taste" or a "polite" (that is, a polished, upper-class) taste; and even of being so informed by the acquired knowledge of the "rules" of a particular art that it becomes a "just taste" or a "correct taste." This new term quickly became a staple in critical discussion, where it obviously served to emphasize the perceiver's point of vantage to a finished artifact. (Note that in 1790 Kant labeled the normative aesthetic response by a deliberately paradoxical phrase: "a pure *judgment* of *taste.*")

The second, and related, word from the Italian is *virtuoso.* This was introduced into the English vocabulary in 1622 by Henry Peacham, in his book on the requisites of an upper-class education that he entitled *The Complete Gentleman.* Men who are "skilled" in such antiquities as "statues, inscriptions, and coins," Peacham says, "are by the Italians termed *virtuosi.*"[7] In the course of the seventeenth century, the term *virtuoso* came to be applied to a mode of life increasingly engaged in by gentlemen of the leisure class who applied themselves to one or both of two pursuits. One pursuit was collecting, and developing a degree of expertise about, the curiosities of natural history and the contrivances of contemporary technology. The other was collecting, and developing an informed taste for appraising, various artifacts, which included an extraordinary range of rarities and bric-a-brac, but most prominently paintings and statuary. By the end of the seventeenth century, the term *virtuoso* had already become derogatory, largely because of the devastating attacks by Restoration wits against the pedantry and fondness for natural and artificial oddities by the science virtuoso. The life-style of the aristocratic art virtuoso nonetheless continued to flourish and expand in the eighteenth century, although now under a new title, this time imported from France, of "connoisseur."

The English painter Jonathan Richardson, with great fanfare, announced in 1719 "a new science to the world" which, he says, since "it is yet without a name," he will call "the SCI-ENCE of a CONNOISSEUR." He points out that in England, unlike in Italy, although there are many "gentlemen of a just and delicate *taste* in musick, poetry, and all kinds of literature . . . very few [are] lovers and connoisseurs in painting." His great endeavor, he says, is "to persuade our nobility and gentry to become lovers of painting and connoisseurs . . . by shewing the dignity, certainty, pleasure and advantage of that science."[8]

Note two features of Richardson's exposition. He points out, first, that in England an aristocratic connoisseurship—which he equates, using our earlier term, with "a just and delicate *taste*"—already exists for poetry and music. He now undertakes to add painting (and, later in his book, sculpture) to this class—thereby linking, for his purposes, four of what were soon to be grouped as the fine arts. He does so, however, not on the ground that these arts possess a common nature or shared objective features, but solely on the ground that they are all capable of a common function or social role—that of yielding to the perceiver what he describes as "at once an intellectual and a sensual pleasure," that is enhanced for "those who have learned to see these things." Second, he reveals that a prime value of connoisseurship, in addition to the refined pleasure that it yields, is its conspicuous uselessness, which makes it an index that one belongs to the leisure class—in his term, to "our nobility and gentry." Connoisseurship, Richardson points out, is "not for the vulgar" (that is, the common people). The fact that it is a nonproductive, nonutilitarian way of employing one's time is what enhances the "dignity" of a connoisseur, making him "always respected and esteemed."[9]

The virtuoso vogue in the seventeenth century (as Walter Houghton has pointed out)[10] had all along been "strongly class-conscious," flaunting a leisure-time avocation free of material and utilitarian ends as a sign of social rank unachievable by what a number of virtuosi, like Peacham, had called "the vulgar" and requiring a cultivated knowledge and taste that serves to distinguish the "polite" class from social climbers. This defensiveness of the landed upper classes against interlopers from below is itself an index to the instability of the established class structure in England, in an era of new wealth acquired by flourishing commercial and manufacturing enterprises. But the rapidly enlarging class of the well-to-do in the eighteenth century were not to be foiled by such defensive tactics. They simply took over from "the nobility and gentry" the cultivation of connoisseurship, in part as a pleasant pursuit to fill a newfound leisure, but also, clearly, because it served as a prominent indicator of the gentlemanly or "polite" status to which they aspired.

3

In his *Spectator* 419 on "Taste," published in 1712, Addison tells his large, primarily middle-class readership that since "*the fine taste* . . . arises very often in conversation, I shall endeavor to give some account of it and to lay down rules . . . how we may acquire that fine taste of writing which is so much talked of among the polite world." Such a deliberate cultivation of connoisseurship in the eighteenth century by a rapidly expanding part of the population resulted in a conspicuous set of social innovations. I refer to the sudden appearance and accelerating development, for the first time in Western history, of a great variety of institutions and arrangements for making one after another of the objects of "fine taste"—that is, products of the diverse arts—accessible, usually for pay, to an ever growing public. I have time to give only a brief overview of this remarkable but neglected social phenomenon, in each of what at that time came to be classified as "the fine arts," that is, the nonutilitarian arts.

And first, *literature*. In the latter seventeenth century, secular literature was still being written largely under the patronage of the nobility and of political parties; an author was supported by writing to order, as an occasion or commission required, or else to gain favor with the patron or patrons on whom he depended for a livelihood. A century later this system had given way to one in which booksellers paid for and published literary works, and so made authors reliant on the sale of their books to the general public. By Dr. Johnson's time, in Germany as well as England, there existed for the first time a reading public in the modern sense, large enough to support, though in many instances on a level of bare subsistence, a substantial number of writers by the books they bought. In this period new literary forms were invented to satisfy the expanding demand—above all the novel, which at first pretended to be both true and edifying, but soon relaxed into the candid condition of being produced to be read merely for the pleasure in the fiction, by a readership now composed in large part by tradesmen, and especially the newly idle wives and daughters of tradesmen. Another commercial institution was invented, the circulating library, to make literature, and especially novels, cheaply available to those who could not afford, or chose not, to buy them outright. This was the age also of the emergence and rapid development of various types of periodical publications. One was the critical review, which served to guide the public in the appreciation and appraisal of works of literature. Another was the magazine, so called because it included a variety of prose and verse forms. A clear indication that such new publications owed part of their appeal to upper-class aspirations is the fact that the first periodical of this latter type, published in the 1690s, was named *The Gentleman's Journal,* and that in the next century the most successful example (it endured until 1914) was named *The Gentleman's Magazine.*[11]

It was, then, in the eighteenth century that literature became a commodity, subject to the exchange values of the marketplace, with all the consequences of such a condition. But for our present purpose, note that both books and magazines incorporated literary forms that were bought to be read by a reader in isolation, for the interest and pleasure of doing so, independently of any practical purpose or specific occasion, and at a distance from their author and his circumstances. It was in 1710 that the term *belles lettres* was imported from France, to signify those literary works that were not doctrinal or utilitarian or instructional, but simply appealed to taste, as writings to be read for pleasure. In the course of time *belles lettres* became simply "literature" and replaced the earlier generic term *poetry,* which was based on the construction model; for in the root sense that endured through the Renaissance, *poetry* signified the art of constructing a "poem"—a word derived from the Greek *poiema*, "a made thing."

Music. Through the Renaissance, composed music (as distinguished from folk music) had been available to a broad, nonaristocratic audience only in churches, or on the occasion of public festivals. The latter seventeenth century, however, saw the emergence of the earliest organizations for making music public—that is, regularly accessible to all who were able and willing to pay to hear it. Examples are the *Abendmusiken* and *Collegia Musica* in various German towns, then in Holland and elsewhere. In Restoration London, regular public concerts came to be offered in a number of taverns; and the first hall specifically designed for public concerts was constructed in the York buildings. The earliest of the great public gardens, Vauxhall, began to provide instrumental and vocal programs of both light and serious music, and was frequented by all classes of citizens, from the high nobility down through merchants and their apprentices—together with the usual camp followers of such diverse crowds. In the process of the eighteenth century, public concerts—music for profit, as a commodity-art—became a matter of course, not only in London (as in other major European cities) but also in cathedral towns, the university towns, the new industrial cities, and even in many villages, where groups of amateur musicians offered performances for a small admission fee. Such concerts included what, in their origin, had been a diversity of compositions to serve different social purposes; all were now equivalently presented, however, for no other end than to provide pleasure to a broad audience—including, specifically, the tired businessman. As one English commentator put it in 1724, music is "a charming Relaxation to the Mind, when fatigued with the Bustle of Business."[12] Various new musical forms, designed to be suitable for performance to a large audience and to be both attractive and intelligible to untrained listeners, were developed to satisfy the growing demand—most prominently, the symphony scored for a large orchestra, which was for the middle-class music public very much what the new novel was for the middle-class reading public.

Painting and sculpture I'll deal with in conjunction. There were contemporary and parallel innovations in the arrangements for providing public access to pictures and statues. The Continental Grand Tour, usually lasting several years and with Italy and Rome as its chief goal, had by the seventeenth century become almost obligatory as a finishing school for the sons of the high aristocracy in England and elsewhere; and some graduates of that school emulated noble or rich Italian collectors of the visual arts—a vogue that had begun in Italy in the early Renaissance—by buying the works they had learned to prize.[13] Enormous collections were gathered—by purchase, or not infrequently as loot following a military conquest—by princes and noble landowners, then by wealthy merchants and industrialists, in many cities of Europe, and notably in London. In England private collectors, from the late seventeenth through the eighteenth centuries, acquired the bulk of the sculpture and paintings that have ever since made that country a major place for the study of the art of Europe, both classical and postclassical.[14]

Some collectors were doubtless, in some part, impersonal connoisseurs of works of painting and sculpture; but their motives were also acquisitive and proprietary, and they were of course very few in number. Our concern is with the growing number of nonowners who visited such collections because of interest in the works themselves. Through most of the seventeenth century, access to the princely galleries had, with few exceptions, been restricted to persons of quality and to qualified scholars. But gradually, as the vogue of art connoisseurship spread, and in response to increasing demands, a number of private galleries were, at first *de facto,* then officially, converted into the first public museums. The British Museum was established as a national institution in 1759, followed in 1773 by the establishment of the Vatican Museum, as well as by the Uffizi gallery in Florence; from then to our own time the public collections have, like insatiable sponges, absorbed ever more of the major works in private hands.[15]

Other institutional innovations served to feed the growing appetite for the visual arts. Attending public auctions of these arts became a popular amusement; Sotheby's was founded in the 1740s, and Christie's in 1762. To visit annual exhibitions sponsored by academies of living painters became nothing short of a craze and filled both building and street with crowds of people. Horace Walpole, with his union of caustic wit and sense of gentility, wrote in 1779 that "the taste for virtù has become universal; persons of all ranks and degrees set up for connoisseurs, and even the lowest people tell familiarly of Hannibal Scratchi, Paul Varnish, and Raphael Angelo."[16] Walpole's comment is a humorous exaggeration of the remarkable diffusion of interest in the visual arts, while his defensive snobbery reminds us of the persisting function of connoisseurship as a sign of social rank. To cite another example: in 1767 Thomas Martyn published in two volumes *The English Connoisseur,* a guide to collections of painting and sculpture "in the palaces and seats of the nobility and principal gentry of England," intended specifically for the instruction of what he calls "the rising Connoisseur." Now, "the rising connoisseur," translated into modern sociologese, is "the upwardly mobile connoisseur"; and Martyn's book is motivated, he tells us, by "the great progress which the polite arts have lately made in England, and the attention which is now paid them by almost all ranks of men."[17]

In sum: during the span of less than one hundred years, an extensive institutional revolution had been effected, with the result that, by the latter eighteenth century, the cultural situation in England (as, to various degrees, in Germany and other countries) was recognizably the present one, with a large, primarily middle-class public for literature, together with public theaters, public concerts of music, and public galleries and museums of painting and sculpture. We now take such a situation so entirely for granted that it requires an effort of the historical imagination to realize the radical difference this made in the social role of the arts and, as a consequence, in what philosophers and critics assumed to be the standard situation when theorizing about them. Through the Renaissance and later, works of music, painting, and sculpture had been produced mainly to order, on commissions by a churchman, prince, wealthy merchant, town council, or guild; very often they were produced for a specific function or occasion, religious or secular; and the accomplished work had been experienced by some members of its audience, no doubt, as the occasion for what we now call an "aesthetic experience," but at the same time as thoroughly embedded in a particular institution or event, and as an integral component in a complex of human activities and functions. Now, however, the new institution of the public concert might include pieces, both vocal and instrumental, that had originally served to intensify sacred feelings in a religious ceremony, or to add splendor and gaiety to a private or public celebration, or to provide melodic rhythms for social dancing—together with new pieces written for the concert hall itself. There exist numerous paintings that represent a room in an eighteenth-century gallery or museum. One can see that they display side by side statuary that was both ancient and recent, pagan and Christian, sacred and profane. And the walls display in close array, extending the length of the room and from floor to ceiling, paintings that were originally made to serve as altar pieces, or else as reminiscences of classical myth, moral allegories, a Flemish bedroom record of a marriage, memorials of historic events, representations of a family estate, or ornaments for a noble salon. All such products, in the new modes of public distribution or display, have been pulled out of their intended contexts, stripped of their diverse religious, social, and political functions, and given a single and uniform new role: as items to be read or listened to or looked at simply as a poem, a musical piece, a statue, a painting.

Suppose, while you are looking at a painting of the Madonna and Child in its original location in a chapel, you are asked: "What's the painting for?" A manifest answer is: "To illustrate, beautifully and expressively, an article of faith, and thereby to heighten devotion." Now suppose that same painting moved to the wall of a museum and hung, let's say, next to a representation of Leda and the Swan. To the question "What's it for?" the obvious answer now is: "To be contemplated, admired, and enjoyed." Note that each of these is a valid answer to the same question—within the institutional setting in which that question is asked.

I have reserved for special treatment *architecture,* the fifth of the standard fine arts, because it is an especially instructive instance of the way in which an altered social role effected a drastic alteration in the conception of a craft. For of all the fine (that is, nonutilitarian) arts, architecture seems the most obviously and thoroughly utilitarian, in that a building is specifically designed to serve as a shelter and to subserve a variety of other purposes—to be a sacred place for worship, to house a great family and its retainers, or to function as headquarters for a political or social or economic body; as well as to announce by its magnitude, formal symbolism, and ornament, the status and wealth of the institution or family for which it is intended. On the Continental Grand Tour in the seventeenth century, however, one aim had been to seek out a diversity of ancient and modern structures simply as instances of architectural achievement. Such a pursuit, hitherto limited to a few members of the aristocracy, grew enormously in the eighteenth century. For this was precisely the period both of the inauguration and the rapid development of a new human activity, and that was the leisure-time journey, not to Italy but within England itself, and for no other purpose than to get acquainted with places and things. Before the end of the century, this activity had become so widespread as to require an invented word: *tourist.* The company of English tourists included increasing numbers of the middle classes. A principal aim of the tour, in addition to viewing picturesque landscapes, was to visit great country houses— many of these soon provided (for a fee, of course) detailed guide books to the estate—in order to admire and judge the works of art, the interior appointments, and the landscaped gardens, and very prominently, the architectural structure itself.[18] It may surprise you, as it did me, to learn that in the year 1775 alone, close to 2,500 tourists visited the famous country estate at Stowe; multiply that number by ten or twelve, to correspond to the increase in the present population of England, and it turns out that the popularity of English tourism, very soon after that activity began, nearly equaled its popularity now. You will recall that the turning point of the novel *Pride and Prejudice,* which Jane Austen began writing in 1798, occurs when Elizabeth Bennet is taken by her aunt and uncle, the Gardiners—who, the author stresses, are "in trade," members of the merchant middle class—on a vacation tour that includes her rejected lover Darcy's great estate of Pemberley, at a time when its owner is supposedly absent.

It is also noteworthy that in the eighteenth century a flourishing market developed for books of engraved views of royal palaces and famous urban and country houses.[19] Buildings can't easily be relocated in museums, but these published engravings served as a museum without walls, hence as yet another vehicle to move works of architecture into their new and widespread social role as, like the products of sculpture and painting, a set of things to be pored over, as such, simply for their capacity to interest and give pleasure to the observer. What had been a utilitarian craft thus became an art—a fine art.

What we find, then, beginning late in the seventeenth century, is the emergence of an astonishing number of institutions for making a diversity of human artifacts public—as commodities, usually for pay—in order to satisfy a burgeoning demand for the delights, but also for the social distinction, of connoisseurship. The sum of these changes constitutes a new "form of life" (in Wittgenstein's phrase) in the leisure-time pursuits both of the high-born and the newly well-to-do. Since humankind is an enquiring and loquacious being, a new form of life calls for an appropriate language—a set of terms for sorting things out and for systematizing and analyzing them in accordance with the altered mode of common or normal experience. In such an enterprise, the normal experience readily becomes the normative experience. The new critical language, accordingly, does not envision a product of art from the traditional point of view of its expert constructor or maker, but from the point of view of the connoisseur, who confronts the work as a completed product which he attends to as an isolated thing, for the sake of the satisfactions that doing so yields. And certain hitherto largely distinct and diversely classified human products—especially poetry, music, painting, sculpture, architecture—since all of them have now acquired, on a broad scale, the same social role as standard objects for connoisseurship, are for the first time gathered together as an entirely distinctive class of things called "the fine arts." Addison, with his customary acumen, identified this new principle of classification when he remarked in *Spectator* 29 that "music, architecture, and painting, as well as poetry and oratory, are to deduce their laws and rules from the general sense and taste of mankind, and not from the principles of those arts themselves." This is a contemporary recognition of the turn from the construction model to the spectator model for the newly identified class of the fine arts; and for the philosophy of this class of objects, the German theorist Baumgarten in the mid-eighteenth century coined the term *aesthetics*.

In such a philosophy, works of fine art, despite their conspicuous differences in physical and other attributes, are naturally enough assumed to share a distinctive quality or essence that enables them to perform their common role as objects of connoisseurship. This role, although often requiring payment of a fee, was, anomalously, not utilitarian or moral but specifically a diversion or escape from ordinary utilitarian and moral interests and pursuits. The essential feature that qualified a product to be accounted a work of fine art was accordingly identified as its inherent capacity to serve as a sufficient and rewarding object of attention as an end in itself—a very elusive, nonmaterial feature that Kant called its "beauty" or "form" or "aesthetic quality."

To put what I have just said in a different philosophical idiom: the condition and status of being a work of art, in accordance with the standard definition of art-as-such, is not an inherent fact but an institutional fact. The most prominent institution that functions to confer this status has become the public museum; the exemplary art-of-arts, which over the centuries had been poetry, has become painting, in which the product is hung on a wall and isolated from its surroundings by a material frame; and the disinterested and absorbed contemplation of an isolated art object—the paradigmatic experience of the theory of art-as-such—is typically a museum experience. The power of being accepted and displayed by a reputable museum to transform a utilitarian object into a work of fine art was melodramatically revealed when Marcel Duchamp took a very homely utility, machine-made and mass-produced—a urinal—from the thousands of its duplicates and had it mounted on a museum wall. Many of us, once the initial shock or indignation or derisive laughter has worn off, succumb to the institutional compulsion, assume the aesthetic attitude, and begin to contemplate the object as such, in its austerely formal and monochromatic harmony.

4

Let me anticipate what some of you are no doubt thinking, and admit that the conditions for the emergence of the theory of art-as-such are not so simple as I have made out. In this short presentation, I have had to omit a number of complications and qualifications. Above all, I have omitted a surprising fact, which becomes evident only if we turn our attention from the sociology of art to intellectual history. I said that the theory of art-as-such was a radical conceptual innovation of the eighteenth century. That assertion is valid, so long as we limit our purview to the basic concepts and operative vocabulary within earlier theories of the arts. But if we take a more comprehensive historical overview, we find that the vantage point, the defining concepts, and the distinctive vocabulary of art-as-such were actually commonplaces—indeed, they were very old and familiar commonplaces; they had functioned, however, not in the traditional philosophy and criticism of the arts, but in alien realms of metaphysics, and especially of theology. These ancient commonplaces were imported into, and specialized for, the theory of fine art—they achieved, that is, a radical novelty of application—only when the new social role of the various arts invited and fostered concepts of a requisite sort. It seems highly likely that, if these concepts and terms had not existed ready-made, modern aesthetics could not have developed so quickly from its beginnings into the complex, complete, and sophisticated form of Kant's *Critique of Judgment*.

I have told this story at some length elsewhere,[20] and have time only to present a few highlights. The prototypical conception of an object that evokes a selfless and absorbed contemplation is Plato's Idea of Ideas—that ultimate essence, uniting Beauty, Goodness, and Truth that Plato posited as the terminus of all human love and desire. The ultimate knowledge, and the supreme human value, Plato says, is "the contemplation with the eye of the mind" of "beauty absolute, separate, simple, and everlasting"—an entity that is "perfect" because, possessing *autarkeia*, it is utterly self-sufficient.[21] Plotinus, following Plato, similarly endowed his Absolute with the attribute of being "wholly self-sufficing," "self-closed," and "autonomous." And in passages of high consequence for later Christian thought—and if I am right, also for modern aesthetics—Plotinus described the highest good of the human soul to be "contemplation" of the essential Beauty and Good which is a state of "perfect surrender" of the self that constitutes "the soul's peace," with "no passion, no outlooking desire . . . reasoning is in abeyance and all Intellection and even . . . the very self." The soul in this contemplation "has in perfect stillness attained isolation."[22]

By one of the strangest developments in intellectual history, this pagan concept of a self-sufficient Absolute Beauty, which is to be contemplated without reference either to the self or to anything beyond its own bounds, became thoroughly identified, early in Christian theology, with the God of the Old Testament, a very personal God. He is described in the Bible as creative, loving, just, and often very angry, but is never said to be beautiful or self-sufficient or an impersonal essence or Absolute. It was St. Augustine who, in his eminently influential expositions of the nature of Christian *caritas*, or love, early in the fifth century, was more than anyone responsible for this fusion of the Christian God and the classical Absolute; and in doing so he promulgated the lexicon of the categories and terms that, some fourteen hundred years later, came to constitute the spectator's vantage and the contemplation model of the theory of art-as-such. Augustine's controlling distinction is between *uti* and *frui*, between loving something for its use and loving something for pure enjoyment, as an end in itself. All the good and beautiful things in this world, he asserts, are to be loved for their utility, as a means to something else. Of all things in the universe, God, and God alone, because He is the ultimate in beauty and excellence, is to be loved with a pure enjoyment, and in a *visio Dei;* that is, in a contemplation of God by "the eye of the mind." And Augustine details the loving contemplation of God's supreme beauty and excellence in terms familiar to us: He is enjoyed as His own end, and *non propter aliud*, for His own sake [*propter se ipsam*], simply for His inherent excellence and, in Augustine's repeated term, *gratis*—that is, gratuitously, independently of our personal interests or of any possible reward.[23] Here are all the elements of the theory of art-as-such; the radical change is the shift of reference from God to a beautiful work of art as the sufficient object of contemplative enjoyment, and not by the eye of the mind but by the physical eye.

The crossing over of these theological terms, especially *contemplation* and *disinterested*, into aesthetic theory occurred, as I have indicated earlier, in 1711 in the book by the Earl of Shaftesbury entitled *Characteristics*. The express subject of Shaftesbury's urbane essays, however, was not aesthetics or art—his book has been preempted by historians of aesthetics only retrospectively—but religion, morals, and the life-style appropriate to a gentleman. Shaftesbury's ideal is the virtuoso ideal of connoisseurship, a mode of contemplation that (in his Platonic way of thinking) applies equally to God, to objects of beauty, and to moral goodness. Shaftesbury's first published work had been an edition of the sermons of Benjamin Whichcote, in which that Neoplatonic theologian had argued that God is to be loved not from a desire for personal gain, nor as "a *Mean*, but [as] an *End*," and "for what he is in himself," in "his own Loveliness, Excellency, and Beauty."[24] In his later *Characteristics*, Shaftesbury imports the rest of Augustine's vocabulary, which he applies primarily to theology and morality, and secondarily to the beauties of nature or of works of art.

I shall cite one German thinker, largely neglected by historians of aesthetics, Karl Philipp Moritz, who in 1785, five years before Kant's *Critique*, published a short essay that is the earliest unqualified presentation of the view of art-as-such. The essay demonstrates that, in little more than seventy years after Shaftesbury, these distinctive theological and moral terms have not only become specialized to the arts but are used to oppose the experience of a work of art to religious and moral experience, as well as to all practical concerns. Only the mechanical or useful arts, Moritz says, have an "outer end"—

that is, an end "outside themselves in something other." He poses instead a contemplation model for discussing the fine arts:

> In the contemplation [*Betrachtung*] of the beautiful object . . . I contemplate it as something which is *completed*, not in me, but *in its own self*, which therefore constitutes a whole in itself, and affords me pleasure *for its own sake* [*um sein selbst willen*].

In adding to this formulation the further concepts of aesthetic disinterestedness and the self-sufficiency of a work of art, Moritz inadvertently reveals the degree to which his views are indebted to the ancient Plotinian and Augustinian representation of the selfless and gratuitous contemplation of the ultimate beauty of God:

> While the beautiful draws our attention exclusively to itself . . . we seem to lose ourselves in the beautiful object; and precisely this loss, this forgetfulness of self, is the highest degree of pure and disinterested pleasure that beauty grants us. In that moment we sacrifice our individual confined being to a kind of higher being. . . . Beauty in a work of art is not pure . . . until I contemplate it as something that has been brought forth entirely for its own sake, in order that it should be something complete in itself.[25]

Kant must surely have studied Moritz's writings—there are many parallels I haven't cited—but he stripped away the patent indicators in Moritz of an origin in a Platonized Christian theology. Other writers of that time, however—like a number of more recent proponents of art-as-such, from Flaubert and Clive Bell through James Joyce and some of the American New Critics—manifest the tendency of a contemplation theory of art to recuperate aspects of its original context in religious devotion. Here is Wilhelm Wackenroder, for example, writing in 1797, seven years after Kant's *Critique*, on the experience of objects of art-as-such; and explicitly, now, in what has become their normative setting in a public museum:

Art galleries . . . ought to be temples where, in still and silent humility and in heart-lifting solitude, we may admire great artists as the highest among mortals . . . with long, steadfast contemplation of their works. . . . I compare the enjoyment of nobler works of art to *prayer*. . . . Works of art, in their way, no more fit into the common flow of life than does the thought of God. . . . That day is for me a sacred holiday which . . . I devote to the contemplation of noble works of art.[26]

Well, what does this excursion into social and intellectual history come to?

The theory of art-as-such consists of assertions that have been claimed, or assumed, by a number of philosophers and critics to be timeless truths about a distinctive class of artifacts. I have proposed, on the other hand, that it is a way of talking about art that emerged at a particular time, as an integral and reciprocative element in an altering form of social life, marked by the development of many new institutions to make highly diverse human products widely public, and for no other ostensible purpose than simply to be attended to for their own sake. I have also proposed that these changes were in part motivated by the prestige of connoisseurship, and of a nonutilitarian aesthetic culture, as a sign of upper-class status; and furthermore, that the determinative idiom and concepts of the new theory were translocated into the realm of art, ready-made, from the realm of a Platonized Christian theology.

I do not, however, mean to assert that this theory of art is, as a consequence, an invalid theory. It describes the way that, in our present circumstances, many of us in fact frequently experience works of art. Furthermore, when a theory of art is put to work in applied criticism, its provenience ceases to matter, and the criterion of its validity becomes the profitability of what it proves capable of doing. (The same holds for some of the profitable theories in the natural sciences, which have also had a strange, and even dubious, provenience.) In criticism, the view of art-as-such has fostered an unprecedented analysis of the complex elements, internal relations, and modes of organization of works of art that has undeniably deepened and subtilized our experience of them. This theory has also been held as their working hypothesis by major modern artists, including such literary masters as Flaubert, Proust, Joyce, and Nabokov.

It is, then, in this heuristic and pragmatic sense, a valid theory; but like all competing views of art, it is also a partial theory. It is a very profitable way of talking, when we want to deal with a work of any of the arts simply in its formal aspects and internal organization. For some kinds of works, this way of talking is relatively adequate. But if we turn to *King Lear,* or Bach's *St. Matthew's Passion,* or the frescoes of Michelangelo (still, happily, in their original situation in the Sistine Chapel)—or for that matter, to Byron's comic masterpiece, *Don Juan*—the view of art-as-such, while it remains pertinent, becomes woefully inadequate. We need to substitute a different perspective, and a very different critical vocabulary, to begin to do justice to the diverse ends and functions of such works, and the patent way that our responses to them involve our shared experiences, appeal to our convictions about the world and our life in that world, implicate our moral interests, and engage our deepest human concerns.

From Addison to Kant: Modern Aesthetics and the Exemplary Art

THE ERA from Addison to Kant was one of unprecedented interest in the fine arts, and of unexampled expansion and innovation in the philosophical and critical theory of the arts. Eighteenth-century theorists had inherited from the Renaissance treatments of a single art, above all of poetry, in which the writers for the most part had explicated and played changes upon the vantage points and analytic terms they had found in their Greek and Roman progenitors. From the time of the Greeks, what we call "the arts" had been classified with crafts such as carpentry and cookery, and had only occasionally and in limited aspects been linked one to another. In the course of the eighteenth century, however, the various arts (especially poetry, painting, sculpture, music, and architecture), so patently diverse in their media and modes, in the skills they require, and in the occasion and social function of individual works, came to be systematized as "the fine arts," or simply as "art."[1] They were treated for the first time, that is, as a single class of products, sharing an essential feature that made them *sui generis*. By the middle of the century, Baumgarten had provided the new science of the arts-in-general with the coined name *aesthetics*, and had made it, enduringly, a part of any philosophical system that undertook to account for our major modes of experiencing and dealing with the world. By the end of the century, Friedrich Schelling, in his *Transcendental Idealism* (1800), made the dialectical process of imagination in producing a work of art into the central and controlling concept of his entire metaphysics—in his words, "the general organon of philosophy and the keystone of its arch."[2]

Despite these drastic changes in the professional philosophy of art, the working premises of practicing critics, through much of the century, continued to be primarily pragmatic, based on Horace's *Art of Poetry* and classical theories of rhetoric, but incorporating concepts derived from Aristotle and Longinus. In general terms: a work of literature or of art was conceived to be, as Aristotle had said, an imitation, but with its materials selected, altered, and ordered in order to achieve predetermined ends, or effects. These ends were to move and give pleasure to the audience; variable stress was also given to the Horatian *utile*, that is, the moral and intellectual improvement of the audience. The excellence of a work, in its specific genre, was theoretically to be measured by the kind and degree of its emotional and pleasurable effectiveness. A primary criterion was that of "truth" to the nature that art imitates; this truth, however, was not verity, but "verisimilitude" or "probability," which is truth adapted to the responsiveness of the audience. That is, the people, objects, and events imitated in a work, though they deviate from history and may violate the known constitution and course of nature, must be so rendered that the audience will accept them as credibly like the world if the work is to achieve its justifying end of effecting pleasurable emotions.

Almost three decades ago, in *The Mirror and the Lamp*, I undertook to chronicle the shift in critical theory, beginning in the latter eighteenth century, from the mimetic and pragmatic orientation to the Romantic, or expressive, orientation. According to this view, a work of poetry or art is not primarily an imitation, but the expression of the emotions or of the feelingful imaginative process of the artist. Its cardinal criterion, consonantly, is no longer its truth, in the sense of a credible correspondence to reality, but its sincerity, or the genuineness of its correspondence to the feelingful state of mind of the artist; often, the work is regarded also as a revelation of the unique personality of the artist. It needs to be stressed, however, that this shift took place by an expansion and change in function of concepts and terms that were already present in the inherited vocabulary of eighteenth-century criticism. The notion, for example, that the language of poetry, in addition to its representational function, can express emotions and manifest the *ethos,* or character, of the speaker, was entirely traditional, though it had earlier been used not to define poetry but to discuss style, or else to specify the matching of an utterance to the state of mind of a character within a poem. And in stressing the requirement that the poet evoke emotions in his audience, pragmatic theorists often added Horace's corollary, *si vis me flere,* that is, "if you wish to move me, you must first yourself be moved." In short, the change from a mimetic and pragmatic to an expressive theory was an evolutionary process, in which, in response to altering social circumstances, sensibility, and artistic practices, certain terms that had hitherto been marginal and subordinate became central and controlling, and so effected an internal revolution in critical theory.

The case, however, is quite different for two other eighteenth-century innovations that are my particular concern here. Both of these introduced new sets of terms, without precedent in the traditional critical vocabulary, for specifying the nature and criteria of a work of art. Both innovations are the achievement mainly of philosophers rather than practicing critics; they did not emerge fully as the express and inclusive premises of critics, and also of artists, until after the Romantic period, in the mid-nineteenth century; and their full effect was delayed until they re-emerged to constitute, in diverse developments, the dominant modes of critical theory and discussion of the arts after the third decade of the present century. If these innovations are taken into account, it can be claimed that eighteenth-century theorists supplemented the traditional repertory of critical discourse with the major alternative concepts that have been exploited by critics and aestheticians up to the very recent past.

1. PARADIGMS OF CRITICISM AND MODELS OF ART

For easy reference, let us call these innovative elements "the contemplation model" and "the heterocosmic model" for a work of art. I cite two twentieth-century examples of each model.

In his influential *Speculations* (1924), T. E. Hulme, after defining *contemplation* as "a detached interest," wrote: "The object of aesthetic contemplation is something framed apart by itself and regarded without memory or expectation, simply as being itself, as end not means, as individual not universal."[3] And in 1960 Jerome Stolnitz began his *Aesthetics and Philosophy of Art Criticism* by defining "the aesthetic attitude" as "disinterested and sympathetic attention to and contemplation of any object of awareness whatever, for its own sake alone." To apprehend a work of art with the attitude appropriate to it, consequently, is to see "the work as a self-contained object which is of interest in its own right." And to talk "about works of art as aesthetic objects" is to talk "about what is within the work itself. . . . [The work] has a significance and value which is inherent in itself alone."[4]

In both these passages the terms are the common currency of modern critical discourse, and the predications are often taken to be timeless truths about the nature and perception of works of art. They are, however, recent and radical novelties in the two-thousand-year history of art criticism. Prior to the eighteenth century, it had occurred to no philosopher or critic to assert that a work of human art is to be attended to with a "contemplation" that is "disinterested," and "for its own sake alone"; or to identify the work as an object "framed apart by itself" and regarded "as being itself, as end not means"; or to distinguish sharply between what is inside and outside a work, and to claim that, since the work is "self-contained," properly aesthetic criticism must confine itself solely to its "inherent," or internal, "significance and value."

The key term in these commentaries is "contemplation," and the shift in theory that the word signals is not a reorganization within the inherited critical system but the introduction of a new paradigm for dealing with a work of art. Traditional critical theory, from Aristotle on, had assumed a construction paradigm. The Greek and Latin terms for "poem" *[poiema, poema]* signified a "made thing"—made, that is, by the poet ("maker") in accordance with an "art" (a craft, or skill) for selecting materials to imitate, and for rendering and ordering these materials toward the end of achieving appropriate effects on the audience. And traditional treatises did not distinguish between their function as a guide to the poet in making a good, or successful, poem and as a guide to the reader in judging whether the made poem is good. This paradigm, which is assumed throughout Aristotle's *Poetics*, becomes blatantly explicit in Horace's *Ars Poetica*, which later critics applied to painting and the other arts as well as poetry. For the *Ars Poetica* is a how-to letter addressed to a poetic novice, advising him how to construct a poem that will achieve maximal and enduring effects on the widest possible audience. In sharp contrast, Hulme and Stolnitz take for granted a perceptual paradigm for art, and within this paradigm they formulate the mode of perception by reference to a contemplation model. That is, they assume that the representative situation, in establishing what constitutes a work of art, is one in which a perceiver confronts a completed work, however it got constructed; and they define the way he perceives that work as a "contemplation" that is "disinterested," or "detached," and is focused exclusively on the isolated object as its own end, or for its own sake.

To introduce the second eighteenth-century innovation by a twentieth-century instance, here is what A. C. Bradley said about the distinctive nature of a poem in an essay written in 1901:

> Its nature is to be not a part, nor yet a copy, of the real world (as we commonly understand that phrase) but to be a world by itself, independent, complete, autonomous; and to possess it fully you must enter that world, conform to its laws, and ignore for the time the beliefs, aims, and particular conditions which belong to you in the other world of reality. . . .
>
> [Poetry and reality] are parallel developments which nowhere meet . . . they are analogues. . . . They differ . . . because they have different *kinds* of existence.[5]

The paradigm is a perceptual one, as in the preceding examples, but Bradley formulates the nature of the perceived poem on a heterocosmic model. He substitutes for the view that a poem is an imitation—"a copy"—of the real world the claim that each poem is its own world, analogous to the ordinary world, but complete in itself, and (in another term unprecedented before the eighteenth century) "autonomous," that is, subject only to laws specific to its individual cosmos.

In the 1920s the novelist and critic E. M. Forster asserted in parallel fashion that the poet's use of words has the power "to create . . . a world" that is governed by laws specific to itself, is complete in itself, is self-referential, and replaces the ordinary truth of correspondence to reality by the poetic truth of self-coherence. Reading the *Ancient Mariner,* for example,

> we have entered a universe that only answers to its own laws, supports itself, internally coheres, and has a new standard of truth. Information is true if it is accurate. A poem is true if it hangs together. Information points to something else. A poem points to nothing but itself. . . . It is not this world, its laws are not the laws of science or logic, its conclusions not those of common sense.[6]

Here we have, then, within the shared perceptual paradigm of a work-in-being, two distinct ways of dealing with art. One deploys a model in which each work is a self-sufficient object that is contemplated for its own sake; the other deploys a model in which each work is a unique, coherent, and autonomous world. My concern is to show—cursorily, in the space available—that: (1) both the contemplative and the heterocosmic models for art were first exploited in the eighteenth century; their novelty, however, was not in their conceptual content but in their application. For both models were imported into the criticism of the arts from theology, where they had been familiar though discrepant commonplaces in formulating the essential nature and activity of God; (2) each model was at first brought to bear primarily on that art to which it was most plausibly applicable, but was later generalized to account for the other arts as well; (3) these two models, although diverse in their original formulations and distinctive features, nonetheless fostered similar assertions about the nature and criteria of works of art—assertions that constitute what I shall call the view of "art-as-such," and that have in large part dominated both the theory of art and the practice of artistic criticism from the 1920s to the present time.

The Contemplation Model

The key terms *contemplation* and *disinterested* had been introduced into contexts that included reference to the arts as early as 1711, in the *Characteristics* of the Earl of Shaftesbury.[7] The first full and systematic treatment of the fine arts exclusively in terms of the contemplation model, however, occurs in a short, densely written essay published in 1785 by a young German thinker, Karl Philipp Moritz. The essay was entitled "On the Unification of All the Fine Arts . . . under the Concept of the Complete-in-Itself"—that is, *des in sich selbst Vollendeten,* which is also translatable as "the perfected in itself." Moritz begins by rejecting the reigning attempts to define the arts as an imitation of nature that is subordinated to the end of giving pleasure to its audience. He sets up a basic opposition between useful objects, which are perceived merely as means to an end outside themselves, hence as "completed" only by achieving that external end, and beautiful works of art, which are perceived as wholes that are complete in themselves. He then proposes the following model for the way in which we perceive a work of art:

> In the contemplation [*Betrachtung*] of the beautiful I roll its end back from me into the object itself; I contemplate it as something which is *completed,* not in me, but *in its own self,* which therefore constitutes a whole in itself and affords me pleasure *for its own sake* [*um sein selbst willen*]. . . . Since the beautiful object is valuable to me more for its own sake, [it] provides me with a higher and more disinterested [*uneigennützigeres*] pleasure than the merely useful object.[8]

The concept of the disinterested "contemplation of a beautiful work of art" thus involves a distinction between what is inside and what is outside the work; in its self-sufficiency, the contemplated object replaces what Moritz calls an "external purposefulness" with an "internal purposefulness" [*innere Zweckmässigkeit*] of all its parts toward the achievement of the perfected whole. Hence the pleasure we experience in contemplating the work is merely supervenient upon an exclusive attention to the self-bounded whole, which is regarded, in Moritz's reiterated phrase, simply "for its own sake."[9]

Where did this complex of new terms for defining a work of art come from? Moritz himself provides the primary clue.

> While its beauty draws our attention exclusively to itself . . . it makes us seem to lose ourselves in the beautiful object; and precisely this loss, this forgetfulness of self, is the highest degree of pure and disinterested pleasure which beauty grants us. In that moment we sacrifice [*opfern auf*] our individual confined being to a kind of higher being. Pleasure in the beautiful must therefore come ever closer to disinterested *love,* if it is to be genuine.[10]

The idiom of self-abandonment, self-loss, and the sacrifice of self to a "higher being" is patently theological; most strikingly, it assimilates the "pure" pleasure in the selfless contemplation of a work of art to a "disinterested *love.*"

In such a passage, as Martha Woodmansee has pointed out, Moritz has translocated into discourse about art the religious terminology of the Quietist creed in which he had been brought up; for in Quietism the primary emphasis—as Moritz himself described it in his autobiographical novel, *Anton Reiser*—had been on "the total annihilation of all so-called selfhood" in "a totally disinterested [*uninteressierte*] love of God," which is "pure" only if it is totally unalloyed by "self-love."[11] In a larger historical purview, however, this concept of the contemplation of a self-sufficient object as the manifestation of selfless love turns out to be a long footnote to Plato. In the *Symposium* Diotima describes to Socrates the ascent of human love from the beauty of sensible objects through ever-higher stages, to culminate in the contemplation of the supersensible Idea of Ideas, which is "beauty absolute, separate, simple, and everlasting," and constitutes also the absolute good. The *summum bonum*—"that life above all others which men should live"—consists in this "contemplation of beauty absolute . . . divine beauty . . . pure and clear and unalloyed," which is viewed not with the bodily eye but "with the eye of the mind." In the *Philebus,* Plato stressed the feature of *autarkia,* or self-sufficiency, of this divine object of contemplation: such a being "always everywhere and in all things has the most perfect sufficiency, and is never in need of anything else."[12] Self-sufficiency is also the prime attribute of the Absolute of Plotinus, whose beauty is "perfect in its purity," and who in his perfection is "wholly self-sufficing," "self-closed," "autonomous," and "most utterly without need." The apex and terminus of all human love, Plotinus says, in passages that became central references for religious contemplatives and are echoed both in Moritz's Quietism and in his aesthetics, is to "contemplate" this "Absolute Beauty" in a "perfect surrender" of the self which is "the soul's peace," since in such contemplation alone there is "no movement . . . no passion, no outlooking desire," but only "perfect stillness."[13]

In the theology of divers Church Fathers, the Absolute Beauty of Plato and Plotinus, impersonal, indifferent, and self-bounded, was merged, very incongruously, with the personal, loving, just, and often angry God of the Old and New Testaments. And with this concept of the biblical Deity as the perfection of both beauty and goodness came the correlative concept that the highest human good is to contemplate this self-sufficient God with a selfless love, not for our sake but purely for His sake. Especially relevant for the Western Church are the views of St. Augustine, who converted the pagan *eros* doctrine into the doctrine of Christian *caritas* which dominated much of Western theology. Augustine deploys an opposition between *uti* and *frui,* "to use" and "to enjoy," to establish two sharply distinct kinds of love: to love something for its use, as means to an end outside itself [*propter aliud*], and to love something in a pure enjoyment [*fruitio*] of it as its own end, and for its own sake. The first class comprehends all the good and beautiful things in the sensible world, whether natural or works of the human arts; all these are to be loved only as means to the end of the supreme beauty and goodness which is God. The second constitutes a unique class: God alone is to be loved with a pure enjoyment, *gratis* (free of profit to the self), and *propter se ipsam* (for His own sake). In this life, such a love manifests itself at its highest in the enjoyment of the supreme beauty in a *visio Dei*, although not with the physical eye, but with the eye of the mind; only in God's own Kingdom will we be capable of that "enjoyment of contemplation [*fructum contemplationis*]" that "will be our reward itself, . . . when we enjoy completely [*perfruamur*] His goodness and beauty."[14]

The Platonic and Augustinian doctrines of a love that terminates in the selfless contemplation and enjoyment of an object of ultimate beauty and value, not for its use but as an end in itself, and for its own sake, constitute both the contemplation model and the distinctive vocabulary of Moritz's theory of art. The difference, to be sure, is a radical one: the Platonic Absolute, and Augustine's God, have been displaced by a human product, the self-sufficient work of art, and the organ of contemplation, the eye of the mind, has become the physical eye. Yet even today, phrases such as "an art lover" and "an amateur of art" serve as indexes to the origins of modern concepts of art in the philosophy and theology of earthly and heavenly love.

The main conduit, however, from the ancient doctrines of selfless contemplation of an otherworldly object to modern aesthetic theory was not Moritz (whose writings have until recently been inadequately heeded) but Immanuel Kant. In his *Critique of Judgment,* published in 1790, five years after Moritz's seminal essay, Kant develops a complex account of how the experience of a distinctive aesthetic perception is "possible," in terms of an interplay of the faculties that the mind brings to all its experience. He simply takes for granted, however, what it is that constitutes the normative aesthetic perception of an object (in his phrase, "the pure judgment of taste") whose possibility he sets out to explain; and the features of aesthetic perception that Kant takes for granted coincide with the contemplation model and the philosophical idiom already established by Moritz. Thus for Kant the pure judgment of taste "combines delight or aversion immediately with the mere *contemplation* [*blossen Betrachtung*] of the object

irrespective of its use or any end." This judgment "is the one
and only disinterested [*uninteressiertes*] and *free* delight," in
that it is "purely contemplative [*bloss kontemplativ*]," hence
without desire, indifferent "to the real existence of the object,"
and totally independent of reference to the "external" ends
of utility, pleasingness, or moral good. The object contemplated, Kant says, is therefore experienced as "purposeful
without a purpose," and "pleases for its own sake [*für sich
selbst gefallt*]."[15]

2. THE WORK AS A WORLD

Three years after his essay of 1785, Moritz, in "The Formative Imitation of the Beautiful," turned from the topic of how
we contemplate a completed work of art to "the question,
how a thing must be created [*beschaffen*] in order not to need
to be useful"; in his answer, he introduces a new order of
concepts. In bringing a work of art into being, the "formative
artist" does not imitate the sensible reality of nature; instead,
he "imitates" the creative power by which nature produces
this reality. (For this transformed sense of the ancient phrase
"to imitate nature" Moritz uses as synonyms *nachstreben, wet-
teifern, nacherschaffen:* to "strive after," "vie with," "create in
the manner of" nature.) The "formative power" of the artist,
penetrating to the "inner being" and internal relations of
creative nature, dissolves the sensible particulars of reality
into "appearance," in order "to form and create" what nature
has left unrealized "into a self-governing [*eigenmächtig*], self-
sufficient whole." In this way the "active power" of the artist
"creates [*schafft*] its own world, in which nothing isolated any
longer has a place, but every thing is, in its own way, a self-
sufficient whole [*ein für sich bestehendes Ganze*]."[16]

Two years later Kant also turned his attention to the mental processes of the artist that bring into being a work that
will satisfy the criteria he has already established by reference to the contemplation model. He introduces a similar
concept:

The imagination (as a productive faculty of cognition) is a powerful agent for the creation [*Schaffung*], as it were, of a second nature out of the material supplied to it by actual nature. . . . We even use it to remodel experience, always following, no doubt, laws that are based on analogy, but still also following principles which have a higher seat in reason . . . with the result that the material can . . . be worked up by us into something else—namely, what surpasses nature.[17]

The radical metaphor in both Moritz and Kant is "create," and, as applied to art in the eighteenth century, this concept has three dimensions of application: the artist is a creator; his creative power resides in a mental faculty, usually identified as the imagination; and the resulting work of art constitutes a new creation—"its own world" or "a second nature." My concern in this paper is with the exploration of the third aspect, the concept that the work of art is its own world. Before turning to this topic, I want to note two important differences between the contemplation model and the creation model as applied to art.

First, although both models originate in views about God, they are based on very divergent concepts of the divine Being which it has been a formidable challenge for theologians to reconcile. The contemplation model, derived from pagan metaphysics, posits a self-bounded and self-sufficient Deity, totally unconcerned for anything beyond Himself, who is to be loved and contemplated entirely for His own sake. The heterocosmic model, on the contrary, posits the God of Genesis, who in a totally other-oriented act wills the creation of a world out of nothing, and outside the limits of His own being. (In Moritz God's creative power has in turn been delegated to a principle, a *natura naturans,* that is active within created nature itself.) In the former theory, God Himself is the prototype for the self-sufficient work of art that demands disinterested contemplation. In the creation theory, it is not the work of art but the artist, or creative "genius," who is godlike (for example, in his freedom from the constitution and laws of this world, and in his power of radical innovation, or "originality"); the work of art is an analogue to God's created world; and the "creative imagination" tends to displace the faculty of reason as the nearest human approximation to the processes of divinity.

Second, in contemplation theory the visual arts, and painting above all, had been the exemplary form. The contemplation of Absolute Beauty by the "eye of the mind," from Plato on, had been based on express analogy with visual perception by the bodily eye.[18] When translated from its other-worldly to a this-worldly form, the representative instances of contemplation became the arts accessible to the eye; only gradually were the categories of the contemplation model expanded to other arts, but perforce in an attenuated form. Even in the present century contemplation theorists tend to advert to painting as the exemplary art. We can understand why. We confront a painting on a wall, sharply demarcated from its surroundings by a material frame and taken in by a glance of the eye. It seems on the face of it plausible to claim that the painting is contemplated as a self-bounded object that is entirely constituted by its components and their internal relations. Such categories, however, become much less plausible when applied to the art of poetry, in which the verbal medium signifies many nonvisual elements, and especially when applied to a long narrative form, such as the *Iliad* or *Paradise Lost,* which is read intermittently and in which the narrative evolves in time.

Even in painting the representational elements, with their seeming reference to things existing outside the frame, have been something of an embarrassment to proponents of aesthetic contemplation. They have focused instead on the elusive, nonrepresentational feature of a painting which they call its "beauty," and which Kant, following Shaftesbury, interchanged with the even more elusive term "form." For example, in his influential little book *Art* (1914), Clive Bell posited that "form," or "significant form," is "the essential quality" of the fine arts, and asserted that "the contemplation of pure form . . . leads to a . . . complete detachment from the concerns of life," and also that "the formal significance of any material thing is the significance of that thing considered as an end in itself," not "as a means to practical ends" in "the world of human business and passion." Bell in turn grades the various arts according to the "purity" of their independence from external reference; at the bottom of this scale is literature, which "is never pure" because "most of it is concerned, to some extent, with facts and ideas."[19] It is precisely the art of literature, however, that was central and exemplary for the alternative theory that a work of art is a created thing that constitutes its own world.

The antecedents of heterocosmic theory emerged in critics of literature who, beginning in the late fifteenth century, reversed the traditional comparison of God the creator to a human artisan by making the portentous comparison of the literary artisan to God the creator—with the cautious quali-fication, however, that while God created this world *ex nihilo*, a poet makes his own world by reworking the materials of God's prior creation.[20] In the sixteenth century the partial parallel between the poet's making and God's creating, with the corollary parallel between God's created world and the poem as "an other nature" or "a second world," occurred frequently enough to be almost a standard topos in literary criticism.[21] But through the seventeenth century this analogy functioned primarily as a topic of praise, designed to defend poetry against its detractors by assigning it a quasi-divine sta-tus.[22] Sir Philip Sidney's *Apologie for Poetry* (c. 1583) is typical. His express aim in introducing this concept is to confound the derogators who have "throwne downe [poetrie] to so ridiculous an estimation." To do so, he traces the etymology of *poet* to the Greek verb *poiein*, "to make," and suggests that the poet's making is parallel to the creative fiat of God in Genesis. While all other arts and sciences have "the workes of Nature" for their "principall object . . . onely the Poet . . . dooth growe in effect another nature." For "the heavenly Maker of that maker . . . set him beyond and over all the workes of that second nature, which in nothing hee sheweth so much as in Poetrie, when with the force of a divine breath he bringeth things forth far surpassing her dooings." But having, as he says, attributed to the poet "so unmatched a praise as the Etimologie of his names wil grant," Sidney goes on to "a more ordinary opening" of his subject, which con-sists in grounding his critical theory on the standard defini-tion of a poem as an imitation designed for external ends:

"Poesie therefore is an arte of imitation, for so *Aristotle* ter-meth it in his word *Mimesis* . . . to speake metaphorically, a speaking picture: with this end, to teach and delight."[23]

Not until the eighteenth century was the divine analogy converted from a topic of laudation into a principle of critical theory, for only then was the concept that a poem is its own world exploited so as to qualify, then to displace, the concept that a poem is a credible imitation of the existing world. The process begins with Addison's defense, in 1712, of "the fairy way of writing"—defined as the presentation of supernatural beings such as "fairies, witches, magicians, demons, and de-parted spirits"—against men of "philosophical dispositions" who object that such poetry "has not probability enough to affect the imagination."[24] Addison's counterclaim, expand-ing on a suggestion by Sir Philip Sidney, is that in reading about such poetic beings, who are entirely the product of the poet's "invention" and "imagination," "we are led, as it were, into a new creation, and see the persons and manners of another species!" The allegorical personification of abstract concepts also "has something in it like creation." In both its nonrealistic and allegorical components, then, poetry

> has not only the whole circle of nature for its province but makes new worlds of its own, shows us persons who are not to be found in being, and represents even the faculties of the soul, with her several virtues and vices, in a sensible shape and character.[25]

After Addison, limited claims that the supernatural and allegorical elements in poetry are not imitations of this world, since they constitute a world of their own, became common among English defenders of such deviations from reality in Ovid, Spenser, Shakespeare, and Milton. For the develop-ment of the heterocosmic model beyond this restricted appli-cation we must turn, as we did for the development of the contemplation model, to German philosophers; first, to Alexander Baumgarten. In 1735 Baumgarten, only twenty-one years of age, published his master's thesis, *Philosophical Reflections on Poetry*. The radical nature of this forty-page essay is veiled by its terse and awkward Latin, its outmoded philo-

sophical terminology, and its deductive procedure for establishing the distinctive features and criteria of poetry.
Baumgarten writes in the method and idiom of "rational philosophy," in the lineage of Descartes, Spinoza, and above all
Leibniz—a mode rigorously systematized by Christian Wolff.
This philosophy had claimed that the faculty of reason, which
employs a deductive logic, is the sole mode for achieving a
kind of knowledge that is "perfect," in the sense that it is
necessarily true; it had, accordingly, relegated the factual and
merely contingent knowledge achievable through sense perception to the status of "an inferior cognition." Baumgarten
undertakes to show that the systematic study of poetry has its
proper place in philosophy, in that a poem provides a mode
of knowledge that possesses its own kind of "perfection"—a
perfection specific to sensory discourse, which can be vali-
dated by criteria that are counterparts of the criteria by which
we validate the logical process for achieving intellectual perfection, or "truth."[26]

Baumgarten sets out from the definition: "By poem we
mean a perfect sensate discourse." He begins, that is, with
the achieved poem-in-being; takes the approach that it is to
be analyzed as a distinctive mode of language, or "discourse"; and sets up as its essential attribute that it is a language of sensory representations which is so developed as to
exploit to the full (that is, "perfectly") its "sensate" or nonlogical potentialities. He explains that this perfection of its possibilities applies to all three aspects of a poem: the objects
that the words represent, the specific "inter-relationships" of
these objects, and the "articulate sounds" that constitute the
verbal medium itself (pars. 6–11). Baumgarten goes on, with
a great show of rigor, to deduce as the "consequences" of this
definition all the distinctive features of a poem. Throughout
he cites classical critics and rhetoricians, Horace's *Ars Poetica*
above all, but his process of reasoning and his overall conclusions are very different from Horace's pragmatic recourse to
the poet's ruling aim to achieve effects on an audience. For
Baumgarten's reasoning is controlled throughout by his
undertaking to show that a poem yields valid knowledge, but
that since this is sensuous as opposed to conceptual knowledge, its features are derivable by systematic parallel and

opposition to the features of logical reasoning. Thus, the elements of logical discourse in philosophy are "conceptually" clear and "distinct," but the representations in poetry are clear in a specifically sensuous way, and are not distinct, but "confused" (that is, fused together, without distinction between essence and accidents). As a consequence, however, the elements of poetry, unlike those of logic, are "vivid" and "lively." Logic is abstract and general, but poetry is determinately particular, individual, specific. Logical concepts are simple and signify essences, but poetic representations are qualitatively rich, abundant, imagistic, and constitute concrete wholes. And as distinguished from rational or philosophic discourse, the sensate language of poetry is densely figurative, and above all metaphorical; it also exploits the pleasurably sensuous appeal of rhythm and meter.

Such conclusions seem to make Baumgarten a Continental Formalist, and even more a New Critic, *avant la lettre*—by some two hundred years. And with good methodological reason. Both Formalists and New Critics, like Baumgarten, take as their premise that poetry is to be dealt with as a distinctive mode of language and—on the assumption that uses of language fall into a bipolar distribution—these theorists proceed, as does Baumgarten, to establish the distinguishing features of poetry, or of literature in general, by systematic opposition to what are held to be the standard features of "practical," or "logical," or "scientific" language. The parallel is especially manifest in John Crowe Ransom who, in a fashion similar to Baumgarten, proposes that poetry is a mode of language that conveys a "kind of knowledge" antithetic to the knowledge provided by science, which is "only the cognitive department of our animal life." And science and works of art, he claims, "between them . . . exhaust the possibilities of formal cognition."[27] Hence, by Ransom's dialectic of contraries, the scientist interests himself "strictly in the universals," but "the artist interests himself entirely in individuals"; science abstracts, but poetry is "knowledge by images, reporting the fulness or particularity of nature." "Science gratifies a rational or practical impulse and exhibits the minimum of perception," as opposed to poetry, which exploits "many technical devices for the sake of increasing the volume of the

percipienda or sensibilia." Among these devices are meter, a
patent fictionality, and figurative language, especially "the
climactic figure, which is the metaphor"; all these features,
by "inviting perceptual attention," serve to weaken "the tyranny of science over the senses."[28] And in a fusion of contemplative and heterocosmic concepts that is frequent in recent
critics, Ransom asserts that when "we contemplate object as
object," under "the form of art," we do so not as in science,
"for a set of practical values," but in order to know the object

> for its own sake, and conceive it as having its own existence;
> this is the knowledge ... which Schopenhauer praised as
> "knowledge without desire." ... The knowledge attained there
> [i.e., "in the poem, or the painting"], and recorded, is a new
> kind of knowledge, the world in which it is set is a new world.[29]

Two centuries earlier Baumgarten had introduced the same
radical metaphor of a poem-as-world into his logic of poetic
knowledge, and had explored its implications beyond any
preceding critic. He was able to do so because he had conveniently at hand the account of God's procedure in creating
this world in the *Theodicea* of the philosopher whom he hails
as "the illustrious Leibniz" (par. 22). In summary: Leibniz
held that God at the creation had in his understanding an
infinite number of model worlds, each of which is a "possible" world. Each possible world, however, is a "compossible" world; that is, it consists only of those essences and
relations of things which are capable of coexisting, by virtue
of the fact that they are mutually consistent. The universal
necessities of logic, based on the Principle of Contradiction,
apply to the entire array of possible worlds. The factual and
contingent truths that apply to the existents, relations, and
events within a possible world, however, are based on an
alternative principle that Leibniz calls "the Principle of Sufficient Reason." And the specific modes in which this Principle manifests itself are not universal, but relative to the
constitution of each model world. As Leibniz put it, with reference to the individual things and laws of order that constitute any possible world: "As there are an infinity of possible

worlds, there are also an infinity of laws, certain ones appropriate to one; others, to another, and each possible individual of any world involves in its concept the laws of its world."[30] The world in which we ourselves live was realized only because God's excellence entailed that, from these alternative models, He bring into existence this world as the best of all possible (which is to say, *com*possible) worlds.

Baumgarten converts Leibniz's cosmogony into poetics by distinguishing between two types of "fictions" in representations of characters, objects, and events. The first type he calls "true fictions" in that, though nonhistorical, they are possible in "the real world in which we find ourselves." The second type are fabulous and mythical elements that violate both the constitution and the causal order of the real world. Justifiable poetic instances of this type, which are necessary to some kinds of poems, he labels "heterocosmic fictions," in the sense that they are capable of coexisting in some other "possible" world. He rejects from poetry only a third class of fictions that he calls "utopian," in the literal sense of belonging "no place"; that is, either because they are logically "self-contradictory," or because they are "mutually inconsistent," such fictions are "absolutely impossible," since they cannot have a place within the coherent constitution of any possible world whatever. And for acceptable "heterocosmic fictions," the justifying criterion is not their "truth" of correspondence to the nature of the real world but a purely internal compossibility, or self-consistency (pars. 51–59).

Baumgarten takes a crucial step when he turns from heterocosmic fictions, or the nonrealistic elements in some poems, to what he calls the "method," or overall principle which determines the "interconnection," or "co-ordination," in "the succession of representations" within any poem whatever; for in this context he extends the heterocosmic analogue to apply to the ordonnance of all works of poetry:

> We observed a little while ago that the poet is like a maker or a creator [*quasi factorem sive creatorem esse*]. So the poem ought to be like a world [*quasi mundus*]. Hence by analogy whatever is evident to the philosophers concerning the real world, the same ought to be thought of a poem (par. 68).

What is evident to the philosophers about the real world, it turns out, is that Leibniz's Principle of Sufficient Reason determines the sequence and interconnections of its elements, together with the assurance that the ultimate "rule" of our mundane order is that "things in the world follow one another for disclosing the glory of the Creator." By analogy, each poetic other-world has its own inherent principle which determines the order and relations of its representations. Baumgarten calls this principle its "theme" [*thema*], and defines a theme as "that whose representation contains the sufficient reason of other representations supplied in the discourse, but which does not have its own sufficient reason in them." The consequence for poetics is that all the elements of a valid poem will either be "determined through the theme," or else "will be connected with it." "Therefore, they will be connected among themselves. Therefore, they follow each other in order, like causes and effects." And the "general rule" for the "method" that orders any poem is that "poetic representations are to follow each other in such a way that the theme is progressively represented in an extensively clearer way" (pars. 66–71).

In sum, what emerges from Baumgarten's parallel-in-opposition between rational logic and what in his later *Aesthetica* he called "esthetico-logic," the "logic of sensuous thinking," is a view that has become familiar in modern criticism. A poem provides sensuous knowledge of its own poetic world—a world governed by laws analogous to causal laws in our world but specific to itself; a world whose "poetic" truth and probability does not consist in a correspondence to the actual world but in the internal coherence of its elements; and a world that is not ordered to an end external to itself but by an internal finality whereby all its elements are subordinate to the progressive revelation of its particular theme.

In his *Aesthetica* of 1750, Baumgarten altered and generalized his definition of a poem as the perfection of sensuous discourse to apply to other arts, and for the first time identified this achieved perfection as beauty: "The aesthetic end is the perfection of sensuous cognition, as such [*qua talis*]; this is beauty" (par. 14). He also applies the term "a new world" [*novus mundus*], passingly, to the realm of nonrealistic fictions into which we are introduced, not only by a writer "whether in verse or prose" but also by "a painter or a sculptor, etc." (par. 592).[31] As in his *Reflections on Poetry*, however, all of Baumgarten's specific analyses of artistic other-worlds are applied only to works of literature and, in considering these, he supplements his earlier work with a larger number of topics derived from classical theories of rhetoric.

In the Swiss-German critics and collaborators Bodmer and Breitinger, a resort to the heterocosmic model effected similar revisions in the standard concepts of the nature and criteria of a poem. Both these critics set out from the reigning premise that a poem is an "imitation of nature," so designed by the poet-maker as to please and be morally useful to the reader. Both were also passionate defenders of Milton's *Paradise Lost* (which Bodmer had translated into German) against detractors such as Voltaire and Gottsched, who had decried Milton's supernatural beings and events, together with his allegory of Sin and Death, as "improbable," in that they do not correspond to the experienced world; their defense of such nonrealistic elements forced Bodmer and Breitinger into a radical modification of their initial premise.

Bodmer's book *The Marvelous in Poetry . . . in a Defense of "Paradise Lost"* appeared in 1740, five years after Baumgarten's *Reflections on Poetry*. Bodmer expressly follows Addison's lead in treating nonnatural invention as "a new creation" that "makes new worlds." He elaborates this suggestive analogue, however, as had Baumgarten, by recourse to the theory of God's creative procedure proposed by Leibniz— "Leibniz," as Breitinger eulogized him, "the great world-sage of our Germany."[32] "The task of the poet," says Bodmer, "is to imitate the powers of Nature in bringing over the possible into the condition of reality." "Every poet who imagines something possible as real . . . imitates Nature and creation." Bodmer, by sleight of words, thereby converts an imitation theory into a creation theory of poetry, in which the poetic world is not a reflection but an analogue of the world that God has brought into being. As he also says:

This mode of creation is the chief work of poetry, which by this very fact distinguishes itself from the writings of historians and natural scientists, in that it always prefers to take the material of its imitation from the possible world rather than from the actual world.[33]

In his *Critische Dichtkunst,* published that same year, Breitinger is even more explicit and detailed in his conversion of poetic imitation into a version of Leibnizian cosmogony. "All the arts," he says, "consist in a skillful imitation of Nature, for the general profit and pleasure of men." But Nature is only one of many possible worlds.

> Nature—or rather the Creator, who works in and through Nature—has from all possible world-structures chosen the present one to bring over into the condition of reality because it was, to his infallible insight, the best of all possible worlds.

Hence, in addition to the present world, "there need to be countless possible worlds, in which there obtain other interrelations and connections of things, other laws of Nature and motion . . . even productions and beings of entirely new and strange kinds." It is precisely these innumerable other worlds which provide the poet with

> the model and materials for his imitation. . . . Since he is capable not only of imitating Nature in the actual, but also in the possible, the power of his art extends as far as the powers of Nature itself. . . . [Indeed] the imitation of Nature in the possible is the chief work that is specific to poetry.[34]

Correlatively to their distinction between the existing world and the poetic world, Bodmer and Breitinger introduce the distinction between "rational truth," which is a truth of correspondence to this world, and "poetic truth," which is a truth of inner coherence, in accordance with whatever mode of sufficient reason governs the compossible world that constitutes a poem. "The poet," Bodmer answers a critic who, as he puts it, seeks "poetry in ontosophy," "troubles himself not at all with rational truth [*das Wahre des Verstandes*]," but only with "poetic truth [*das poetische Wahre*]."

This poetic truth is not without a certain reason and order; it has for the imagination and the senses its sufficient ground, it has no internal contradiction, and one part of it is grounded in the other. . . . For our part, we will look for metaphysics among the teachers of metaphysics, but demand from poets nothing more than poetry; in this we shall be satisfied with the probability and reason that lies in its coherence with itself.[35]

Breitinger, like Bodmer, sets up a distinction between "historical" or "rational" truth and "poetic" or "imaginative" truth, then goes on to analyze—as had Baumgarten, but in much greater detail—the internal organization of a poem in a way that parallels Leibniz's view of the empirical order of the existing world:

I regard the poet as a wise creator of a new ideal world or of a new interrelation [*zusammenhang*] of things, who not only has the right and the power to impart probability to those things which do not exist, but also possesses so much understanding that, in order to achieve his dominant intention [*Absicht*], he binds to one another his individual intentions in such a way that one must always serve as a means to the others, but all together must provide a means to the dominant intention. Accordingly, in this poetic world, as in the actual world, all things must be grounded in one another according to time and place, and the concordance of these toward a single end [*Zwecke*] constitutes precisely the perfection of the whole.[36]

As in Baumgarten, the inference drawn from the heterocosmic model is that the prime criterion of "perfection" in a poem is the interdependence and consistency of its elements, and the subordination of all the elements to an internal end.

One other important point: it is clear that like Baumgarten, the Swiss critics, who had adduced the concept of a poem as its own world in order to justify the invention of nonrealistic characters and events, extended the analogue to the overall organization of all well-contrived poems. As Breitinger explicitly says in *Critische Dichtkunst*:

What is poetic invention [*Dichten*] other than to form in the imagination new concepts and ideas of which the originals are

to be sought not in the actual world, but in some other possible world-structure? Every single well-invented poem is
therefore to be regarded in no other way than as the history
of an other possible world. In this respect the poet alone
deserves the name of *poietes,* that is, of a creator.[37]

And Bodmer in 1741 extended the heterocosmic model from
poems to a work of prose fiction, Cervantes's *Don Quixote:*

> The author, as the father and creator [of his characters], has
> determined and ordered them and all their destiny; not, how-
> ever, without a distinct plan of inter-related intentions, which
> conduct his work to its primary end.[38]

If we turn again to Karl Philipp Moritz's essay of 1788,
"The Formative Imitation of the Beautiful," we find two
important innovations upon the views of these earlier theorists:

(1) For Bodmer and Breitinger, as for Baumgarten, the
exemplary heterocosmic art had been literature. That is, they
introduced the concept of the poem as its own world in order
to account for and justify deviations from the experienced
world in the components and ordonnance of works of literary
art, and especially in the persons, events, and organization
of extended narrative forms. Moritz, however, specifically
expands the heterocosmic analogue to apply to the arts of
music, sculpture, and painting, as well as literature.[39]

(2) In Moritz, the conception of a work of art as a self-
sufficient and self-governing world is stripped of its residual
references to the imitation of nature and to the ends of
effecting pleasure and moral utility;[40] as a result, the heterocosmic model falls into coincidence with the contemplation
model, in terms of which the work of art is apprehended
disinterestedly, entirely for its own sake. Moritz in fact adverted
to the analogue of creation, we remember, precisely in order
to explain how a work gets produced which "does not need
to be useful." The "formative genius" himself, it turns out,
can create his beautiful work only at a time when, by "annul-
ling every trace of self-interest," his "restless activity gives place
to quiet contemplation." The consequence that Moritz draws

from his claim that the artist, emulating creative nature, "creates his own world" is specifically that this artistic otherworld is to be apprehended with a "*calm contemplation . . . as a single great whole . . .* in which all relationship stops," because "the genuine work of art . . . complete in itself, has the end and intention [*den Endzweck und die Absicht*] of its being solely in itself." The beautiful object thus requires that it "be contemplated and perceived, just in the same way in which it is produced, purely for its own sake."[41]

3. ART-AS-SUCH

In mid-nineteenth-century France, the contemplation and heterocosmic models were often conjoined in the loose-boundaried movement known by its catch phrase, "Art for Art's Sake." In this movement the original theological context of these models re-emerged, in a displaced form, to constitute a religion of art and a morality of life for art's sake. Flaubert wrote in 1857, "Life is a thing so hideous that the only way to endure it is to escape it. And one escapes it by living in art."[42] And Flaubert, in employing the analogue between divine and artistic creation, also adopted the ancient theological notion that God is both transcendent and immanent, both concealed and revealed in His created world, when he said about the literary heterocosm:

> An author in his book must be like God in the universe, present everywhere and visible nowhere. Art being a second Nature, the creator of that Nature must behave similarly. In all its atoms, in all its aspects, let there be sensed a hidden, infinite passivity.[43]

"Poetry," said Baudelaire, "is that in which there is more of reality, it is that which is not completely true except in *an other world*." The creative imagination "has taught man the moral sense of color, contour, of sound and perfume."

> It decomposes the entire creation and . . . creates a new world, it produces the sensation of the new. As it has created the

world (one can indeed say this, I believe, even in a religious sense), it is just that it should govern its world. . . . The imagination is the queen of the true, and the *possible* is one of the provinces of the true.[44]

In a poem, furthermore, any requirements of "teaching," "truth," and "morality" are "heresies," for poetry "has no end except itself; it cannot have any other end."[45] Poetry, Mallarmé likewise asserts, is "close to creating." But for Mallarmé, to create a poem is to unrealize and abolish the natural objects that are its materials; hence, "Equivalent to creation: the notion of an object, escaping, which fails to appear."[46] Baudelaire's concept of "la poésie pure" (independent of an external end, or of awareness of an audience, or of the passions of the poet) and Mallarmé's concept of "l'oeuvre pure" (not needing a reader, and in which the poet "disappears," leaving the textual work "anonyme et parfait")[47] are both patently a reincarnation of the self-sufficient Deity of a Platonized Christianity—existing in the purity and perfection of a total lack of reference to, or concern for, anything outside itself—in the mode of being of a sacred work of art.

The claim that a work of art is a world created by the artist, which at the time of its origin had been felt to verge on blasphemy, has in our time become a commonplace of critical discourse. It is not surprising that Vladimir Nabokov, a fervent advocate of the autonomy of art, opened his lectures on the novel at Cornell with the premise that

the work of art is invariably the creation of a new world, so that the first thing we should do is to study that new world as closely as possible, approaching it as something brand new, having no obvious connections with the world we already know.[48]

It is something of a surprise, however, to find a critic of the opposite persuasion, the Marxist Georg Lukács, also asserting that

every work of art must present a circumscribed, self-contained and complete context with its own *immediately* self-evident movement and structure. . . . Thus every significant work of art creates its "own world." Characters, situations, actions, etc. in each have a unique quality unlike that in any other work of art and entirely distinct from anything in everyday reality. The greater the artist . . . the more pregnantly his fictional "world" emerges through all the details of a work.

It turns out, however, that by endowing its "exemplary men and situations" with "the greatest possible richness of the objective conditions of life," the great bourgeois novelist in fact "makes his 'own world' emerge as the reflection of life in its total motion, as process and totality"—a "reflection," that is, of the alienation, contradictions, and progressive evolution of bourgeois society.[49] In both Nabokov and Lukács the exemplary heterocosmic art remains, as it had been originally, literary narrative; but Wassily Kandinsky indicates how all-inclusive the scope of the analogue has become by applying it not only to paintings, but to nonrepresentational paintings:

> Painting is a thundering collision of different worlds, intended to create a new world in, and from, the struggle with one another, a new world which is the work of art. . . . The creation of works of art is the creation of the world.[50]

I shall end by turning back to the two twentieth-century theorists with whom I introduced the topic of the poem-as-world in order to stress this point: the heterocosmic model, despite its differences from the contemplation model in its theological prototype, and in the particular art to which it was initially applied, eventuated in the same philosophical idiom—the idiom of art-as-such—for specifying the defining features and primary criteria for a work of art. Thus A. C. Bradley, from his premise that a poem is "a world by itself, independent, complete, autonomous," educes the philosophical consequences that the experience of a poem "is an end in itself," with an "intrinsic value" that excludes reference to "ulterior ends"; that the purely "poetic worth" of a poem "is to be judged entirely from within"; hence, that "it makes no direct appeal to [the] feelings, desires, and purposes" of ordi-

nary life, "but speaks only to contemplative imagination."[51]
Bradley's title is "Poetry for Poetry's Sake," and he explicitly
undertakes to rid the earlier French doctrine of the extrava-
gance of its claim that "Art is the whole or supreme end of
human life." He nonetheless guards the self-bounded integrity of a poem by prohibitions against such "heresies" as "the
heresy of the separable substance" (that is, of a paraphrasa-
ble content), as well as against reference to the "emotions and
conditions" of the poet himself, which "are poetically irrelevant."[52]

E. M. Forster similarly entitled one of his essays "Art for
Art's Sake," and he described the world of a poem as subject
only "to its own laws" and to a standard of truth that is not
of external reference but of internal consistency: it "supports
itself, internally coheres." "A poem is absolute. . . . It causes
us to suspend our ordinary judgments." The sole analogue
to the self-sufficing "internal" order and harmony of a work
of art, he says, is "the divine order, the mystic harmony, which
according to all religions is available for those who can contemplate it." And in opposition to "the demand that literature should express personality," Forster contends that "during
the poem nothing exists but the poem. . . . It becomes anonymous," on the basis of the theological concept that "to forget its Creator is one of the functions of a Creation."[53] In
Bradley's essay of 1901, and Forster's essays of the 1920s, we
patently move from the theory of Art for Art's Sake to the
premises and categories that were to recur in the New Criticism, in its view, as Cleanth Brooks put it, that, as opposed to
propositional assertions about the world, the "coherence" of
a poem consists in "the unification of attitudes into a hierarchy subordinated to a total and governing attitude," which
in its unity constitutes "a simulacrum of reality,"[54] and also
in its zealous defense of the boundaries of the autonomous
and self-contained poem by quasi-theological prohibitions (in
the lineage of Poe, Baudelaire, and Bradley) against the heresy of paraphrase, the intentional fallacy, and the affective
fallacy.

By identifying their theological origins, I do not mean to
derogate the practical value of the contemplation and het-

erocosmic models for art. Once adapted to aesthetics and criticism, what matters is not their provenience but their profitability when put to work in clarifying the features both of a work of art and of our experience of that work. Both these models have amply demonstrated their profitability for the applied criticism of literature and the other arts. Their focus on the aesthetic objects as such, especially in the last half-century, has greatly enlarged our repertory of terms and distinctions for analyzing a work of art as constituted by distinctive elements, ordered into coherence by internal relations, and made integral by subordination to an internal end. But to suggest the limits of the view of art-as-such—for, as in all theories of art, the sharpness of its focus imposes limitations on its scope and adequacy—let me put this question. Why should the claim—radically opposed to all traditional views about the nature and value of art—that a work is to be contemplated for its own sake as a self-sufficient entity, severed from all relations to its human author, to its human audience, and to the world of human life and concerns, serve as the very ground for attributing to art its supreme human value?

The appeal of this view, I suggest, is not primarily empirical, for it accords only with selective aspects of our full experience of great works of art. Its primary appeal consists rather in its profound metaphysical and theological pathos. It is the same pathos that empowers the concept, which has endured from Plato through the Christian centuries, that perfection and ultimate value inhere solely in a metaphysical absolute or deity who is purely otherworldly, serenely integral, self-sufficient and self-bounded, and for those reasons, to be contemplated and revered about everything in the fragmented, incoherent, and conflict-ridden world in which we find ourselves. The attraction that many of us feel to the theory of art-as-such, if I am not mistaken, is the attraction that it shares with this concept, and with its frequent complement: that even in his seemingly other-oriented act of creation, the inscrutable deity brought into being a world that he then left to its own destiny, remaining himself—as James Joyce, echoing Flaubert, put it in describing "the mystery of esthetic like that of material creation"—remaining himself "invisible, refined out of existence, indifferent, paring his fingernails."[55]

III. The New
and Newer Criticism

Five Types of Lycidas

 MOST MODERN CRITICS base their theories on the proposition that a poem is an object in itself. And all critics endorse enthusiastically at least one statement by Matthew Arnold, that the function of criticism is "to see the object as in itself it really is." The undertaking is surely valid, and laudable; the results, however, are disconcerting. For in this age of unexampled critical activity, as one poetic object after another is analyzed under rigidly controlled conditions, the object proves to be highly unstable, and disintegrates. In the pages of the critics we increasingly find, under a single title, not one poem but a variety of poems.

Milton's *Lycidas* is a convenient case in point, because it is short enough to be easily manageable, has been explicated many times, and is almost universally esteemed. If not every reader goes all the way with Mark Pattison's judgment that it is "the high-water mark of English Poesy," still critics agree about its excellence as closely as they ever do in evaluating a lyric poem. My point is that, on the evidence of their own commentaries, critics agree about the excellence of quite different poems. They present us not with one *Lycidas* but with discriminable types of *Lycidas*—five types, I have announced in my title. I feel confident that with a little more perseverance I could have distinguished at least seven, to equal William Empson's types of ambiguity. But in these matters, distinctions, as Mr. Empson's procedure demonstrates, can be rather arbitrary. And even five types of *Lycidas* are enough to confront the literary theorist with an embarrassing problem: Is a poem one or many? And if it is one, how are we to decide which one?

1

For the first type, take *Lycidas* as it was commonly described in the period between the first volume of Masson's monumental *Life of Milton* (1859) and the critical age ushered in by T. S. Eliot and I. A. Richards a generation ago. This traditional reading (in which I was educated) was conveniently epitomized by J. H. Hanford in his *Milton Handbook*. Individual discussions varied in emphasis and detail; but when in that lost paradise of critical innocence readers looked at *Lycidas*, they agreed that they saw an elegiac poem about Edward King, a contemporary of Milton's at Christ's College, who had been drowned when his ship suddenly foundered in the Irish Sea. To depersonalize his grief and elevate its occasion, Milton chose to follow the elaborate conventions of the pastoral elegy, as these had evolved over the 1800 years between the Sicilian Theocritus and the English Spenser; he ended the poem with a traditional consolation at the thought of Lycidas resurrected in heaven, and found in this thought the strength to carry on his own concerns. In two passages, many commentators agreed—they often called them digressions—Milton uttered his personal concerns in a thin fictional disguise. In one of these, Milton expressed his own fear that "th' abhorred shears" might cut him off before he could achieve the poetic fame to which he had dedicated his life. In the other, Milton, through St. Peter, voiced a grim warning to the corrupt English clergy of his time.

Writing in 1926, on the extreme verge of the New Criticism, Professor Hanford was so imprudent as to close his discussion with the statement that "*Lycidas* bears its meaning plainly enough on its face." It contains, to be sure, a minor verbal crux or two, such as the nature of the "two-handed engine at the door"; but, he roundly asserted, "there has been little room for disagreement regarding its larger features."

Only four years later E. M. W. Tillyard published in his

Milton an analysis of *Lycidas* which in its opening tucket sounded the new note in criticism:

> Most criticism of *Lycidas* is off the mark, because it fails to distinguish between the nominal and the real subject, what the poem professes to be about and what it is about. It assumes that Edward King is the real, whereas he is but the nominal subject. Fundamentally *Lycidas* concerns—[1]

But before we hear what *Lycidas* is really about, we ought to attend to Tillyard's distinction between "nominal" and "real" poetic meaning. For this modern polysemism, which splits all poems—or at least the most noteworthy poems—into two or more levels of meaning, one overt and nominal (which other readers have detected) and the other covert but essential (whose discovery has usually been reserved for the critic making the distinction), is extraordinarily widespread, and we shall find it repeatedly applied to *Lycidas*. The lamination of poetic significance is variously named. Tillyard elsewhere distinguishes between conscious and unconscious, and direct and oblique meanings. Other critics make a parallel distinction between manifest and latent, ostensible and actual, literal and symbolic, or particular and archetypal significance. And at the risk of giving away a trade secret, it must be confessed that most of the time, when we critics come out with a startling new interpretation of a well-known work, it is through the application of this very useful interpretative stratagem.

The procedure is indispensable in analyzing works for which there is convincing evidence that they were written in the mode of allegory or symbolism. But it is worth noting that the distinction was developed by Greek commentators, interested in establishing Homer's reputation as a doctor of universal wisdom, who dismissed Homer's scandalous stories about the gods as only the veil for an esoteric and edifying undermeaning. The same strategy was adapted by Philo to bring the Old Testament into harmony with Greek philosophy, and by the Church Fathers to prove that the Old Testament prefigured the New Testament, and by medieval and Renaissance moralists in order to disclose, behind Ovid's pagan and ostensibly licentious fables, austere ethical precepts and anticipations of the Christian mysteries. From the vantage of our altered cultural prepossessions, it appears that the distinction between nominal and real meaning has not infrequently been used as a handy gadget to replace what an author has said with what a commentator would prefer him to have said.

We are braced now for Tillyard's disclosure of the real subject of *Lycidas*. "Fundamentally *Lycidas* concerns Milton himself; King is but the excuse for one of Milton's most personal poems." The main argument for this interpretation is that *Lycidas* is generally admitted to be a great poem, but "if it is great, it must contain deep feeling of some sort"; since this feeling is obviously not about King, it must be about Milton himself. Milton, Tillyard maintains, expresses his own situation and feelings and attitudes, not only in the obviously allegorical passages about driving afield and piping with Lycidas, or in the passages on fame and the corrupt clergy which had been called personal by earlier critics, but from beginning to end of the poem. How radical Tillyard's formula is for translating objective references to subjective equivalents is indicated by his analysis of the poem's climactic passage:

> The fourth section purports to describe the resurrection of Lycidas and his entry into heaven. More truly it solves the whole poem by describing the resurrection into a new kind of life of Milton's hopes, should they be ruined by premature death or by the moral collapse of his country. . . . Above all the fourth section describes the renunciation of earthly fame, the abnegation of self by the great egotist, and the spiritual purgation of gaining one's life after losing it.[2]

Only such an interpretation, Tillyard claims, will reveal the integrity of the poem, by making it possible "to see in *Lycidas* a unity of purpose which cannot be seen in it if the death of King is taken as the real subject." Furthermore, the value of the poem really resides in the ordered and harmonized mental impulses for which the objective references are merely a projected correlative: "What makes *Lycidas* one of the greatest poems in English is that it expresses with success a state of mind whose high value can hardly be limited to a particular religious creed."

From this interpretation and these grounds of value John Crowe Ransom (to speak in understatement) disagrees. His premise is that "anonymity . . . is a condition of poetry." Milton very properly undertook to keep himself and his private concerns out of his memorial verses, and to do so assumed the identity of a Greek shepherd, the "uncouth swain" of the last stanza, who serves as a dramatis persona, a "qualified spokesman" for the public performance of a ritual elegy. As for the problem with which Tillyard confronted us—if the passion is not for King, for whom can it be except Milton himself?—Ransom solves it by dissolving it. There is no passion in the poem, and so no problem. "For Lycidas [Milton] mourns with a very technical piety." The pastoral conventions are part of the poetic "make-believe," and the whole poem, whatever more it may be, is "an exercise in pure linguistic technique, or metrics; it was also an exercise in the technique of what our critics of fiction refer to as 'point of view.' "

This is the poem, at any rate, that Milton set out to write and almost succeeded in writing. But his youth and character interfered and forced into the writing three defiant gestures of "rebellion against the formalism of his art." One of these is the liberty he took with his stanzas, which are almost anarchically irregular and include ten lines which do not rhyme at all. Another is St. Peter's speech; in Ransom's comment on this passage, we hear a voice out of the past—the Cavalier critic gracefully but firmly putting the stiff-necked and surly Puritan in his place: it expresses, he says, "a Milton who is angry, violent, and perhaps a little bit vulgar . . . Peter sounds like another Puritan zealot, and less than apostolic." The third instance of Milton's self-assertion is his "breach in the logic of composition"; that is, he shifts from the first-person monologue with which the poem opens to dialogues with Phoebus and others, then abruptly to the third person in the last stanza, where the uncouth swain is presented in "a pure narrative conclusion in the past [tense]." It follows that Ransom's concluding evaluation turns Tillyard's precisely inside-out. The sustained self-expression, on which Tillyard had grounded both the unity and excellence of the elegy, according to Ransom breaks out only sporadically, and then so as to violate the integrity and flaw the perfection of the poem. "So *Lycidas,* for the most part a work of great art, is sometimes artful and tricky. We are disturbingly conscious of a man behind the artist."

One might, of course, demur that given Ransom's own criteria, two of the items he decries as arrogant gestures of Milton's originality are exactly those in which he closely follows established conventions. The scholarly annotators—at whom, as he passes, Ransom turns to smile—tell us that the models for Milton's stanzas, the elaborate *canzone* employed by several Italian lyrists of the sixteenth century, were not only variable in structure, but also included unrhymed lines for the sake of that seeming ease and freedom which is the aim of an art that hides art. As for St. Peter's diatribe, Milton inherited the right to introduce rough satire against the clergy into a pastoral from a widespread convention established by Petrarch, who was hardly vulgar, nor a Puritan, nor even a Protestant. In Ransom's third exhibit, one element—Milton's putting the elegy into a narrative context in the conclusion, without a matching narrative introduction—is not, apparently, traditional. But it is at any rate odd to make Milton out to assert his own egoism in the passage that specifically assigns the elegy to another person than himself; a person, moreover, who is the entirely conventional rural singer of a pastoral elegy.

But this begins to seem captious, and does not represent the measure of my admiration for the charm and deftness of Mr. Ransom's essay, which thrusts home some important and timely truths about the dramatic construction of *Lycidas* by the artful device of overstatement. It is, one might hazard, a virtuoso exercise in critical point of view.

Let the commentary by Cleanth Brooks and John Hardy, in their edition of Milton's *Poems* of 1645, represent *Lycidas,* type four. At first glance it might seem that to these explicators the poem is not really about King, nor about Milton, but mainly about water. They turn to the first mention of water in lines 12–14 and discover at once the paradox that the "tear," which is the "meed" paid to Lycidas by the elegiac singer, is of the same substance, salt water, as the "wat'ry bier," the sea on which the body welters. As the poem develops, they say, "the 'melodious tear' promises to overwhelm the 'sounding Seas.'" For the tear is the elegy itself, which derives its inspiration from the "sacred well" of the muses, and flows on through a profusion of fountains, rivers, and streams, in richly ambiguous interrelations of harmonies, contrasts, and ironies, until, by the agency of "resurrection images," all of which "have to do with a circumvention of the sea," we are transferred to a transcendent pastoral realm where Lycidas walks "other streams along" and the saints wipe the tears forever from his eyes.

The base of the critical operation here is the assumption that "the 'poetry' resides in the total structure of meanings." The primary component in this structure is "imagery," of which the component parts are so organically related, through mutual reflection and implication, that it does not matter where you start: any part will lead you to the center and the whole. The key to both the form and value of *Lycidas,* then, which Tillyard had found in the ordering of mental impulses, and Ransom in the all-but-successful maintenance of impersonal elegiac conventions, Brooks and Hardy locate in the evolution and integration of the imagery: "*Lycidas* is a good poem not because it is appropriately and simply pastoral and elegiac—with ... all the standard equipment—but because of its unique formal wholeness, because of the rich 'integrity' of even such a single figure as that in the lines 'He must not flote upon his wat'ry bier / Unwept. . . .'"[3]

It turns out, however, that these images are only provisionally the elements of the poem, since in Milton they are used as vehicles for a more basic component, "certain dominant, recurrent symbolic motives." The fact, hitherto mainly overlooked, is that "Milton is a symbolist poet to a considerable extent."[4] Accordingly we must again, as in Tillyard's essay, penetrate the ostensible meaning to discover the real meaning of *Lycidas,* though a real meaning which in this case is an abstract concept. "What," they ask, "is the real subject" of *Lycidas?*

If Milton is not deeply concerned with King as a person, he is deeply concerned, and as a young poet personally involved, with a theme—which is that of the place and meaning of poetry in a world which seems at many points inimical to it.

Specifically, the early part of the poem presents the despairing theme that nature is neutral, emptied of the old pastoral deities ("to say nymphs are ineffectual is tantamount to denying their existence"); and this concept is transcended only by the movement from philosophic naturalism to Christian supernaturalism, in the pastoral imagery of the conclusion in heaven.

Perhaps other readers share my disquiet at this discovery. Leaving aside the validity of assuming that *Lycidas* is essentially a symbolist poem of which the real subject is a theme, there remains the difficulty that the theme seems to be startlingly anachronistic. Milton, we are told, writing in 1637, and echoing a complaint about the nymphs which is as old as Theocritus' first Idyll, presents us with the world-view involving "an emptied nature, a nature which allows us to personify it only in the sense that its sounds seem mournful. . . . The music of nature . . . has also been stilled." But wasn't it Tennyson who said this, in an elegy published in 1850?

> And all the phantom, Nature, stands—
> With all the music in her tone,
> A hollow echo of my own,—
> A hollow form with empty hands.

As for the concept imputed to Milton, with respect to the place of poetry in an inimical world, that "Nature is neutral: it is not positively malignant, but neither is it beneficent"— isn't this exactly the thesis laid down in 1926 by I. A. Richards in a very influential little book, *Science and Poetry*? In our own age, Mr. Richards said,

> the central dominant change may be described as the *Neutralization of Nature,* the transference from the Magical View of the world to the scientific. . . . There is some evidence that Poetry . . . arose with this Magical View. It is a possibility to be seriously considered that Poetry may pass away with it.[5]

At any rate, it is by a notable sleight of explication that Brooks and Hardy convert to the real meaning that Nature does not sympathize with the poet's sorrow and "has no apparent respect for the memory of Lycidas" the very passage in which Milton explicitly states the contrary: that nature, which had responded joyously to Lycidas's soft lays when he was alive, now mourns his death:

> Thee Shepherd, thee the Woods, and desert Caves,
> With wilde Thyme and the gadding Vine o'ergrown,
> And all their echoes mourn.

We go on to the fifth type of *Lycidas,* the archetypal version, which entered the critical ken after the vogue of the writings in comparative anthropology of James G. Frazer and in analytical psychology of C. G. Jung. This mode of criticism, like the last, begins by isolating images or patterns of imagery; now, however, the focus is on images that reflect the agents and events of myth or folklore. The favorite legends are those that (according to some folklorists) concern beings who were once nature deities—the dead and risen gods of Syria, Egypt, and Greece associated with the dying or reaping of the crops in the fall and their revival in the spring.

Richard P. Adams, investigating "The Archetypal Pattern of Death and Rebirth in *Lycidas,*" discovers that the poem is throughout "a remarkably tight amalgam of death-and-rebirth imagery." These images begin with the initial reference to the evergreen plants, the laurel, myrtle, and ivy, and continue through the allusions to the hyacinth, the rose, and the violet, which had their mythical genesis in the blood of a mortal or deity. The many water-images are here interpreted as fertility symbols; the allusion to the death of Orpheus is said to bring in a myth whose similarities to "the deaths of Adonis, Attis, Osiris, and other fertility demigods have been pointed out by modern scholars"; while the poet's speculation that the body of Lycidas perhaps visits "the bottom of the monstrous world" parallels the descent into water and the dragon fight "which is often a feature of death-and-rebirth cycles."[6]

Adams is content with a fairly traditional interpretation of the subject of *Lycidas:* Milton's concern was not with Edward

King, but "with the life, death, and resurrection of the dedicated poet, and specifically with his own situation at the time." Northrop Frye, however, in his essay on "Literature as Context: Milton's *Lycidas*," contends that the "structural principle" of the poem, the formal cause which "assimilates all details in the realizing of its unity," is "the Adonis myth," and that "Lycidas is, poetically speaking, a god or spirit of nature, who eventually becomes a saint in heaven." The archetypal reading here provides us with a new principle of unity, a new distinction between ostensible and implicit meaning, and a new version of what the poem is really rather than nominally about. In an earlier essay, Frye put the matter bluntly: "Poetry demands, as Milton saw it, that the elements of his theme should be assimilated to their archetypes. . . . Hence the poem will not be about King, but about his archetype, Adonis, the dying and rising god, called Lycidas in Milton's poem."[7]

2

It will not do to say, as one is tempted to say, that these five versions of *Lycidas* really give us the same poem, in diversely selected aspects and details. The versions differ not in selection or emphasis, but in essentials. Each strikes for the heart of the poem; each claims to have discovered the key element, or structural principle, which has controlled the choice, order, and interrelations of the parts, and which establishes for the reader the meaning, unity, and value of the whole. Nor will it help put Humpty Dumpty together again to carry out the proposal we sometimes hear, to combine all these critical modes into a single criticism which has the virtues of each and the deficiency of none. To provide a coherent reading, a critical procedure must itself be coherent; it cannot be divided against itself in its first principles. A syncretic criticism is invertebrate, and will yield not an integral poem but a ragout.

When there is such radical and many-sided disagreement about the real but nonliteral and esoteric meaning of the poem, the best hope of remedy, I think, lies in going back to Milton's text and reading it with a dogged literalness, except when there is clear evidence that some part of it is to be read allegorically or symbolically. This is what I propose, very briefly, to attempt. In a way, this puts me in a favorable position. A drawback in writing as a new critic is that it would be embarrassing to come out with an old reading; while I can plead that I have deliberately set out to labor the obvious, and can take comfort from the number of earlier critiques with which I find myself in agreement.

Looked at in this way, *Lycidas* turns out to be in some sense— although in some cases a very loose sense—about Edward King, about Milton, about water, about the problem of being a poet in an inimical world; and it is undoubtedly about at least one God (Christ) who died to be reborn. But it is about none of these in the central way that it is about certain other things that, to the literal-minded reader, constitute the essential poem Milton chose to write.

First, it is about—in the sense that it presents as the poetic datum, or Milton's elected fiction—a nameless shepherd, sitting from morn to evening in a rural setting and hymning the death of a fellow poet-pastor, who is not Edward King but, specifically, Lycidas. The reason all our interpreters except Ransom treat the stated elegist rather casually, if at all, is that they tend to take as premise that a poem is an object made of words, or "a structure of meanings." So indeed it is. But as a starting point for criticism, it would be more inclusive and suggestive to say that a poem is made of *speech,* because the term "speech" entails a particular speaker. In *Lycidas* the speaker is an unnamed rustic singer whose speech refers to a state of affairs, describes the appearance and quotes the statements of other speakers, including Phoebus, Camus, and St. Peter, expresses his own thoughts and changing mood, and conveys, by immediate implication, something of his own character. The poem is therefore clearly a dramatic lyric, with a setting, an occasion, a chief character, and several subordinate characters (who may, however, be regarded as representing the speaker's own thoughts, objectified for dramatic purposes as standard personae of the pastoral ritual).

Tillyard is surely right, as against Ransom (and earlier, Dr. Johnson), in finding deep feeling in the poem, but he confronts us with the spurious alternative that the feeling must be either about King or about Milton himself. The feeling is occasioned by the death of Lycidas and the thoughts plausibly evoked by that event; and it is experienced and expressed not by Milton, but by a singer Milton is at considerable pains to identify as someone other than himself. Precisely what Milton himself thought and felt during the many hours— probably days—in which he labored over *Lycidas,* despite Tillyard's assurance, is beyond all but the most tenuous conjecture; although it is safe to say that, among other things, he was thinking how he might put together the best possible pastoral elegy. But we know precisely what the uncouth swain thought and felt, because the expression of his thoughts and feelings constitutes the poem, from the bold opening, "Yet once more, O ye Laurels . . . ," up to, but not including, the closing eight lines, when the author takes over as omniscient narrator: "*Thus* sang the uncouth Swain. . . ."

Readers of the poem at its first appearance knew that it was one of thirteen *Obsequies to the Memorie of Mr. Edward King,* and undoubtedly some also knew that the J. M. who signed the last obsequy was John Milton, whose circumstances and relations to King bore some resemblance to those presented in the poem. Such knowledge, however, does not displace but adds a particular historical reference to the two chief persons of the literal poem. *Lycidas* is not simply "about" King; it is a public ceremonial on the occasion of King's death, and the decorum of such a performance requires that the individual be not only lamented but also honored. And how could King be honored more greatly than to be made an instance of the type of poet-priest, identified by the traditional name "Lycidas," and to be lamented by a typical pastoral singer— in Ransom's phrase, a "qualified spokesman" for the public performance of a ritual elegy—whose single voice is resonant with echoes of poets through the ages mourning other poets untimely cut off? My insistence here may seem to be much ado about trivia, and, provided we are ready to fill out the details when pertinent, it can be a harmless critical shorthand to say that it is Milton who sings a lament for Edward King. But entirely to disregard these elementary circumstances may be the beginning of critical arrogance, which can end in our substituting our own poem for the one Milton chose to write.

The pastoral singer sets out, then, both to lament and to celebrate Lycidas. But consideration of this particular death raises in his mind a general question about the pointless contingencies of life, with its constant threat that fate may slit the thin-spun thread of any dedicated mortal prior to fulfillment and so render profitless his self-denial. This doubt, it should be noted, is not an ulterior "theme" beneath the ostensible surface of the poem. It is, explicitly, a topic in the thought of the lyric speaker, a stage in his soliloquy, which the speaker's continued meditation, guided by the comments of other imagined characters, goes on to resolve. This turn away from Lycidas to the circumstance of those who have survived him is not insincere, nor does it constitute a digression or an indecorously personal intrusion. It is entirely natural and appropriate; just as (to borrow a parallel from J. M. French) it is altogether fitting and proper for Lincoln, in the course of the *Gettysburg Address,* to turn from "these honored dead" to concern for "us the living."[8] After all, the doubts and fears of the lyric speaker concern the insecurity of his own life only insofar as he, like Lycidas, is a member of the genus Poet, and concern the class of poets only insofar as they share the universal human condition.

While initially, then, we may say that the presented subject of *Lycidas* is a pastoral singer memorializing the death of a dedicated shepherd poet-and-priest, we must go on to say that—in a second and important sense of "subject" as the dynamic center, or controlling principle, of a poem—its subject is a question about the seeming profitlessness of the dedicated life and the seeming deficiency of divine justice raised by that shocking death in the mind of the lyric speaker. That the rise, evolution, and resolution of the troubled thought of the elegist is the key to the structure of *Lycidas,* Milton made as emphatic as he could. He forced it on our attention by the startling device of ending the elegy, in a passage set off as a stanza in ottava rima, not with Lycidas, but with the elegist himself as, reassured, he faces his own destiny with confidence. But there is no occasion for Lycidas to feel slighted by this dereliction, for has he not been left in heaven, entertained and comforted by a chorus of saints, and given an office equivalent to St. Michael's, as a guardian of the western shore?

3

If this, in barest outline, is the subject and the structural principle of the poem, what are we to make of the thematic imagery that, in the alternative interpretation by Brooks and Hardy, motivates and controls its development?

Lycidas indeed, as these critics point out, incorporates many water and sheep-and-shepherd images; it also has song-and-singer images, flower images, stellar images, wide-ranging geographical images, even a surprising number of eye, ear, and mouth images. The usual strategy of the imagist critic is to pull out a selection of such items and to set them up in an order that is largely independent of who utters them, on what occasion, and for what dramatic purpose. Freed from the controls imposed by their specific verbal and dramatic contexts, the selected images readily send out shoots and tendrils of significance, which can be twined into a symbolic pattern—and if the critic is sensitive, learned, and adroit, often a very interesting pattern. The danger is that the pattern may be largely an artifact of the implicit scheme governing the critical analysis.

From our elected point of view, the images in *Lycidas* constitute elements in the speech—some of it literal and some figurative, allegoric, or symbolic—that serve primarily to express the perceptions, thoughts, and feelings of the lyric speaker. These images constitute for the reader a sensuous texture, and they set up among themselves, as Brooks and Hardy point out, various ambiguities, contrasts, and harmonies. But in *Lycidas,* the procession of images is less determining than determined. If they steer the meditation of the speaker, it is only insofar as they cooperate in doing so with more authoritative principles: with the inherited formulas of the elegiac ritual, and with these formulas as they in turn (in Milton's inventive use of pastoral conventions) are subtly subordinated to the evolving meditation of the lyric speaker himself. In effect, then, the imagery does not displace but corroborates the process of feelingful thought in the mind of a specified character. This, it seems to me, is the way Milton wrote *Lycidas*; there is no valid evidence, in or out of the poem, that he constructed it—as T. S. Eliot might have done—out of a set of ownerless symbols which he endowed with an implicit dynamism and set to acting out a thematic plot.

For the mythic and archetypal interpretation of *Lycidas*, as it happens, there is a more plausible basis in Milton's ideas and characteristic procedures. As a Christian humanist of the Renaissance, Milton was eager to save the phenomena of classical culture, and thus shared with the modern archetypist an interest in synthesizing the ancient and modern, the primitive and civilized, pagan fable and Christian dogma, into an all-encompassing whole. And Milton knew, from divers ancient and Renaissance mythographers, about the parallel to the death and resurrection of Christ in ancient fables and fertility cults—about what in *Paradise Lost* he called the "reviv'd Adonis" (IX, 440), and the "annual wound" of Thammuz, identified with Adonis by the Syrian damsels who lamented his fate "in amorous ditties all a Summer's day" (I, 446–52). But these facts are not adequate to validate a reading of *Lycidas* as a poem that is really about Adonis, or any other pagan fertility god. In *Lycidas* Milton makes no allusion whatever to Adonis, and he refers to Orpheus only to voice despair that even the Muse his mother was helpless to prevent his hideous death. In his references to these fables in *Paradise Lost,* Milton specifies that the story of the Garden of revived Adonis is "feign'd," lists Thammuz-Adonis among the "Devils [adored] for Deities," and describes the mother of Orpheus as "an empty dream" (VII, 39). For though a humanist, Milton is a Christian humanist, to whom revelation is not one more echo of archetypal myths but the archetype itself, the one Truth, which had been either corrupted or distortedly foreshadowed, "prefigured," in various pagan deities and fables. There is a world of difference between Milton's assumption that there is only one religion and Blake's archetypal assertion that "All Religions are One."

By conflating Christian and non-Christian story into equivalent variations on a single rebirth pattern, the tendency of an archetypal reading is to cancel dramatic structure by flattening the poem out, or even—in the extreme but common view that we get closer to the archetype as we move back along the scale toward the vegetational cycle itself—by turning the poem inside out. For if we regard the rebirth theme as having been revealed in the opening passage on the unwithering laurel, myrtle, and ivy, and as merely reiterated in later passages on Orpheus, on water, on sanguine flowers, and in the allusion to Christ and the risen Lycidas, then the denouement of the poem lies in its exordium and its movement is not a progress but an eddy.

The movement of *Lycidas,* on the contrary, is patently from despair through a series of insights to triumphant joy. We can put it this way: read literally, the elegy proper opens with the statement, "Lycidas is dead, dead ere his prime"; it concludes with the flatly opposing statement, "Lycidas your sorrow is *not* dead." Everything that intervenes has been planned to constitute a plausible sequence of thoughts and insights that will finally convert a logical contradiction into a lyric reversal by the anagnorisis, the discovery, that for a worthy Christian poet-priest a seeming defeat by death is actually an immortal triumph.

Milton achieves this reversal by a gradual shift from the natural, pastoral, and pagan viewpoint to the viewpoint of Christian revelation and its promise of another world, the Kingdom of Heaven. He carefully marks for us the stages of this ascent by what, to contemporary readers, was the conspicuous device of grading the levels of his style. For as Milton said in the treatise *Of Education,* issued seven years after *Lycidas,* decorum (including "the fitted stile of lofty, mean, or lowly" to the height of the matter) "is the grand master peece to observe." The problem of stylistic decorum had been particularly debated in connection with the pastoral, which had troubled Renaissance theorists by the duplicity of its stylistic requirements, since it typically dealt with high matters under the lowly guise of a conversation between two uncouth swains. Milton's comment on the fitted style probably was an echo of Puttenham's statement that "decencie," or "decorum"—the just proportioning of the "high, meane, and base stile"—is "the chiefe praise of any writer"; and Puttenham had also pointed out that, though the normal level of pastoral was the "base and humble stile," the form was often used "under the vaile of homely persons and in rude speeches to insinuate and glaunce at greater matters."[9]

Accordingly Milton's singer opens the poem with a style higher than the pastoral norm: "Begin, and somewhat loudly sweep the string" is what he bids the muses, echoing the *"Sicelides Musae, paulo maiora canamus"* with which Virgil had elevated the pitch of his Fourth, or "Messianic," Eclogue. (Puttenham had remarked concerning this pastoral that, because of its lofty subject, "Virgill used a somewhat swelling stile" and that under the circumstances, "this was decent."[10]) The initial level of *Lycidas* suffices for the early pastoral and pagan sections on sympathizing nature, the nymphs, and the death of Orpheus. But this last reference evokes the despairing thought: What boots the ascetic life for those who, like Lycidas, stake everything on a treacherous future? The immediate comfort is vouchsafed to the singer in a thought in which the highest pagan ethics comes closest to the Christian: the distinction between mere earthly reputation and the meed of true fame awarded by a divine and infallible judge. The concept is only tangentially Christian, however, for the deities named in this passage, Phoebus and Jove, are pagan ones. Nevertheless, "that strain," the singer observes, "was of a higher mood," and he therefore readdresses himself to Arethuse and Mincius, waters associated with the classical pastoralists, as a transition back to the initial key: "But now my *Oat* proceeds. . . ."

The next modulation comes when St. Peter raises by implication the even more searching question why a faithful shepherd is taken early, while the corrupt ones prosper. He himself gives the obscurely terrifying answer: the two-handed engine stands ready to smite at the door; infallible justice dispenses punishment as well as rewards. This time the "dread voice" has been not merely of "a higher mood," but of an entirely different ontological and stylistic order, for it has "shrunk" the pastoral stream and frightened away the "Sicilian Muse" altogether. It is not only that the voice has been raised in the harsh rhetoric of anger, but that it belongs to a pastor, and expresses a matter, alien to the world of pagan pastoral. A

Christian subject is here for the first time explicit. The appearance and speech of Peter, although brought in, as Milton said in his subtitle, "by occasion," is far from a digression. It turns out, indeed, to be nothing less than the climax and turning point of the lyric meditation, for without it the resolution, inadequately grounded, would seem to have been contrived through Christ as a patent *Deus ex machina*. The speech of Peter has in fact closely paraphrased Christ's own pastoral parable (John 9:39–41; 10:1–18), addressed to the Pharisees, in which He too had denounced those who remain blind to the truth, who climb into the sheepfold, and who abandon their sheep to the marauding wolf, and had then identified Himself as the Good Shepherd who lays down His life for His sheep—but only, He adds, "that I might take it again." Once Christ, the shepherd who died to be born again, is paralleled to the dead shepherd Lycidas, though by allusion only, the resolution of the elegy is assured—especially since Peter, the Pilot of the Galilean Lake, is the very Apostle who had been taught by Christ, through faith and force of example, to walk on the water in which he would otherwise have drowned (Matthew 14:25–31). The elegiac singer, however, is momentarily occupied with the specific references rather than the Scriptural overtones of Peter's comment, with the result that the resolution, so skillfully planted in his evolving thought, is delayed until he has tried to interpose a little ease by strewing imaginary flowers on Lycidas's imagined hearse. But this evasion only brings home the horror of the actual condition of the lost and weltering corpse. By extraordinary dramatic management, it is at this point of profoundest depression that the thought of Lycidas's body sinking to "the bottom of the monstrous world" releases the full implication of St. Peter's speech, and we make the leap from nature to revelation, in the great lyric peripety:

Weep no more, woful Shepherds weep no more,
For *Lycidas* your sorrow is not dead,
Sunk though he be beneath the watry floar . . .
So *Lycidas*, sunk low, but mounted high,
Through the dear might of him that walk'd the waves. . . .

This consolation is total, where the two earlier ones were partial. For one thing, we now move from the strict judgment of merit and demerit to the God who rewards us beyond the requirements of justice by the free gift of a life eternal. Also, the elegist has had the earlier promises of reward and retribution by hearsay from Apollo and Peter, but now, in a passage thronged with echoes from the Book of Revelation and soaring, accordantly, into an assured sublimity of style, he has his own imaginative revelation, so that he, like St. John in that Book, might say: "And I saw a new heaven and a new earth." His vision is of Lycidas having lost his life to find a better life in a felicity without tears; in which even that last infirmity of noble mind, the desire for fame, has been purged "in the blest Kingdoms meek of joy and love," the earthly inclination to Amaryllis and Neaera has been sublimated into the "unexpressive nuptial Song" of the marriage of the Lamb, and the pastoral properties of grove, stream, and song serve only to shadow forth a Kingdom outside of space and beyond the vicissitude of the seasons. But the meditation of the lyric singer, as I have said, is ultimately concerned with the dead as they affect the living; so, by way of the Genius of the shore, we redescend to the stylistic level of plain utterance and conclude with the solitary piper at evening, facing with restored confidence the contingencies of a world in which the set and rise of the material sun are only the emblematic promise of another life.

4

We are all aware by now of a considerable irony: I undertook to resolve the five types of *Lycidas* into one, and instead have added a sixth. But of course, that is all a critic can do. A critique does not give us the poem, but only a description of the poem. Whatever the ontological status of *Lycidas* as an object-in-itself, there are many possible descriptions of *Lycidas*—as many, in fact, as there are diverse critical premises and procedures that can be applied to the text.

In the bewildering proliferation of assumptions and procedures that characterizes the present age, we need a safeguard against confusion, and a safeguard as well against the
skeptical temptation to throw all criticism overboard as a waste
of time. I would suggest that we regard any critique of a poem
as a persuasive description; that is, as an attempt, under the
guise of statements of fact, to persuade the reader to look at
a poem in a particular way. Thus when a critic says, with
assurance, "A poem means *X*," consider him to say: "Try
reading it as though it meant *X*." When he says, "*Lycidas* is
really about Milton himself," quietly translate: "I recom-
mend that you entertain the hypothesis that *Lycidas* is about
Milton, and see how it applies." From this point of view, the
best interpretation of *Lycidas*—we can say, if we like to use
that philosophical idiom, the reading that approximates most
closely to *Lycidas* as an object-in-itself—is the one among the
interpretations at present available that provides the best fit
to all the parts of the poem in their actual order, emphases,
and emotional effects, and which is in addition consistent with
itself and with what we know of Milton's literary and intellectual inheritance and his characteristic poetic procedures.[11]

The persuasive description of *Lycidas* that I have sketched
must be judged by the degree to which it satisfies these criteria of correspondence and coherence. To be sure it has a
serious handicap, when measured against the startling discoveries in recent years of what *Lycidas* is really about. It is
singularly unexciting to be told at this date that *Lycidas* is really
what it seems—a dramatic presentation of a traditional pastoral singer uttering a ritual lament and raising in its course
questions about untimely death and God's providence which
are resolved by the recognition that God's Kingdom is not of
this world. But surely this is the great commonplace in terms
of which Milton, as a thoroughly Christian poet, inevitably
thought. We cannot expect his innovations, on this crucial
issue, to be doctrinal; the novelty (and it is entirely sufficient
to make this an immense feat of lyric invention) consists in
the way that the pastoral conventions and Christian concepts
are newly realized, reconciled, and dramatized in the minute
particulars of this unique and splendid poem.

I would not be understood to claim that the alternative

readings of *Lycidas* I have described are illegitimate, or their discoveries unrewarding. They freshen our sense of old and familiar poems, and they force readers into novel points of vantage that yield interesting insights, of which some hold good for other critical viewpoints as well. I am as susceptible as most readers to the charm of suddenly being brought to see a solidly dramatic lyric flattened into an ornate texture of thematic images, or to the thrill of the archetypal revelation whereby, as Jane Harrison described it, behind the "bright splendors" of "great things in literature" one sees moving "darker and older shapes." But in our fascination with the ultraviolet and infrared discoveries made possible by modern speculative instruments, we must take care not to overlook the middle of the poetic spectrum. The necessary, though not sufficient, condition for a competent reader of poetry remains what it has always been—a keen eye for the obvious.

Postscript to "Five Types of Lycidas"

In the essay I wrote a quarter century ago, I emphasized the drastic changes effected in our reading of *Lycidas* by alternative critical perspectives—in other words, by diverse hypotheses as to the principle that controls the choice, order, and interrelations of the parts of the poem and serves to account for the nature and degree of its poetic success. In the present critical climate, however, in which we hear frequent claims that all literary texts disseminate themselves into a range of undecidable and inescapably contradictory meanings, one needs to emphasize the other side of the matter; and that is, the uniformity of the interpretive premises that are shared by all the critics represented in this volume, whatever the diversity of their critical hypotheses, and including the authors of the six essays, published during the last two decades, that have been added to the present edition.[1]

The most important of these premises is that the sentences of Milton's poem have a determinable meaning—even though in some instances that meaning is determinably ambiguous or multiplex—which qualified readers are capable of understanding in approximately the same way. To this view the essay by Stanley Fish might be regarded as an exception by those who know Fish's claim, in his theoretical writings, that there are a number of possible "interpretive strategies," each of which creates its own distinctive text by "constituting" both the formal properties and the meanings of the sequence of verbal signs on a page. In the course of evolving his theory, however, Fish has gone on to assert that in his applied criticism, such as his essay on *Lycidas,* he operates—he in fact suggests that he cannot help but operate—as a member of a particular "interpretive community," specified as the community of "academic literary criticism," whose shared assumptions and procedures make possible a common understanding of the meanings of a text.[2] To this latter view I agree—with the important proviso, however, that there is abundant evidence that the practice of the English language that we, as an "interpretive community," have inherited is continuous enough with the practice that Milton had himself inherited to provide adequate assurance that our understanding of the language of *Lycidas* can approximate the meanings that Milton expressed and intended his readers to understand.

The issue is confused by the fact that what we call "the interpretation of a poem" involves two discriminable though interrelated processes. One of these is *linguistic* interpretation: making sense of the English sentences (or, in a current parlance, "the speech acts") that compose a text, in the order of their occurrence. The other is *critical* interpretation: making sense of *Lycidas* as a poem, by applying to it an artistic hypothesis concerning the principle that controls the poem's overall structure and specifies the relations among its component elements. The matter is complicated by the phenomenon that linguistic interpretation and critical interpretation are co-responsive and interdependent, with the result that (as I tried to show in my essay) linguistic meanings are altered by the particular critical hypothesis that a reader brings to bear on the poem. But what the critics in this volume say about *Lycidas* demonstrates that linguistic meanings, while to a considerable degree acquiescent to different artistic hypotheses, are nonetheless recalcitrant to demands that are inordinate. The common core of recalcitrant linguistic meanings, established by the shared practice, or "strategy," that constitutes what we call understanding the English language, is adequate to disqualify some critical interpretations of the poem as too strained to be tenable, and also to provide a common ground on which critics can share insights and argue reasonably about interpretive disagreements, not only within the same critical perspective, but to a lesser extent between diverse critical perspectives.

To cite one instance: in line 8 Milton writes, "For Lycidas is dead, dead ere his prime." In line 166 he writes, "For Lycidas your sorrow is not dead." Taken as isolated assertions, these sentences signify a flat logical contradiction. All the critical essayists manifest their common understanding of the assertive meaning of these sentences. What they undertake is to demonstrate, by a critical interpretation applied to the intervening sentences—each in terms appropriate to his or her proposed artistic hypothesis—that these contradictory assertions in fact express a lyric peripety, either by virtue of a change of view in the lyric speaker attendant on a discovery or on a breakthrough to a higher mode of knowledge, or else by the triumph of one side in a conflict of opposing forces.

This brings me to another important premise which is shared by the interpreters of the poem: the critical assumption that we should undertake to read a poem as a unified whole—that is, as having an apt beginning and a middle section that leads coherently to a resolution which, since it requires nothing to follow it, satisfies us that the poem is complete. The degree to which the poem is a coherent and sufficient unity serves as a prime, though not a sufficient, criterion of its poetic value. If a critic, like G. Wilson Knight in his essay on Milton in *The Burning Oracle*, discovers that *Lycidas*, while "exquisite in parts," is "an accumulation of magnificent fragments," then the poem is deemed to be deficient in an essential aspect of its artistry.

The essayists added to this edition all assume and apply this presumption of artistic unity—most of them, presumably, on the implicit ground that Milton in all probability undertook to write a unified poem. They also concur that, whatever the seeming dislocations and disruptions between one and another of its parts, *Lycidas*, when read from the appropriate critical viewpoint, turns out to have an adequate integrity. The principle and locus of this integrity, however, differs according to the kind of hypothesis posited by the critical expositor. It is found, for example, to consist in the plausible sequence of consciousness through which the lyric speaker, by rising gradually through the Old Testament doctrine of vengeance to the Christian revelation of mercy and redemptive love, comes to accept in his life (and to resolve for the writing of his poetry) the violent onslaughts of reality upon the pastoral dream. Alternatively, the unity is located in an intricately modulated three-part evolution; this evolution is variously described as a movement of the speaker's state of mind, and of his view of the content of poetry, from innocence through experience of a fallen world to a wiser innocence, or as an Hegelian dialectical process, involving the possibility of writing poetry, from thesis through antithesis to synthesis, or as a typological succession from the prefigurations in the pagan pastoral through the higher types of Old Testament pastoralism to the ultimate antitypes of the Christian pastoral truth. From a third critical viewpoint the unity consists in the coherent stages exhibited in the progressive education of "the swain" as a poet, which, though complete in *Lycidas* itself, is in turn taken to reflect Milton's own poetic maturation to the point at which he is ready to undertake an epic poem.

In this respect also Stanley Fish's essay might seem an exception, for in it he derogates "the seekers of unity" who strive in vain to domesticate the repeated disruptions that breach the logic of the poem. Fish makes clear, however, that what he rejects are the efforts "to put the poem together" by reference to a "unified consciousness" which is expressed by "an integrated and consistent first person voice." He himself substitutes a critical hypothesis which he describes as a revival, "but with a difference," of John Crowe Ransom's argument that the poem's discontinuities "reflect a tension between anonymity and personality." The application of this hypothesis results in an interpretation which in effect replaces the evolving consciousness of the lyric speaker with an alternative principle of poetic unity: Fish views the "plot" of the poem as an *agon,* a contest for "control over the poem" between "the first person voice" and the many other voices that break into its utterance. According to this reading, *Lycidas* "begins in digression" ("the first person voice," Fish explains, "is the digression"), proceeds through successive disjunctions which function "relentlessly" to deny "the privilege of the speaking subject, of the unitary and separate consciousness," and ends with "the great vision" in which, the personal voice having at last been totally silenced, the poem "is finally, and triumphantly, anonymous." The narrative coda, since it is spoken by "an unidentified third person voice," confirms the integrity of the overall plot by its function as "the perfect conclusion to a poem in which the personal has been systematically eliminated."

The boundaries of what I have called a "type" of *Lycidas* are sufficiently loose to make it a matter of individual judgment whether to classify Fish's essay, or any of the added essays, as an additional type or else as a variant on an existing type. No matter what type of critical hypothesis a reader may apply to the poem, however, he will find in each of the essays, with its expert application of an alternative perspective, valuable insights into the components and artistry of the poem. But with all the dazzling virtuosity of modern critical analytics, we need to keep in mind what Isabel MacCaffrey in her essay calls "the relevance, not only of the poem's form, but of its theme to ourselves." The calm accents and sublime assurance of the voice which, after facing up to the intervening horrors, recounts the concluding vision enforces our imaginative participation in the experience of that vision, whether or not we share its supporting creed that a bright reversion in the sky will make abundant recompense for the tears we shed in this earthly life.

Critics who propose a new reading of *Lycidas* still tend to justify their enterprise as a discovery of what *Lycidas* is really about. One thing its language is undeniably about is death, and how to cope in a world where the threat of death is constant, and may strike early and in stark violation of our human sense of merit and justice. Whatever the values of structure and intricate relations of detail one discovers in the poem, to overlook the enduring human relevance of the subject to which this artistry has been applied is to leave out what is essential to the power that has made *Lycidas* the lyric of lyrics, a standing challenge to critics and readers of English poetry.

Positivism and the Newer Criticism

D ESPITE THE MODEST CLAIM of its subtitle, Philip Wheelwright's *The Burning Fountain: A Study in the Language of Symbolism* pretty well epitomizes the major concepts, preoccupations, and procedures of the Newer Criticism of the 1950s. Its starting point is the antithesis between literal or "stenolanguage"—the language of science—and expressive or "depth language"—the language common to poetry, myth, religion, and metaphysics. Expressive language is opposed to that of science, not in lacking cognitive reference, but in possessing such "translogical" attributes as plurisignation (Wheelwright's useful substitute for Empson's "ambiguity"), a variability of meaning according to the context, the possibility of fusing universal and particular in a single concrete universal, freedom to transgress the law of contradiction by the use of "the paradox of depth," and a cognitive and assertive mode (hence a special truth-value) transcending the propositions and methods of verification proper to science. The meanings of this expressive language are the products of an imaginative activity which enters into our creative perception of the world by particularizing and intensifying an object, by imposing aesthetic distance, by fusing diverse objects into metaphor, and by envisioning the archetypal significance in the single object. Metaphor is analyzed in detail as essentially "a tension which is maintained among . . . heterogeneous elements," and the archetype as a transient image which is apprehended as a "preconsciously rooted" and hereditary symbol of something universal and enduring. The opinion that the same archetypes appear in both myth and poetry motivates a sustained excursion into the nature of the primitive world view, the relations of ritual, myth, and poetry, and the origins of tragedy in the ritual celebrating the death and rebirth of a vegetation god. Poetic images, particularly those of an archetypal nature, often occur in significant patterns; here Wheelwright introduces the concept of multiple levels of meaning, in which the author's surface-story may either be reinforced or counterpointed by the unconscious depth-meanings of this "thematic imagery." In the course of the book, all these concepts are applied to writings ranging from Buddha's Fire Sermon through the *Oresteia* to the *Four Quartets.*

None of these ideas or methods will be novel to anyone in touch with recent criticism but Professor Wheelwright, a trained logician as well as a sensitive and wide-ranging student of literature, develops them with acuteness and precision, and applies them deftly and, often, illuminatingly. As a philosopher, he also defines and systematizes what are often unexamined and scattered assumptions, and grounds them on his own version of an existentialist theory of man and his position in the universe.

I do not propose to consider here any of the interesting questions that suggest themselves about the truth of Wheelwright's various propositions about language or poetry. Criticism, as we are fond of saying these days, is not autotelic; if that is so, it is a practical science, and the cardinal question is not the theoretical one of whether, in its individual positions, a critical theory is true or false, but a pragmatic one—the kind of work that, taken all in all, it is equipped to do. And the admirably synoptic and representative character of Wheelwright's book raises a problem of general scope: How far will a criticism take us, in which the principal, almost the sole, instruments are the analysis of language, meanings, images, and archetypes?

There is no denying the valuable insights made possible by this distinctively modern combination of semantics, cultural

anthropology, and depth psychology, nor the vitality and
health of a movement that has perhaps generated more energy
and excitement than any in English history—including even
the criticism of the Age of Dryden, when the triumphant
mastery of Neoclassic concepts and methods coincided with
the electrifying rediscovery of Longinus. There is a bracing,
stout-Cortez air in much recent critical writing which communicates itself to the reader. To be sure, the thematic or
archetypal discoveries sometimes strike that reader as meanings made by an interpretative *acte gratuit.* Thus Wheelwright finds in

> Golden lads and girls all must
> As chimney-sweepers, come to dust,

a suggestion of the archetype of the vegetational cycle of death
and rebirth, on the evidence of the occasional practice in
Shakespeare's day of dressing the leader of May Day revels
as a chimney sweep. And in Cleopatra's death scene, he detects
not only the archetype of the four elements, in the movement from Cleopatra's earlier earth-and-water imagery to an
air-and-fire imagery (p. 130), but also (by adverting to the
mythic and esoteric uses of the serpent as a symbol of the
rounding of death into life) an archetypal significance in
Cleopatra's asp as representing "at once the sharp tooth of
death and the symbol of new life" (p. 151). But these are
understandable results of the exuberant handling of a novel
critical concept which, in time, will work out its own discipline. What the Oedipus Complex was to the 1920s, the dying-
to-be-resurrected vegetation god is now; and we may expect
in the latter instance a similar qualification by sober second
thought.

Even in its more restrained applications, however, there is
something incomplete and lopsided in a too exclusively imagistic critical procedure. It is not only that a poetic part is
taken for the whole, but that the poem is turned upside-down
and inside-out in a peculiar way. Or in other terms, infrared
and ultraviolet significances are seen as though they constituted the whole spectrum. This effect is especially marked in
the treatment of narrative or dramatic poems. The Shake-

speare criticism of Dr. Johnson, whatever its deficiencies from our point of view, even now comes much closer to the actual experience of seeing a play produced, or of reading it in a relatively anastigmatic fashion, than do some of the recent commentaries. Wheelwright still makes passing use of such seemingly indispensable concepts as plot and character (however little grounds these nonlinguistic concepts have in his approach to literature as a special kind of language system). But he magnifies certain aspects of diction—thematic and archetypal imagery—into the rivals and peers of the characters in action. For example, in *Romeo and Juliet* Wheelwright finds that the surface meaning, the "literal story" of descent from happiness to adversity, is in a state of tension with the contrary movement of a "para-plot of religious redemption"—a plot that exists only in the implications of the imagery. In more extreme critics, Lear and Macbeth are elbowed entirely off the stage by bloodless abstractions; the true protagonists turn out to be the vehicles of Shakespeare's figures of speech, which are conceived to be endowed with a kind of implicit dynamism and to participate in a plot that is a "symbolic action," or an "inherent dialectic," or a "drama of meanings."

Such a distortion of poetic structure is not incidental, but the result of a radical deficiency in the bases of an exclusively symbolic critical theory. Wheelwright's book is of special interest because it displays so clearly an important cause of this widespread bias in modern criticism. For *The Burning Fountain,* like a number of contemporary documents, while seemingly self-sufficient, is really one side in a philosophical dispute. Viewed in its historical context, it is seen to be, no less than the essays of Sidney and of Shelley, a Defense of Poetry, though this time not against Puritan or Utilitarian detractors, but against the logical positivists and the challenge, explicit or implicit, posed to poetry by a semantics based on the language of science. Wheelwright's critique of this semantics is detailed and cogent. The so-called laws of thought are really conventional rules governing logical symbols and their manipulation; these rules are adapted to the specific requirements of science, with its necessary emphasis on "operables" and public verifiability; and the language of science is only a highly specialized limit of symbolization, at the extreme from the language of poetry. Wheelwright quotes from Bertrand Russell, in his late period of logical positivism, the comment that "the play *Hamlet* consists entirely of false propositions, which transcend experience. ... The propositions in the play are false because there was no such man. ... The fundamental falsehood in the play is the proposition: the noise 'Hamlet' is a name." This is an amusing parallel to Jeremy Bentham's contention, a century and a quarter earlier, that "the poet always stands in need of something false. ... Truth, exactitude of every kind, is fatal to poetry." Both statements demonstrate the gross unaptness of a positivistic theory of language, with its simple criterion of "either true or false," to works whose very essence is not correspondence to fact, but feigning, imaginative invention, "imitation."

By merely converting his refutation of the semantics of scientific language into the principles of his own poetic theory, however, Wheelwright remains, in an important sense, a prisoner to the theory he opposes. For he accedes to its view that poetry is to be regarded primarily as a mode of discourse, and accepts as his own primitive proposition the typical positivistic opposition between scientific and expressive language, by which maneuver poetry, metaphysics, and religion all get lumped at the expressive end of a simple bipolar distribution of all language. Wheelwright's deliberate procedure of letting the opposition dictate the terms is obvious in what he calls his "dialectical" method for setting up the bases of his own scheme. The method consists of systematically positing the contrary for each assumption of logical positivism, and then adopting these contraries as the actual principles of expressive language. Thus: instead of the ideal of univocality, that of plurisignation; instead of the law of contradiction, the paradoxical assertion of simultaneous opposites; instead of operational truth, a higher truth, shared by poetry, philosophy, and religion, verifiable only in an intuitive and emotional depth-experience.

It is no wonder that a theory so thoroughly controlled, even if in negative fashion, by the alien requirements of a scientific logic and semantics should turn out to be less than adequate to illuminate the nature and structure of poems. Especially is it a dubious service to poetry—or to religion and metaphysics—to fall into the positivist's trap by conflating these several enterprises. Each one is grounded in human needs which each satisfies in its own distinctive way. A scheme that attributes to each its specific ends and procedures, and which is no less ready to oppose poetry to religion and to metaphysics than to science, will serve all three better than a scheme that confounds their special qualities and powers by regarding them as a single mode of depth-language, aiming at a single kind of ill-defined and highly attenuated "truth."

In short, an adequate theory of poetry must be constructed, not by a strategy of defense and limited counterattack on grounds chosen by a different discipline, but by a positive strategy specifically adapted to disclose the special ends and structures and values, not only of poetry as such, but of the rich diversity of individual poems. What is needed is not merely a "metagrammar" and a "paralogic." What is needed, and what the present yeasty ferment in criticism may well portend, is, simply, a poetic.

Northrop Frye's Anatomy of Criticism

Periodically since the renaissance, important intellectual developments outside the field of literature have produced books on literary criticism—usually with words like *poetics, elements, principles,* or *science* in the title—which reformulate literary theory from first principles, in order to accommodate existing materials to the new concepts. In sixteenth-century Italy a number of treatises attempted to adjust Aristotle's *Poetics* to the doctrines and literary forms of a Christian culture. In the mid-eighteenth century Lord Kames set out to assimilate the psychology of sensation and association to Neoclassical literary theory by ascending "to principles from facts and experiments," in the hope by this procedure to convert the new science of mind into "the science of criticism." Coleridge's *Biographia Literaria* was the product of his persistent attempt to act as "the arbitrator between the old school and the new school," and to bring inherited critical concepts into line with the idealism and organicism of contemporary German philosophy. Some thirty-five years ago I. A. Richards, in his *Principles of Literary Criticism,* restated traditional critical ideas in terms both of the psychology of impulse and equilibrium and of the new and exciting field of semantics. Looked at in the light of these works, Northrop Frye's *Anatomy of Criticism: Four Essays* is an attempt to resystematize the field of criticism so as to save the existing phenomena, yet to work in the implications for literary analysis of three recent and interrelated developments: depth psychology, the theories of ritual and myth in Frazer and other cultural anthropologists, and the revival of serious interest in medieval symbology.

Professor Frye has written a big, packed, compendious, and audacious book. He undertakes specifically a "science" of criticism which, following the model of the modern natural sciences, is constructed on the basis of "an inductive survey of the literary field." His aim is to achieve what criticism has always lacked, a body of knowledge which, like any genuine science, will be systematic, coherent, and progressive (pp. 6–11). This knowledge is not to be exclusive but "synoptic"; that is, it will incorporate everything that is valid in existing approaches to literature. Aristotelian poetics, aesthetic criticism, literary history and scholarship, the new criticism of text and texture, the newer criticism of myth and archetype, medieval hermeneutics—all are accepted and given their due places in a single critical system. Frye puts his claim modestly: the book consists of tentative "essays . . . on the possibility of a synoptic view." But it is clear that, however subject to refinement and expansion, these essays are conceived as the prolegomena to any future criticism. The book considers all varieties of literature, from the simplest and most "naïve" to the most sophisticated and complex, and it moves from the elementary treatment of metrics and sonantal patterns, through the analysis of images and symbols, to the consideration of character types, narrative structures, and genres. Constantly it yields a freshness of insight by cross-cutting the traditional perspectives and stereotypes of criticism. It is a strikingly original achievement, of bewildering scope and complexity. And it raises a host of questions which will provide topics of literary debate for years to come; the book will be attacked and it will be defended, but it will not be ignored. All a reviewer can do, after a preliminary reading, is to identify a few of the larger issues that it so spectacularly raises.

First is the question of the synoptic system itself. In Frye's conspectus, the field of criticism falls into a diagrammatic form with multilateral symmetries. There are, for example, five modes of criticism, in parallel with five phases of symbolism;

then three kinds of archetypes, each exhibited in seven matched categories, and falling, in their narrative forms, into the four cardinal *mythoi* (comedy, romance, tragedy, and satire), arranged in a circle so that each has two neighbors and an antithetic form; furthermore, each *mythos* incorporates, *mutatis mutandis,* the same four character types, and is subdivided into six phases or species; these in turn divide neatly down the middle, three approximating ever more closely to the myth-form on the right and three to the myth-form on the left; and so on. The whole is reminiscent of the medieval encyclopedic tables designed to comprehend the *omne scibile;* instinctively, though in vain, the reader looks for an appendix that will open out into a square yard of tabular diagram.

Undeniably, systematic classification is necessary to order and make manageable any field of knowledge, and it can be charged that any classification, however, indispensable, to some extent falsifies the phenomena it subsumes. The solution to this difficulty lies in keeping the system as open and flexible as possible, and in maintaining a balanced responsiveness between the categories and the data. Systems that are too elaborately symmetrical tend to keep order by tyrannizing over the unruly facts. And once you begin an intricately ordered pattern, it seeks closure by reproducing mirror images of itself:

> Grove nods at grove, each alley has a brother;
> And half the platform just reflects the other.

The danger is that when the total gridwork is completed, not only have you a place for everything but every place must have a something; and that thing automatically inherits a complex set of attributes, correspondences, clan relationships, and oppositions. In its fearful symmetry Frye's critical system repeatedly raises the question: To what extent are the inevitable sequences of repetitions, variations, parallels, and antitypes genuine discoveries, and to what extent are they artifacts of the conceptual scheme?

A second matter which is bound to become a *causa belli* is Frye's contention that evaluation must be strictly excluded from a critical theory, either in its premises or in its application to individual works of literature. His point appears to be that a science of literature, like all sciences, must be objective, that all evaluations are "subjective," an "illusion of the history of taste," and that all hierarchies of literary values express concealed—and temporary—social or moral prejudices. Criticism as systematic knowledge "should show a steady advance toward undiscriminating catholicity." The critic, Frye says, finds Milton a more rewarding poet than Blackmore, but he cannot prove it. For there is a total antithesis between critical theory, which is a world of language, and the "direct experience" of a poem, which is an unmediated response of the nervous system in which "every act is unique and classification has no place" (pp. 20–28). According to Frye's view, it seems, "critical evaluation" becomes a contradiction in terms.

Let it be said that there are considerable grounds for Frye's impatience with the usual role of evaluation in theory: the violent fluctuations in literary tastes and fashions; the persistent tendency to build into an ostensibly universal theory of poetry the passing preferences of a poet or a critic or an age; the projection of contemporary ethical, social, or religious prepossessions in the form of a postulated "great tradition" of literature. But Frye seems to me to put the part for the whole. Theory certainly differs from direct literary experience, but the total separation between them is, in practice, neither possible nor desirable to maintain. A well-grounded theory opens our senses to literary possibilities, and, as Coleridge said, though meditation (theory) without observation is vacuous, observation without meditation is blind. Near the beginning of his book, Frye cites the opening words of Aristotle's *Poetics* as the model for his own approach: "Our subject being poetry, I propose to speak not only of the art in general but also of its species . . . [and] of the structure of plot required for a good poem." A *good* poem; that is, good *as* a poem, according to properly artistic criteria which are founded not on submerged moral and social premises but on the choice and order of elements required to maximize the effects the poem is designed to achieve.

At any rate, if in his own theory Frye tries to be a scientist, evaluation is always breaking through, even the kind of evaluation that implies a literary hierarchy: "Aristophanes' . . .

greatest comedy," "one of the greatest masterpieces of tragic irony in literature, Plato's *Apology*," "the greatest contemporary tragedian, Racine. . . ." And ironically enough, the whole book serves, in effect, to transvaluate established literary values, by putting not only primitive but "popular" literary phenomena on an equivalence with Homer and Shakespeare as the basis for critical generalizations—including melodrama, soap operas, advertising copy, science fiction, nursery rhymes, college yells, and political cartoons.

It is safe to predict that the storm center of debate about the *Anatomy of Criticism* will be its adoption of the medieval doctrine of four-level meaning, regarded as applicable to all works of literature, no matter how literally the poet may have intended his work to be read. Some form of polysemism, indeed, is necessary to Frye's thesis that all forms of criticism—including textual, thematic-image, and myth criticism—discover meanings that are simultaneously and objectively existent in any poem. As Frye points out, he modifies the medieval conception of the levels in order to incorporate some peculiarly modern concepts. For example, he interprets the "literal" level so as to involve the current view of a poem *qua* poem, or self-contained universe of discourse; and he translates the medieval moral and tropological level into the archetypal mode of reading, which discovers the ritual-and-myth patterns that constitute the underground of even the most sophisticated literary structures. Of the four levels, the archetypal level has the central role and is given the most prominence and space; it also raises the most basic and troublesome questions.

We may take for our example Frye's treatment of comedy. Comedy has been a notably stable literary form, and on the literal and "rhetorical" level Frye looks across standard critical concepts and classifications to make many fresh and valid literary discoveries concerning recurrent stylistic devices, situations, character types, and plot forms. He identifies, for instance, the function of "the green world" in comedies such as *As You Like It, A Midsummer Night's Dream,* and *The Winter's Tale,* in which the cruelties, conflicts, and injustices of the ordinary world are magically dissolved, all enmities reconciled, and all lovers united. Or he emphasizes, most reveal-ingly, the importance of an organized society in comedy, and the frequency and import of the comic conclusion in a social ritual such as a wedding, a feast, or a dance. Some of these insights may have been effected or expedited by his archetypal bias, but however discovered, they are verifiable on the literal level as literary conventions, or recurrent comic elements and devices.

Then, however, Frye bids us to "stand back" in order, undistracted by surface details, to discern the archetypal organization of a work—its inevitable understructure of generic shapes and its pattern of ritual action and myth. From this distance we find, for example, the shape of the Proserpine myth and its associated ritual of death and rebirth in Shakespeare's Hero, Imogen, and Hermione, and in Spenser's Florimell; in Esther Summerson's attack of smallpox and in the shooting of Lorna Doone; eventually we discover that even Richardson's Pamela and the Belinda of Pope's *The Rape of the Lock* are "Proserpine figures," or archetypal earth goddesses (pp. 138, 183). And at a still further remove we see that the ritual pattern of all comedies recapitulates the "mythos of spring" and the eternal rhythm of the natural cycles.

Unlike most other archetypal critics, Frye explicitly disavows the standard attempts to give a causal explanation for the recurrence of archetypes. Jung's "collective unconscious" (in effect, a theory of the inheritance of acquired mental characteristics) is "an unnecessary hypothesis"; the ritual origin of dramatic forms is merely speculative history; and archetypal patterns are not, like conventions, dependent on the mimicry of literary originals. The patterns, Frye says, are simply there, "however they got there" (pp. 108–12). Which brings up the questions: How do we know they are there? What is the evidence for the existence of an archetype? And these take us back to Frye's conception of a science of criticism.

The qualifications he cites for a science are coherence, inclusiveness, and the possibility of progress. Many pseudo-sciences, however, exhibit these attributes. Astrology, physiognomy, and the theory of humours were systematic theories that undertook to comprehend all relevant phenomena, and all showed great possibilities for development through the centuries. What seems indispensable to a genuine science is a fourth qualification: it sets out from and terminates in an appeal to facts which enforce agreement from all sane, knowledgeable, and disinterested witnesses, in independent observations. It is relevant to inquire whether Frye's literary data do enforce agreement from all qualified readers. Are they discoverable by independent observations? Could even an initiate predict, in advance of publication, that Frye would discover (p. 190) "displaced" forms of the dragon-killing myth in the cave episode in *Tom Sawyer* and in the hero's release from the labyrinth of past time in Henry James's *The Sense of the Past*?

The concept of "displacement" is, of course, taken from Freud, and it is instructive to consider Freud's canons of natural, or unintended, symbolic meaning, which include all the standard interpretative devices used by symbolist critics of literature. Freud's system permits him to apply alternatively, according to circumstance, the canon of literal meaning (A is A), displacement or substitution (A is B), condensation (A is A + B + C + D . . .), and inversion or transvaluation (A is the contrary of A). It may be that such rules of reasoning are necessitated by the inherent nature of symbolism, whether in the sleeping or waking (i.e., literary) dream, but they serve incidentally to leave considerable room for logical maneuver between the Law of Contradiction and the Law of Excluded Middle. The cardinal mode of proof, however, in Freud's theory as in all theories of natural symbolism, is analogical. The implicit canon here is that analogy justifies identification: if A is in some respects like B, then A is identifiable as B. This appears to be the standard formula of archetypal reasoning. If the stories of Hermione, Esther Summerson, Pamela, and Belinda are in some respects like the Proserpine archetype, then these stories are all instances of the Proserpine archetype (e.g., Frye, pp. 136–46).

Here it must be observed that the patterns of events in these diverse actions can be made to coincide only on a high level of abstraction, and abstraction, as Frye says in another context, implies "the leaving out of inconvenient elements." Even if we grant, in the first place, that these heroines are all Proserpine figures who act out a ritual death, when we have made that discovery, our task as practical critics has not even begun. For few works differ more radically from each other in constitution, characterization, qualitative feel, and emotional effect than do *The Winter's Tale, Bleak House, Pamela,* and *The Rape of the Lock,* and the job of a practical critic is to account for each work in its minute particularity. But beyond this, the odd thing about evidence for an archetype is not that you cannot prove that it is present, but that you cannot help proving it, and that there is no way of disproving it. Any extended and complex literary work can, by the omission of unsuitable elements, be made to resemble almost any archetypal shape. Since there is no firm possibility of negative observations, archetypal statements are empirically incorrigible, and incorrigible statements are not good grounds for a science of criticism; one may doubt whether many archetypal statements are even, in the strict sense, significant empirical propositions. This point is perhaps implicit in Frye's assertion that "it is not sufficient to use the text as a check on commentary," for "the poet unconsciously meant the whole corpus of his possible commentary" (p. 342).

Consider a parallel instance. I am not one of those who find four-leaf clovers, but my wife is. I search a bed of clover diligently for fifteen minutes without finding a one, and she stoops casually down and picks two. I have to admit that, though I hadn't seen them, the four-leaf clovers were actually there. Again: I have never noticed that the world is full of quincunxes. Then I read Sir Thomas Browne, who points them out everywhere, and—well, yes, I have to admit that, in a way, the quincunxes are actually there, too. But they are not there in the way that four-leaf clovers are there, but only in the way that circles, triangles, and dodecagons can also be shown to be there, given the prepossession and the will. And so with any conceptual scheme that uses distant analogy as proof and possesses built-in expedients for universal application. The same literary work in which the archetypist discovers a seasonal myth will turn out to have a quite different pattern of subsurface meaning when analyzed by a Freudian, a Marxist, a Nietzschean, or a Hegelian critic.

As a science, accordingly, a thoroughgoing archetypal theory of literature does not resemble physics, chemistry, or biology nearly so much as it resembles alchemy. In its complete philosophical form, alchemy also relied on a universal system of correspondences among the physical, mental, moral, and divine worlds, and interpreted analogy as identity and parallelism as proof. There is a further similarity in the drastic reductive tendency of both conceptual systems. On Frye's fourth, or anagogical, level of reading, any one poem, as I understand it, is seen to incorporate the universe: its language becomes the Logos, and its protagonist becomes all mankind, envisioned as a Man-God (pp. 115ff.). And on the third, or archetypal, level, we also find a steady regress to unity. The individual comedy, for example, falls together with other comedies into one basic comic pattern; the comic pattern in turn plays variations on the spring mythos; the spring mythos is referred back to the vernal segment of the seasonal cycle, and eventually falls into place with romance (summer), tragedy (autumn), and irony and satire (winter) in a unitary process which is continuous, complete, and self-sufficient, and is represented by that ancient figure of perfection, the circle. Any work of literature, therefore, which to the short-sighted reader seems to have its own beginning, middle, and end, turns out in the longer view to be only a phase in a single pattern of death and rebirth whose end is always in its beginning.

Frye maintains that criticism, like science, needs such "a central hypothesis" in order to see individual phenomena "as parts of a whole" (p. 16), and that the only cure for the endless proliferation of conflicting literary commentary is the view that "criticism has an end in the structure of literature as a total form" (p. 342). But the regress to one hypothetical *Urmythos* behind the multitude of individual literary phenomena does not correspond to the ever widening generality of the sequence of physical hypotheses, from Kepler to Newton to Einstein; nor does the concept of an archetype of archetypes have the function in criticism of Einstein's unified-field theory in physics. Its function, in fact, is not scientific but metaphysical, and its relation to literary particulars is like the relation of the one to the many in Neoplatonic philosophy, in which the method of reasoning is a steady movement from the multitude of particulars back, through a progressively narrowing sequence of types, to the One or the Absolute. This yields a "certainty," indeed; but it is not the certainty of empirical proof, it is the security of an ultimate abiding place for the monistic compulsion of the human spirit.

What I have said about the *Anatomy of Criticism* will be misunderstood if it is taken as an attempt to refute or disparage this notable book. My intention is rather to isolate and identify the nature of its particular achievement. On the literal level, or in its many other aspects which can be translated into literal terms, it provides as large and varied a body of critical insights as any book in recent years. Many of these can be looked upon as valid elements in a science of criticism, according to the criterion for a science which, Aristotle suggests, is the only one an educated man will apply: that it yield just so much precision and certainty as the nature of a particular subject will admit. As for the remainder, though it is not science, it is a thing no less valid or rare—it is wit, "a combination of dissimilar images, or discovery of occult resemblances in things apparently unlike." When we are shown that the circumstances of Pope's giddy and glittering Augustan belle have something in common with the ritual assault on a nature goddess, that Henry James's most elaborate and sophisticated social novels share attributes with barbaric folk tales, and that the ritual expulsion of the *pharmakos*, or scapegoat, is manifested alike in Plato's *Apology*, in *The Mikado*, and in the treatment of the umpire in a baseball game, we feel that shock of delighted surprise which is the effect and index of wit. Such criticism is animating; though only so, it should be added, when conducted with Frye's special *brio*, and when it manifests a mind that, like his, is deft, resourceful, and richly stored. An intuitive perception of similarity in dissimilars, Aristotle noted, is a sign of genius and cannot be learned from others. Wit criticism, like poetic wit, is dangerous, because to fall short of the highest is to fail dismally, and to succeed, it must be managed by a Truewit and not by a Witwoud.

Professor Frye argues eloquently that the theory and practice of literary criticism is a humanistic and liberal pursuit; and one of the functions of both criticism and a liberal culture, as Matthew Arnold pointed out, is a free and disinterested play of mind. The *Anatomy of Criticism* is a remarkable instance of that free and delightful play of ideas around literature which has always been a distinction of the urbane and civilized mind.

IV. Doing Things with Texts: Theories of Newreading

The Deconstructive Angel

> DEMOGORGON.—If the Abysm
> Could vomit forth its secrets:—but a voice
> Is wanting. . . .
>
> —Shelley, *Prometheus Unbound*

WE HAVE BEEN INSTRUCTED these days to be wary of words like *origin, center,* and *end,* but I will venture to say that this session had its origin in the dialogue between Wayne Booth and myself which centered on the rationale of the historical procedures in my book *Natural Supernaturalism.* Hillis Miller had, in all innocence, written a review of that book; he was cited and answered by Booth, then recited and re-answered by me, and so was sucked into the vortex of our exchange to make it now a dialogue of three. And given the demonstrated skill of our chairman in fomenting debates, who can predict how many others will be drawn into the vortex before it comes to an end?

I shall take this occasion to explore the crucial issue that was raised by Hillis Miller in his challenging review. I agreed with Wayne Booth that pluralism—the bringing to bear on a subject of diverse points of view, with diverse results—is not only valid, but necessary to our understanding of literary and cultural history: in such pursuits the convergence of diverse points of view is the only way to achieve a vision in depth. I also said, however, that Miller's radical statement, in his review, of the principles of what he calls deconstructive interpretation goes beyond the limits of pluralism, by making impossible anything that we would account as literary and cultural history.[1] The issue would hardly be worth pursuing on this public platform if it were only a question of the soundness of the historical claims in a single book. But Miller considered *Natural Supernaturalism* as an example "in the grand tradition of modern humanistic scholarship, the tradition of Curtius, Auerbach, Lovejoy, C. S. Lewis,"[2] and he made it clear that what is at stake is the validity of the premises and procedures of the entire body of traditional inquiries in the human sciences. And that is patently a matter important enough to warrant our discussion.

Let me put as curtly as I can the essential, though usually implicit, premises that I share with traditional historians of Western culture, which Miller puts in question and undertakes to subvert:

1. The basic materials of history are written texts; and the authors who wrote these texts (with some off-center exceptions) exploited the possibilities and norms of their inherited language to say something determinate, and assumed that competent readers, insofar as these shared their own linguistic skills, would be able to understand what they said.

2. The historian is indeed for the most part able to interpret not only what the passages that he cites might mean now, but also what their writers meant when they wrote them. Typically, the historian puts his interpretation in language which is partly his author's and partly his own; if it is sound, this interpretation approximates, closely enough for the purpose at hand, what the author meant.

3. The historian presents his interpretation to the public in the expectation that the expert reader's interpretation of a passage will approximate his own and so confirm the "objectivity" of his interpretation. The worldly-wise author expects that some of his interpretations will turn out to be mistaken, but such errors, if limited in scope, will not seriously affect the soundness of his overall history. If, however, the bulk of his interpretations are misreadings, his book is not to be accounted a history but an historical fiction.

Notice that I am speaking here of linguistic interpretation, not of what is confusingly called "historical interpretation"—

that is, the categories, topics, and conceptual and explanatory patterns that the historian brings to his investigation of texts, which serve to shape the story within which passages of texts, with their linguistic meanings, serve as instances and evidence. The differences among these organizing categories, topics, and patterns effect the diversity in the stories that different historians tell, and which a pluralist theory finds acceptable. Undeniably, the linguistic meanings of the passages cited are in some degree responsive to differences in the perspective that a historian brings to bear on them; but the linguistic meanings are also in considerable degree recalcitrant to alterations in perspective, and the historian's fidelity to these meanings, without his manipulating and twisting them to fit his preconceptions, serves as a prime criterion of the soundness of the story that he undertakes to tell.

One other preliminary matter: I don't claim that my interpretation of the passages I cite exhausts everything that these passages mean. In his review, Hillis Miller says that "a literary or philosophical text, for Abrams, has a single unequivocal meaning 'corresponding' to the various entities it 'represents' in a more or less straightforward mirroring." I don't know how I gave Miller the impression that my "theory of language is implicitly mimetic," a "straightforward mirror" of the reality it reflects,[3] except on the assumption he seems to share with Derrida, and which seems to me obviously mistaken, that all views of language that are not in the deconstructive mode are mimetic views. My view of language, as it happens, is by and large functional and pragmatic: language, whether spoken or written, is the use of a great variety of speech-acts to accomplish a great diversity of human purposes; only one of these many purposes is to assert something about a state of affairs; and such a linguistic assertion does not mirror, but serves to direct attention to selected aspects of that state of affairs.

At any rate, I think it is quite true that many of the passages I cite are equivocal and multiplex in meaning. All I claim—all that any traditional historian needs to claim—is that, whatever else the author also meant, he meant, at a sufficient approximation, at least *this,* and that the "this" I specify is sufficient to the story I undertake to tell. Other historians, having chosen to tell a different story, may in their interpretation identify different aspects of the meanings conveyed by the same passage.

That brings me to the crux of my disagreement with Hillis Miller. His central contention is not simply that I am sometimes, or always, wrong in my interpretation, but instead that I—like other traditional historians—can never be right in my interpretation. For Miller assents to Nietzsche's challenge of "the concept of 'rightness' in interpretation," and to Nietzsche's assertion that "the same text authorizes innumerable interpretations [*Auslegungen*]: there is no 'correct' interpretation."[4] Nietzsche's views of interpretation, as Miller says, are relevant to the recent deconstructive theorists, including Jacques Derrida and himself, who have "reinterpreted Nietzsche" or have written "directly or indirectly under his aegis." He goes on to quote a number of statements from Nietzsche's *The Will to Power* to the effect, as Miller puts it, "that reading is never the objective identifying of a sense but the importation of meaning into a text which has no meaning 'in itself.'" For example: "Ultimately, man finds in things nothing but what he himself has imported into them." "In fact interpretation is itself a means of becoming master of something."[5] On the face of it, such sweeping deconstructive claims might suggest those of Lewis Carroll's linguistic philosopher, who asserted that meaning is imported into a text by the interpreter's will to power:

> "The question is," said Alice, "whether you *can* make words mean so many different things."
> "The question is," said Humpty Dumpty, "which is to be master—that's all."

But of course I don't at all believe that such deconstructive claims are, in Humpty Dumpty fashion, simply dogmatic assertions. Instead, they are conclusions which are derived from particular linguistic premises. I want, in the time remaining, to present what I make out to be the elected linguistic premises, first of Jacques Derrida, then of Hillis Miller, in the confidence that if I misinterpret these theories, my errors will soon be challenged and corrected. Let me eliminate suspense by saying at the beginning that I don't think that their radically skeptical conclusions from these premises are wrong. On the contrary, I believe that their conclusions are right—in fact, they are *infallibly* right, and that's where the trouble lies.

1

It is often said that Derrida and those who follow his lead subordinate all inquiries to a prior inquiry into language. This is true enough, but not specific enough, for it does not distinguish Derrida's work from what Richard Rorty calls "the linguistic turn"[6] which characterizes modern Anglo-American philosophy and also a great part of Anglo-American literary criticism, including the "New Criticism," of the last half-century. What is distinctive about Derrida is first that, like other French structuralists, he shifts his inquiry from language to *écriture*, the written or printed text; and second that he conceives a text in an extraordinarily limited fashion.

Derrida's initial and decisive strategy is to disestablish the priority, in traditional views of language, of speech over writing. By priority I mean the use of oral discourse as the conceptual model from which to derive the semantic and other features of written language and of language in general. And Derrida's shift of elementary reference is to a written text which consists of what we find when we look at it—to *"un texte déjà écrit, noir sur blanc."*[7] In the dazzling play of Derrida's expositions, his ultimate recourse is to these black marks on white paper as the sole things that are actually present in reading, and so are not fictitious constructs, illusions, phantasms; the visual features of these black-on-blanks he expands in multiple dimensions of elaborately figurative significance, only to contract them again, at telling moments, to their elemental status. The only things that are patently there when we look at the text are "marks" that are demarcated, and separated into groups, by "blanks"; there are also "spaces," "margins," and the "repetitions" and "differences" that we find when we compare individual marks and groups of marks.

By his rhetorical mastery Derrida solicits us to follow him in his move to these new premises, and to allow ourselves to be locked into them. This move is from what he calls the closed "logocentric" model of all traditional or "classical" views of language (which, he maintains, is based on the illusion of a Platonic or Christian transcendent being or presence, serving as the origin and guarantor of meanings) to what I shall call his own graphocentric model, in which the sole presences are marks-on-blanks.

By this bold move Derrida puts out of play, before the game even begins, every source of norms, controls, or indicators which, in the ordinary use and experience of language, set a limit to what we can mean and what we can be understood to mean. Since the only givens are already existing marks, "*déjà écrit*," we are denied recourse to a speaking or writing subject, or ego, or cogito, or consciousness, and so to any possible agency for the intention of meaning something ("*vouloir dire*"); all such agencies are relegated to the status of fictions generated by language, readily dissolved by deconstructive analysis. By this move he leaves us no place for referring to how we learn to speak, understand, or read language, and how, by interaction with more competent users and by our own developing experience with language, we come to recognize and correct our mistakes in speaking or understanding. The author is translated by Derrida (when he's not speaking in the momentary shorthand of traditional fictions) to a status as one more mark among other marks, placed at the head or the end of a text or set of texts, which are denominated as "bodies of work identified according to the 'proper name' of a signature."[8] Even syntax, the organization of words into a significant sentence, is given no role in determining the meanings of component words, for according to the graphocentric model, when we look at a page we see no organization but only a "chain" of grouped marks, a sequence of individual signs.

It is the notion of "the sign" that allows Derrida a limited opening-out of his premises. For he brings to a text the knowledge that the marks on a page are not random markings, but signs, and that a sign has a dual aspect as signifier and signified, signal and concept, or mark-with-meaning. But these meanings, when we look at a page, are not there, either as physical or mental presences. To account for significance, Derrida turns to a highly specialized and elaborated use of Saussure's notion that the identity either of the sound or of the signification of a sign does not consist in a positive attribute, but in a negative (or relational) attribute—that is, its "difference," or differentiability, from other sounds and other significations within a particular linguistic system.[9] This notion of difference is readily available to Derrida, because inspection of the printed page shows that some marks and sets of marks repeat each other, but that others differ from each other. In Derrida's theory "difference"—not "the difference between a and b and c . . ." but simply "difference" in itself—supplements the static elements of a text with an essential operative term, and as such (somewhat in the fashion of the term "negativity" in the dialectic of Hegel) it performs prodigies. For "difference" puts into motion the incessant play [*jeu*] of signification that goes on within the seeming immobility of the marks on the printed page.

To account for what is distinctive in the signification of a sign, Derrida puts forward the term "trace," which he says is not a presence, though it functions as a kind of "simulacrum" of a signified presence. Any signification that difference has activated in a signifier in the past remains active as a "trace" in the present instance as it will in the future,[10] and the "sedimentation" of traces which a signifier has accumulated constitutes the diversity in the play of its present significations. This trace is an elusive aspect of a text which is not, yet functions as though it were; it plays a role without being "present"; it "appears / disappears"; "in presenting itself it effaces itself."[11] Any attempt to define or interpret the significance of a sign or chain of signs consists in nothing more than the interpreter's putting in its place another sign or chain of signs, "sign-substitutions," whose self-effacing traces merely defer laterally, from substitution to substitution, the fixed and present meaning (or the signified "presence") we vainly pursue. The promise that the trace seems to offer of a presence on which the play of signification can come to rest in a determinate reference is thus never realizable, but incessantly deferred, put off, delayed. Derrida coins what in French is the portmanteau term *différance* (spelled -*a*nce, and fusing the notions of differing and deferring) to indicate the endless play of generated significances, in which the reference is interminably postponed.[12] The conclusion, as Derrida puts it, is that "the central signified, the originating or transcendental signified" is revealed to be "never absolutely present outside a system of differences," and this "absence of an ultimate signified extends the domain and play of signification to infinity."[13]

What Derrida's conclusion comes to is that no sign or chain of signs can have a determinate meaning. But it seems to me that Derrida reaches this conclusion by a process which, in its own way, is no less dependent on an origin, ground, and end, and which is no less remorselessly "teleological," than the most rigorous of the metaphysical systems that he uses his conclusions to deconstruct. His origin and ground are his graphocentric premises, the closed chamber of texts for which he invites us to abandon our ordinary realm of experience in speaking, hearing, reading, and understanding language. And from such a beginning we move to a foregone conclusion. For Derrida's chamber of texts is a sealed echo-chamber in which meanings are reduced to a ceaseless echolalia, a vertical and lateral reverberation from sign to sign of ghostly nonpresences emanating from no voice, intended by no one, referring to nothing, bombinating in a void.

For the mirage of traditional interpretation, which vainly undertakes to determine what an author meant, Derrida proposes the alternative that we deliver ourselves over to a free participation in the infinite free-play of signification opened out by the signs in a text. And on this cheerless prospect of language and the cultural enterprise in ruins Derrida bids us to try to gaze, not with a Rousseauistic nostalgia for a lost security as to meaning which we never in fact possessed, but instead with "a Nietzschean *affirmation,* the joyous affirmation of the play of the world and of the innocence of becoming, the affirmation of a world of signs without error [*faute*], without truth, without origin, which is offered to an active interpretation. . . . And it plays without security. . . . In absolute chance, affirmation also surrenders itself to *genetic* indeterminacy, to the *seminal* chanciness [*aventure*] of the trace."[14] The graphocentric premises eventuate in what is patently a metaphysics, a world view of the free and unceasing play of *différance* which (since we can only glimpse this world by striking free of language, which inescapably implicates the entire metaphysics of presence that this view replaces) we are not able even to name. Derrida's vision is thus, as he puts it, of an "as yet unnamable something which cannot announce itself except . . . under the species of a non-species, under the formless form, mute, infant, and terrifying, of monstrosity."[15]

2

Hillis Miller sets up an apt distinction between two classes of current structuralist critics, the "canny critics" and the "uncanny critics." The canny critics cling still to the possibility of "a structuralist-inspired criticism as a rational and rationalizable activity, with agreed-upon rules of procedure, given facts, and measurable results." The uncanny critics have renounced such a nostalgia for impossible certainties.[16] And as himself an uncanny critic, Miller's persistent enterprise is to get us to share, in each of the diverse works that he criticizes, its self-deconstructive revelation that in default of any possible origin, ground, presence, or end, it is an interminable free-play of indeterminable meanings.

Like Derrida, Miller sets up as his given the written text, "innocent black marks on a page"[17] which are endowed with traces, or vestiges of meaning; he then employs a variety of strategies that maximize the number and diversity of the possible meanings while minimizing any factors that might limit their free-play. It is worthwhile to note briefly two of those strategies.

For one thing Miller applies the terms *interpretation* and *meaning* in an extremely capacious way, so as to conflate linguistic utterance or writing with any metaphysical representation of theory or of "fact" about the physical world. These diverse realms are treated equivalently as "texts" which are "read" or "interpreted." He thus leaves no room for taking into account that language, unlike the physical world, is a cultural institution that developed expressly in order to mean something and to convey what is meant to members of a community who have learned how to use and interpret language. And within the realm of explicitly verbal texts, Miller allows for no distinction with regard to the kinds of norms that may obtain or may not obtain for the "interpretation" of the entire corpus of an individual author's writings, or of a single work in its totality, or of a particular passage, sentence, or word within that work. As a critical pluralist, I would agree that there is a diversity of sound (though not equally adequate) interpretations of the play *King Lear,* yet I claim to know precisely what Lear meant when he said, "Pray you undo this button."

A second strategy is related to Derrida's treatment of the "trace." Like Derrida, Miller excludes by his elected premises any control or limitation of signification by reference to the uses of a word or phrase that are current at the time an author writes, or to an author's intention, or to the verbal or generic context in which a word occurs. Any word within a given text—or at least any "key word," as he calls it, that he picks out for special scrutiny—can thus be claimed to signify any and all of the diverse things it has signified in the varied forms that the signifier has assumed through its recorded history; and not only in a particular language, such as English or French, but back through its etymology in Latin and Greek all the way to its postulated Indo-European root. Whenever and by whomever and in whatever context a printed word is used, therefore, the limits of what it can be said to mean in that use are set only by what the interpreter can find in historical and etymological dictionaries, supplemented by any further information that the interpreter's own erudition can provide. Hence Miller's persistent resource to etymology— and even to the significance of the shapes of the printed letters in the altering form of a word—in expounding the texts to which he turns his critical attention.[18]

Endowed thus with the sedimented meanings accumulated over its total history, but stripped of any norms for selecting some of these and rejecting others, a key word—like the larger passage or total text of which the word is an element—becomes (in the phrase Miller cites from Mallarmé) a *suspens vibratoire*,[19] a vibratory suspension of equally likely meanings, and these are bound to include "incompatible" or "irreconcilable" or "contradictory" meanings. The conclusion from these views Miller formulates in a variety of ways: a key word, or a passage, or a text, since it is a ceaseless play of anomalous meanings, is "indeterminable," "undecipherable," "unreadable," "undecidable."[20] Or more bluntly: "All reading is misreading." "Any reading can be shown to be a misreading on evidence drawn from the text itself." But in misreading a text, the interpreter is merely repeating what the text itself has done before him, for "any literary text, with more or less explicitness or clarity, already reads or misreads itself."[21] To say that this concept of interpretation cuts the ground out from under the kind of history I undertook to write is to take a very parochial view of what is involved; for what it comes to is that no text, in part or whole, can mean anything in particular, and that we can never say just what anyone means by anything he writes.

But if all interpretation is misinterpretation, and if all criticism (like all history) of texts can engage only with a critic's own misconstruction, why bother to carry on the activities of interpretation and criticism? Hillis Miller poses this question more than once. He presents his answers in terms of his favorite analogues for the interpretive activity, which he explores with an unflagging resourcefulness. These analogues figure the text we read as a Cretan labyrinth, and also as the texture of a spider's web; the two figures, he points out, have been fused in earlier conflations in the myth of Ariadne's thread, by which Theseus retraces the windings of the labyrinth, and of Arachne's thread, with which she spins her web.[22] Here is one of Miller's answers to the question, Why pursue the critical enterprise?

> Pater's writings, like those of other major authors in the Occidental tradition, are at once open to interpretation and ultimately indecipherable, unreadable. His texts lead the critic deeper and deeper into a labyrinth until he confronts a final aporia. This does not mean, however, that the reader must give up from the beginning the attempt to understand Pater.

> Only by going all the way into the labyrinth, following the
> thread of a given clue, can the critic reach the blind alley,
> vacant of any Minotaur, that impasse which is the end point
> of interpretation.[23]

Now, I make bold to claim that I understand Miller's passage, and that what it says, in part, is that the deconstructive
critic's act of interpretation has a beginning and an end; that
it begins as an intentional, goal-oriented quest; and that this
quest is to end in an impasse.

The reaching of the interpretive aporia or impasse precipitates what Miller calls "the uncanny moment"—the moment
in which the critic, thinking to deconstruct the text, finds that
he has simply participated in the ceaseless play of the text as
a self-deconstructive artifact. Here is another of Miller's
statements, in which he describes both his own and Derrida's
procedure:

> Deconstruction as a mode of interpretation works by a careful
> and circumspect entering of each textual labyrinth. . . . The
> deconstructive critic seeks to find, by this process of retracing,
> the element in the system studied which is alogical, the thread
> in the text in question which will unravel it all, or the loose
> stone which will pull down the whole building. The decon-
> struction, rather, annihilates the ground on which the build-
> ing stands by showing that the text has already annihilated
> that ground, knowingly or unknowingly. Deconstruction is not
> a dismantling of the structure of a text but a demonstration
> that it has already dismantled itself.[24]

The uncanny moment in interpretation, as Miller phrases it
elsewhere, is a sudden *"mise en abyme"* in which the bottom
drops away and, in the endless regress of the self-baffling
free-play of meanings in the very signs which both reveal an
abyss and, by naming it, cover it over, we catch a glimpse of
the abyss itself in a "vertigo of the underlying nothingness."[25]

The "deconstructive critic," Miller has said, *"seeks* to find"
the alogical element in a text, the thread which, when pulled,
will unravel the whole texture. Given the game Miller has set
up, with its graphocentric premises and freedom of interpretive maneuver, the infallible rule of the deconstructive quest

is, "Seek and ye shall find." The deconstructive method works, because it can't help working; it is a can't-fail enterprise; there is no complex passage of verse or prose which could possibly serve as a counter-instance to test its validity or limits. And the uncanny critic, whatever the variousness and distinctiveness of the texts to which he applies his strategies, is bound to find that they all reduce to one thing and one thing only. In Miller's own words: each deconstructive reading, "performed on any literary, philosophical, or critical text . . . reaches, in the particular way the given text allows it, the 'same' moment of an aporia. . . . The reading comes back again and again, with different texts, to the 'same' impasse."[26]

It is of no avail to point out that such criticism has nothing whatever to do with our common experience of the uniqueness, the rich variety, and the passionate human concerns in works of literature, philosophy, or criticism—these matters are among the linguistic illusions that the criticism dismantles. There are, I want to emphasize, rich rewards in reading Miller, as in reading Derrida, which include a delight in his resourceful play of mind and language and the many and striking insights yielded by his wide reading and by his sharp eye for unsuspected congruities and differences in our heritage of literary and philosophical writings. But these rewards are yielded by the way, and that way is always to the ultimate experience of vertigo, the uncanny *frisson* at teetering with him on the brink of the abyss; and even the shock of this discovery is soon dulled by its expected and invariable recurrence.

I shall cite a final passage to exemplify the deft and inventive play of Miller's rhetoric, punning, and figuration, which gives his formulations of the *mise en abyme* a charm that is hard to resist. In it he imposes his fused analogues of labyrinth and web and abyss on the black-on-blanks which constitute the elemental given of the deconstructive premises:

> Far from providing a benign escape from the maze, Ariadne's thread makes the labyrinth, is the labyrinth. The interpretation or solving of the puzzles of the textual web only adds more filaments to the web. One can never escape from the labyrinth because the activity of escaping makes more laby-

rinth, the thread of a linear narrative or story. Criticism is the production of more thread to embroider the texture or textile already there. This thread is like the filament of ink which flows from the pen of the writer, keeping him in the web but suspending him also over the chasm, the blank page that thin line hides.[27]

To interpret: Hillis Miller, suspended by the labyrinthine lines of a textual web over the abyss that those black lines demarcate on the blank page, busies himself to unravel the web that keeps him from plunging into the blank abyss, but finds he can do so only by an act of writing which spins a further web of lines, equally vulnerable to deconstruction, but only by another movement of the pen that will trace still another inky net over the ever-receding abyss. As Miller remarks, I suppose ruefully, at the end of the passage I quoted, "In one version of Ariadne's story she is said to have hanged herself with her thread in despair after being abandoned by Theseus."

3

What is one to say in response to this abysmal vision of the textual world of literature, philosophy, and all the other achievements of mankind in the medium of language? There is, I think, only one adequate response, and that is the one that William Blake made to the Angel in *The Marriage of Heaven and Hell*. After they had groped their way down a "winding cavern," the Angel revealed to Blake a ghastly vision of hell as an "infinite Abyss"; in it was "the sun, black but shining," around which were "fiery tracks on which revolv'd vast spiders." But no sooner, says Blake, had "my friend the Angel" departed, than "this appearance was no more, but I found myself sitting on a pleasant bank beside a river by moon light, hearing a harper who sung to a harp." The Angel, "surprised asked me how I escaped? I answered: 'All that we saw was owing to your metaphysics.'"

As a deconstructive Angel, Hillis Miller, I am happy to say, is not serious about deconstruction, in Hegel's sense of "serious"; that is, he does not entirely and consistently commit himself to the consequences of his premises. He is in fact, fortunately for us, a double agent who plays the game of language by two very different sets of rules. One of the games he plays is that of a deconstructive critic of literary texts. The other is the game he will play in a minute or two when he steps out of his graphocentric premises onto this platform and begins to talk to us.

I shall hazard a prediction as to what Miller will do then. He will have determinate things to say and will masterfully exploit the resources of language to express these things clearly and forcibly, addressing himself to us in the confidence that we, to the degree that we have mastered the constitutive norms of this kind of discourse, will approximate what he means. He will show no inordinate theoretical difficulties about beginning his discourse or conducting it through its middle to an end. What he says will manifest, by immediate inference, a thinking subject or ego and a distinctive and continuant ethos, so that those of you who, like myself, know and admire his recent writings will be surprised and delighted by particularities of what he says, but will correctly anticipate both its general tenor and its highly distinctive style and manner of proceeding. What he says, furthermore, will manifest a feeling as well as thinking subject; and unless it possesses a superhuman forbearance, this subject will express some natural irritation that I, an old friend, should so obtusely have misinterpreted what he has said in print about his critical intentions.

Before coming here, Miller worked his thoughts (which involved inner speech) into the form of writing. On this platform, he will proceed to convert this writing to speech; and it is safe to say—since our chairman is himself a double agent, editor of a critical journal as well as organizer of this symposium—that soon his speech will be reconverted to writing and presented to the public. This substitution of *écriture* for *parole* will certainly make a difference, but not an absolute difference; what Miller says here, that is, will not jump an ontological gap to the printed page, shedding on the way all the features that made it intelligible as discourse. For each of his readers will be able to reconvert the black-on-blanks back into speech, which he will hear in his mind's ear; he will perceive the words not simply as marks nor as sounds, but as already invested with meaning; also, by immediate inference, he will be aware in his reading of an intelligent subject, very similar to the one we will infer while listening to him here, who organizes the well-formed and significant sentences and marshals the argument conveyed by the text.

There is no linguistic or any other law we can appeal to that will prevent a deconstructive critic from bringing his graphocentric procedures to bear on the printed version of Hillis Miller's discourse—or of mine, or of Wayne Booth's—and if he does, he will infallibly be able to translate the text into a vertiginous *mise en abyme*. But those of us who stubbornly refuse to substitute the rules of the deconstructive enterprise for our ordinary skill and tact at language will find that we are able to understand this text very well. In many ways, in fact, we will understand it better than while hearing it in the mode of oral discourse, for the institution of print will render the fleeting words of his speech by a durable graphic correlate which will enable us to take our own and not the speaker's time in attending to it, as well as to reread it, to collocate, and to ponder until we are satisfied that we have approximated the author's meaning.

After Hillis Miller and I have pondered in this way over the text of the other's discourse, we will probably, as experience in such matters indicates, continue essentially to disagree. By this I mean that neither of us is apt to find the other's reasons so compelling as to get him to change his own interpretive premises and aims. But in the process, each will have come to see more clearly what the other's reasons are for doing what he does, and no doubt come to discover that some of these reasons are indeed good reasons in that, however short of being compelling, they have a bearing on the issue in question. In brief, insofar as we set ourselves, in the old-fashioned way, to make out what the other means by what he says, I am confident that we shall come to a better mutual understanding. After all, without that confidence that we can use language to say what we mean and can interpret language so as to determine what was meant, there is no rationale for the dialogue in which we are now engaged.

Behaviorism
and Deconstruction

MY PREDICTION that other contributors would be drawn into the dialogue between Wayne Booth, Hillis Miller, and myself has been fulfilled sooner than I expected. We already have strong rejoinders from James Kincaid and Morse Peckham, and the discussion bids fair to continue until a drop in subscriptions impels the editors to cry, "Hold, enough!" Kincaid's contribution raises issues about the role of generic preconceptions in interpretation that I hope other writers will be moved to consider. I want to address myself to what Morse Peckham has said about pluralism, deconstructive criticism, and the question of validity in interpretation.

Let me try to focus the discussion by enlarging upon a distinction I made earlier. The issue between pluralism and deconstructive interpretation is obscured by lumping together three diverse applications of the term "interpretation":

1. The historical interpretation of a series of literary, philosophical, historical, and other texts.
2. The interpretation of a single text in its entirety; for example, Wordsworth's *Prelude*, Schiller's *Aesthetic Education of the Human Race*, Hegel's *Phenomenology*, Shakespeare's *King Lear*. My view is that in both these modes of interpretation, our quest for a full and multi-dimensional understanding not only justifies but requires the

bringing to bear, whether on a series of texts or on a single text, of a plurality of perspectives which select different aspects of the texts for consideration and organize and relate these aspects in a variety of rewarding ways. This type of critical pluralism differs from Hillis Miller's deconstructive pluralism, which asserts that all cultural histories and all critiques of a single text are arbitrary determinations of an indeterminable suspension of meanings, imposed by the individual historian's or critic's will to power over his texts. My contention is that, on the contrary, expert readers of history and of literary criticism possess and apply criteria—which under challenge can be made explicit—for deciding between principled or unprincipled, controlled or arbitrary, sound or unsound, penetrating or silly interpretations, be they in the Marxist, Freudian, archetypal, Auerbachian, Abramsian, or any other interpretive mode. In addition, although each perspective, when soundly applied, brings out aspects of the subject matter that others minimize or overlook, we possess other criteria—such as relative adequacy to the details and complexity of the texts and to their historical situations—which enable us to assess an interpretation within one perspective as better history or criticism, taken all in all, than an interpretation in a different perspective.

3. The interpretation of the meaning of a single passage, consisting of a sentence or linked sequence of sentences, which the historian or critic quotes in order to exemplify, illustrate, and confirm his historical or critical claims. Now, there do exist—and in the era since Surrealism, in ever-increasing numbers and varieties—texts composed of passages which have been deliberately written in order to mislead and baffle the reader, or to leave him suspended in a tangle of unresolvable alternatives, contradictions, and "aporias." But we have convincing grounds for believing that the great majority of serious writers who are cited by traditional historians wrote passages with the intention that they be understood by a qualified reader. My contention is that such passages have a determinate and determinable meaning. Hillis Miller

ascribes to me the view that this meaning is "obvious or univocal."[1] I hold, in fact, that a cited passage is often in various degrees vague, ambiguous, or multiply meaningful—how could someone who dealt, as I have, with Hegel's *Phenomenology* think otherwise?—but they are *determinably* so. In addition, many cited passages undoubtedly have further meanings which the historian doesn't specify because they are irrelevant, but not destructive, to the case he is making. The historian presents his interpretations of these passages to competent readers, in the knowledge that their interpretations will tend to confirm or disconfirm his case, to the extent that they match or differ from his. In doing so, however, the historian makes a crucial presupposition: that the reader sets himself to make out what the writer of the text said, and not (like a deconstructionist) to demonstrate what can be made out of the text.

The core of meaning in a single utterance, as interpreted by a reader who undertakes to understand what its author said, is not subject to a plurality of interpretive perspectives, for that reader shares with the author the mastery of the same implicit rules, without which a language would not exist, and which make it possible for us to say what we mean and to understand what someone else says. We can interpret variously, yet profitably, the overall structure, or "meaning," of *King Lear*. But when Lear says, "Pray you, undo this button," or again, "As flies to wanton boys are we to the gods; / They kill us for their sport," there is no ground in the constitutive rules of English for a difference between a Marxist, Freudian, or archetypal interpretation of his utterance. All readers of Elizabethan English know what Lear meant—to put it more specifically, we know what Shakespeare meant Lear to mean—however variously we may relate this meaning, according to our critical stance, to the evolving characterization of Lear, or to the play of imagery in the rest of the text, or to what we posit as the organizing principle of the drama as a whole.

This question of the meaning of an utterance or cited passage is the focus of my contention with Hillis Miller. His extreme theoretical claim seems to be that no textual passage has a determinable meaning, but simply sets off a free play, or *suspens vibratoire,* of innumerable significations. His more moderate claim, implicit in his practice in deconstructing a particular passage, is that it generates a large but specifiable set of meanings, accumulated through the ages by the words and morphemes that constitute the passage, which are equivalently relevant yet mutually baffling, so that they inevitably precipitate, in a reader who has freed himself from linguistic delusions, an uncanny moment of aporia or the revelation of a semantic abyss.

In his commentary on these matters, Morse Peckham discriminates between historical interpretation, the interpretation of "complex literary texts," and the interpretation of a single utterance. He undertakes to show, however, that if we determine "what interpretational behavior is in ordinary, mundane, routine verbal interaction" (p. 803), exemplified by what happens in the case of one representative utterance, we can establish the principles of valid interpretation in all three applications of the term.

In his conclusions, by and large, Peckham is on the side of the angels, which should of course be interpreted to mean that he mainly agrees with me rather than with Hillis Miller. The theory of language and meaning, however, on which Peckham bases his conclusions, differs radically from my own. I want to identify some of these differences and then to show why, as it seems to me, Peckham's behavioral theory of language neither clarifies nor helps to resolve the points at issue between traditional cultural history and Miller's deconstructionism.

Peckham's wide-ranging essay incorporates five claims that bear closely on these issues:

1. A representative case of ordinary verbal interaction is one in which Professor Booth goes into "his usual coffee shop" and says to the waiter, "I'd like a cup of coffee, please" (p. 804). The "methodology of the waiter" in responding to this utterance is identical with the method of the historian in interpreting any passage that he cites.
2. The procedure by which an experienced waiter suc-

ceeds in instructing an apprentice how to respond behaviorally to Booth's utterance establishes the procedure for the valid historical interpretation and explanation of the relationships among a selected body of texts.

3. Abrams's behavior in *Natural Supernaturalism* is to disengage "the Fall-Redemption semiotic pattern from a series of texts" and to identify it "as a Christian pattern which was continued in the post-Christian period by a semiotic transformation which he calls secularization of the pattern" (pp. 806–7). Since this interpretive behavior is no less valid than the waiter's, his historical claim is sound, though a bit obvious.

4. Since a sign is essentially "a figure to which there is a response" which has been "acquired by learning processes," deconstructionists such as Derrida and Miller don't in fact deconstruct a text; instead, they deconstruct "an individual's ability to respond." We find parallel techniques for "deconstructing meaning" in the mantra, in various mystic disciplines, and in the use of marijuana or LSD. In fact, "were Miller consistent he would rapidly be reduced either to catatonia or to speaking in tongues" (pp. 813–14).

5. Nonetheless, Peckham urges Miller to be less timid in his enterprise and, in effect, to sin harder. The virtue of deconstructionism is that it is part of a growing "analytic" movement which may finally succeed in destroying the continuing Romantic ideology of "secular redemptionism" which has often "in the past 190 years . . . turned into brutal and bloody authoritarianism," as exemplified by the horrors "perpetrated by Hitler and Stalin" (pp. 815–16).

I shall comment briefly on these five matters in turn.

1

In dealing with language and meaning, Morse Peckham belongs to the class of thinkers that A. O. Lovejoy called *esprits simplistes*. That is, he is impatient with the clutter and tangle of our experience in using language and is convinced that a few simple principles underlie the seeming disorder and complexities. Like that of most such thinkers in our time, Peckham's approach is modeled on the natural sciences, and he looks for the principles of meaning in the overt and regular, hence empirically observable and predictable, behavior of speakers when they talk and auditors when they respond to what they hear. He is also what William James calls "tough-minded" rather than "tender-minded." Accordingly, Peckham employs two key operative terms in dealing with language, meaning, and interpretation; one of these is *behavior*, and the other is *control*. Thus: "The ability to use the spoken language" is the ability "to control behavior by means of verbal instructions and to be controlled by the same means" (p. 804). "Language controls behavior" (p. 805). "Culture consists of instructions for controlling behavior" (p. 809). "Ideologies" are means for "controlling human behavior," and are reinforced by "redundancy," that is, the frequency with which they occur (pp. 815–16, 809). In consonance with these views, Peckham asserts that "the meaning of a sign is the response to that sign or, to be a touch more precise, is the determination of the appropriate response." In the representative instance of Booth's request for a cup of coffee, the meaning of Booth's utterance is the behavior of the waiter (who has learned to control "his response to [this] semiotic pattern") in bringing Booth a cup of coffee (p. 805).

Note that, given his theoretical orientation, Peckham's choice of a representative utterance in "ordinary . . . verbal interaction" is patently slanted. His paradigmatic example is the utterance, specifically, of an order (not the kind of order an officer gives an enlisted man, or a parent gives his child, but the kind involved when we order from a menu), and an adequate analysis of the meaning of this special type of speech-act has to take into account the behavior of the waiter. The situation in which Booth's order is appropriately uttered is an institutional one, a restaurant, in which Booth, as a patron, is privileged to order food and drink and the waiter, in taking the job, has assumed the obligation to act in accordance with such orders. To understand the meaning of Booth's "I'd like a cup of coffee, please," uttered in such a situation, involves knowing that it is a polite way of ordering which expresses Booth's desire for a cup of coffee and his intention that the utterance will get the waiter to bring the coffee to him.

Even in this slanted instance, however, I think it misleading to say that the meaning of Booth's utterance is the waiter's response, including his behavior in bringing the coffee. Let us suppose that a non-English-speaking onlooker, who like Peckham is a linguistic behaviorist, somehow guesses that Booth's utterance is an order and observes the behavior of the waiter in order to discover what the utterance meant. The waiter picks up a fork that Booth happens to have dropped on the floor, empties an ashtray, brings Booth a cup of coffee, and lights a cigarette for Booth's table companion. There is no way the observer can know which of these actions constitutes the meaning of Booth's utterance, unless he knows in advance what the utterance means. Or suppose that Booth has mistaken for the waiter a man in evening dress who is in fact the inordinately proud and hot-tempered ambassador from Transylvania. The response of this man is to pick up a pot of coffee and pour it over Booth's head. This responsive behavior, although entirely appropriate from the point of view of the choleric ambassador, in no way alters the meaning of Booth's utterance. The ambassador in fact responds as he does precisely because he has already understood Booth's utterance (and has resented its implication as to his menial relation to its speaker), just as we amused onlookers from a nearby table know that Booth's order has misfired because we understood its meaning the instant it was uttered—and, I would add, just as Peckham knows where to look for a behavioral criterion of the meaning of Booth's order, because he knows in advance the meaning of the order whose criterion he seeks. All of us know its meaning because we have mastered the English language and so know how to apply the implicit rules governing the use of the words that constitute Booth's order, including the implicit rules that constitute the institutional situation of restaurant-patron-waiter in which such an order is appropriately uttered.

Peckham claims that my "behavior" in dealing with the quotations in *Natural Supernaturalism* is the same, in methodology and validity, as the interpretive behavior of Booth's waiter. But the great bulk of the utterances in my quotations—and no less, of the utterances constituting Peckham's own essay—do not consist of orders, requests, or commands. Instead, they consist of assertions, descriptions, judgments, exclamations, approbations, condemnations, and many other kinds of speech-acts, the meanings of which are not related to my interpretive behavior, even in the indirect way in which the meaning of Booth's order is related to the future behavior of his waiter.

Take, for example, some of the quotations with which, at the beginning of the book, I introduce a major topic. Wordsworth writes that Paradise and groves Elysian need not be "A history only of departed things, / Or a mere fiction of what never was,"

> For the discerning intellect of Man,
> When wedded to this goodly universe
> In love and holy passion, shall find these
> A simple produce of the common day.

Coleridge writes that the condition he calls "Joy"

> is the spirit and the power,
> Which, wedding Nature to us, gives in dower
> A new Earth and New Heaven. . . .

In Hölderlin's novel *Hyperion* the poet-protagonist cries out:

> Let the new world spring from the root of humanity! . . . They will come, Nature, thy men. A rejuvenated people will make thee young again, too, and thou wilt be as its bride.

And in one of his *Fragments* Novalis asserts: "The higher philosophy is concerned with the Marriage of Nature and Mind." My "behavior" in selecting and aligning these and other passages does not constitute their meaning. Instead I treat them as I do because, by applying my acquired linguistic skill, I have understood their meaning. What can be said, although only in a very loose sense, to control my behavior in composing this part of the book is my overall plan for the work, my decision to present a particular Romantic *topos* at this point, and my judgments as to how to do so lucidly and effectively. I present the quotations as instances of this *topos*, by virtue of the fact that their meanings overlap in relevant aspects, and in the confidence that a competent reader, applying the linguistic skill that he shares with me, will interpret each of them very much as I do.

The focal issue between Hillis Miller and myself is whether I am justified in saying that these quotations determinately mean at least what I say they mean, or whether what I say they mean is the imposition of my will upon a suspension of indefinite yet conflicting significations. It doesn't seem to me that Morse Peckham's behavioral theory of meaning is of any help in this dispute. In specifying the meaning of an utterance, the only relevant "response" by the reader is not the behavior which may be its consequence, but his understanding of what it is that the writer has said.

2

We move from the verbal interpretation of a single utterance or textual passage to the larger question of "historical interpretation," in which an historian asserts specified relations—and proposes explanations for these relations—between passages he has selected from a great variety of texts, written by many individuals at diverse times and places. Here too I don't see what we learn about the criteria for the validity of an historian's procedure from Peckham's claim that "the *model* for 'the historical interpretation of texts' is historical interpretation in ordinary verbal behavior"—the "historical interpretation of texts" being translated, in Peckham's favored terms, as "a semiotic transformation of the norm of [the historian's] response behavior, which is historically controlled" (p. 809).

Peckham offers as his "model" another aspect of his paradigmatic case of Booth's ordering a cup of coffee. The nature of the historical control of interpretation is exemplified by the behavior of an experienced waiter who is "training an apprentice waiter and . . . instructs him verbally in his duties, in how he should control his behavior in this semiotic matrix" (p. 806). But surely the apprentice waiter already knows how to understand English, or at least another language such as French or Italian. He therefore brings to the situation a knowledge of what counts as an order, and unless he is moronic, he already knows what, in general, are the responsibilities of a waiter in carrying out an order. If the apprentice speaks only a foreign language, the experienced waiter teaches him, not how to control his behavioral responses, but what the nearest equivalents are in his native tongue to the orders he is apt to hear in English. In neither case will the waiter teach the apprentice the meaning of an order by instructions that take the form: "If the customer utters the locution, 'Bring me a cup of coffee' (or the equivalent locutions X, Y, Z) you will respond by the following pattern of behavior." Instead, he will no doubt instruct the novice in the niceties of his response to an order whose meaning he already knows—for example, not to put his thumb inside the cup of coffee nor allow it to spill into the saucer, always to serve it over the patron's left shoulder, and so on.

In a refinement of this instance, Peckham assumes that the veteran "tells his apprentice waiter that in serving Professor Booth it is quite unnecessary to take him cream, for the Professor never uses it"; in giving these instructions, Peckham concludes, the waiter generates "an historical explanation and justification for the appropriate response to Professor Booth's request for coffee" (p. 808). It seems to me, however, that all the waiter does is to specify in Booth's order what Booth has left unspecified. An order for a cup of coffee can be carried out by bringing either black coffee or coffee with cream. The waiter, from his prior knowledge of Booth's habits, infers that his taste in coffee hasn't changed, hence specifies that when he simply orders coffee he wants to be brought black coffee.

But how can this justified inference from a single individual's more specific orders in the past serve as the methodological "model" for the validity of my historical procedure in *Natural Supernaturalism*? There I undertake to show, for example, that the passages from various writers that I cited above overlap in meaning with many other passages in the Romantic era, and that all predicate the power of the human mind, in interaction with outer nature, to make the old world into a new and better world. Then, by making reference to scores of intervening passages selected from writers over the centuries, I assert that these Romantic passages reformulate the apocalyptic predictions in the Bible that the old world will be remade into a new heaven and new earth; the major change in this reformulation is that the Romantic writers secularize the Christian apocalypse by attributing its achievement not to a relief expedition from the sky, but to a potential of power within the human mind and imagination. I confirm my assertion that the Romantic passages are naturalized restatements of Christian apocalypse by pointing to the analogues between what each predicts or anticipates, as well as to the striking continuance of such figures for the coming change as the marriage of the protagonists and the advent of a new heaven and earth; but above all, I confirm it by citing the claims by all the major Romantic writers—often explicit, and elsewhere clearly implied—that what they were doing was specifically to translate the mythical truths or "picture-thinking" of Christian apocalyptic doctrine into the higher truth of their own conceptual, nonsupernatural language. Between such complex interpretive and evidential procedures on the part of a cultural historian and the instructing of an apprentice waiter in the rudiments of his job, the alleged parallel in method reduces pretty much to the obvious fact that in both cases we make use of knowledge acquired in the past to make sense of something we confront in the present.

3

After the extraordinarily varied and complex goings-on that Wayne Booth, with a consummate *esprit de finesse*, has distinguished in *Natural Supernaturalism*, it is at first refreshing to be told by Morse Peckham that my behavior in that book was simply to disengage the Fall-Redemption semiotic pattern, to identify it as originally Christian, and to show that this pattern, in a secular transformation, was central to the Romantic period and has persisted since. But even cursory second thought reveals that this summation of the book simply won't do. It isn't only that it omits a large part of the subject matter which is remotely, or not at all, connected with the Fall-Redemption pattern; the description of the pattern itself is radically reductive, to an extent that not only greatly distorts what the book undertakes to show but also opens the way to false conclusions.

The biblical and exegetical version of what Peckham calls the "Fall-Redemption pattern" was a history of the creation of man and of a paradisal world and of the fall of man into evil and suffering in a blasted world, together with the prophecy of a Messianic coming (or Second Coming) that will inaugurate an apocalyptic conclusion in which, after a millennial Kingdom of God on earth, man reborn will inherit a new earth and heaven which is as good as, or even better than, the Paradise he has lost. *Natural Supernaturalism* undertakes to tell a story that shows, among many other things, the highly various elements in pagan metaphysics and esoteric thought which interacted with this pattern; its division (apparent even in the Bible) between describing the history of mankind as a whole and posing the possibility of redemption in this life for each individual man; and the diversity of views as to what is in fact signified by the terms "fall," "evil," "redemption," and "apocalypse." The book also undertakes to indicate how individual Romantic writers incorporated various elements from this mixed tradition of the design of history and of the individual life in a great variety of works, including metaphysical systems, autobiographies and biographies, "universal histories" of the past and future of the human race, symbolic and allegorical poems, and prose romances. Conspicuous Romantic innovations, common to all these writings, was not only the attribution of the apocalyptic capacity to man's own mind, but also the transformation of the circular design of Paradise, Paradise lost, and Paradise regained into a spiral form. To conflate all of these highly diverse matters into a single Fall-Redemption pattern opens the way to misleading generalizations and mistaken claims—one of which I will mention in my concluding section.

4

In comparing the practice of deconstruction to the regimen of the mantra, and its results to the effects of using pot and LSD, Peckham is much more severe than I was in my discussion of this movement and, even allowing for hyperbole, less than fair. As practiced by Derrida and Hillis Miller, deconstruction is not at all, as these parallels imply, an irruption of irrationalism into philosophy and literary criticism; on the contrary, it is a thoroughly rational and very sophisticated mode of thought. I would restate Peckham's description of its procedure and effect in this way. The skills that we ordinarily and unreflectively bring into play when interpreting the language we hear or read are remarkably subtle and sure; yet—despite the fact that their sureness is supported by a lifetime of interplay with other users of language, and by our ability to recognize and correct our errors—our confidence in these skills is vulnerable when subjected to a determined assault by a radical linguistic skepticism. The reason our confidence is vulnerable is that when our interpretations are so challenged, there is no way to "prove" that our interpretation is right, in the ordinary logical or scientific sense of demonstrating that it must be accepted by all reasonable people. When our interpretations are challenged in this radical way we are, in the last analysis, reduced to the claim that we are competent in the language we interpret. From this point of view, deconstruction can be characterized as the systematic deployment, from what I've called a "graphocentric premise," of a variety of strategems for destroying our confidence in the interpretive skills that we in fact manifest, whose results are largely confirmed by other interpreters who share our condition of undeconstructed innocence.

5

Peckham maintains that in the past 190 years the persistence of the Romantic Fall-Redemption pattern has often turned "into brutal and bloody authoritarianism," such as the horrors perpetrated by Hitler and Stalin (pp. 815–16). This claim, I think, is a dramatic demonstration of the failure to make essential distinctions. It makes sense only if by "the Fall-Redemption pattern" Peckham refers exclusively to the belief in historical apocalypse, and specifically to its millennial or chiliastic component; that is, the prophecy of a Messiah who, by a prodigious display of violence, will annihilate the old order and replace it by a thousand-year Kingdom of God on earth. As I pointed out in *Natural Supernaturalism*, the chiliastic myth has periodically empowered revolutionary movements in which a self-identified elite, God's Saints, anticipate His own imminent and wrathful coming by undertaking to destroy the corrupt existing order, root and branch. This chiliasm was manifested, for example, in northern Europe during the fifteenth and sixteenth centuries, in revolutionary movements led by the elect, including John of Leyden, the "Messiah of the Last Days"; it appeared again during the civil war in England, in such radical millenarian sects as the "Fifth Monarchy Men." And it reappeared in America during crises such as the Civil War; "The Battle Hymn of the Republic," for example, is a song of pure chiliastic expectation and violence, taken wholesale from the Book of Revelation. I also pointed out that the secular forms of chiliasm replaced God's supervisory providence by an immanent historical dialectic, or else by the "iron laws" of history, but that these inevitabilities, no less than scriptural authority, guaranteed an impending liquidation of all existing institutions in which the clairvoyant elect are invited to take an immediate and violent part. The chiliastic pattern is discernible in Marx's combination of history and prophecy, and plays a more prominent role in what Peckham calls "vulgarized Marxism" (p. 815); it manifests itself even in Hitler's undertaking to bring into being a "thousand-year Reich," which was, by distant derivation, his secular version of the millennial Kingdom of the Book of

Revelation. I am less ready than Peckham to make the blanket appraisal that the consequences of the pervasive chiliastic myth in Western culture have been exclusively evil; but I certainly agree that it has helped bring huge disasters, destruction, and suffering upon mankind.

The early days of the French Revolution were a time of widespread millennial expectations in Western Europe— expectations that, in their buoyant youth, the Romantic writers in Germany and England enthusiastically shared. But when they perceived the violent and authoritarian consequences of the Revolution in the Reign of Terror and the French wars of aggression, these writers recoiled in dismay. A major enterprise in *Natural Supernaturalism* is to show how Romantic writers, each in his own way, tried to reconstitute the grounds of hope for human amelioration by transferring them from historical inevitability to the mind of individual man— as the German philosopher C. L. Reinhold put it, by transferring the arena from "political revolutions" to "revolutions of the spirit"—and by proposing that only through a radical alteration of his own moral, cognitive, and imaginative consciousness can man effect a new and better life in a new and better world. The Romantic "Fall-Redemption pattern," thus, far from being a type of historical chiliasm, was precisely a reaction against militant historical chiliasm. And the central Romantic interpretation of the "fall" of man and of the nature of "evil," or the essential human malaise, was that man, by his selfhood or radical egoism, has become multiply fragmented, and so has fallen into a condition of conflict with himself, of enmity with other men, and of alienation from his natural environment. The revolution of moral consciousness on which the Romantic writers pin their hope, correspondingly, is one that will effect an inclusive reintegration of man with himself, with his fellows, and with the natural world.

The aim of deconstructive interpretation, as Hillis Miller both describes and illustrates it, is to conduct us to the discovery that every text by which our culture is transmitted deconstructs itself, in a *mise en abyme* in which, through the self-canceling play of unrestricted meanings, we glimpse the groundless abyss in a "vertigo of the underlying nothingness." To the results of this relentless "deconstruction," "dismantling," "subversion," or "undermining" of structured meanings Miller does not hesitate, in his writings and conversation, to apply Nietzsche's term "nihilism"—a stage which Nietzsche himself claimed he had passed through to an affirmation of life, but in which, at least for the time being, Miller seems contented to dwell.

Morse Peckham concludes by giving his approval to the deconstructive critic because, albeit unknowingly, he participates in an "analytic tradition" which promises finally to destroy the Romantic ideology of Fall-Redemption, to which Peckham attributes major responsibility for the authoritarian horrors of the last two centuries. It may be that Peckham proffers this appraisal ironically, and if so, I apologize to him for missing the cues. Now, I do not mean to be alarmist; I in fact believe that deconstruction as a program will soon pass on, leaving behind the many perceptive insights into the workings of language that it has effected by the way. But assuming that Peckham is unironic in his conclusion, I want to pose to him the following question. Which of the following alternatives is more apt to open a cultural vacuum that will be filled by power-hungry authoritarians who have no doubts about what they want nor scruples about how to get it: A systematic and sustained enterprise to deconstruct the grounds of all truths or values asserted by our culture-bearing texts, and to subvert even our confidence that we can communicate determinately with each other? Or a reformulated version of the central Romantic hope that, by a revolution of mind and heart, man may yet achieve unity with himself, community with his fellow men, and reconciliation with a nature in which, because it has been humanized, he can feel at home?

How to Do Things with Texts

THE AGE OF CRITICISM, which reached its zenith in the mid-decades of this century, has given way to the Age of Reading, and whereas the American New Critics and European formalists of the Age of Criticism discovered the work-as-such, current literary theorists have discovered the reader-as-such. This reader, as everyone knows who has kept even cursorily in touch with the latest Paris fashions, is not the man he used to be. He is a wraith of his old self, stripped of everything human, as part of a systematic dehumanizing of all aspects of the traditional view about how a work of literature comes into being, what it is, how it is read, and what it means.

For purpose of comparison, let me sketch the salient and persistent features of the traditional, or humanistic paradigm of the writing and reading of literature. The writer is conceived, in Wordsworth's terms, as "a man speaking to men." Literature, in other words, is a transaction between a human author and his human reader. By his command of linguistic and literary possibilities, the author actualizes and records in words what he undertakes to signify of human beings and actions and about matters of human concern, addressing himself to those readers who are competent to understand what he has written. The reader sets himself to make out what the author has designed and signified, through putting into play a linguistic and literary expertise that he shares with the author. By approximating what the author undertook to signify the reader understands what the language of the work means.

In our Age of Reading, the first casualty in this literary transaction has been the author. To the noninitiate, it is bemusing to observe the complacency with which authors of recent books and essays announce their own demise. "It is about time," says Michel Foucault, "that criticism and philosophy acknowledged the disappearance or the death of the author." "As institution," according to Roland Barthes, "the author is dead: his civil status, his biographical person, have disappeared." The necrology extends to the human reader, and indeed to man himself, who is reduced to an illusion engendered by the play of language, or as Foucault puts it, to "a simple fold in our knowledge," destined to "disappear as soon as that knowledge has found a new form." In these new writings about reading, accordingly, the author deliquesces into writing-as-such and the reader into reading-as-such, and what writing-as-such effects and reading-as-such engages is not a work of literature but a text, writing, *écriture*. In its turn the text forfeits its status as a purposeful utterance about human beings and human concerns, and even its individuality, becoming simply an episode in an all-encompassing textuality—dissolved, as Edward Said has remarked, into "the communal sea of linguicity." Consonantly, the relations between authors which had traditionally been known as "influence" are depersonalized into "intertextuality," a reverberation between ownerless sequences of signs.

It might be expected that, evacuated of its humanity, reading-as-such would become an interplay of bloodless abstractions. Quite to the contrary. We find in French structuralist criticism and its American analogues that reading is a perilous adventure—not of a soul among masterpieces, but of the unsouled reading-process as it engages with the text-as-such. Persistently this inhuman encounter is figured in a rhetoric of extremity, as tense with the awareness of risk and crisis; anguished by doubts about its very possibility; meeting everywhere in the "*action du signifiant*" with violence, disruption, castration, mysterious disappearances, murder, self-destruction; or as overcome by vertigo as the ground falls away and leaves it suspended over an abyss of recessive meanings in a referential void. In this Gothic context of the horrors of reading it is a relief to come upon Roland Barthes's *The Pleasure of the Text*, with its seeming promise to revive the notion, as old as Aristotle and Horace, that the distinctive aim of a literary work is to give pleasure to its readers. But then we find in Barthes's account that the pleasure is not in the artful management of the human agents, interactions, and passions signified by the text, but in the engagement with the text-as-such, and that Barthes adapts the traditional concept to current connoisseurs of textuality by a running conceit sustained by double entendres, in which textual pleasure is assimilated to sexual pleasure; the prime distinction is between the mere *plaisir* effected by a comfortably traditional text and the orgasmic rapture, *jouissance,* in the close encounter with a radical "modern" text which, by foiling the reader's expectations, "brings to a crisis his relations with language." It seems safe to predict that the innocent reader, seduced by Barthes's erotics of the text, who engages with a *nouveau roman* is in for a disappointment.

My concern, however, is with the strategy and the rhetorical tactics of structuralist criticism only as a background for considering three current writers who put forward radical new ways of reading texts. One, Jacques Derrida, is a French philosopher with an increasing following among American critics of literature; by pressing to an extreme the tendencies of structuralism, Derrida proposes a mode of reading which undermines not only the grounds of structuralism itself, but the possibility of understanding language as a medium of decidable meanings. The other two, Stanley Fish and Harold Bloom, are Americans who set their theories of reading in opposition to what they decry as the antihumanism of structuralist procedures. All three are erudite, formidable, and influential innovators who found their strategies of reading on an insight into a neglected aspect of what enters into the interpretation of a text. These theorists differ, we shall see, in essential respects, but they share important features which are distinctive of current radicalism in interpretation. In each, the theory doesn't undertake simply to explain how we in fact read, but to propagate a new way of reading that subverts accepted interpretations and replaces them with unexpected alternatives. Each theory eventuates in a radical skepticism about our ability to achieve a correct interpretation, proposing instead that reading should free itself from illusory linguistic constraints in order to become liberated, creative, producing the meanings that it makes rather than discovers. And all three theories are suicidal; for as the theorist is aware, his views are self-reflexive, in that his subversive process destroys the possibility that a reader can interpret correctly either the expression of his theory or the textual interpretations to which it is applied.

It is worth noting that such Newreading—by which I denote a principled procedure for replacing standard meanings by new meanings—is by no means recent, but had many precedents in Western hermeneutics. We find such a procedure, for example, in ancient Greek and Roman attempts to uncover the deep truths hidden within Homer's surface myths and fictions, and to moralize the immoral tales of Ovid; we find it also in the reinterpretations of the Old Testament by writers of the New Testament, as well as by Jewish Kabbalists; we find a similar procedure in medieval and later exegetes of the many-leveled allegorical meanings in the entire biblical canon. These old reinterpretive enterprises, however diverse, all manifest three procedural moments, or aspects: (1) the interpreter indicates that he understands the standard, or accepted meanings of a text or passage (called by biblical exegetes "the literal meaning"); (2) he replaces, or at least supplements, these standard meanings by new meanings; (3) he mediates between these two systems of signification by setting up a transformational calculus which serves to convert the old meanings into his new meanings. We can, I think, discern a parallel procedure in our current Newreaders. In considering their proposals, I shall ask the following questions. What sort of things does each Newreader undertake to do with texts? By what transformational devices does he manage to do these things? And then there is the general question: What is there about the way language functions that enables a Newreader to accomplish the surprising things he does with texts?

1. THE SCIENCE OF NESCIENCE: JACQUES DERRIDA

How is one to make entry into the theory of Jacques Derrida, the most elusive, equivocal, and studiously noncommittal of philosophical writers? I shall try to break through with a crashing generalization: as a philosopher of language, Derrida is an absolutist without absolutes.

Derrida proposes that both the Western use of language and philosophies of language are "logocentric"; that they are logocentric because essentially "phonocentric" (that is, giving priority and privilege to speech over writing); and that language is thereby permeated, explicitly and implicitly, by what, in a phrase from Heidegger, he calls "the metaphysics of presence." By "presence"—or in alternative terms, a "transcendental signified" or "ultimate referent"—he designates what I call an absolute; that is, a foundation outside the play of language itself which is immediately and simply present to us as something ultimate, terminal, self-certifying, and thus adequate to "center" the structure of the linguistic system and to guarantee the determinate meaning of an utterance within that system. The positing of some form of presence, it is suggested, is the expression of a desire—which is the motivating desire of metaphysics—to establish a conceptual replacement for the certainty about language and meaning provided by the myth in *Genesis* of language as originated and guaranteed by a divine, hence absolute, authority, or else by the theological view that language is certified by the omnipresence of the Logos. In a remarkable series of readings of diverse texts, philosophical and literary, Derrida subtly uncovers the presupposition that there is an absolute foundation for language, and displays the internal paradoxes and self-contradictions that are attendant upon such a presupposition. The quest for presence, then, is doomed to unsuccess, whether that supposed absolute is the presence of his meaning to the consciousness of the speaker at the instant of his utterance; or Platonic essences that underwrite the significations of verbal names; or a fixed and simple referent, "the thing itself," in the world "outside of language"; or Heidegger's "Being" as the ultimate ground of signification and understanding. But having, in the critical aspect of his reading of texts, dismantled the traditional absolutes, Derrida remains committed to absolutism; for he shares the presupposition of the views he deconstructs that to be determinately understandable, language requires an absolute foundation, and he maintains that, since there is no such ground, there is no stop to the play of undecidable meanings: "The absence of a transcendental signified extends the realm and the play of signification to infinity." In this aspect of his dealings with language, Derrida's writings present variations on a Nietzschean theme: Absolutes, though necessary, are dead, therefore free play is permitted.

It should be remarked, however, that the philosophy of language offers an alternative to the supposition that language requires an absolute foundation in order to be determinately meaningful. This alternative sets out from the observation that in practice language often works, that it gets its job done. We live a life in which we have assurance that we are able to mean what we say and know what we mean, and in which our auditors or readers show us by their verbal and actional responses whether or not they have understood us correctly. This alternative stance takes as its task not to explain away these workings of language, but to explain how it is that they happen, and in instances of failure, to inquire what it is that has gone wrong. A prominent recent exemplar of this stance is the *Philosophical Investigations* of Ludwig Wittgenstein. There are similarities between Wittgenstein's views of language and Derrida's, in the critical aspect of Derrida's reading of philosophical texts. Like Derrida, for example, Wittgenstein insists that it is not possible to use language to get outside "the limits of language"; he holds that the concept that language directly represents reality is simply "a picture that holds us captive"; he rejects the account of the meaning of an utterance in terms of the objects or processes to which its words refer, or as equivalent to the conscious state of the speaker of the utterance; and, in his own way, he too deconstructs the traditional absolutes, or "essences," of Western metaphysics. He also rejects as futile the quest for an ultimate foundation for language. Philosophy, he says, "can in the end only describe" the "actual use of language," for it "cannot give it any foundation"; in giving reasons for the working of language, "the spade turns" before we reach an ultimate reason. But Wittgenstein's stance is that language is "a practice" that occurs as part of a shared "form of life," and that this practice works; as he puts it, "this game is played." His *Investigations* are designed to get us to recognize when language works, and when it doesn't—"when language is like an engine idling, not when it is doing work"—to get us to understand how the slippage occurred.

Derrida of course acknowledges that language works, or as he puts it, that it "functions"—that we constantly perform what we take to be successful speech-acts and successful instances of oral communication, and that a written text is *lisible,* "legible," that is, strikes us as having determinably specific meanings. But he accounts for this working as no more than "the *effects* of ideality, of signification, of meaning and of reference"—effects which are engendered by the play of differences within language itself; he then proceeds to "deconstruct" these effects by undertaking to show that, since they lack a ground in presence, their specificity of meaning is only a simulation. Derrida's procedure might be summarized as follows. He agrees that language works, then asks, "But is it possible that it really works?" He concludes that, lacking an ultimate ground, it is absolutely not possible that it works, hence that its working is only a seeming—that, in short, though texts may be legible, they are not intelligible, or determinately significant.

Of each of the traditional terms and distinctions used to analyze the working of language—terms such as *communication, context, intention, meaning,* and oppositions such as speech-writing, literal-metaphorical, nonfictional-fictional—Derrida requires not only that they be grounded in absolute presence, but also that they be certified by criteria of what he calls "ideal purity" and "ultimate rigor" if they are to be determinately used and understood. For example: in order to communicate "a determinate content, an identifiable meaning," each of these words must signify a concept "that is unique, univocal, rigorously controllable," and its contextual conditions of use must be "absolutely determinable" and "entirely certain"; while the utterance of a determinate speech act must be tied to "the pure singularity of the event." Of course such analytic words cannot meet these criteria of absolute fixity, purity, and singularity, nor can any words, for it is an essential condition of a language that a finite set of words, manageable in accordance with a finite set of regularities, be capable of generating an unlimited variety of utterances adaptable to an unlimited diversity of circumstances, purposes, and applications. But Derrida's all-or-none principle admits of no alternative: failing to meet absolute criteria which language cannot satisfy without ceasing to do its work, all spoken and written utterances, though they may give the "effect" of determinate significance, are deconstructable into semantic indeterminacy.

Derrida describes his "general strategy of deconstruction" as a mode of "double writing": it first "inverts" the hierarchy of the terms in standard philosophical oppositions such as speech-writing, signifier-signified, then it "displaces" what was the lower term in the hierarchy (or a derivative from that term) "outside the oppositions in which it was held." The latter move generates, in place of the standard terms used to analyze the workings of language, a set of new terms which, he says, are neither words nor concepts, neither signifiers nor signifieds. These invented pseudo-terms, however, although "displaced" from their locus within the system of language, nonetheless are capable of producing "conceptual effects"; and these effects operate in two dimensions. On the one side, they account for the fact that texts are "legible," yielding the effects of seemingly determinable meanings. On the other side, they serve as what I have called a set of transformers, which Derrida employs to "disseminate" these effects into their deconstructed alternatives.

The chief transformer is *différance*—Saussure's key term "*différence*," twice-born and respelled with an *a*—which conflates "difference" and "deferment." In one aspect of its functioning, the "differences" among signs and among the conditions of their use explain how they generate their apparently specific significations; in its deconstructive aspect, it points to the fact that, since these significations can never come to rest in an absolute presence, their specification is deferred from substitute sign to substitute sign in a movement without end. Similarly with the other nonwords for nonentities with which Derrida replaces standard terms for dealing with language; in place of the spoken utterance or written text, the "general text" or "proto-writing"; in place of the word, "mark" or "grapheme"; in place of significance, "dissemination" or a large number of other "nicknames" that Derrida resourcefully coins, or else adapts to his equivocal purpose from common usage. All in their double function account for the legibility of a text at the same time that they "open" the apparent closure of the text "*en abyme,*" into the abyss of an endless regress of ever-promised, never-delivered meaning.

Derrida emphasizes that to deconstruct is not to destroy; that his task is to "dismantle the metaphysical and rhetorical structures" operative in a text "not in order to reject or discard them, but to reconstitute them in another way"; that he puts into question the "search for the signified not to annul it, but to understand it within a system to which such a reading is blind." He can in fact be designated as, on principle, a double-dealer in language, working ambidextrously with two semantic orders—the standard and the deconstructed. He writes essays and books, and engages in symposia and in debates, that put forward his deconstructive strategy and exemplify it by deconstructing the texts of other writers. In this deconstruction of logocentric language he assumes the stance that this language works, that he can adequately understand what other speakers and writers mean, and that competent auditors and readers will adequately understand him. In this double process of construing in order to deconstruct he perforce adopts words from the logocentric system; but he does so, he tells us, only "provisionally," or *sous rature,* "under erasure." At times he reminds us of this pervasive procedure by writing a key word but crossing it out, leaving it "legible" yet "effaced"—an ingenious doublespeak, adapted from Heidegger, that enables him to eat his words yet use them too.

Derrida's double-dealing with texts is all-inclusive, for he is aware that his deconstructive reading is self-reflexive; that, although "exorbitant" in intention, it cannot in fact escape the orbit of the linguistic system it deconstructs. "Operating necessarily from the inside," as he says, "the enterprise of deconstruction always in a certain way falls prey to its own work." The invented nonwords which serve as his instruments of deconstruction not only are borrowed from language, but are immediately reappropriated into language in the process of their "iteration" (in Derrida's double sense of being "repeated" and therefore "other" than absolutely self-identical). And the deconstructive reading these instruments effect, he says, is a "production," but "does not leave the text. . . . And what we call production is necessarily a text, the system of a writing and a reading which we know is ordered by its own blind spot." Even as they are put to work on a text, accordingly, the deconstructive instruments deconstruct themselves, as well as the deconstructed translation of the original text which Derrida, as deconstructor, has no option except to write down as still another deconstructible text.

Derrida's critical lexicon, therefore, as Gayatri Spivak, his translator, has said, "is forever on the move." In the consciously vain endeavor to find a point outside the logocentric system on which to plant his deconstructive lever, he leaps from neologism to neologism, as each sinks beneath his feet *en abyme*. His deconstructive enterprise thus is a bootstrap operation, a deliberate exercise in ultimate futility, in a genre of writing he has almost singlehandedly invented—the serious philosophy of the absurd. The most earnest and innovative passages in Derrida are those that, on the surface, seem at best playful and at worst embarrassingly arch—passages that deploy grotesque puns, distorted words, false etymologies, genital analogues, and sexual jokes; which insist on our attending to the shapes of printed letters, play endless tricks with Derrida's own name and with his written signature; or collocate wildly incongruous texts. In such passages—extended to the length of a nonbook in his *Glas*—Derrida is the Zen master of Western philosophy, undertaking to shock us out of our habitual linguistic categories in order to show what cannot be told without reappropriation into those categories: what it is to experience a text not as conveying significance, but as simply a chain of marks vibrating with the free and incessant play of *différance*.

Occasionally, however, Derrida ventures the attempt to tell what can't be told, that is, to make his deconstructive concepts, although "in intimate relationship to the machine whose deconstruction they permit," nonetheless "designate the crevice through which the yet unnameable glimmer beyond the closure can be glimpsed." This glimpse is of an apocalyptic new world which, he prophesies, will be effected by the total deconstruction of our logocentric language-world—"the ineluctable world of the future which proclaims itself at present, beyond the closure of knowledge," hence cannot be described but only "proclaimed, *presented,* as a sort of monstrosity."

To realize the inclusiveness of the new world thus proclaimed, we need to keep in mind what Derrida calls "the axial proposition" in *Of Grammatology,* his basic theoretical work: *Il n'y a pas d'hors-texte,* "there is no outside-the-text." Like all Derrida's key assertions, this sentence is multiple in significance. In one aspect, it says we can't get outside the written text we are reading—it is a closure in which both its seeming author and the people and objects to which the text seems to refer are merely "effects" engendered by the internal action of *différance.* In another aspect, it says that there is nothing in the world that is not itself a text, since we never experience a "thing itself," but only as it is interpreted. In this inclusive rendering, then, all the world's a text, and men and women merely readers—except that the readers, according to Derrida, as "subjects," "egos," "cogitos," are themselves effects which are engendered by an interpretation; so that in the process of undoing texts, we undo our textual selves. The apocalyptic glimpse, it would seem, is of a totally textual universe whose reading is a mode of intertextuality whereby a subject-vortex engages with an object-abyss in infinite regressions of deferred significations.

At the end of his essay "Structure, Sign and Play," Derrida hazards his most sustained trial in the vain attempt to put names to "the as yet unnameable which cannot announce itself except . . . under the formless form, mute, infant, and terrifying, of monstrosity." The annunciation is of "a world of signs without error, without truth, without origin, which is offered to an active interpretation," in which one "plays without security" in a game of "absolute chance, surrendering oneself to *genetic* indeterminacy, the *seminal* chanciness of the trace." Derrida suggests that we at least try to overcome our age-old nostalgia for security, with its hopeless dream of an absolute ground in "full presence, the reassuring foundation, the origin and end of the play," and to assume instead toward this prophecy of deconstruction triumphant the nonchalance of the *Übermensch*, "the Nietzschean *affirmation,* the joyous affirmation of the freeplay of the world." If one cannot share the joy, one can at least acknowledge the vertigo effected by Derrida's vision, yet take some reassurance in the thought that, even in a sign-world of absolute indeterminacy, it will presumably still be possible to achieve the "effect" of telling a hawk from a handsaw, or the "effect," should the need arise, of identifying and warning a companion against an onrushing autobus.

2. READING BETWEEN THE WORDS: STANLEY FISH

Of the deconstructive "interpretation of interpretation" Derrida remarks that it "attempts to pass beyond man and humanism." Stanley Fish represents his theory of reading as a ringing defense against "the dehumanization of meaning" in the "formalism" of current linguistics and stylistics, as well as in structuralist criticism, which raises "the implied antihumanism of other formalist ideologies to a principle." Such theory "is distinguished by what it does away with, and what it does away with are human beings." Fish himself undertakes to explain meaning by reference to "the specifically human activity of reading," proposing as his humanistic "point of departure the interpretive activity (experience) by virtue of which meanings occur." His model for interpretation is that of a reader who confronts the marks on a page and generates meanings by his informed responses to it. In the traditional humanistic view, it will be recalled, there is an author who records what he undertakes to signify, as well as a reader who undertakes to understand what the author has signified.

In terms of this paradigm, Fish's rehumanization of reading is only a half-humanism, for it begins by diminishing, and ends by deleting, the part played by the author. In Fish's later writings, we shall see, the reader becomes the only begetter not only of the text's meanings, but also of the author as the intentional producer of a meaningful text.

Fish differs from other systematic Newreaders in that, instead of setting up a matrix of transformers—a set of revisionary terms—he proposes a "method" or "strategy" which is in fact a set of moves to be enacted by the reader in the process of construing a text. These moves are such as to yield meanings which are always surprising, and often antithetic to, what we have hitherto taken a text to mean. As the key to his method, he proposes that we replace our usual question while reading—"What does this sentence (or word, phrase, work) mean?"—by what he calls "the magic question," namely: "What does this sentence do?" The result of this magic question, if persistently applied by readers, is that it "transforms minds."

In all Fish's expositions of his method, however, "the key word," as he himself remarks, "is, of course, experience"; and what in fact works the transformative magic is his major premise, express and implied, "Reading is an experience." On the common assumption that the term "experience" can be predicated of any perception or process of which one is aware, this assertion seems self-evident, and innocent enough; it can, however, lead to dubious consequences when posed as the premise from which to draw philosophical conclusions. Take, for example, one of Fish's favorite sources of sentences to demonstrate his method of reading, Walter Pater's "Conclusion" to *The Renaissance*. In one virtuoso paragraph, Pater begins by casually positing that the perception of all "external objects" is an "experience," then dissolves the experience of each object "into a group of impressions," translates this into "the impression of the individual in his isolation," and reduces it "to a single sharp impression" in a fleeting moment, bearing traces of "moments gone by"; to this, he asserts, "what is real in our life fines itself down." From the premise that everything we perceive is our experience, Pater has taken us headlong down the metaphysical slope to his conclusion of a solipsism of the specious present—that one can validly assert reality only for one's single sense impression in a fugitive "Now!" The example should make us wary about the consequences for interpretation that Fish deduces from his premise that reading is an experience, and what he proposes as its immediate corollary—that "the meaning of an utterance . . . is the experience—all of it."

One conclusion that Fish draws from this claim that meaning is all of a reader's experience (all the experience, as he qualifies it, of a "competent" or "informed" reader) is that, since the "response includes everything" and is a "total meaning experience," you can't make valid use of the traditional distinction between subject matter and style, "process and product (the how and the what)" in an utterance. Another and related conclusion is that you can't distinguish, within the totality of a declarative sentence, what is being asserted. He excerpts, for example, from Pater's "conclusion" to *The Renaissance:* "That clear perpetual outline of face and limb is but an image of ours." In standard stylistic analysis, he says, this is "a simple declarative of the form X is Y." He then analyzes the experience of reading the sentence in accordance with the question, "What does it do?" and finds that "in fact it is not an assertion at all, although (the promise of) an assertion is one of its components. It is an experience; it occurs; it does something; . . . [and] what it does is what it means." Turn Fish's method of reading back upon his own writing (I find nothing in the method to prevent our doing so) and we get the interesting result that his assertion about Pater's sentence—"In fact it is not an assertion at all . . ."—is in fact not an assertion at all, but only an evolving experience effectuated in a reader.

I want to focus, however, on an important aspect of Fish's strategy for transforming accepted meanings. He supplements his basic equation of meaning with the reader's total response by proposing a start-stop-extrapolate method in reading:

> The basis of the method is a consideration of the *temporal* flow of the reading experience. . . . In an utterance of any length, there is a point at which the reader has taken in only the first

word, and then the second, and then the third, and so on, and the report of what happens to the reader is always a report of what has happened to *that point*. (The report includes the reader's set toward future experiences, but not those experiences.)

What happens at each stopping point, then, is that the reader makes sense of the word or words he has so far read, in large part by surmising what will come next. These surmises may, in the text's sequel, turn out to have been right, but they will often turn out to have been wrong; if so, "the resulting mistakes are part of the experience provided by the author's language, and therefore part of its meaning." Thus "the notion of a mistake, at least as something to be avoided, disappears." And the point at which "the reader hazards interpretive closure" is independent of the "formal units" (such as syntactical phrases or clauses) or "physical features" (such as punctuation or verse lines) in the text written by the author; the method in fact creates what the reader takes to be formal features of the text, "because my model demands (the word is not too strong) perceptual closures and therefore locations at which they occur." In reading the sentence from Pater's *Renaissance,* for example, Fish hazards brief perceptual closures after each of the four opening words: "That clear perpetual outline. . . ."

It is apparent that by Fish's start-stop strategy, a large part of a text's meaning consists of the false surmises that the reader generates in the temporal gaps between the words; and this part, it turns out, constitutes many of Fish's new readings. To cite one instance: Fish presents a three-line passage from Milton's *Lycidas* which describes one consequence of Lycidas's death:

> The willows and the hazel copses green
> Shall now no more be seen,
> Fanning their joyous leaves to thy soft lays.

Although, he tells us, it is *"merely* a coincidence" when a perceptual closure coincides with a formal unit or physical feature such as the end of a verse line, it happens in this instance that the reader's process of making sense "will involve the assumption (and therefore the creation) of a completed assertion after the word 'seen' " at the end of the second line; he will then hazard the interpretation that these trees, in sympathy with the death of Lycidas, "will wither and die (will no more be seen by anyone)." And though this interpretation will be undone "in the act of reading the next line," which reverses it by going on to say that they "will in fact be seen, but they will not be seen by Lycidas," the false surmise remains part of the text's meaning.

I recall a new reading of the closing couplet of *Lycidas* which William York Tindall of Columbia proposed to me many years ago. Tindall suggested the following perceptual closures (I cite the first edition of 1637):

> At last he rose, and twitch'd. His mantle blew.
> To morrow to fresh Woods, and Pastures new.

Those who know Bill Tindall may suspect he was not wholly serious in this proposal. Yet according to Fish's strategy, it is the way a first reader might hazard his perceptual closures. The thought that, even after subsequent correction, this misreading remains an element in the poem's meaning is to me disquieting.

I have myself tried, by way of experiment, to read in accordance with Fish's method. By stern self-discipline, I managed to read word by word and to impose frequent perceptual closures, resisting the compulsion to peek ahead in order to see how the phrases and clauses would work out in the total sentence. And instead of suspending judgment as to meaning until the semantic *Gestalt* was complete, I solicited my invention to anticipate possible meanings and actuated my will to fix on a single one of these possibilities. The result was indeed an evolving sequence of false surmises. I found, however, that the places where I chose to stop rarely coincided with the stopping-places of Stanley Fish, and that my false surmises rarely matched his, especially in the startling degree to which they diverged from what actually followed in the text. What am I to conclude? A possible conjecture is that Fish himself has not always resisted the impulse to peek

ahead; that in fact many of his novel readings are not prospective, but retrospective; that in local instances they are the
result of a predisposition to generate surprising meanings
between the words; and that in large-scale instances, when
he presents a new reading of a total literary work, they are
the result of a predisposition to generate a system of surprising meanings of a coherent sort.

In his earlier writings, despite some wavering as to what is
implied by his use of the term "method," Fish represented
his analyses primarily as a description of what competent
readers in fact do; its aim was simply to make "available to
analytic consciousness the strategies readers perform, independently of whether or not they are aware of having performed them." In his recent theoretical writings, however,
Fish asks us to take his method not as "descriptive" but "pre-
scriptive"; its aim now is to persuade us to give up reading in
our customary way and instead to "read in a new or different
way." Fish's current views are an extreme form of methodological relativism, in which the initial choice of a method of
reading is "arbitrary," and the particular method that the
reader elects creates the text and meanings that he mistakenly thinks he finds. "Interpretive strategies" are procedures
"not for reading (in the conventional sense) but for writing
texts, for constituting their properties and assigning their
intentions." "Formal units," and even "the 'facts' of grammar," are "always a function of the interpretive will one brings
to bear; they are not 'in' the text." It turns out, indeed, that
there is nothing either inside or outside the text except what
our elected strategy brings into being, for "everyone is continually executing interpretive strategies and in that act constituting texts, intentions, speakers, and authors." Starting with
the premise that the meaning is all of a reader's experience
of a text, we have plunged down the metaphysical slope to
the conclusion that each reader's optional strategy, by determining his responsive experience, creates everything but the
marks on the page, including the author whose intentional
verbal acts, we had mistakenly assumed, effectuate the text
as meaningful discourse.

From this position Fish draws the consequence that, since
all reading strategies are self-confirming, there is no "right

reading" of any part of a text; there are only agreements among readers who belong to an "interpretive community" which happens to share the same strategy. And with his usual acumen, Fish acknowledges that the reading strategy he himself proposes is no less "arbitrary" in its adoption and therefore no less a "fiction" than alternative ways of reading; his justification for urging it upon us is that it is "a superior fiction." It is superior because it is "more coherent" in the relation of its practice to its principles, and because "it is also creative." Insistence on a "right reading" and "the real text" are

> the fictions of formalism, and as fictions they have the disadvantage of being confining. My fiction is liberating. It relieves me of the obligation to be right (a standard that simply drops out) and demands only that I be interesting (a standard that can be met without any reference at all to an illusory objectivity). Rather than restoring or recovering texts, I am in the business of making texts and of teaching others to make them by adding to their repertoire of strategies.

In these claims Fish does his own critical practice less than justice. Many of his close readings of literary texts effect in his readers a shock of recognition which is the sign that they are not merely interesting, but that they are right. In such readings, however, he escapes his own theory and reads as other competent readers do, only more expertly than many of us; his orientation to the actual process of reading serves in these instances to sensitize him to nuances effected by the author's choice and order of words that we have hitherto missed. And even when, in conformity with his stated strategy, Fish creates meanings by reading between the words, the new readings are often, as he claims, interesting. They are interesting because they are bravura critical performances by a learned, resourceful, and witty intelligence, and not least, because the new readings never entirely depart from implicit reliance on the old way of reading texts.

I remain unpersuaded, therefore, that the hermeneutic circle is inescapably, as Fish represents it, a vicious circle—a closed interplay between a reader's arbitrary strategy and his interpretive findings. I persist in the assurance that a competent reader of Milton, for example, develops an expertise in reading his sentences in adequate accordance both with Milton's linguistic usage and with the strategy of reading that Milton himself deployed, and assumed that his readers would deploy. This expertise is not an arbitrary strategy—though it remains continuously open to correction and refinement—for it has a sufficient warrant in evidence that we tacitly accumulate in a lifetime of speaking, writing, and reading English, of reading English literature, of reading Milton's contemporaries, and of reading Milton himself. Those who share this assurance set themselves to read Milton's text, not as a pretext for a creative adventure in liberated interpretation, but in order to understand what it is that Milton meant, and meant us to understand. For our prepossession is that, no matter how interesting a critic's created text of Milton may be, it will be less interesting than the text that Milton himself wrote for his fit readers though few.

3. THE SCENE OF LITERATURE: HAROLD BLOOM

Harold Bloom's theory of reading and writing literature centers on the area that Derrida and the structuralists call "intertextuality." Bloom, however, employs the traditional term "influence," and presents his theory in opposition against "the antihumanistic plain dreariness of all those developments in European criticism that have yet to demonstrate that they can aid in reading any one poem by any poet whatsoever." "Poems," he affirms, "are written by men"; and against "the partisans of *writing* . . . like Derrida and Foucault who imply . . . that language by itself writes the poem and thinks," he insists that only "the human writes, the human thinks." Unlike Stanley Fish, then, Bloom restores the human writer as well as reader to an effective role in the literary transaction. But if Fish's theory is a half-humanism, Bloom's is all-too-human, for it screens out from both the writing and reading of "strong"

literature all motives except self-concern and all compunction about giving free rein to one's will to power:

> the living labyrinth of literature is built upon the ruin of every
> impulse most generous in us. So apparently it is and must
> be—we are wrong to have founded a humanism directly upon
> literature itself, and the phrase "humane letters" is an oxy-
> moron. . . . The strong imagination comes to its painful birth
> through savagery and misrepresentation.

Like many recent critics, Bloom posits a great divide in
literary history and locates it in the seventeenth century; his
innovation is to account for this division as the change from
the relative creative nonchalance of a Homer, Dante, or
Shakespeare in "the giant age before the flood" to the acute
anxiety of influence suffered by all but a very few poets since
the Enlightenment. A modern, and therefore "belated," poet
awakens to his calling when irresistibly seized upon by one or
more poems of a precursor or father-poet, yet experiences
that seizure as an intolerable incursion into his imaginative
life-space. The response of the belated writer is to defend
himself against the parent-poem by distorting it drastically in
the process of reading it; but he cannot escape the precursor,
for he inevitably embodies its distorted form into his own
attempt at an absolutely original poem.

Bloom's theory, as he points out, is a revision for literary
criticism of what Freud sardonically called "the Family
Romance." The relation of reader and poet to his parent-
precursor, as in Freud's Oedipal relationship, is ambivalent,
compounded of love and hate; but in Bloom's detailed
descriptions of reading and writing, love enters only to weaken
the result of the process, while the aspect of hate, jealousy,
and fear is alone given a systematic and creative role to perform. This role is to deploy, with unconscious cunning, a set
of defensive tactics, "the revisionary ratios," which are in fact
aggressive acts designed to "malform" the precursor in the
attempt to disestablish its "priority" over the latecomer, both
in time and in creative strength. "Every act of reading is . . .
defensive, and as defense it makes of interpretation a necessary misprision. . . . Reading is therefore misprision—or mis-

reading." And since "every poem is a misinterpretation of a parent poem," he concludes that "the meaning of a poem can only be another poem." "There are no right readings"; the sole alternative is between "weak mis-readings and strong mis-readings." A weak misreading attempts, although unavailingly, to get at what a text really means in itself; it is the product of an inhibiting timidity, or at best of an excess of "generosity" toward the parent-poet. A misreading is strong, hence creative and valuable, in proportion to the boldness with which the reader's emotional compulsions are licensed to do violence to the text that he strives to overcome.

It is sometimes argued against Bloom's theory that his claim, "all reading is misreading," is incoherent, on the ground that we cannot know that a text has been misread unless we know what it is to read it correctly. This argument overlooks an interesting feature of Bloom's theory, that is, its quasi-Kantian frame of reference. At times Bloom's idiom corresponds closely enough to Kant's to qualify, in Bloom's terms, as a "deliberate misprision" of Kant's epistemology. Terms that recur on almost every page in which Bloom discusses misreading are "necessity," "necessary," "necessarily," "must be." Such terms are to be taken seriously; they signify an *a priori* necessity. In Bloom's theory, that is, the compulsive revisionary ratios through which we experience a poem correspond, in Kant's philosophy, to the cognitive forms of space, time, and the categories that the mind inescapably imposes on all its experience of the world. Consequently Bloom's reader can only know the phenomenal poem constituted by his own revisionary categories; he cannot possibly get outside these categories to know the noumenal *Ding an sich*, or what Bloom calls "the poem-in-itself" or the "poem-as-such."

But Bloom's aim, he says, is not simply to propose "another new poetics," but to establish and convert us to "a newer and starker way of reading poems." The product of this new way of reading is "an antithetical practical criticism, as opposed to all the primary criticisms now in vogue."

Let us give up the failed enterprise of seeking to "understand" any single poem as an entity in itself. Let us pursue instead the quest of learning to read any poem as its poet's

deliberate misinterpretation, *as a poet,* of a precursor poem or
of poetry in general.

Bloom therefore, like Derrida and Fish, proposes a way of
reading a text that will displace the meanings that "primary,"
or traditional readers have hitherto found in it. As applied
in his reading, Bloom's revisionary ratios in effect function
as an inventory of transformers for translating accepted
meanings into new meanings; he conveniently presents a one-
page table of his transformers which he calls "The Map of
Misprision." And such is the virtuosity of these devices that
they cannot fail to effect Bloom's antithetic meanings; in his
own repeated assertion, "It must be so."

In this analysis I deliberately enact the role that Bloom, in
a phrase from Blake, calls "the Idiot Questioner," whose
presence as an aspect of his own mind Bloom recognizes but
sternly represses. (In the present instance "the Idiot Questioner" can be translated as a stolid inquirer into the credentials of a critic's interpretive procedures.) Pursuing such an
inquiry, I note that Bloom, in his tetralogy of books on the
theory and practice of antithetic criticism, sets up six revisionary ratios which he names "clinamen," "tessera," "ken-
osis," and so on. He goes on to assimilate each of these ratios
to a variety of other reinterpretive devices—to a Freudian
defense-mechanism; to a concept of the Hebrew Kabbalists;
to one of the rhetorical tropes such as synecdoche, hyperbole, metaphor; and to a recurrent type of poetic imagery.
These amalgamated transformers are not only versatile
enough to establish each of Bloom's new readings, but also
antithetical enough to convert any possible counterevidence
into a confirmation of his own reading.

Take, for example, the Freudian mechanisms of defense—
which Bloom calls "the clearest analogues I have found for
the revisionary ratios"—as he applies them to interpret any
poem as a distorted version of a precursor-poem. If the belated
poem patently echoes the parent-poem, that counts as evidence for the new reading; although, Bloom asserts, "only
weak poems, or the weaker elements in strong poems, immediately echo precursor poems, or directly allude to them." If
the later poem doesn't contain such "verbal reminders," that

counts too, on the basis of the mechanism of repression—the belated poet's anxiety of influence has been strong enough to repress all reference to his predecessor. And if the belated poem differs radically from its proposed precursor, that counts even more decisively, on the basis of the mechanism of "reaction formation"—the poet's anxiety was so intense as to distort the precursor into its seeming opposite. This power of the negative to turn itself into a stronger positive manifests itself frequently in Bloom's applied criticism. For example, the opening verse paragraph of Tennyson's *Tithonus* has traditionally been read as expressing the aged but immortal protagonist's longing for death. Bloom, however, reads it antithetically as a revision, or

> swerve away from the naturalistic affirmations of Words-worth and of Keats. What is absent in these opening lines is simply all of nature; what is present is the withered Tithonus. As Tennyson's reaction-formation against his precursors' stance, these lines are a rhetorical irony, denying what they desire, the divination of a poetic survival into strength.

Perhaps so; but it will be noted that the reaction-transformer charters the antithetic critic to speak without fear of contradiction, while stranding his Questioner in a no-win position.

Bloom's theory, like that of other Newreaders, is self-referential, for he does not exempt his own interpretations from the assertion that all readings are misreadings. In his recent books on Yeats and Stevens, he often writes brilliant critiques that compel assent from a "primary" critic like myself. The extent of Bloom's own claim for these readings, however, is that they are strong misreadings, in that they do violence to the texts they address, by virtue of his surrender to his need for autonomy and to his anxieties of the influence exerted on him by his critical precursors. And in lieu of any possible criterion of rightness, such readings can be valuable only to the degree that they are "creative or interesting misreadings." By their strength, he says, such readings will provoke his critical successors to react by their own defensive misreadings, and so take their place within the unending accumulation of misreadings of misreadings that constitute the history both of poetry and of criticism, at least since the Enlightenment.

While acknowledging that his theory "may ask to be judged, as argument," Bloom also insists that "a theory *of* poetry must belong *to* poetry, must *be* poetry" and presents his work as "one reader's critical vision" bodied forth in "a severe poem." Let me drop my role as Idiot Questioner of Bloom's evidential procedures to read him in this alternative way, as a prose-poet who expresses a founding vision of the Scene of Literature. In the main, this has been traditionally conceived as a republic of equals composed, in Wordsworth's phrase, of "the mighty living and the mighty dead" whose poetry, as Shelley said, "is the record of the best and happiest moments of the happiest and best minds." In Bloom's bleak re-vision, the Scene of Literature becomes the arena of a savage war for *Lebensraum* waged by the living poet against the oppressive and ever-present dead—a parricidal war, in which each newcomer, in his need to be self-begotten and self-sufficient, undertakes with unconscious cunning to mutilate, murder, and devour his poetic father. The poet's prime compulsions are like those of the Freudian Id, which demands no less than everything at once and is incapable of recognizing any constraints on its satisfactions by moral compunction, logical incompatibility, or empirical impossibility. And the poetic self remains forever fixed at the Oedipal stage of development; for Bloom explicitly denies to the poet "as poet" the Freudian mechanism of sublimation, which allows for the substitution, in satisfying our primordial desires, of higher for lower goals and so makes possible the growth from the infantile stage of total self-concern to the mature recognition of reciprocity with other selves. The war of which each poem is a battleground is ultimately futile, not only because every poet is inescapably fathered by precursors but also because, according to Bloom, his will to priority over his precursors is, in deep psychic fact, a defense against acknowledging his own human mortality. The conflict, furthermore, is doomed to terminate in the death of poetry itself, for the population of strong poets will soon usurp so much of the available living-space that even the illusion of creative originality will no longer be possible.

In Bloom's own idiom of rhetorical tropes, one can say of

his critical poem about poetry that it is a sustained synecdoche which puts a part for the whole. By this device, and by his subsidiary device of strong hyperbole, Bloom compels us to face up to aspects of the motivation to write and misread poems—self-assertiveness, lust for power and precedence, malice, envy, revenge—which canonical critics have largely ignored. To those of us who yield ourselves to Bloom's dark and powerful eloquence, the Scene of Literature will never look the same again; such a result is probably the most that any writer compelled by an antithetical vision can hope to achieve. But the part is not the whole. What Bloom's point of vantage cannot take into account is the great diversity of motives for writing poetry, and in the products of that writing, the abundance of subject matters, characters, genres, and styles, and the range of the passions expressed and represented, from brutality and terror and anguish, indeed, to gaiety, joy, and sometimes sheer fun. In sum, what Bloom's tragic vision of the literary scene systematically omits is almost everything that has hitherto been recognized to constitute the realm of literature.

On the basis of Bloom's critical premises, I am of course open to the retort that I have misread both his criticism and our heritage of literary texts. But knowing from experience Bloom's geniality to his own critical precursors, I am confident that he will attribute my misreading to an amiable weakness—to my fallacy, that is, of misplaced benevolence.

4. NEWREADING AND OLD NORMS

I shall conclude by considering briefly my third question: What makes a text so vulnerable to the diverse things that Newreaders do with it? The chief reason is that our use and understanding of language is not a science but a practice. That is, what we call "knowing a language" is not a matter of knowing that or knowing why, but of knowing how, of having acquired a skill. We are born into a community of speakers and writers who have already acquired this skill, and we in turn acquire it by interplay with these others, in which we learn how to say what we mean and how to understand what others have said by a continuous process of self-correction and refinement, based on what are often very subtle indications of when and in what way we have gone wrong.

The successful practice of language depends on our mastery of linguistic uniformities that we call conventions, or norms, or rules. Linguistic rules, however, differ radically from the rules of chess or of a card game, to which they are often compared. The rules that constitute these games are stipulated in an authoritative code to which we can refer in order to resolve disputes. The use and understanding of language, on the other hand, depends on tacit consensual regularities which are multiplex and fluid; except in very gross ways, these regularities are uncodified, and probably uncodifiable. In our practice, therefore, we must rely not on rules, but on linguistic tact—a tact that is the emergent result of all our previous experience with speaking, hearing, writing, and reading the language.

Stanley Fish seems to me right in his claim that the linguistic meanings we find in a text are relative to the interpretive strategy we employ, and that agreement about meanings depends on membership in a community which shares an interpretive strategy. But if we set out not to create meanings, but to understand what the sequence of sentences in a literary work mean, then we have no choice except to read according to the linguistic strategy the author of the work employed, and expected us to employ. We are capable of doing so, because an immense store of cumulative evidence provides assurance that the authors of literary texts belonged to the linguistic community into which we were later born, and so shared our skill, and the consensual regularities on which that skill depends, with some divergencies—which we have a variety of clues for detecting—which are the result both of the slow change of communal regularities in time and of the limited innovations which can be introduced by the individual author.

When a Newreader, on the basis of his contrived interpretive strategy, asserts that a passage means something radically different from what it has been taken to mean, or else that it means nothing in particular, we lack codified criteria to which we can appeal against the new interpretation; in the last analysis, we can only appeal to our linguistic tact, as supported by the agreement of readers who share that tact. But such an appeal has no probative weight for a reader who has opted out of playing the game of language according to its constitutive regularities; nor is the application of our own inherited practice verifiable by any proof outside its sustainedly coherent working. All we can do is to point out to the Newreader what he already knows—that he is playing a double game, introducing his own interpretive strategy when reading someone else's text, but tacitly relying on communal norms when undertaking to communicate the methods and results of his interpretations to his own readers.

We can't claim that the Newreader's strategy doesn't work, for each of these ways of doing things to texts indubitably works. Allowed his own premises and conversion procedures, Derrida is able to deconstruct any text into a suspension of numberless undecidable significations, Fish can make it the occasion for a creative adventure in false surmises, and Bloom can read it as a perverse distortion of any chosen precursor-text. These substitute strategies in fact have an advantage which is a principal cause of their appeal to students of literature. Our inherited strategy, although it has shown that it can persistently discover new meanings even in a classic text, must operate always under the constraint of communal regularities of usage. Each new strategy, on the other hand, is a discovery procedure which guarantees new meanings. It thus provides freshness of sensation in reading old and familiar texts—at least until we learn to anticipate the limited kind of new meanings it is capable of generating; it also makes it easy for any critical follower to say new and exciting things about a literary work that has been again and again discussed. But we purchase this advantage at a cost, and ultimately the choice between a radical Newreading and the old way of reading is a matter of cultural cost-accounting. We gain a guaranteed novelty, of a kind that makes any text directly relevant to current interests and concerns. What we lose is access to the

inexhaustible variety of literature as determinably meaningful texts by, for, and about human beings, as well as access to
the enlightening things that have been written about such
texts by the humanists and critics who were our precursors,
from Aristotle to Lionel Trilling.

Construing and Deconstructing

THIS AGE of critical discourse is the best of times or it is the worst of times, depending on one's point of view; but there is no denying that it is a very diverse and lively time. Never have the presuppositions and procedures of literary criticism been put so drastically into question, and never have we been presented with such radical alternatives for conceiving and making sense of literary texts. Among the competing theories of the last several decades we find reader-response criticism (itself divisible into a variety of subspecies), reception criticism, anxiety-of-influence criticism, structuralist criticism, semiotic criticism, and—most ominous to many traditional ears—deconstructive criticism. It was not many years ago that announcements of jobs for professors of literature began to be supplemented by requests for professors of literary criticism. Now we find increasing requests for professors of the theory of criticism—professors, that is, whose profession is metacriticism.

The new theories are diverse in principles and procedures, but in their radical forms they converge in claims that have evoked indignation from many traditional critics. One claim is that it is impossible even to identify anything called "literature" by establishing boundaries, or specifying features, which set it off from other forms of writing. Another and related claim is that criticism is in no way attendant upon or subordinate in function to the literature that, over the centuries since Aristotle, critics have set themselves to classify, analyze, and elucidate; criticism, it is now often said, is a mode of writing that does not discover, but "produces," the meanings of the texts that it engages, hence is equally entitled to be "creative." Most dismaying to traditionalists is the claim, diversely argued, that no text, either in its component passages or as an entity, has a determinable meaning and therefore that there is no right way to interpret it; all attempts to read a text are doomed to be misreadings.

Among these innovations in literary theory and practice, the signs are that deconstruction, based primarily on writings of Jacques Derrida since the late 1960s, will be predominant. Within the last ten years deconstructive criticism has generated a flood of books and articles which exemplify it, describe it, attack it, or defend it; the articles appear not only in several journals devoted primarily to deconstruction, but increasingly in the most staid of publications, including the alleged stronghold of the critical establishment, *PMLA*. Its focal center in America has been Yale University, whose faculty includes those exponents whom their colleague, Geoffrey Hartman, has genially labeled "boa deconstructors"— especially Derrida himself, Paul de Man, and J. Hillis Miller. Radiating from that center, the movement has captivated, in varying degree, a number of younger teachers of literature and many among the brightest of graduate students, including some who have written their theses under my direction. By J. S. Mill's maxim that the opinions of bright people between twenty and thirty years of age is the best index to the intellectual tendencies of the next era, it seems probable that the heritage of deconstruction will be prominent in literary criticism for some time to come.

I shall try to locate the deconstructive enterprise on the map of literary theory by sketching its overlap with, as well as its radical departures from, traditional treatments of literature. It is impossible to do so except from some point of view. I shall try to make allowances for mine, which is that of a traditionalist who has staked whatever he has taught or written about literature, and about literary and intellectual history, on the confidence that he has been able to interpret the textual passages he cited with a determinacy and an accuracy sufficient to the purpose at hand.

1

One must approach deconstructive literary criticism by way of the writings of Jacques Derrida, the founder, namer, and prime exemplar of deconstruction-in-general. To be brief about so protean, oblique, and tactically agile a writer cannot escape being selective and reductive. It seems fair to say, however, that in terms of the traditional demarcations among disciplines, Derrida (though he has commented on some literary texts) is to be accounted a philosopher, not a literary critic, and that his writings undertake to reveal the foundations presupposed by all precedent Western philosophies and ways of thinking, to "undermine" or "subvert" these foundations by showing that they are illusions engendered by desire for an impossible certainty and security, and to show the consequences for writing and thinking when their supposed foundations are thus undermined.

Some commentators on Derrida have remarked in passing that Derrida's conclusions resemble the skeptical conclusions of David Hume. I want to pursue this comparison; not, however, in order to show that, despite his antimetaphysical stance, Derrida ends in the classical metaphysical position called radical skepticism, but in order to bring out some interesting analogues between the procedures of these two very diverse thinkers. These analogues will highlight aspects of Derrida's dealings with language, emulated by some of his followers in literary criticism, which are inadequately stressed, both by proponents who assert that Derrida has totally revolutionized the way we must from now on read texts and by opponents who assert that Derrida cancels all criteria of valid interpretation, in an anarchical surrender to textual "freeplay."

We can parallel three moments in the overall procedures of Hume and Derrida:

(1) The point of departure in Hume's *Treatise of Human*

Nature is that "nothing is ever really present with the mind but its perceptions," which consist of "impressions" that are "immediately present to our consciousness" and the "ideas" that are the fainter replica of these impressions.[1] Beginning with these as the sole givens which can be known with certainty, Hume proceeds to show that, in all reasoning and knowledge concerning "matters of fact," we can never get outside the sense-impressions which were his starting point, nor establish the certainty of any connections between the single sense-impressions which constitute immediate awareness. He thus disintegrates all grounds for certain knowledge about the identity of any two impressions separated in time, about the existence of material objects in an external world, about the relation of cause and effect between any two occurrences, and about the reality even of "personal identity" or a conscious "self." All these entities and relations, Hume contends, since they cannot be established by demonstrative reasoning from his premised single impressions, are the products of the "imagination" and of "custom," and have the status not of knowledge but merely of "fallacies," "fictions," or "illusions."

To Derrida's way of thinking, Hume's starting point in the *hic et nunc* of a nonmediated, hence certainly known perception would be a classic example of the way Western philosophy, in all its forms, is based on a "presence," or indubitable founding element independent of language; so that Hume's skeptical conclusions from this given, to Derrida, would be merely a negative counterpart of the cognitive dogmatism that it challenges. As Derrida has put it: "Perception is precisely a concept, a concept of an intuition or of a given originating from the thing itself, present itself in its meaning, independently from language, from the system of reference."[2] Hence, he declares, "I don't believe that anything like perception exists." Instead of positing a foundational given, Derrida establishes a point of view. "The axial proposition of this essay," he declares in *Of Grammatology*, is "that there is nothing outside the text" ["*il n'y a rien hors du texte*," or alternatively, "*il n'y a pas de hors-texte*"[3]]. This assertion is not offered either as the point of departure or as the result of a philosophical demonstration. It functions as an announcement of where Derrida takes his stand, and that is within the workings of language itself, in order to show us what standard philosophical problems, premises, and intellection look like when viewed from this stance and point of vantage. In many of its consequences, nonetheless, Derrida's counterphilosophical linguistic ploy converges with those of Hume's skeptical philosophy. Hume, premising only single impressions, showed that there is no way to establish identity or causal connections among impressions, nor to match impressions to material objects, a world, or a self to which we have access independently of impressions. Derrida, taking his stand within language, disperses the seemingly determinate meanings of terms such as "identity," "cause," "material objects," "the external world," "the self," and shows that there is no way to match such terms to a reality to which we have access independently of the language we use to represent it.

Derrida's way of carrying out his project is to offer "readings" of passages in Western thinkers, from Plato to the ordinary-language philosopher John Austin, in order to reveal their common "logocentrism." This term denominates his claim that Western philosophical discourse—and indeed all modes of discourse, since none can escape the use of terms whose significance is "sedimented" by their role in the history of philosophy—is predicated on the existence of a logos. The logos is Derrida's overall term for an absolute, or foundation, or ground, whose full, self-certifying "presence" is assumed to be given in a direct cognitive encounter which is itself unconditioned by the linguistic system that incorporates it, yet relies on it as a foundation. Such a presence, for example, is sometimes posited as an immediately known intention or state of consciousness in a speaker while speaking, or as an essence, or as a Platonic Form accessible to mental vision, or as a referent known in its own being; in any case, it constitutes a "transcendental signified" which, though inevitably represented by a signifier, is regarded as an unmediated something that is unaffected by the signifying system which represents it.

Derrida's readings are oriented toward showing that any philosophical text can be shown to rely on a ground which is indispensable to its argument, its references, and its conclusions, but turns out to be itself groundless, hence suspended over an "abyss." Derrida's view, furthermore, is that a logos-centered philosophy is a voice-centered philosophy. In consequence, one of his characteristic procedures, often misunderstood, is to overcome Western "phonocentrism" (the reliance on the speaking voice as the linguistic model) by positing an admittedly nonexisting "arche-écriture," or "writing-in-general." By asserting the "priority" of writing (in the sense of writing-in-general) both to speech and to writing (in the ordinary sense of putting words on paper), Derrida is not claiming that the invention of writing preceded speech in history; he is deploying a device designed to get us to substitute for the philosophical idiom of speaking the alternative idiom of writing, in which we are less prone to the illusion, as he conceives it, that a speaker in the presence of a listener knows what he means independently of the words in which he expresses it, or that he establishes the meaning of what he says to the listener by communicating his unmediated intention in uttering it.

From his elected stance within language, Derrida replaces the view that language developed by a matching of words to the given world by positing an internal linguistic principle of "*différance*." This term, like "writing-in-general," is offered as a heuristic fiction, in which the *a* in the written form, Derrida tells us, indicates the conflation of the incompatible senses of the French word *différer* as "to differ" and "to defer." In accordance with the insight of the linguist Saussure that both a signifier and what it signifies are constituted not by their inherent features, but by a network of "differences" from other signifiers and signifieds, Derrida posits *différance* as generating internally the differential verbal signs, while deferring the presence of what they signify through endless substitutions of signifiers whose ultimate arrest in a determinate and stable meaning or reference never is, but is always about to be. For according to Derrida, in the lack of any possible "transcendental," or extralinguistic referent unconditioned by the differential economy of language, there is no stopping the play of meanings. In one of Derrida's formulations: "The absence of the transcendental signified extends the domain and the interplay of signification *ad infinitum*."[4]

Or, in another of his punning, deliberately contrarious terms, which in this case exploits a double etymology, any text, under radical inquisition, "disseminates": it sows its seed, and in that process loses its seeming semantic determinacy, by scattering into a regress which inevitably involves an "aporia"—that is, a deadlock between incompatible meanings which are "undecidable," in that we lack any certain ground for choosing between them.

(2) Having reached his skeptical conclusions, Hume finds himself, he tells us, in a condition of "melancholy" and "despair," "affrighted and confounded with that forelorn solitude, in which I am plac'd in my philosophy."[5] Hume's solitude is beyond solipsism, for the solipsist is certain at least of the reality of his conscious self, while Hume is reduced to knowing only present perceptions which yield no implication of a conscious self that knows. From this dire condition he finds himself rescued not by further reasoning, but by the peremptory intrusion of a life-force—"an absolute and uncontrollable necessity" that he calls "nature." "Nature herself . . . cures me of this philosophical melancholy and delirium. . . . I dine, I play a game of back-gammon, I converse, and am merry with friends; and when after three or four hours' amusement, I wou'd return to these speculations, they appear so cold, and strain'd, and ridiculous, that I cannot find in my heart to enter into them any farther." Hume finds that he cannot live in accordance with his skeptical philosophy; yet his impulse to philosophical reasoning is no less compelling than his instinct to participate in human society in accordance with its shared beliefs. As a consequence, Hume finds himself living (and recommends that others should also live) a double life: the life of human society, and the life of the reason that disintegrates all the beliefs on which social life is based into fictions and illusions: "Here then I find myself absolutely and necessarily determin'd to live, and talk, and act like other people in the common affairs of life." Yet "in all the incidents of life we ought still to preserve our skepticism. If we believe, that fire warms, or water refreshes, 'tis only because it costs us too much pains to think otherwise."[6]

Derrida's conduct of language is analogous to Hume's double mode of necessarily continuing to live in accordance with shared beliefs that he is rationally compelled to subvert. Derrida in fact describes the deconstructive enterprise as a deliberate and sustained duplexity—"a double gesture, a double science, a double writing."[7] And in reading texts there is a double procedure, "two interpretations of interpretation," which play a simultaneous role in life, and which, though irreconcilable, permit no option between them:

> There are more than enough indications today to suggest we might perceive that these two interpretations of interpretation—which are absolutely irreconcilable even if we live them simultaneously [*même si nous les vivons simultanément*] and reconcile them in an obscure economy—together share the field which we call, in such a problematic fashion, the human sciences.
>
> For my part, although these two interpretations must acknowledge and accentuate their difference and define their irreducibility, I do not believe that today there is any question of *choosing*. . . .[8]

We mistake Derrida's own procedure if we overlook the fact that his deconstructive readings of philosophical passages involve both these interpretive modes and consist of a deliberate double-reading—we may denominate them as reading$_1$ and reading$_2$—which are distinguishable, even if they are irreconcilable, sometimes concurrent, and always interdependent. Reading$_1$ finds a passage "lisible" and understandable, and makes out, according to a procedure that Derrida shares with common readers, the determinate meanings of the sentences he cites. (For convenience let us say that in reading$_1$ he *construes* the passage.) Reading$_2$, which he calls a "critical reading," or an "active interpretation," goes on to disseminate the meanings it has already construed.

Derrida accounts for the possibility of reading$_1$ by attributing to *différance* the production of the "effect" in language of a fundamental presence—not a real presence, or freestanding existent, but one that is simply a "function" of the differential play—as well as the production of all the other "effects" on which the common practice of reading depends, including the "effects" of a conscious intention, of a specific speech act, and of a determinate meaning or reference.[9] In this way, he explains, "the metaphysical text is *understood;* it is still readable, and remains to be read."[10] And this standard reading and understanding, though only an initial "stage," is indispensable to the process of deconstruction.

For example: most of Derrida's *Of Grammatology* presents readings of selected passages from Rousseau's *Essay on the Origin of Language*. In great part Derrida, with no lack of assurance, construes these passages as conveying determinate meanings, with tacit confidence that his own readers will assent to his construal—a confidence I find well founded, because Derrida is an uncommonly proficient and scrupulous reader of texts in the standard fashion. In this process, he attributes the writing of the *Essay* to an individual named "Rousseau," and has no hesitation in specifying what "Rousseau affirms . . . unambiguously," or what "Rousseau says . . . clearly in the *Essay*" and "also invariably says . . . elsewhere" (pp. 173, 184), nor in attributing what the text says to Rousseau's "intention" to say it, or to what it is that "Rousseau wishes to say." In the course of this reading $_1$, Derrida paraphrases Rousseau's assertions and identifies recurrent "themes" in variant phrasings of the same assertion (p. 195; see also p. 133); undertakes to establish the time of his life in which Rousseau wrote the *Essay* on the basis of two kinds of evidence, which he describes as either "internal" or "external" to the *Essay* itself (pp. 171, 192); and, though he detects "massive borrowings" in the *Essay* from earlier writers, affirms the essential "originality" of Rousseau as a theorist of language (pp. 98, 272, 281). Derrida also accepts as accurate some interpretations of Rousseau's text by earlier commentators, but corrects others which he describes, politely, as the result of "hasty reading" (pp. 189, 243). And he is able to find Rousseau's text "readable" in this fashion because the language that Derrida has inherited, despite some historical changes, is one that he possesses in common with Rousseau; as Derrida puts it: "Rousseau drew upon a language that was already there—and which is found to be somewhat our own, thus assuring us a certain minimum readability of French literature" (p. 160).

Thus far, Derrida's reading proceeds in a way that is congruent with the theories of many current philosophers that communication depends on our inheritance of a shared language and shared linguistic practices or conventions, and that when, by applying the practice we share with a writer, we have recognized what he intended to say, then we have understood him correctly. Many of these philosophers also agree with Derrida that there is no extralinguistic, nonconventional foundation for our linguistic practice which certifies its rules and their application and guarantees the correctness of a reader's interpretation; in justifying an interpretation, when we have exhausted appeals to shared, though contingent, linguistic and social conventions, in Wittgenstein's phrase, "the spade turns." Derrida's radical innovation does not, therefore, consist in his claim that no such foundation exists, but in his further claim that such a foundation, though nonexistent, is nevertheless indispensable, and that in its absence there is no stopping the continuing dissemination of construed meanings into undecidability.

In accordance with this view, Derrida designates his reading $_i$—the determinate construal of the "legibility" of passages in Rousseau—as no more than a "strategic" phase which, though indispensable, remains "provisional" to a further "critical," or deconstructive reading (pp. 99, 149). One of Derrida's moves in this critical reading is to identify strata, or "strands" in Rousseau's text which, when read determinately, turn out to be mutually contradictory (pp. 200, 237, 240, 245). A number of earlier commentators, of course, have found Rousseau's linguistic and social theories to be incoherent or contradictory, but have regarded this feature as a logical fault or else as assimilable to an overall direction of his thinking. Derrida, however, regards such self-contradictions not as logical mistakes which Rousseau could have avoided, but as inescapable features not only in Rousseau's text but in all Western texts, since all rely on a fixed logocentric ground yet are purely conventional and differential in their economy. In his critical "subreading" of Rousseau's texts, Derrida asserts that their determinate reading always leaves an inescapable and ungovernable "excess" or "surplus" of signification, which is both the index and the result of the fact that "the writer writes *in* a language and *in* a logic whose proper system, laws, and life his discourse by definition cannot dominate absolutely"; a critical reading must aim at detecting the "relationship, unperceived by the writer, between what he commands and what he does not command" (p. 158). Derrida's reading $_2$ of Rousseau thus repeatedly uncovers an opposition of meanings between what Rousseau "wishes to say" and what "he says without wishing to say it," or between what Rousseau "declares" and what the text "describes" without Rousseau's wishing to say it (pp. 200, 229, 238). What Rousseau declares and wishes to say is what is construed by a standard reading; what the text ungovernably goes on, unbeknownst to the writer, to say is what gets disclosed by a deeper deconstructive reading.

Derrida's commentary on John Austin, an ordinary-language philosopher who disclaims any extralinguistic foundation for the functioning of language, couches Derrida's views in terms which bring them closer to the idiom familiar to Anglo-American philosophers. In discussing Austin's theory of a performative speech-act, Derrida points out that all words and verbal sequences are "iterable," or repeatable in diverse linguistic and social circumstances, with a consequent diversity both in the nature of the speech-act and the signification of its words. Derrida construes Austin to make the claim that the total verbal and social context, in a clear case, establishes for certain the nature and communicative success of a speech-act. Derrida's counterclaim is that we never find an absolutely clear case, in that we can never know for certain that all the necessary and sufficient conditions for determining a specific and successful performative have in fact been satisfied. (In Derrida's parlance, no context is ever "saturated," so as to make it "entirely certain," or "exhaustively determinable," which is "the sense required by Austin."[11]) He stresses especially Austin's reiterated references to the intention of the speaker—necessary, for example, in order to determine a speaker's sincerity and seriousness—as a condition for the success of a speech-act. The speaker's intention, Derrida asserts, is a condition whose fulfillment neither the speaker nor his auditor can know with certainty and one that cannot control or "master" the play of meaning. Derrida's conclusion is that there can be no "communication," as he puts it,

"that is unique, univocal, rigorously controllable, and trans-
mittable," and no way of achieving certainty about the "purity,"
in the sense of "the absolutely singular uniqueness of a speech
act."[12] To this conclusion Austin himself would surely agree.
Language, as a shared conventional practice, cannot provide
grounds for absolute certainty in communication; even in the
clearest case, it always remains possible that we have got an
interpretation wrong. Language nonetheless is adequate for
communicating determinate meanings, in that the shared
regularities of that practice can provide, in particular circumstances, a warranted assurance about what someone has
undertaken to say. For Derrida, however, it is a matter of all-
or-nothing; there is no intermediate position on which a
determinate interpretation can rest, for if no meanings are
absolutely certain and stable, then all meanings are unstable
and undecidable. "Semantic communication," or the successful achievement of a performative or other speech-act, is
indeed an "effect"; but it is, he says, "only an effect," and as
such incapable of arresting the dispersal of signification in "a
dissemination irreducible to *polysemy*."[13]

In the process of his critical reading, Derrida identifies
various features of a philosophical text which inescapably
"exceed" the limits of what its writer set out to assert. One of
these features is the use in the argument of key equivocations
that cannot be used to specify one meaning without involving
the opposed meaning. In Rousseau's theory of language, for
example, the argument turns on the duplicitous word *supplement* (meaning both something added to what is itself complete and something required to complete what is insufficient);
in reading other authors, Derrida identifies other Janus-faced
terms such as *pharmakon* and *hymen*. Another feature is the
presumed reliance of a text on a logical argument which turns
out to involve nonlogical "rhetorical" moves. Prominent in
Derrida's analysis of the inherent rhetoricity of philosophical
reasoning is the disclosure of the role of indispensable metaphors that are assumed to be merely convenient substitutes
for literal or "proper" meanings, yet are irreducible to literal
meanings except by applying an opposition, metaphoric/lit-
eral, which is itself a consequence of the philosophy which
presupposes it. A third feature is the unavoidable use in a

text of what are presumed to be exclusive oppositions; Derrida undertakes to undermine such oppositions by showing that their boundaries are constantly transgressed, in that each of the terms crosses over into the domain of its opponent term. Prominent among the many unsustainable oppositions to which Derrida draws our attention is that of inside/outside, or internal/external, as applied to what is within or outside the mind, or within or outside the system of linguistic signs, or within or outside a text (a book, a poem, or an essay) which is ostensibly complete in itself.

Derrida's view of the untenability of the distinction between what is inside or outside a text has had, as we shall see, an especially important impact on the procedures of deconstructive literary criticism. "What used to be called a text," Derrida says, has "boundaries," which were thought to demarcate "the supposed end and beginning of a work, the unity of a corpus"; such a designation, however, applies only on the condition that "we accept the entire conventional system of legalities that organizes, in literature, the framed unity of the corpus," including the "unity of the author's name . . . registration of copyright, etc."[14] Derrida's double-reading, reading$_1$ and reading$_2$, in fact produces two texts. One is the text, such as Rousseau's *Essay,* which he reads by accepting, in a provisional way, the standard conventions and legalities that establish as its boundaries the opening and closing lines of its printed form. Text$_2$ is produced "by a sort of overrun [*débordement*] that spoils all these boundaries and divisions and forces us to extend the accredited concept, the dominant notion of a 'text,' of what I still call a 'text,' for strategic reasons." This second text is "no longer a finished corpus of writing" by a particular author, but a text as an aspect of textuality in general—of "a differential network, a fabric of traces referring endlessly to something other than itself, to other differential traces." Text$_2$, however, does not simply annul the constraints and borders that function in the reading of text$_1$ for, though it "overruns all the limits assigned to it so far," it does so not by "submerging or drowning them in an undifferentiated homogeneity, but rather making them more complex."[15]

This last quotation brings out what commentators overlook who claim that Derrida's emphasis on "freeplay" in language is equivalent to "anything goes in interpretation," and that is his repeated emphasis that a deconstructive reading$_2$ does not cancel the role of intention and of the other conventions and legalities that operate in a determinate reading of a limited text, but merely "reinscribes" them, as he puts it, so as to reveal their status as no more than "effects" of the differential play.[16] Derrida insists that the standard mode of "doubling commentary"—a commentary, that is, which simply undertakes to say in other words what it is that the author undertook to say—"should no doubt have its place in a critical reading." "To recognize and respect all its classical exigencies [i.e., of reading$_1$] is not easy and requires all the instruments of traditional criticism. Without this recognition and this respect, critical production [i.e., reading$_2$] would risk developing in any direction at all and authorize itself to say almost anything."[17]

The deliberate anomaly of Derrida's double interpretive procedure, however, is patent. He cannot demonstrate the impossibility of a standard reading except by going through the stage of manifesting its possibility; a text must be read determinately in order to be disseminated into an undecidability that never strikes completely free of its initial determination; deconstruction can only subvert the meanings of a text that has always already been construed. And even if a reader has been persuaded that Derrida has truly discovered a force in language (seemingly unsuspected, or at least unexploited, before Nietzsche) which forces him to overrun all the constraints and borders of standard construal, he has no option except to begin by construing a text, including Derrida's own text; or more precisely, his only option is whether or not to read French, or English, or any other natural language.

(3) In addition to subverting all the convictions of our common life and common thought, then to asserting the inescapable need for a double life and double thinking, Hume's epistemology contains a third moment that has an analogue in Derrida's theory of language. This is the moment when Hume turns his skepticism back upon itself, by what he calls "a reflex act of the mind" upon "the nature of our under-

standing, and our reasoning." In doing so he finds himself involved in "manifest absurdities" and "manifold contradictions," including the absurdity that his skeptical argument has no recourse except to use reason itself in order "to prove the fallaciousness and imbecility of reason." Hence "the understanding . . . entirely subverts itself, and leaves not the lowest degree of evidence in any proposition, either in [skeptical] philosophy or common life."[18] As the only reasonable way to cope with the diverse illogicalities of his philosophical and his social life, Hume recommends that we replace "the force of reason and conviction" by an attitude of insouciance—"a serious good-humor'd disposition" and a "careless" [i.e., carefree] conduct of philosophy, and a diffidence about the conclusions reached by that philosophy. "A true skeptic will be diffident of his philosophical doubts, as well as of his philosophical conviction."[19]

In a parallel way, Derrida turns deconstruction back upon itself. Since, he says, it has no option except to take all "the resources of subversion" from the logocentric system that it subverts, "deconstruction always in a certain way falls prey to its own work." Even the assertion that the play of writing is incomprehensible by the categories of "the classical logos" and "the law of identity" cannot escape reference to the logocentric logic that it flouts; and "for the rest," he allows, "deconstruction must borrow its resources from the logic it deconstructs." In addition, as Derrida says, his own deconstructive "production is necessarily a text."[20] Hence in his writing about writing, Derrida has no option except to "communicate" his views in language intended to be understood determinately by his readers, knowing that, to the extent that his own text is understood, it becomes a victim of the dissemination it asserts. The "work of deconstruction," then—since it is forced to use linguistic tools which are themselves deconstructed by the work they perform, in a play of illogicalities which cannot be named except by the logic it undermines—cannot escape the "closure" of logocentrism; it can only provide the "crevice through which the yet unnamable glimmer beyond the crevice can be glimpsed." And to this glimpse of what Derrida can designate only by terms borrowed from the logocentric system—"the freeplay of the world," "*genetic* indetermination," "the *seminal* adventure of the trace"—he too recommends that we assume an attitude. This is not, in his case, Hume's attitude of urbane "carelessness," but a Nietzschean attitude of gaiety: a "joyous affirmation" which is "without *nostalgia*," "with a certain laughter and with a certain dance."[21]

Where, according to Derrida, does deconstruction leave both our ordinary use of language and the philosophical and other specialized uses of language? Apparently, pretty much where they are now. He disclaims any possibility of a superior truth which would allow us to replace, or even radically to reform, our current linguistic procedures. "Deconstruction," he insists, "has nothing to do with destruction." "I believe in the necessity of scientific work in the classical sense, I believe in the necessity of everything which is being done."[22] He does not, he says, "destroy" or set out to "discard" concepts; he merely "situates" or "reinscribes" them in an alternative system of *différance*, in order to reveal that they indeed function, but only as "effects" which lack absolute foundation in an ontological given. What he can be said to reveal, in a change of vocabulary, is that the communicative efficacy of language rests on no other or better ground than that both writers and readers tacitly accept and apply the regularities and limits of an inherited social and linguistic contract.

2

Derrida has attracted little sustained comment from English and American philosophers, and that comment has been, with few exceptions, dismissive. One reason is that his writings, in addition to being abstruse, variable in procedure, and inveterately paradoxical in the give-yet-take of their "double gestures," are also outlandish. I do not mean only in the sense that they employ what, to the mainstream Anglo-American philosopher, is the foreign idiom of continental philosophy from Hegel through Heidegger. They are outlandish also because there is an antic as well as a sober side to Derrida's philosophical writings. He likes to give rein to his inventive playfulness in order to tease, or outrage, philosophers who regard the status and role of philosophy with what he takes to be excessive seriousness. He is fond—increasingly in recent publications—of exploiting Janus-faced neologisms, deliberately farfetched analogues, bizarre puns, invented etymologies, straight-faced and often sexual jokes, and dexterous play with his own signature, and also of intercalating incongruous texts by diverse authors, in order to shake, shock, or beguile us out of our ordinary assurance about the enabling conditions that establish the limits of a textual entity or yield a determinate and stable interpretation.

It is not on Anglo-American philosophy but on Anglo-American literary criticism that Derrida has had a strong and increasing effect. Some reasons for this specialized direction of influence are obvious. Derrida's examples of textual readings became widely available to English readers in the 1970s, when what was called the "New Criticism" was some forty years old. The New Criticism was only the most prominent mode of a procedure that had dominated literary criticism for almost a half-century, namely the elaborate explication, or "close reading," of individual literary texts, each regarded as an integral and self-sufficient whole. A representative New Critic defined a literary work as a text that, in contradistinction to "utilitarian" discourse, uses a language that is metaphorical and "ambiguous" (that is, polysemous, multiply meaningful) rather than literal and univocal, to form a structure which is a freestanding organization of ironies and paradoxes, instead of a logically ordered sequence of referential assertions. By the mid-1970s this once-innovative critical procedure had come to seem confining, predictable, stale. The very features of what Derrida calls his "style" of philosophical reading which made him seem alien to Anglo-American philosophers—his reliance on the elaborate analysis of particular texts, his stress on the covert role of metaphor and other rhetorical figures, his dissemination of ostensibly univocal meanings into paradoxes and aporias—made his writings seem to Anglo-American critics to be familiar, yet generative of radically novel discoveries. Far from offering his style of reading philosophical texts as a model for literary criticism, however, Derrida has emphasized its subversion of the metaphysical concepts and presuppositions that occur in all modes of discourse without exception: there are no features, metaphorical or other, which distinguish a specifically literary use of language; and dissemination, he insists, is "irreducible" to polysemy (a set of determinate meanings), for dissemination is an "overloading" of meanings in an uncontrollable "spread" that cannot be specified as a finite set of determinate signifieds.[23] Critical followers of Derrida have nonetheless assimilated deconstruction to their pre-existing critical assumptions and procedures. The result has been in various degrees to domesticate, naturalize, and nationalize Derrida's subversiveness-without-limit, by accommodating it to a closer reading of individual works which serves to show, as Paul de Man has put it, that new-critical close readings "were not nearly close enough."[24] The process is well under way of providing a rival deconstructive reading for each work in the literary canon which had earlier been explicated by one or another New Critic.

What we tend to blanket as deconstructive criticism is in fact highly diverse, ranging from an echoing of distinctive Derridean terms—"presence," "absence," "difference," "efface-ment," "aporia"—in the process of largely traditional explication, through foregrounding the explicit or implied occurrence in a work of a Derridean theme (especially the theme of writing, or inscription, or decoding), to a radical use of Derridean strategies to explode into dissemination both the integrity and the significance of the literary text that it undertakes to explicate. Instead of generalizing, I shall ana-lyze a single example of the radical type—the reading of Wordsworth's "A Slumber Did My Spirit Seal" by one of the "boa deconstructors," J. Hillis Miller, in an essay of 1979 entitled "On Edge: The Crossways of Contemporary Criti-cism." I choose this instance because Miller presents his read-ing explicitly "to 'exemplify,' " as he says, the deconstructive mode of literary interpretation;[25] because Wordsworth's poem is only eight lines long, so that we can have the entire text before us as we go along; because Miller specifies some of the theoretical underpinning of his enterprise and is a lucid and lively expositor of its results—and also, I admit, because some of these results will be so startling to Oldreaders as to inject drama into my presentation. My intention is not polemical, but expository, to bring into view some of the unexpressed, as well as explicit, procedures in this instance of radical literary deconstruction; if my tone is now and then quizzical, that is because it would be both disingenuous and futile to try to conceal my own convictions about the limits of a sound interpretation.

3

> A slumber did my spirit seal;
> I had no human fears:
> She seemed a thing that could not feel
> The touch of earthly years.
>
> No motion has she now, no force;
> She neither hears nor sees;
> Rolled round in earth's diurnal course,
> With rocks, and stones, and trees.

The "battle" between the earlier, metaphysic-bound reading and the deconstructive reading, Miller says, is joined in the alternative answers they offer to the question, "What does this given poem or passage *mean*?" (p. 101). Early on in answering this question, he shows that the poem means to him very much what I and other Oldreaders have hitherto taken it to mean. I quote from Miller's deft and lucid exposition of this moment in his deconstructive double-reading:

> This beautiful, moving, and apparently simple poem was written [by Wordsworth] at Goslar in Germany in the late fall or early winter of 1798–1799. . . .
>
> To have no human fears is the same thing as to have a sealed spirit. Both of these are defined by the speaker's false assumption that Lucy will not grow old or die.[26]
>
> . . . the shift from past to present tense [between stanza 1 and

stanza 2] . . . opposes then to now, ignorance to knowledge, life to death. The speaker has moved across the line from innocence to knowledge through the experience of Lucy's death.

The poem expresses both eloquently restrained grief for that death and the calm of mature knowledge. Before, he was innocent. His spirit was sealed from knowledge as though he were asleep, closed in on himself. . . . Lucy seemed so much alive . . . that she could not possibly be touched by time, reach old age, and die. . . . Then Lucy seemed an invulnerable young "thing"; now she is truly a thing, closed in on herself, like a stone . . . unable to move of her own free will, but unwillingly and unwittingly moved by the daily rotation of the earth (pp. 102–4).

Thus far Miller, with no want of assurance, has read the text, in its parts and as a whole, as having determinate meanings. He has, to use my term, construed the text and gone on to explicate the implied purport of these meanings in ways closely tied to the construal. Here are some features of Miller's reading $_1$:

(1) He accepts the historical evidence that the poem was written by an individual, William Wordsworth, during a particular span of time, 1798 to 1799. And in the assurance with which he construes the poem, it seems that Miller assumes, as standard readers do, that Wordsworth deployed an acquired expertise in the practice of the English language and of short lyric poems, and that he wrote his text so as to be understandable to readers who in turn inherit, hence share, his competence in the practice of the language and the conventions of the lyric.

(2) By implicit reference to this common practice, Miller takes it that, whatever the intended thematic relation to other Lucy poems, Wordsworth undertook to write a poem, beginning with the words "A slumber" and ending with the words "and trees," which can be understood as an entity complete in itself.

(3) Miller takes the two sentences which constitute the poem to be the utterance of a particular lyric speaker, the "I" of the text, and to be about a girl, who is referred to by the

pronoun "she." And he takes the tense of the verbs in the first sentence-stanza ("did . . . seal," "had," "seemed") as signifying an event in the past, and the tense of the verbs in the second sentence-stanza ("has . . . now," "hears," "sees") as signifying a state of affairs in the present—the sustained "now," that is, of the speaker's utterance.

(4) He takes the three clauses in the first sentence, although they lack explicit connectives, to be related in such a way that the assertions in the second and third clause make more specific, and give reasons for, the assertion in the first clause, "A slumber did my spirit seal." As Miller puts it, perhaps a bit flatly, "the second line . . . repeats the first, and then lines three and four say it over again" (p. 103). Miller also takes the assertions in the first sentence plainly to imply that the girl was then alive, and the assertions in the second sentence (augmented by the stanza-break) to imply that the girl is now dead.

(5) So far, I think, most standard readers of the poem will concur. Miller also goes on to specify the lyric speaker's state of feeling, now that the girl is dead. Since the second stanza does not advert to the speaker's own feelings, but leaves them to be inferred from the terms with which he asserts a state of affairs, the text allows standard readers considerable room for variance in this aspect of interpretation.[27] Miller's statement on this issue seems to me sensitive and apt: "The poem expresses both eloquently restrained grief for that death and the calm of mature knowledge" (p. 103).

(6) Note also that Miller reads the poem as a verbal presentation of a human experience which, as he says, is both "beautiful" and "moving"; that is, its presentation is ordered—especially in the sharp division of the stanzas between the situation then and the situation now—so as to effect an emotional response in the reader. That experience might be specified as the shocking discovery, by a particular person in a particularized instance, of the awful suddenness, unexpectedness, and finality of death.

These are features of Miller's reading of Wordsworth's lyric, phase one: the determination of specific meanings in the poem read as an entity. Phase two, the deconstructive reading, follows from Miller's claim that, since literature is not "grounded in something outside language," the determinate bounds of its meanings are "undermined by the text itself," in a "play of tropes" that "leaves an inassimilable residue or remnant of meaning . . . making a movement of sense beyond any unifying boundaries" (p. 101). The intrinsic anomaly of the deconstructive procedure is apparent: in claiming that a determinate interpretation is made impossible by the text, Miller has already shown that it is possible, for he deconstructs a text that he has already determinately construed.

We find the same double-reading—the first performed, but declared to be in some sense impossible, the second held to be made necessary by the text itself—in Paul de Man, whose deconstructive criticism is often said to be closest in its "rigor" to the model of reading established by Derrida himself. As it happens, in an essay of 1969 entitled "The Rhetoric of Temporality," de Man dealt with this very poem by Wordsworth; and he there construes the text in a way that, for all its difference in idiom, emphasis, and nuance, approximates the way that Miller, and I, and almost all traditional readers, construe it. In the two stanzas,

> we can point to the successive description of two stages of consciousness, one belonging to the past and mystified, the other to the *now* of the poem, the stage that has recovered from the mystification of a past now presented as being in error; the "slumber" is a condition of non-awareness. . . .
>
> The curious shock of the poem . . . is that this innocuous statement ["She seemed a thing . . ."] becomes literally true in the retrospective perspective of the eternal "now" of the second part. She now has become a *thing* in the full sense of its word.

De Man also reads the poem as the utterance of its first-person speaker whose responses we can infer from the way he describes the situation then and the situation now:

> The stance of the speaker, who exists in the "now," is that of a subject whose insight is no longer in doubt. . . . First there was error, then the death occurred, and now an insight into the rocky barrenness of the human predicament prevails.[28]

In this early essay de Man goes on to describe the poem he has so read as, in a special sense, an "allegory." He thus opens the way to the intricate deconstructive strategy exemplified in his later *Allegories of Reading* (1979): "The paradigm for all texts consists of a figure (or a system of figures) and its deconstruction." But such a reading engenders a second-order "narrative" which he calls an "allegory"—of which the tenor, by the inherent nature of discourse, is invariably the undecidability of the text itself: "Allegories are always allegories of metaphor and, as such, they are always allegories of the impossibility of reading."[29]

To return to Miller's engagement with Wordsworth's text: I shall first list some of the significations into which (forced, he asserts, by an "inassimilable residue" in the text itself) he disperses the meaning that he has already construed as "apparently simple"; I shall then go on to inquire into the operations which enable him to arrive at these multiplex and self-conflicting significations.

(1) "An obscure sexual drama is enacted in this poem. This drama is a major carrier of its allegorical significance" (p. 105). Miller explains that he applies " 'allegorical' in the technical sense in which that term is used by Walter Benjamin or by Paul de Man," with temporal reference to "the interaction of two emblematic times," that of stanza one and that of stanza two (p. 104).

(2) "The possession of Lucy alive and seemingly immortal is a replacement for [Wordsworth's] lost mother," who had died when he was eight years old. It follows that Lucy's "imagined death is a reenactment of the death of the mother," hence a reenactment of the loss of "that direct filial bond to nature" which his mother, while alive, had established for him (p. 106).

(3) "Lucy was [line 3] a virgin 'thing.' " In fact she was, by Miller's account, a very young virgin thing, in that she was viewed by the adult and knowledgeable male "speaker of the poem" as possessing a "prepubertal innocence." Consonantly Miller interprets "the touch of earthly years," line 4, to be "a form of sexual appropriation"; but since time is the death-bringing aspect of nature ("earthly years"), that touch is also "the ultimate dispossession which is death." Yet, since Lucy

had died so young as to remain intact, "to be touched by earthly years is a way to be sexually penetrated while still remaining virgin" (p. 107).

(4) "The speaker of the poem" (signified by "I,") is not, as it initially seemed, "the opposite of Lucy, male to her female, adult knowledge to her prepubertal innocence." In Miller's disseminative reading of the speaker's temporal transition to knowledge in the second stanza, he becomes "the displaced representative of both the penetrated and the penetrator, of both Lucy herself [thus also of the mother whom Lucy has replaced] and of her unravishing ravisher, nature or death." "The speaker's movement to knowledge," Miller remarks, "as his consciousness becomes dispersed, loses its 'I' " (p. 108). The I-as-construed, we can add, is dispersed not only into a "he" (the knowledgeable male), but also into a "she," a "they" (Lucy and his mother), and, as the representative of nature, an "it."

(5) "Lucy is both the virgin child and the missing mother. . . . Male and female, however, come together in the earth, and so Lucy and the speaker are 'the same.' . . . The two women, mother and girl child, have jumped over the male generation in the middle. They have erased its power of mastery, its power of logical understanding, which is the male power *par excellence*" (p. 108).

(6) Climactically, in his deconstructive second-reading, Miller discovers that the poem "enacts one version of a constantly repeated occidental drama of the lost sun. Lucy's name of course means light. To possess her would be a means of rejoining the lost source of light, the father sun as logos, as head power and fount of meaning. . . . Her actual death is the loss both of light and of the source of light. It is the loss of the logos, leaving the poet and his words groundless. . . . As groundless, the movement is, precisely, alogical" (pp. 109–10). The poem thus allegorically re-enacts the inescapable dilemma of our logocentric language, and that is the reliance on a logos, or ground outside the system of language which is always needed, always relied on, but never available.[30] From this ultimate alogicality stem the diverse aporias that Miller has traced. As he puts it: "Whatever track the reader follows through the poem he arrives at blank contradictions. . . . The

reader is caught in an unstillable oscillation unsatisfying to the mind and incapable of being grounded in anything outside the activity of the poem itself" (p. 108).

4

Now, what are the interpretive moves by which Miller deconstructs his initial construal of the poem into this bewildering medley of clashing significations? In a preliminary way, we can describe these moves as designed to convert the text-as-construed into a pre-text for a supervenient over-reading that Miller calls "allegorical." There are of course precedents for this tactic in pre-deconstructive explications of literary texts. The old-fashioned close reader, however, undertook to over-read a text in a way that would enlarge and complicate the significance of the text-as-construed into a richer integrity; the novelty of Miller's deconstruction is that in his over-reading he "undermines," as he says, the text, then detonates the mine so as to explode the construed meaning into what he calls, in one of his essays, "an undecidability among contradictory alternatives of meaning."

Miller's first move is to identify in Wordsworth's poem an "inter-related set of binary oppositions. These seem to be genuinely exclusive oppositions, with a distinct uncrossable boundary line between them" (p. 102). He lists almost a score of such oppositions; among the more obvious ones are "slumber as against waking; male as against female; sealed up as against open; . . . past as against present; . . . self-propulsion as against exterior compulsion; . . . life as against death." About such linguistic oppositions Miller, following the example of Derrida, makes a radical claim. This is not the assertion, valid for standard readers, that the boundary between such opposed terms is not a sharp line, but a zone, and that the locus of this boundary is not fixed, but may shift between one utterance and another. Miller's claim is that the seeming boundary between each pair of these terms dissolves into what he calls an inevitable "structure of chiasmus"; that as a result there is "a constant slipping of entities across borders into their opposites" so as to effect a "perpetual reversal of properties"; and that this "cross over" is forced on the reader by a "residue" of meaning within the text of Wordsworth's poem itself (pp. 110, 107, 101).

When we examine Miller's demonstrations of these crossovers and reversals, however, we find, I think, that they are enforced not by a residue of meaning in the two sentences of Wordsworth's "A Slumber," but only by these sentences after they have been supplemented by meanings that he has culled from diverse other texts. Miller acquires these supplementary meanings by his next move; that is, he dissolves the "unifying boundaries" of the poem as a linguistic entity so as to merge the eight-line text into the textuality constituted by all of Wordsworth's writings, taken together. ("His writing," Miller explains, ". . . is what is meant here by 'Wordsworth' " [p. 106].) This maneuver frees "A Slumber" from the limitations involved in the linguistic practice by which Miller himself had already read the text as a specific *parole* by a specified lyric speaker. Miller is now licensed, for example, to attribute to the "I" in line 1, initially construed as a particular speaker, and the "she" in line 3 and elsewhere, initially construed as a particular girl, any further significances he discovers by construing, explicating, and over-reading passages that occur elsewhere in Wordsworth's total oeuvre.

By way of brief example: Miller reads "other texts both in poetry and prose" as providing evidence that Wordsworth (whom he now identifies with the unspecified "I" of the poem) "had as a child, and even as a young man, a strong conviction of his immortality," and that this conviction "was associated with a strong sense of participation in a nature both enduringly material, therefore immortal, and at the same time enduringly spiritual, therefore also immortal" (p. 103). Miller reads other passages in Wordsworth as evidence that "nature for Wordsworth was strongly personified," though "oddly, personified as both male and female, as both father and mother." He cites as one instance of the latter type of personification the passage of *The Prelude* in which the "Infant Babe," learning to perceive the world in the security of his mother's arms, and in the assurance of her nurturing love, comes to feel in his veins "The gravitation and the filial bond / Of nature, that connect him with the world." Miller interprets this statement to signify that the "earth was [to Wordsworth] the maternal face and body." In other episodes in *The Prelude* and elsewhere, on the other hand, nature is "a frightening male spirit threatening to punish the poet for wrongdoing," hence representative of his father. Miller points out that "Wordsworth's mother died when he was eight, his father when he was thirteen," leaving Wordsworth feeling abandoned by the death of the former and irrationally guilty for the death of the latter. He then cites another passage, this time not directly from Wordsworth but from his sister Dorothy's journal, in which she describes how she and her brother lay down in a trench, and Wordsworth "thought that it would be as sweet thus to lie so in the grave, to hear the *peaceful* sounds of the earth and just to know that our dear friends were near"; this remark Miller identifies with Wordsworth's "fantasy" of Lucy lying in the earth in stanza two of "A Slumber" (p. 107).

It is only by conflating the reference and relations of the "I" and "she" in "A Slumber" with these and other passages that Miller is able to attribute to Wordsworth's text the oscillating, contrarious meanings that Lucy alive was a replacement for the lost mother, while her death re-enacts the death of the mother, hence the loss of the "filial bond to nature" which his mother had established for him; and the further meaning that Wordsworth's "only hope for reestablishing the bond that connected him to the world is to die without dying, to be dead, in his grave, and yet still alive, bound to maternal nature by way of a surrogate mother, a girl who remains herself both alive and dead, still available in life and yet already taken by Nature" (p. 107). And it is only by merging the reference of the "I" with other passages, interpreted as expressing Wordsworth's sense of participation in an enduring, immortal nature, or as signifying Wordsworth's experience of a nature which is male and his father as well as female and his mother, that Miller achieves the further range of simultaneous but incompatible meanings that "the speaker of the poem rather than being the opposite of Lucy, male to her female . . . is the displaced representative . . . of both Lucy herself and of her unravishing ravisher, nature or death" (p. 108).

It might seem that Miller acts on the interpretive principle that whenever Wordsworth uses a narrative "I" or "she" in a poem, the pronouns inescapably carry with them reference to everything the author has said, in any of his texts, about himself and any female persons and about their relations to each other and to nature. In fact, however, Miller's procedure is constrained in various ways. It is constrained by Miller's tacit requirement of some connection to partial aspects of the text as initially construed, as well as by his tacit reliance on plausible bridges for the crossovers between the "I" and "she" and the various personages and relationships that he finds, or infers, elsewhere in Wordsworth's writings. These are primarily doctrinal bridges, whose validity Miller takes for granted, which serve to warrant his "allegorical" reading—in other words, to underwrite his over-readings of the text of "A Slumber." Some underwriters remain implicit in Miller's essay. He relies throughout, of course, on the views, terms, and strategies of Derrida. He patently accepts Freud's doctrines about the unconscious attitudes of a male to his mother, father, and lover, and the disguised manifestations of these attitudes in the mode of symbolic displacements, condensations, and inversions. And in his discussion of Wordsworth's lyric as simultaneously affirming and erasing "male mastery" and the male "power of logical understanding," Miller manifests a heightened consciousness of the relations of men to women in a patriarchal society, as delineated in recent feminist criticism.

Some of his connective bridges, however, Miller explicitly identifies; and one of these is Martin Heidegger's assertions about the use of the word "thing" in German. I want to dwell on this reference for a moment, as representative of the way Miller both discovers and corroborates some startling aspects of the allegorical significance of "A Slumber" as "an obscure sexual drama."

Miller cites (and construes determinately) a passage in which Heidegger points out that in German, we do not call a man a thing [*Der Mensch ist kein Ding*]; and that "only a stone, a

clod of earth, a piece of wood are for us such mere things."
We do, however, "speak of a young girl who is faced with a
task too difficult for her as being a young thing, still too young
for it [*eine noch zu junges Ding*]" (p. 104). This is a striking
quotation, with its parallel (of the sort Miller is often and
impressively able to introduce) between Heidegger's "a stone,
a clod of earth, a piece of wood" and Wordsworth's triad,
"with rocks, and stones, and trees." As Miller implies, this
sexual asymmetry in the application of the term "young thing"
applies to English as well as German. Among speakers of
English, women as well as men are apt to refer to inexperienced or innocent girls, but not to inexperienced or innocent
boys, as "young things." On this feature of the language Miller
largely relies for important elements in his sexual drama. By
referring to her as "a thing," the speaker invests the girl with
a virginal innocence—a "prepubertal innocence," in fact—
which nature tries, only half in vain, to violate; by the same
epithet, he implicitly stresses his own male difference, and
claims superiority over the young virgin in knowledge, experience, physical attributes, and logical power; only to have
the oppositions dissolved and the claims controverted by
implications derived from crisscrossing "A Slumber" with other
texts in Wordsworth.

There comes to mind a familiar folk song in English, not
cited by Miller, whose parallel to Miller's disseminative second-reading of "A Slumber" seems a good deal closer than
the German passage in Heidegger. In this song the term
"young thing" is again and again applied to a girl who resists
(or seems to resist) the advances of an importunate and experienced male. Her age—or rather ages—are compatible with
her being prepubertal, nubile, and maternal too:

> Did she tell you her age, Billy boy, Billy boy,
> Did she tell you her age, charming Billy?
> She's three times six, four times seven,
> Twenty-eight and near eleven,
>   She's a young thing, and cannot leave her mother.

In the concluding stanza the young thing is represented as
vulnerable, acquiescent, yet unpenetrated by her lover:

> Did she light you up to bed, Billy boy, Billy boy,
> Did she light you up to bed, charming Billy?
> Yes, she lit me up to bed,
> But she shook her dainty head,
>   She's a young thing, and cannot leave her mother.[31]

Now, what is the relevance of the gender-specific uses of "young thing," whether in German or English, to the third line of Wordsworth's poem—which does not call the girl a "young thing" at all, nor even simply "a thing," but that term as qualified by a clause Miller had initially construed to signify that she was a thing so vital "that she could not possibly be touched by time, reach old age, and die"? To Oldreaders like myself, they have no relevance whatever. But to a second-order reading which has deliberately cut itself free from the limitations in construing the poem as a specific lyric *parole*, such uses help to endow the text with a diversity of contradictory sexual significations.

There remains the last feature that I have listed in Miller's deconstructive reading of "A Slumber," the discovery of a general aporia that underlies and necessitates all the local aporias; and to track down this discovery requires us to identify a final interpretive operation. This move (already suggested by Miller's reference to the use of *junges Ding* in German, and by his comment [p. 109] that Wordsworth's "identifying the earth with a maternal presence" repeats a trope that exists "in the Western tradition generally") is to dissolve linguistic boundaries so as to merge "A Slumber" not only with Wordsworth's other writings, but into the textuality constituted by all occidental languages taken together. In this all-embracing linguistic context, by way of the etymological link between "Lucy" (a name not mentioned in the poem) and the Latin *lux,* or light, the death of the girl is read as enacting "a constantly repeated occidental drama of the lost sun . . . the father sun as logos, as head power and fount of meaning" (p. 109).

The implicit warrant for this over-reading of the "she" in "A Slumber" is a remarkable essay by Derrida, "White Mythology: Metaphor in the Text of Philosophy." There Derrida undertakes to show that metaphysics is inescapably

metaphorics, and that the founding metaphors of philosophy are irreducible. All attempts to specify the literal meaning, in implicit opposition to which a metaphor is identified
as metaphoric, and all attempts to translate a metaphor into
the literal meaning for which it is held to be a substitute, are
incoherent and self-defeating, especially since the very distinction between metaphoric and literal meaning is a product
of the philosophical system it purports to found, or "sub-
sume." Derrida stresses particularly the reliance of traditional philosophical systems on metaphors, or "tropes," in
which terms for visual sense-perception in the presence or
absence of light are applied in what purports to be the mental or intellectual realm. Philosophers claim, for example, that
they see the meaning or truth of a proposition, or they distinguish clear and distinct from obscure ideas, or they appeal to
contemplative vision and to the natural light of reason; all
are instances of standing at gaze before something which
compels belief, in the way that we are supposedly compelled
to believe in the presence of a thing perceived by our sense
of sight. Such mental tropes, like their visual correlates, must
assume a source of light, which is ultimately the sun; and
with his customary wit, Derrida names this key trope (that is,
"turn") of Western thought—which as metaphor is also an
instance of what are traditionally called "flowers of rhetoric"—the "heliotrope"; that is, a kind of sunflower of rhetoric. But the visible sun, itself ever turning, rises only to set
again; similarly, the philosophical tropes turn to follow their
analogous sun, which appears only to disappear, even though,
as the source of light, it constitutes the necessary condition
for the very opposition between seeing and not-seeing, hence
between presence and absence. The sun thus serves Derrida
himself as a prime trope for the founding presence, or logos,
which by our logocentric language is ever-needed and always-
lost.

Miller, it is evident, has plucked Derrida's heliotrope and
carried it over, via the unnamed Lucy, into the text of
Wordsworth's poem. (Derrida himself remarked, possibly by
way of warning, that "the heliotrope may always become a
dried flower in a book";[32] it may become, that is, a straw-
flower.) As a radically deconstructive critic of literature, Miller

always knows in advance that any literary text, no less than any metaphysical text, must be an allegorical or "tropological" vehicle whose ultimate tenor is its constitutional lack of a required ground. And by ingeniously transplanting the heliotrope, he is indeed enabled to read the death of the "she" in Wordsworth's short lyric as an allegory for "the loss of the logos, leaving the poet and his words groundless" (p. 109).

5

Miller introduces his exemplary analysis of Wordsworth's poem in the middle of an essay which begins and ends with a discussion of literary study in the university, and in the course of this discussion he raises a pressing issue for the teaching of literature. He divides the "modes of teaching literature and writing about it" into two kinds. One kind is the deconstructive "mode of literary study I have tried to exemplify"; the other comprehends all the more traditional modes. And, he declares, "both can and should be incorporated into college and university curricula" (p. 111).

I am not at all opposed to incorporating deconstructive theory and deconstructive critical practice as subjects for study in university curricula. They have become the focus of the kind of vigorous controversy which keeps a discipline from becoming routine and moribund, and have had the salutary result of compelling traditionalists to re-examine the presuppositions of their procedures and the grounds of their convictions. The question is: when, and in what way, to introduce this subject?

Miller's answer is to incorporate it at all stages, "from basic courses in reading and writing up to the most advanced graduate seminars." The basic courses are presumably freshman and sophomore courses. Such early and reiterative presentation of the subject would seem to rest on the conviction that Derrida's theory, which deconstructs the possibility of philosophical truth, is itself the truth about philosophy, and furthermore, a theory capable of being taught before students have read the philosophy on which it admittedly depends even as it puts that philosophy to radical question. And how are we to introduce Derrida's theory and practice of deconstructing texts to novices at the same time that we are trying to teach them to write texts that will say, precisely and accurately, what they mean, and to construe, precisely and accurately, the texts that they read? In his sustained "double gestures" Derrida is an equilibrist who maintains a precarious poise on a tightrope between subverting and denying, between deconstructing and destroying, between understanding communicative "effects" and dissolving the foundations on which the effects rely, between deploying interpretive norms and disclaiming their power to "master" a text, between decisively rejecting wrong readings and declaring the impossibility of a right reading, between meticulously construing a text as determinate and disseminating the text into a scatter of undecidabilities. In this process Derrida is also a logical prestidigitator who acknowledges and uses, as a logocentric "effect," the logic of noncontradiction, yet converts its either / or into a simultaneous neither / nor and both / and, in a double gesture of now-you-see-it, now-you-don't, of giving and taking back and regiving with a *différance*. I find it difficult to imagine a population of teachers of composition and reading who are so philosophically adept and pedagogically deft that they will be able to keep novices from converting this delicate equilibristic art into a set of crude dogmas; or from replacing an esteem for the positive powers of language by an inveterate suspicion of the perfidy of language; or from falling either into the extreme of a paralysis of interpretive indecision or into the opposite extreme of interpretive abandon, on the principle that, since both of us lack a foundation in presence, my misreading is as good as your misreading.

Miller's recommendation to teach deconstruction as a subject to advanced students—after, it is to be hoped, a student has become competent at construing a variety of texts, and knowledgeable about traditional modes of literary criticism, and has also achieved the philosophical sophistication to understand the historical position and the duplexities of Derridean deconstruction—seems to me unobjectionable. No student of literature, in fact, can afford simply to ignore deconstruction; for the time being, it is the focus of the most basic and interesting literary debate. And it is only fair to add that, if a graduate student elects to adopt, in whole or part, this strategy for liberating reading from traditional constraints, it offers, in our institutional arrangements for hiring and advancing faculty, certain practical advantages. It guarantees the discovery of new significations in old and much-criticized works of literature, hence is eminently publishable; and while, because of the built-in conservatism of many literary departments, it still incurs institutional risks, it increasingly holds out the promise of institutional rewards.

As a long-time observer of evolving critical movements and countermovements, I am not disposed to cavil with this latest innovation; I do want, however, to express a few caveats. In appraising the old against the new mode of teaching and writing about literature, Hillis Miller declares that the old mode, since it is "controlled by the presupposition of some center," "already knows what it is going to find," while the deconstructive mode "is more open to the inexhaustible strangeness of literary texts" (p. 110). I recognize the justness of the second clause in this claim, but not of the first. As Miller's reading of "A Slumber" demonstrates, deconstruction has indeed proved its ability to find strange meanings that make the most ingenious explorations of new-critical Oldreaders seem unadventurous—although it should be noted that deconstructive readings are adjudged to be strange only by tacit reference to the meanings of the text as already construed. But surely it is deconstructive criticism, much more than traditional criticism, which is vulnerable to Miller's charge, in his first clause, that it "already knows what it is going to find." Whatever their presuppositions, traditional modes of reading have amply demonstrated the ability to find highly diverse structures of meaning in a range of works from Wordsworth's "A Slumber" through Shakespeare's *King Lear,* George Eliot's *Middlemarch,* and the rhymes of Ogden Nash. But as Miller himself describes deconstruction, it "attempts to show that in a given work of literature, in a different way in each case," following out "the play of tropes leads to . . . the experience of an aporia or boggling of the mind" (p. 101). This presupposition makes a deconstructive reading not merely goal oriented, but single-goal-oriented. The critic knows before he begins to read what, by deep linguistic necessity, he is going to find—that is, an aporia—and sure enough, given the freedom of interpretive maneuver that deconstruction is designed to grant him, he finds one. The readers of radically deconstructive critics soon learn to expect that invariable discovery. So one of my caveats is this: for all the surprising new readings achieved en route, I do not see how Derrida's counterphilosophical strategy, when transposed to the criticism of literature, can avoid reducing the variousness of literary works to allegorical narratives with an invariable plot.

Another caveat: to be successful in his chosen métier, the apprentice needs to approximate the proven strengths of the masters of deconstruction: their wide-ranging and quite traditional learning, for example; their quick eye for unexpected similarities in what is taken to be different and of differences in what seems to be the same; their ingenuity at finding openings into the linguistic substructure of a work and resourcefulness at inventing diverse tactics in the undeviating deconstructive quest; and not least, the deftness, wit, and wordplay which often endow their critical writings with their own kind of literary value.

My third warning is this: Derrida is careful to point out, as I have said, that deconstruction does not destroy, and cannot replace, traditional humanistic pursuits, including presumably literary criticism; nor can it, as his own theory and practice demonstrate, dispense with a determinate construal of a text, as a necessary stage toward disseminating what has been so construed. Above all, then, the young practitioner needs to be sure that he establishes his credentials (as Derrida, Miller, de Man, and other adepts have impressively established theirs) as a proficient, acute, and sensitive construer and explicator of texts in the primary mode of literary understanding. Otherwise, as traditional literary readings may degenerate into exercises in pedantry, so deconstructive readings may become a display of modish terminology which never engages with anything recognizable as a work of literature.

My final point has to do with the difference between traditional and deconstructive motives for reading literature, and

the distinctive values that each reading provides. To read a
text in the traditional way, as a work of literature, is to read
it as a human document—a fictional presentation of thinking, acting, and feeling characters who are enough like ourselves to engage us in their experiences, in language which is
expressed and ordered by a human author in a way that moves
and delights the human reader. Deconstructive critics, if they
acknowledge such features at all, treat them as unauthored,
linguistically generated illusions, or "effects." Literature has
survived over the millennia by being read as a presentation
of human characters and matters of human interest, delight,
and concern. It is far from obvious that the values in such a
reading can for long be replaced by the value, however
appealing in its initial novelty, of reading literature as the
tropological vehicle for a set of conundrums without solutions.

I am reassured, however, by the stubborn capacity of construed texts to survive their second-order deconstruction.
When, for example, I turn back from Miller's essay to
Wordsworth's "A Slumber," I find that it still offers itself, not
as a regress of deadlocked "double-binds," but as what
Wordsworth's friend Coleridge found it to be when he called
it a "sublime elegy," and what Miller himself at first found it
to be, when he described it as a "beautiful" and "moving"
poem—beautiful in the terse economy, justness, and ordering of its verbal expression, and moving in that it presents a
human being at the moment in which he communicates the
discovery, in a shocking instance, of the suddenness, unexpectedness, and finality of death. Let's put the text to trial:

> A slumber did my spirit seal;
> I had no human fears:
> She seemed a thing that could not feel
> The touch of earthly years.
>
> No motion has she now, no force;
> She neither hears nor sees;
> Rolled round in earth's diurnal course,
> With rocks, and stones, and trees.

A Colloquy on Recent Critical Theories

Question: In "Behaviorism and Deconstruction" (1977) you wrote that you expected deconstruction to pass on soon. Do you see that prophecy coming true?

Answer: It probably hasn't reached its climacteric, although things turn faster and faster in the carousel of literary theory these days. Look at the New Criticism, which came into dominance in the thirties. It reigned—though not unchallenged—a good quarter-century before there appeared a serious rival in Frye's archetypal criticism. If I were forced to guess, I would say that deconstruction will be crescent for another five or ten years, after which it will pass on; but it won't pass away. In the Hegelian term, it will be *aufgehoben;* that is, it will be canceled, yet survive at another level. That higher level is the traditional way of reading works of literature, which has shown over the centuries a powerful survival value. Because it has enormous inertia (based, I believe, on its grounding in enduring human concerns and needs), traditional criticism assimilates innovations and continues on, although sometimes with important and positive differences.

It's now the fashion to derogate the New Criticism. We forget that the sustained close reading of literary texts had almost no precedent before the New Critics showed us how to do it. I was in mild opposition to some manifest deficiencies of the New Criticism during the earlier part of my critical career. I must say now, however, that there isn't anyone I know who teaches literature or writes about it who hasn't learned a lot from the New Criticism. Because I manifest a skeptical stance toward the radical claims or procedures of deconstruction, don't assume that I think that everything the deconstructionists say is wasted. Deconstruction raises important questions and has some important things to tell us, too.

Question: Wouldn't the deconstructionists concede your point about the staying power—or inertia, or durability—of traditional criticism? They often say that there's no escaping the metaphysics that underlies traditional criticism. Why do they try to escape a tradition that they themselves acknowledge cannot finally be escaped?

Answer: If you return to the fountainhead, Derrida himself, he would indeed claim that there is no escaping Western metaphysics, because it is involved in our very language: the minute you use language you accede to its fallacy of presence, the ground for which there is no ground, always needed but never in fact available. But I don't think he means that we can never get rid of a particular philosophical position within that overall frame.

In any case, I think that many of Derrida's followers are less consistently aware than he is of the implications of their position, which makes everything that they themselves say vulnerable to deconstruction. For Derrida, the writing in which you undermine any other piece of writing is equally subject to being undermined. That's a persistent admission on his part, and he means it; but some of his followers seem to make truth-claims without awareness of the rebound, or ricochet, of their operations upon themselves. Perhaps because it's a rather unpleasant thing to contemplate: what's the use of deconstructing others if you're deconstructing yourself in the process?

Question: I've heard it suggested that certain kinds of literature bring about certain kinds of theories about literature. People have proposed that modern literature helped bring about the New Criticism, which was promoted by critics who were also modern poets. If the same thing can be said of deconstruction—that it was the natural product of certain kinds of postmodern literature, criti-fiction and so on—is its usefulness limited to helping us understand that particular kind of literature, or can it be useful in dealing with other kinds?

Answer: I agree that deconstruction feeds upon certain phenomena in literature of the last couple of decades or more. Whether that's a sufficient explanation of its emergence or vogue is another question. You can easily move to a higher explanatory level and claim that certain kinds of postmodern literature and deconstruction are both manifestations of a skepticism about the bases of Western culture that is part of the intellectual ambience of our time: the literature undertakes to subvert the basic assumptions and conventions on which earlier literary documents were built, and the criticism undertakes to subvert the bases of all earlier modes of reading and of Western thinking in general.

But at any rate they do feed on each other. Derrida learned from Barthes, while Barthes, who before his death became more deconstructive in his mode, picked up ideas from Derrida. Barthes's early criticism was based in large part on experimental fiction like the *nouveau roman,* which undertakes to subvert prominent features of the implicit social contract involved in storytelling which had been the grounds of almost all earlier fiction. But both deconstructive literature and deconstructive criticism flourish because they appeal to the temper of the times—a dangerous temper, one that worries me—in which we tend to be much more hospitable to negative modes of thinking and writing than to positive modes.

A vigorous culture can never do without the negatives; traditionalists need to be driven to re-examine and reconstitute their premises and to refresh their procedures. But the negative seems to be what at present absorbs the interest and enthusiasm of many of the younger intellectuals—graduate students, teachers, writers. Sometimes the ready hospitality to negative ideas appears to me to be ominous; but it's reassuring to remember the attested power of traditional criticism to adapt itself to—even, selectively, to absorb—ideas which seem to threaten its own survival.

I think that deconstruction leaves radically out of account features of works of literature which have been essential to their survival as presentations of human matters and concerns which themselves embody human values. That doesn't mean, however, that deconstruction, *en passant*, may not reveal other features of these works which have been neglected. My own position is that of a critical perspectivist; it seems to me that a new mode of criticism, insofar as it has validity, throws a strong shaft of light on features in literature we're apt to have overlooked or insufficiently stressed, but throws into shadow, even into darkness, things which have hitherto been central in our view of literature. In the process of achieving its own aims, deconstruction has in fact been constructive; for example, in drawing attention to the subtle play in a literary work of figurative language, concealed rhetorical devices and modes, and so on. The claim of a radically deconstructive critic, following Derrida's lead, is that these figures uncontrollably get out of hand and subvert the very grounds of the literary document within which they were meant to be constructive. I don't agree to the force of this claim; it can be maintained only by setting up a rationale for waiving the rules for the practice of writing and understanding language on which the deconstructor himself tacitly relies, in presenting his own claims in language that he intends his readers to understand. But I believe nonetheless that one can profit from a deconstructive critic's sensitivity to certain aspects of the play of language, which goes beyond the range of perception of the New Critics, however much they did to open our eyes to the play of figuration in a literary text.

Question: Speaking of the relatively hospitable climate that Derrida has found among literary critics, can you explain the neglect of Derrida by Anglo-American philosophers?

Answer: Neglect, or sometimes contempt. The standard procedure in philosophy is to read other philosophers to get at the content of their thought by looking through their language to the doctrines, and the arguments for those doctrines, that the language is taken more or less transparently to convey. Derrida's procedure is quite different. Derrida insists that language, even at its most abstract and logical, is never transparent to meaning; he reads selected passages of a philosophical text minutely, with close attention to the play of language and figuration as indiscriminable from the doctrines and arguments—and indeed, as ultimately subversive of the doctrines and arguments. Such close reading, which foregrounds the linguistic medium itself, seems strange, or aberrant, to most American philosophers, but much more familiar to literary critics nurtured on the close reading of the New Criticism. So, once we got habituated to the repertory of special terms, neologisms, and analytic maneuvers that Derrida deploys, what he was doing did not seem all that strange to us.

The relatively few Anglo-American philosophers who take Derrida seriously enough to read him with some care interpret his central assertion about the lack of "presence," hence of a "ground," in metaphysics to be coincident with the assertion by American pragmatists, and one especially familiar in Anglo-American philosophy since Wittgenstein, that there is no ultimate "foundation" on which metaphysical truth-claims can rest. This seems to me to be on the right track. The distinctive and radical aspect of Derrida's thinking, however, as I put it in 1979 (in "How to Do Things with Texts"), is that he "is an absolutist without absolutes"; that is, though he denies the possibility of the traditional metaphysical claim that there is an absolute foundation for valid knowledge, he tacitly accepts the metaphysical assumption that such an absolute foundation is indispensable to valid truth-claims and indeed indispensable to all determinate communication that is more than an illusory "effect" of the internal, differential play of language. Derrida's "dissemination" of seemingly determinate meanings, like his subversion of metaphysical claims to an absolute truth, rests on this presumption of the indispensability, yet radical absence, of an absolute foundation for language. To this, I think, the proper response is that a language is a highly complex conventional practice that requires no ontological or epistemological absolute or foundation in order to do its work; furthermore, that we have convincing evidence that as speakers or auditors, writers or readers, we share the regularities of this practice in a way that makes possible determinacy of communication and also makes it possible to utter assertions that can not only be understood determinately, but adjudged validly to be true or false. Such understanding can never be absolutely certain, nor can the asserted truths be absolute truths; understanding can at best be an adequate or practical assurance, and the truths practically certain within the limits of a given frame of reference. That is simply our human condition. But we should not let what Derrida calls our human "nostalgia" for absolute certainties blind us to the fact that, as an inherited and shared practice, and despite the attested failures in some attempts at communication, language in fact can work, can work determinately, and can work wonderfully well—in literature as in other modes of discourse.

Question: Do you think there's any truth to the charge that deconstruction, despite its distressed, radical rhetoric, actually shelters conservative ideas about literature and literary criticism, especially by isolating the literary work from life in a way that's comfortable for at least some old New Critics? Does the "autonomous" literary work that we heard so much about from the New Criticism reappear as the self-reflexive, self-subversive work—a work that talks mainly about itself—that we're hearing about now?

Answer: Yes, in a way. One of the standard claims in post-structuralism generally is that literature and criticism can't be distinguished, that they're both equally creative, equally interesting, equally figurative, equally fictive, and so on. But then, as you suggest, many critics—such as Hillis Miller—are writing deconstructive close readings of the same literary texts that the New Critics wrote new-critical close readings of. Such deconstructors, like the New Critics, are thereby—in a way— maintaining the autonomy of the work they're dealing with, both by separating it from specific relevance to human life and human concerns and by treating it as a self-sufficient, self-reflexive linguistic entity.

In a way, and up to a point: there is always, in other words, a point at which Miller, for example, crosses over. He first deals with Wordsworth's "A Slumber Did My Spirit Seal" as a separate poem—an independent textual entity. But then he goes on to dissolve its boundaries and to merge it first into all of Wordsworth's other writings, then into the differential play of language throughout the Western world. It's only in the initial moment, or aspect, of his criticism that Miller resembles a new-critical close reader of an autonomous text, before he proceeds to dissolve that text into what Edward Said has called the sea of textuality. But of course he continues to sustain the view that a literary text, as a self-enclosed play of linguistic *différance,* makes none but illusory references to the experienced world, human life, and human concerns.

Question: At the end of your essay "Behaviorism and Deconstruction: A Comment on Morse Peckham's 'The Infinitude of Pluralism,' " you write of a "central Romantic hope" for the reintegration of the self, of the self with a community, and of the self with a humanized nature. Deconstruction, you say there, is a "subversive" kind of criticism leading to "cultural vacuum"—refuting Peckham's notion that deconstruction, despite its problems, may at least manage to destroy the sometimes violent and authoritarian side of the Romantic ideology of "secular redemptionism" [reprinted in this volume, pp. 266–68]. In some respects J. Hillis Miller's criticism seems to fit this Romantic pattern. His use of violent analysis to move the reader to the abyss of underlying nothingness perpetuates a revolution of the spirit in the affirmation of a personal code, thus allowing him to say, "I believe in the traditional canon of English literature and the validity of the determinate text" ("The Function of Rhetorical Study at the Present Time," in *The State of the Discipline 1970s–1980s,* ed. Jaspar P. Neel [New York, 1979], p. 12). The ultimate outcome of the secular ritual of repeatedly affirming the unit of the self over the abyss sounds much like the Romantic affirmation you have described: "life, love, liberty, hope, and joy." Can't one see Miller within the Romantic tradition?

Answer: I haven't seen the essay you allude to, but it doesn't surprise me to find Hillis Miller reaffirming the traditional literary canon and the determinacy of a text. As you suggest, he can be viewed as recapitulating the process of many Romantic writers in England and America, who moved from a literal belief in violent revolution as carrying out the millenarian prophecies of the Bible to a translation of central elements of biblical and exegetical ethics into a secular, humanistic ethos. I think I'm right in saying that Hillis Miller is the son of a preacher, and he is certainly imbued with the humanistic ethos derived in many ways from certain values which, in the Bible, are grounded in divine revelation. When Miller adopts his heroic central figure—Poulet once, Derrida now—he speaks at first almost like John the Baptist. Whether the evangel is consciousness criticism or deconstruction, his initial tone tends to be evangelistic. But when the chips are down, Miller is very much a middle-of-the-road humanist who shares the central ethos of Western humanism. I think that's the post-theological heritage that the moral and other values of our civilization rest on, and I have the strongest confidence that Miller rests there, too.

In the earlier period of his enthusiasm for Derrida, I think that Miller tended to stress, and laud, some negative, countercultural implications of deconstruction. But it doesn't surprise me if he now moves to a more conservative or centrist position. In terms of the figure in my essay, of Derrida's tightrope act, one might say that Miller now stresses the right-hand side, in which Derrida affirms and uses the logocentric "effects" of a construable determinacy of meaning, of the existence of a canon of discrete and distinctive literary works, etc., where earlier Miller had stressed the left-hand side, whereby all such effects subvert, disseminate, and deconstruct themselves.

Question: In "What's the Use of Theorizing . . . ?" you claim, with certain reservations, that all applied criticism presupposes a theory of criticism. Can you explain why your own self-proclaimed pluralism is not as limited by its presuppositions as the kinds of criticism you attack for their narrowness?

Answer: Yes, I did say, and do believe, that any set of critical observations by a practicing critic involves general, or theoretical, presuppositions, even though the critic may seem to eschew a general theory of literature. Matthew Arnold, for example, who always denigrated abstract theorizing about art, quite clearly presupposes certain premises which are distinctively Arnoldian premises about literature, very different from those of other critics, including many critics in his own time such as Oscar Wilde. And of course that generalization applies to my own preferred critical practice no less than to the practice of others. There's no way for any of us to escape the limitations of a particular set of presuppositions—what for short I call a "critical perspective"—because the very sharpness of focus that a perspectival view makes possible also blurs, or conceals, what lies outside its purview. When I proclaim myself a "pluralist" in criticism, I mean to affirm my belief in the usefulness—in fact, indispensability—of diverse sets of critical presuppositions or perspectives, if we are to see literature in the round, rather than in two-dimensional flatness.

Some of us critics are very reluctant to give up the idea that we can somehow invent *one* set of critical premises and procedures that will tell us the whole story about literature. Historically, that has never happened, nor do I think it possible. Anybody who tries to be eclectic and all-inclusive ends up mashing everything together—instead of an egg you get an egg salad. I don't think we should be nonplussed by the recognition that our preferred premises can never yield everything. Why should we want to believe that one set of theoretical presuppositions will suffice to reveal the whole story about something so richly textured, so complexly structured, so diverse in the human interests it can appeal to and in its relevance to matters of human concern, and so interinvolved in both its causes and effects with other cultural factors, as literature? I'm not bothered by thinking that whatever I myself have to say about literature is only one part of the story—of a story, in fact, which has no conclusion. From my preferred, broadly humanistic premises, I decry the radical exclusiveness of certain opposing views, and even mutter darkly about their implicit threats to the very fabric of our culture. But in a more genial humor I recollect my principles as a pluralist, and say that I welcome well-considered alternative viewpoints and often find that I can learn something of substantial value from them. And since I'm now speaking in my genial humor, I'll add that this statement applies to deconstruction.

Question: How would you characterize Northrop Frye's attempt to construct a single inclusive system of criticism?

Answer: I think it's an admirable synoptic enterprise, but in some sense futile. He has made a remarkably strong and persistent effort to show how everything valid that's been revealed about literature by alternative critical premises and analytic procedures is subsumable under his own archetypal theory. But the minute they are subsumed, they can no longer play the role they played in earlier theories. They're now playing a different, circumscribed role within his particular overview of literature.

It's an admirable overview, however. It places all individual literary works within a world of imagination, wherein human needs and desires project a realm of archetypes which reshape the experienced world, yet remain relevant both to ordinary life and ordinary human concerns. Frye traces his basic conceptions back to Blake, but they seem to me no less close to Shelley's views, in his *Defence of Poetry*, that all great works of literature reflect an enduring realm of Neoplatonic archetypes. But whatever his precursors, Frye's treatment of literature is remarkable both for its originality and for its comprehensiveness. When I reviewed *The Anatomy of Criticism* many years ago [see pp. 223–33 in this volume], I drew attention to its limitations as well as to its strengths. Let me affirm now my overall judgment that in that book, and in the many writings which have followed it, Frye has proved himself to be the most innovative, learned, and important literary theorist of my generation.

Nevertheless Frye's system can't achieve what it sets out to achieve. That is, it cannot, by assimilating them all, displace all alternatives. Take a basic premise of the New Criticism, that what matters in reading poetry is to come to terms with the autonomous and unique organization of an individual work in isolation. Frye's theory is antipodal, in that it moves from the individual back to the universal. The work is viewed as participating in an imaginative universal, or archetype, and that archetype is conceived as having its place in the total and enduring structure of the imaginative world, with its seasonal analogues and so on. Now, Frye is so flexible and acute a critic that I am sure that if he chooses to, he can operate to great effect as either a New Critic or an archetypal critic. But even Frye can't operate, coherently, as an archetypist in such a way as to achieve the critical results made possible by the special premises and methods of the New Criticism.

Question: Might it be possible that the presuppositions of your own views have biased your conclusions about Romanticism? Since your approach in *Natural Supernaturalism* seems to assume the values of Western religion, for example, is it any surprise that it ends up in the realm of the Romantic positives, which are transformations of those religious values?

Answer: As a matter of biographical fact, my thinking, of which *Natural Supernaturalism* was the published product, developed in the opposite direction: First I found what I call "the positives" (the chief moral and cultural values) that were assumed and affirmed by many Romantic poets, and only gradually did I come to see how deeply they were grounded in certain values of the religious tradition, of which they constitute, in part, a secularized translation. These values, of course, are in that aspect culture-bound, but many of them are not simply Hebraic-Christian values; they have equivalents in other major religions. Furthermore, we mustn't forget that the values of much Western theology are not simple derivatives from the Bible, but were biblical concepts as reinterpreted and expanded in terms of the philosophy of the Greeks and Romans. So that the primary Romantic values had a mixed origin; and they seem to me to remain central to a humane view of life and to be relevant among the criteria by which to judge literature—as T. S. Eliot put it, not to judge whether a work of literature is literature, but to judge whether a work of literature is great literature.

One other thing. There are numerous elements in the Western religious tradition which I find abhorrent and which have had disastrous implications in history—they have fostered fanaticism, tyranny, cruelty, internecine warfare. Radical antinomianism, for example, is a recurrent strain in that tradition. Another is a literal apocalypticism, or chiliasm, which in times of stress has led people to pin their fanatical loyalty to a messianic leader of what Rufus Jones has called "an apocalyptic relief expedition from the sky." So it is a question of which values from the inherited tradition you select. I think it a good thing that many major Romantic poets turned from their early faith in a chiliastic recovery of Eden by bloody violence to a belief in an imaginative transformation of the self that would make one see the old world in a new way, and to act accordingly. Some historians regard that change as no more than a weak retreat from political radicalism to political reaction. But I think it undeniable that some of the greatest Romantic poets, including Blake, Hölderlin, Wordsworth, Coleridge, Shelley, wrote their best poetry after abandoning their literal faith in an apocalypse by violence for a metaphorical faith in an apocalypse by imagination.

Question: Changes in theories of literature seem to change the shape of literary history. The New Criticism, for example, devalued Romanticism, while Frye's archetypal criticism makes Blake central to Romanticism and Romanticism central to literary history. Is deconstruction changing our view of Romanticism?

Answer: It's hard to see how it could do so without being unfaithful to its own premises, which make it radically ahistorical. It dissolves not only the boundaries between literature and nonliterature in any one period, but also the boundaries between one writer and another and between one period and another. Writing, that is, is always writing; its constitution is always the same play of *différance,* it always exhibits logocentrism, and it is always ultimately self-subversive. Of course, there is the conservative right-hand side of Derrida's equilibrium, which acknowledges the standard distinction between distinct works, individual writers, and various periods on the level of logocentric "effects": but Derrida recognizes and uses such effects only "provisionally," or "strategically," as a stage toward disseminating them. Since a major thrust of deconstruction is to convert all antitheses into chiasmus, and to dissolve temporal as well as all other "boundaries," I don't see how any thoroughgoing follower of Derrida can have anything in particular to say about Blake, Romanticism, or any individual writer and any literary period. Except, of course, to the degree that a deconstructive critic forgets his own premises. Fortunately, all of us theorists sometimes escape from our premises long enough to say things which, however inconsistent, are insightful and important.

Question (continued): Under the influence of deconstruction, isn't it natural to value Blake more than Wordsworth? Complaints about Wordsworth seem to have increased sharply—it no longer seems undiplomatic to launch an outright attack on his self-contradictions—while I've heard it said more than once that Blake may have been the first deconstructionist. He seems so aware of the pitfalls of language and so playfully wily in confronting them. Wordsworth's linguistic earnestness makes him an easy target of deconstruction instead of a paradigm. How true is the generalization that literary history under deconstruction favors the writers who reflect its concerns with and attitudes toward language?

Answer (continued): You persuade me of the need to make a distinction between deconstructive procedures in reading that I neglected in my previous answer. Derrida clearly, in his readings, distinguishes his treatment of writers whom we may for convenience call "paradigmatic," from his treatment of other writers. Paradigmatic writers he construes as asserting, or at least implying, doctrines about language and metaphysics and central Western concepts which approximate his own views—even though I think he would not want to call his own views "truths." Among his paradigmatic writers are of course Nietzsche, and also Mallarmé—in fact, it is my impression that Derrida's typical essays on writers ordinarily called "literary" are not radically deconstructive, but stop at the stage of reading these writers paradigmatically or at tracing approvingly their way of playing with key metaphysical concepts and distinctions.

In his deconstructive essays, Hillis Miller seems to follow Derrida's differential way of treating paradigmatic and non-paradigmatic writers, but he applies the distinction within the literary realm as well as outside it. For Miller as for Derrida, Nietzsche is clearly and reiteratively paradigmatic. And within literature itself, Miller treats Wallace Stevens, for example, primarily as paradigmatic. That is, he for the most part stops at reading—in my sense of construing—selected textual passages from Stevens as anticipating what he presents as deconstructive truths about language and metaphysical concepts. His analysis of Wordsworth's "A Slumber," on the other hand, is devoted to showing how that poem, when read allegorically by an unmystified reader, can't help but manifest the deep truth of the death of the "logos," and thereby undoes itself despite itself. Which can, I think, be translated to say, in my terms, that its implicit allegorical meanings inadvertently but inescapably undo its construed meaning.

But to the thrust of your question: deconstructive critics indeed seem to set higher value on paradigmatic writers whom they can construe, and not simply allegorize, as anticipating their own convictions about language. But there's another factor involved in their choice of writers to write critical essays about, and that is the challenge of taking a writer who seems canonical, straightforward, and resistant to deconstruction, and then showing how his texts unknowingly deconstruct themselves. I'm very dubious indeed that Blake, for all his controverting standard uses of language, can be read by a deconstructor as paradigmatic; beyond most poets, he is an essentialist who claims that his fundamental assertions disclose presence. Another major poetic text of the Romantic era, Byron's *Don Juan*, is of a more paradigmatic order. It is easy to show that in many passages in *Don Juan*, Byron can be construed as deliberately subverting not only the poem's own narrative premises, but also major concepts and oppositions in Western metaphysics—so easy, in fact, that it doesn't present much of a challenge. Wordsworth, in his seriousness of asseveration, presents a much more inviting challenge.

We find a parallel in the evolution of the New Criticism. Cleanth Brooks, like his colleagues, began by reading Donne as a paradigmatic exemplar of the major literary virtues of ambiguity, symbolic imagery, irony, and paradox, and used those criteria to derogate poets of the reigning canon—Milton, Romantic and Victorian poets—as writers who are defective because unironic, committed to forthright assertions, and unparadoxical. But as time went on, Brooks delighted in taking up the challenge of demonstrating that such canonical poems as Milton's *Lycidas*, Wordsworth's *Intimations Ode*, and Tennyson's *Tears, Idle Tears* can also be accounted great poems, insofar as they in fact embody features, overlooked both by critical precursors and by the poets themselves, of ambiguity, symbolic imagery, irony, and paradox.

Question: Do you think that the deconstructionist interpretation of a text has any cognitive value beyond correctly "construing," as you say, the primary meaning of the text? To put it another way, do you learn anything from the specifically deconstructionist moves involved in Miller's reading of

Wordsworth's "A Slumber Did My Spirit Seal," or are you merely entertained by them?

Answer: I've already said that I have learned things I value both from the analytic procedures and verbal play of Derrida. (I find particularly notable the essay called "White Mythology.") I have also profited from the writings of de Man, Miller, Barbara Johnson, and other expert practitioners of the deconstructive craft. Some things I've learned are positive; others (no less valuable to me) are negative, in that they've forced me to redefine and defend my own critical stance, and led me to try to identify the moves which enable deconstructors to achieve their startling new readings.

Miller's essay on "A Slumber" I chose for commentary, as I have said, in part because it is so extreme an instance of radically deconstructive criticism. One of its inherent values consists in Miller's flair for language and the zest he communicates in his own ingenuity at finding in Wordsworth's little poem a galaxy of meanings that no one hitherto has in the least suspected. (I shudder to think what we may expect in a similar vein from deconstructive critics who lack Miller's talents, learning, flair, and, the *sine qua non,* his tact and sensitivity in reading a text on the primary level of construing.) But in this particular instance of the deconstructive, or "allegorical" phase of Miller's criticism, I can't say I've learned anything that I consider valid about the meaning of Wordsworth's poem, except insofar as his claims have driven me back to scrutinize the text itself.

It's worth noting that, according to its own frequently given account, poststructuralist literary criticism aims to be "productive" and autonomous rather than auxiliary, with a function no less creative and interesting than that of the literary work to which it ostensibly directs its attention. To the degree to which deconstructive criticism in fact accords with its own statement of its function, it is a mode of what Aristotle called epideictic rhetoric. That is, it belongs in the class of display oratory, of which the aim is to celebrate an occasion such as the Fourth of July. The orator doesn't really undertake to tell us anything we don't know already about his ostensible subject, the Fourth of July; instead, he sets out to show how well he can meet a ritual emergency which has evoked innumerable earlier orations and to display his own invention, verbal and rhetorical skills, and aplomb for the admiration and delight of his audience.

Question: Would you clarify the difference in the role that construing a text plays in more traditional criticism as against deconstructive criticism?

Answer: At the level of construing a text, the reader makes out what the sentences of a text signify, in the order in which those sentences occur. He does so on the supposition, for which we have convincing grounds in our experience in learning, using, and understanding a language, that he shares with the writer of the text certain conventions governing the practice of the language which enable him to understand what, on this primary level, the writer undertook to say.

All of us, including deconstructive critics, have to construe a text such as Wordsworth's "A Slumber," or else we're simply not reading English: and although no construal is ever capable, by reference to an infallible criterion (what Derrida calls "a transcendental referent") of being absolutely provable beyond any possibility of error, we are capable in most instances of achieving adequate assurance about its construed meaning, which is confirmed by substantial agreement with other competent construers. But construal of a poem merges, without sharp boundary, into what I have called "explication," which poses questions about the kind of poem it is, what is central to the poem, how it is structured, what effects its author undertook to achieve, etc. In this aspect of what we loosely call "interpreting" a poem, criticism begins to become variable, and by that fact, more interesting. You get, for example, the application to the construed poem of diverse critical perspectives, as well as favored value-concepts, such as the ambiguity, irony, and paradox of the New Criticism. (In "Five Types of *Lycidas*" [reprinted in this volume], an essay written decades before the emergence of deconstruction, I pointed out how radically different are the explications effected by applying to a single text diverse critical perspectives and criteria.) Here we find the area of critical disagreement widening, and a diminishing consensus about the criteria for deciding between alternative explications; I've always liked the formulation of F. R. Leavis that, in this aspect of his procedure, a critic who proposes an explication learns to expect from another critic at most the qualified agreement, "Yes, but. . . ." By and large, however, the mixed class of what Hillis Miller called traditional critics agree in keeping the text-as-construed a primary reference—that is, they would reject an explication which is patently out of keeping with the construal; a traditional critic will also agree that many of the reasons offered by another critic, even for a radically alternative explication, may be sound reasons, even though he regards them as falling short of being convincing reasons. The deconstructive critic, however, rejects both the reference to the construed text and the standard reasons for justifying an explication, as illusory "constraints" on reading which are overcome by an inherent force, or "surplus of meaning," which is beyond any possibility of control by either the writer or the reader of the poem.

(Let me interject, by the way, that although New Critics tended to regard the "interpretation"—constituted by the construal and the explication of a text—as the be-all and end-all of criticism, literary critics before, during, and since that era have fortunately continued to carry on the traditional enterprises of enhancing our understanding of individual works of literature by bringing them into various relations with other works, other genres, other modes of discourse, the life and times of the author, and the intellectual, social, and economic as well as literary history of the West.)

I have said that a standard move of the deconstructive critic, in establishing a requisite freedom of interpretive maneuver, is to make the text-as-initially-construed (and in part explicated) into a pre-text for interpretive over-reading—often this over-reading is labeled "allegorical" and is imposed entirely independently of any evidence that the author intended his work to be an allegory. This move has some, though only partial, parallels in more traditional critical procedures. Let's take a very simple case. A Freudian critic comes across Blake's gnomic lines:

> Can Wisdom be put in a silver rod?
> Or Love in a golden bowl?

Aha! A rod is convex and a bowl is concave; we all know what such shapes symbolize; we can now proceed to over-read what Blake meant according to Freudian mechanisms, independently of what Blake may have consciously undertaken to say. Notice that this interpretation begins by construing the determinate meanings of *rod* and *bowl*, which become a pretext for the over-reading, and that the Freudian critic would agree that if he has misconstrued the primary meanings of *rod* or *bowl*, then his symbolic over-reading is also mistaken. Notice also that our postulated critic proposes that his symbolic over-readings of Blake's sentences constitute their determinately right, or deeper meanings, even though these meanings are supervenient on the construed meanings.

It is with this last claim that the deconstructive critic radically disagrees. His or her allegorical over-reading of the construed text "produces" a disseminative "overloading" (Derrida's terms)—an endless scatter of meanings which are "undecidable," rather than determinately multiplex, or "polysemantic." That is, the construed text, as over-read deconstructively, has no determinately right meaning, nor even a limited set of specific meanings; it disseminates, allegorically, into an indefinitely open set of inevitably contradictory possibilities.

(By the way, my intention is to use the term "over-reading" noninvidiously, for convenience of exposition. I would be glad to reverse the implicit diagrammatic polarity, and trade the metaphor of over-reading for the metaphor of under-reading. This change to under-reading is compatible with the deconstructive claim to *under*mine meaning and would also cancel the built-in implication of "over-reading" that to read deconstructively is to do something excessive. I must point out, however, that the change would also cancel the implication that deconstruction is a mode of higher criticism. I leave the choice between these directional metaphors to the deconstructive critics.)

Question (continued): When you say that deconstruction can produce traditionally acceptable or genuine readings in passing, do you mean that these insights occur despite the theory rather than because of it? Just what is it that you claim to have learned from a deconstructor such as Derrida?

Answer (continued): A deconstructive reader, even in his disseminative phase, establishes a mode of reading which (I quoted Derrida as saying in my essay) is relatively, but not entirely, free from the "legalities" that constrain the initial phase that I call construing. Furthermore, deconstruction is in principle a mode of double-dealing with texts, in which you can take or leave (rather, take-and-leave) such constraints. Both in principle and in practice, then, deconstruction can produce readings that are sound according to traditional criteria of interpretation.

Besides, there are things one can learn from what Derrida calls his "style." Some of his characteristic modes of verbal and rhetorical play are very infectious. I would not, for example, be prepared to avow that my own procedures in the present dialogue have in no instance been affected by Derrida's proclivity, rejecting the "logocentric" logic of either-or, to speak and write in a way which, instead of being either serious or nonserious, is at the same time *neither* serious nor nonserious and *both* serious and nonserious. I leave the decision to my auditors as to which of my assertions from this platform were intended to be taken as entirely serious. (Including, of course, what I've just asserted.)

Question: You distinguish between construing, explicating, and disseminating a literary text. How would you respond to Stanley Fish's claim that all aspects of interpreting a text are relative to a particular strategy, which is an arbitrary, or at least an optional, strategy? To Fish, even what you call "construing a text" deludedly thinks it finds shared meanings which are in fact projected on an empty text by members of an interpretive community who simply happen to share a certain strategy of interpretation.

Answer: Those issues are too complex to be fully discussed here. But let me propose some crude headings for a response to Fish's claim. I have said in an essay ("How to Do Things with Texts," [reprinted in this volume]), that Fish seems to me right in his claims that the meanings of a text are relative to an interpretive strategy and that agreement about meanings depends on our joint membership in a community which shares an interpretive strategy. It's a question, however, of how extensive that community is and whether it includes the writer, as well as the reader, of a text. Take Milton's *Lycidas* as an example. In construing the sentences of Milton's text, we have excellent grounds for the assurance (based on reading Milton, Milton's contemporaries, and writers before and after Milton) that he belongs to our interpretive community, which is no less extensive than all those who speak, write, and understand English; that Milton used his inherited expertise in the conventional regularities of the English language to write texts (admittedly, on a high level of complexity) meant to be determinately construable by competent readers; hence that we, as members of Milton's community—making allowance for limited and largely discoverable historical shifts in the conventions of the language—by applying our shared expertise, are for the most part quite able to construe what Milton undertook to mean by the sentences he wrote.

It is our diversity of interpreting *Lycidas* on the level I have called "explication" that gives some plausibility to Fish's claim that there are an indefinite number of interpretive communities, each of which produces its own poem. (A fuller discussion would need to point out that the distinction between construing and explicating is not sharp-boundaried but nonetheless useful for exposition; also that even the phase of construal is to some degree responsive to a particular explication, yet recalcitrant to excessive explicative distortion.) In explicating *Lycidas* as a poem, for one thing, we have less grounds for assurance than we have in construing its component sentences as to just what poetic conventions Milton deployed, though we do have a number of sound clues to their nature. Also, as I pointed out in "Five Types of *Lycidas*," a number of critics have chosen to explicate *Lycidas* by applying a diversity of critical perspectives independently of any clues about Milton's own artistic intentions. You can, if you want to use Fish's concepts, say that the set of new-critical explicators of *Lycidas,* the set of archetypal critics, the set of more or less Freudian critics, as well as the set of old-fashioned critics like myself who undertake to read *Lycidas* "with the same spirit that its author writ," each constitutes a distinct explicative community; that these communities have all been institutionalized in the Academy; that the diverse critical perspectives adopted by these communities produce what I have called diverse "types" of *Lycidas,* with identifiable family resemblances among the instances of each type; and that individual critics within an explicative community are much more apt to agree with each other than with someone who applies a radically different critical perspective.

To bring an over-hasty discussion to a hasty conclusion: In construing Milton's text, we have no interpretive option except whether to resign from the ongoing community of speakers, writers, and readers of English into which we, like Milton, were born. In the phase of explicating a construed text, however, we can distinguish a variety of loosely constituted subcommunities; and in this aspect of critical interpretation, it makes sense to say that readers have a choice among available interpretive strategies.

Question: While you obviously believe that it is possible for an author to communicate a meaning and for a reader to get that meaning, you have on at least one occasion characterized metaphors as inherently inadequate:

> The human compulsion not only to say, do, and make but also to understand what we say, do, and make enforces a discourse about these processes and products of consciousness, intention, purpose, and design. This discourse unavoidably involves metaphors whose vehicles are natural or artificial objects, and since none of these objects runs on all fours with the human primitives it undertakes to define and take into account, each metaphor, however pertinent, remains inadequate. It is because a number of metaphorical vehicles are pertinent, yet no one is adequate, that the history I undertook to narrate [in *The Mirror and the Lamp*] displays the recurrent

emergence, exploitation, displacement, and supplementation of constitutive metaphors; this historical process seems to me to be in the long run profitable to understanding, in that it provides . . . a vision in depth in place of the two-dimensional vision of the complex realities with which the metaphors engage ("A Reply," in *High Romantic Argument: Essays for M. H. Abrams*, ed. by Lawrence Lipking [Ithaca, N.Y., 1981], p. 173).

Answer: Your quotation occurs in a context in which I was explaining why none of the "constitutive metaphors" that are applied to works of art, since their vehicles are natural or artificial objects, can equate exactly with the human, intentional, and purposive procedures by which a work of art is designed and produced. But the point can be generalized. I quote Coleridge as saying that "no simile runs on all four legs." That is, no figurative term squares exactly with whatever it is you're applying it to; otherwise, you wouldn't be able to recognize that it's figurative. So I agree with Derrida that we can't dispense with metaphors, and also that there's always a discrepancy, which he calls a "surplus," or "excess," between a metaphor and its application.

I don't agree, however, that this discrepancy, or excess, in the vehicle of a metaphor is uncontrollable by a user of the metaphor, or by the listener or reader who understands how he's applying it—that the excess, by an internal energy, runs wild and inescapably goes on to say what the user of the metaphor doesn't want to say. In *The Mirror and the Lamp* I described, for example, the way in which later users explored the implications of discrepancies in organic metaphors, as applied to the production and internal organizations of works of art, which earlier users of such metaphors, in the contexts of their usage, overrode as unintended and irrelevant. But when I read a user of organic metaphors such as Coleridge, I recognize what he intended that metaphor to signify—I understand what, in the context of Coleridge's *parole,* the metaphor means. At the same time, I recognize potentialities in the features of the organic vehicle of the metaphor that Coleridge did not call into play; and on investigation, I find that later writers did exploit these features in their *paroles.*

The process of the surplus getting out of control, that is, is a historical process, which I discover by examining a sequence of textual *paroles* by a variety of writers. I don't find that process necessarily occurring, despite the writer's intention, in every *parole* by every user of an organic metaphor on every occasion of its use; nor do I see how such a conclusion follows from the fact that in no metaphoric vehicle do all the features equate exactly with its tenor—with what someone in a particular context uses it to say.

Question: J. Hillis Miller confessed his willingness to say that metaphors signify a finite set of meanings. If so, aren't you and he agreeing?

Answer: I'm not familiar with the statement of Miller's that you allude to. But insofar as he undertakes to describe or paraphrase what any text, or metaphoric segment of a text, signifies, he has no recourse except to list a number of determinate meanings, which he presents to be determinately understood by us, his readers. You cite him as saying that this set, or scatter, of determinate meanings is finite; but as his analysis of Wordsworth's "A Slumber" demonstrates, it's a very large set, and probably an open set; I feel quite certain that if Miller should return to the poem, he could, by the freedom of interpretive maneuver he permits himself, readily make new discoveries of signification. But whether it is finite or not, the important features of his set of meanings, on which Miller indubitably insists, is that the set is very large, inevitably includes aporias, and is undecidable—that is, there is no valid reason whatever for choosing between incompatible alternatives.

We know, both from the texts written by some authors and from what they say about their own writings, that some literary works are intentionally written to be read in precisely this way, so that we can't in fact be said properly to understand such works except if we read them as signifying an indefinite set of undecidable and mutually incompatible meanings; this is a literary genre energetically exploited by some writers of the present era. The novelty of the deconstructive claim is that all literary works are instances of this genre, no matter how lucid, determinate, and coherent are the meanings that an author undertook to express in a work. The model of writing that a deconstructive critic presupposes is that of a power struggle between what a writer tries to use language, in his *parole,* to mean and what language, by an internal compulsion which manifests itself by an "excess" in the *parole,* goes on willy-nilly to mean—a struggle in which language ineluctably overcomes all attempts by the writer to control its unruly differential energy. This model seems to me to be radically unapt for our actual linguistic practice; but it serves as an effective rationale for the surprising semantic discoveries of a determined deconstructive reader.

Question: You have described yourself as, among other things, a cultural historian. Can you use your distinction— the distinction between the level of construing and explicating a text, and the second level on which the text-as-construed is used as a pre-text—to compare your role as an interpreter with the role of deconstructive critics? For example, would it be fair to say that you, as a cultural historian, substitute "real world" for "text" in the distinction I have described? And if so, that you confine yourself to the level of construing and explicating the real world, whereas deconstructors and fiction writers begin with a text and move up to the level of using it merely as a pre-text for a supervenient allegory?

Answer: I do not, in *Natural Supernaturalism,* claim to be interpreting "the real world." The materials that I interpret are texts and passages from texts. I construe them and explicate them in a determinate way; and on the basis of identifying in these texts certain thematic similarities, and changes in those themes over time, I develop a complex narrative history not about reality, but about altering human views concerning the nature of reality—about (to mention only one of many such themes) the overall form of the past, the present condition, and the future of the human race. The soundness of the history I relate—as a pluralist I hold that it can be a sound history, even if it is only one of diverse possible histories—depends on the representativeness of the texts I choose, given the focus of my undertaking, and above all, on the validity of my determinate readings of those texts. I don't deny that there are meanings of the same texts which, since they fall outside my purview, I do not explore; my implicit claim is only that by and large, and whatever else they mean, the texts that I cite at least mean, determinately, what I interpret them to mean.

An added comment. I think that I recognize in the way you pose your question a widespread current assumption that, since we can say, sensibly enough, that we interpret the world and also that we interpret a text, then an interpretation of a text is subject to no more "constraints" than is an interpretation of the natural world. Where this parallel fails is in ignoring the fact that the language of a text is a medium specifically developed to convey meaning, and that the text was written by an author who undertook to say something determinate by his use of that medium. The constitution of reality, or the natural world, lacks those distinctive and essential features for the determination of meaning—except, of course, for a theologian who believes, as many have indeed believed, that the world is the great book of nature, whose true meanings can be interpreted by cracking the code which determines the significations that its divine Author intended it to convey.

Question: Most of your published work is about Romantic writers. Do you see any Romantic tendencies in yourself and your work?

Answer: I'm not sure by what criteria I'd qualify as a Romantic or a non-Romantic. But I think that my writings about selected writers of the era between the French Revolution and the third or fourth decade of the nineteenth century manifest a strong sympathy with many of their characteristic enterprises. This applies above all to the great Romantic undertaking, in a time of social, cultural, and moral crisis and demoralization—many writers agreed with Wordsworth that it was without precedent a time of "dereliction and dismay"—to reconstitute the grounds of social, cultural,

and moral values in the West by translating the earlier theological concepts into primarily secular terms. In *Natural
Supernaturalism* I traced this enterprise, as variously, and
sometimes explicitly, proposed by many writers, whether in
poems, novels, philosophy, or history. This is a common feature, for example, in Romantic works otherwise as diverse as
Wordsworth's *Prelude,* Hegel's *Phenomenology,* Hölderlin's prose
romance *Hyperion,* and Shelley's *Prometheus Unbound.*

Question: J. Hillis Miller said in answer to a question about
his reading of a poem by Yeats that a traditional historical
reading of that poem would be an incompetent or wrong
reading. Would you say that his reading of "A Slumber Did
My Spirit Seal" is incompetent or wrong?

Answer: Competency or incompetency in reading are terms
that apply within a particular frame of reference. When he
operates within the limits of traditional construal and explication, Miller has shown himself to be a competent traditional reader; when he operates with the freedom established
by deconstructive premises, he has shown himself to be a
competent disseminative reader. I don't, as you know, subscribe to the premises that serve to justify such freedom of
interpretive procedure. But no gong rings in heaven or hell
to proclaim that the premises and practices of deconstruction
are wrong or wicked; nor do I know of a knock-down argument guaranteed to convince critics of the deconstructive
persuasion that they are on a hopelessly wrong track. I point
out to deconstructionists, for example, how easy it is, given
the requisite learning and wit, to produce sensationally novel
readings when their elected premises permit them to operate
with such minimal constraints. Deconstructionists counter that
my inordinate constraints are illusions engendered by a logocentrism from which I can't possibly escape, and which prevent me from discovering in a text anything more interesting
than the reflection of my own projected illusions.

Now, how am I to argue against that? It's of no rational or
practical use to hurl epithets and call down anathema, as some
conservative critics do. What I first try to do is to understand

what it is that competent deconstructors are actually doing, on what premises, and what it is that makes it, to such obviously intelligent, learned, and sensitive critics, seem worth doing. Then (as in my essay on *Construing and Deconstructing* and in this discussion) I point out what seem to me anomalies in the theory and extravagances in the practice of deconstruction. In doing that, I solicit my wit and marshal rhetorical resources such as irony and *reductio* to highlight and exaggerate such features. But as I suggested at the end of the essay, the choice between a radically deconstructive and a more traditional mode of reading is a choice between premises which can't be conclusively argued by logic alone, because it involves a choice between values—it is a matter, as I said in an earlier essay ("How to Do Things with Texts" [reprinted in this volume]), of "cultural cost-accounting." Even so, if I should say to Hillis Miller that ultimately such a choice entails whether or not to be a communicant in a society held together by our capability to say determinately what we mean and to understand (actually, and not merely as a provisional stage of illusionary effects to be noted and transcended) what someone else has said—well, I'm quite sure that Miller would produce reasons for denying that his own choice of a deconstructive mode of reading entails so drastic a consequence.

Question (continued): If Derrida or Miller shows that he can competently construe the text before deconstructing it, does that competence determine the competence of his deconstructive interpretation?

Answer (continued): If a deconstructive critic doesn't demonstrate competence at the primary aspect of reading that I called construing a text and explicating it in a way closely tied to that construal, he cannot be competent in what follows, because (as Derrida himself is careful to point out, in the passage I quoted in my essay) the effects of "classical exigencies" that constrain what he calls "traditional criticism" not only precede but, in ways that he leaves indefinite, continue to exert some kind of control over a second-order dissemination; otherwise the latter reading would, as he says, "authorize itself to say almost anything." Those classical exigencies, in my view, are grounded on solid evidence that authors largely share with their readers the regularities that govern the practice of a language and the evidence that most authors have in fact exploited their expertise in those conventional regularities to write texts designed to be determinately understandable by their readers.

In his disseminative commentary on Wordsworth's "A Slumber," Miller continues to rely, in however loose and tenuous a fashion, on some of the constraints that determine his initial construal. And even when he claims for his second-order deconstructive reading the feature that he regards as its special value, its openness "to the inexhaustible strangeness of literary texts," he uses "strangeness" in tacit opposition to the meanings we (and he) expect in the standard reading of a text; by what other criterion can he adjudge the disseminated meanings to be "strange"? So Miller's radically deconstructive reading is dependent upon standard reading not only in its initial phase, and (in undefined ways) in its disseminative phase, but also in his very attempt to argue the virtues of his deconstructive way of reading.

Question: You claimed that you have tried objectively to understand the premises, procedures, and reasons for the appeal of deconstructive criticism, and then went on to suggest that to choose it involves, in a final analysis, the choice whether or not to participate in a community for which the capability to communicate determinately constitutes an indispensable bond. But is that claim of objectivity sincere, and are the alternatives that you suggest alternatives in which you genuinely believe? Might it not be the fact, as deconstructionists often assert, that your claim is a façade, and that your reasoning is in fact a rationalization of your nostalgia for a lost certainty of presence, involving a variety of rhetorical ploys that are motivated by anger (which is in turn a result of your terror) at the deconstructive demonstration that all our Western talking, writing, and thinking is suspended over an abyss by its reliance on a ground which deconstruction shows to be in fact groundless?

Answer: I am familiar with the charge by some deconstructionists that any attempt by a nondeconstructionist to understand their position objectively and to argue against it rationally can never be anything other than a rationalization for metaphysical nostalgia and cultural terror. That seems to me to be itself a rhetorical device to put all possible opponents in an untenable position. As a literary and intellectual historian, and as a theorist of language and of literary criticism, I have tried to emulate the procedure that J. S. Mill, in a great essay, attributed to Coleridge: When confronted with a position, posed by highly intelligent thinkers, which seems to me mistaken, I try to "look at it from within . . . to see it with the eyes of a believer in it; to discover by what apparent facts it was at first suggested, and by what appearances it has . . . been rendered . . . credible."

This is the third public occasion on which I have tried to come to terms with deconstructive theory and with radical deconstructive criticism. Each time, as the result of continued reading and reflection, I think that, in the Coleridgean sense, I understand it better and find in it, as I said, interesting and even profitable insights. But I nonetheless remain radically unpersuaded. So far as I am able to assess my motives, I remain unpersuaded on grounds of experience and reasoning and also (as I have said) of my commitment to certain social and cultural values; but not because of my nostalgia for a demolished ontological ground of absolute certainty in which I have never, in my maturity, invested any belief, nor of my abject terror at a conclusive demonstration that our culture is suspended by a network of illusions over a linguistic and intellectual *abyme*.

But I do confess to occasional fits of anger, or rather of irritation, at some deconstructive moves, such as the one you describe, designed proleptically to put out of play any possibility of validly reasoned grounds for opposing it. By way of conclusion, let me specify another such move. I have said that deconstructive theory proposes a model for the relation of a speaker or writer to language which seems to me to be very defective—the model, that is, of a power struggle between unequal antagonists in which the inherent differential energy of language ineluctably overcomes any effort by a user to master it, by disseminating what he says into an undecidable *suspens vibratoire* which includes significations that controvert what the user has undertaken to say. Some poststructuralists have translated the metaphor of power struggle into a metaphor of *Machtpolitik,* and have extended it from the relation between the writer and his linguistic medium to the relation between a written text and its interpreter. They assert that to interpret a text as signifying what its writer undertook to mean is nothing other than to succumb to the "author's" illegitimate claim to "authority," or "authoritarianism," over both his text and his reader. But to set ourselves to make out what someone has undertaken verbally to convey is simply to try to understand him or her, and the attempt to understand each other's utterances, whether spoken or written, seems to me indispensable to the maintenance of anything we can account a human community. I am thus irritated whenever I encounter this rhetorical move, by a play on words, to put anyone who tries to understand what someone else has tried to communicate into the humiliating posture of obsequiousness to an arrogated authoritarianism.

On Political Readings of Lyrical Ballads

"Why this is ideology, nor am I out of it."

THE CRITICISM OF WORDSWORTH, which took a linguistic turn in the New Criticism of the 1930s, and even more
sharply in the semiotics and the deconstructive criticism of
the 1970s, has in the present decade taken a decidedly political turn. This sudden left-face in the march of Wordsworth
studies, especially of the earlier poetry, is indicated by the
prevalence of the term *politics* in the titles of books and essays,
such as "The Politics of 'Tintern Abbey,' " "Criticism, Politics, and Style in Wordsworth's Poetry," *Wordsworth's Second
Nature: A Study of the Poetry and Politics.* Three books, all published between 1983 and 1986, although they do not feature
the word in their titles, are drastically political in their treatment of Wordsworth: Heather Glen's *Vision and Disenchantment,* Jerome McGann's *The Romantic Ideology,* and Marjorie
Levinson's *Wordsworth's Great Period Poems.* I want to address
two questions with respect to this recent critical direction:
What are the premises and procedures of a radically political
criticism? And what does such criticism make of the poems
in the *Lyrical Ballads* of 1798, but especially of "Tintern
Abbey"?

My discussion is not intended to apply overall to the current movement called the New Historicism. That term covers
a broad range of overlapping critical enterprises. One wing
(its practitioners tend to identify themselves as "new histori-
cists" and to use "power" as their critical leitmotif) is mainly

in the lineage of Michel Foucault; the other wing (its exem-
plars are apt to call what they do "political criticism" and to
use "ideology" as their leitmotif) is more distinctly in the lineage of Karl Marx. My concern is with the sons of Karl rather
than with the sons (and daughters) of Michel, and of these,
primarily with some radical, or all-out representatives of that
critical mode.

At first view, political criticism seems merely an intensified
form of a prominent feature in earlier Wordsworth studies.
For no other major poet has been more persistently treated
from the vantage of his politics than has Wordsworth, in his
shift from revolutionary radicalism to Tory conservatism, by
a line of critics from his contemporaries to such distinguished recent commentators as Carl Woodring, David Erdman, and E. P. Thompson. Closer inspection, however, reveals
an important shift in focus, assumptions, and methods among
recent political critics. It seems to me misleading to claim flatly,
as Stephen Greenblatt does, that "the traditional historical
approach to literature . . . finds history to lie outside the texts,
to function in effect as the object to which signs in the text
point."[1] This description doesn't do justice to many historical
critics, all the way back from Leslie Stephen to Ian Watt and
David Erdman, who not only advert to social and political
history as circumstances that shape a literary work, but also
identify implicit social and political structures and values that
are inscribed within the literary works themselves. But
Greenblatt is revealing when he goes on to specify a newer
approach that finds history "in the artworks themselves, as
enabling condition, shaping force, forger of meaning." The
view that history, not the author, shapes a literary work and
forges its meaning is indeed the crucial feature in the shift
from traditional historical criticism both to the New Historicism and to the New Politicalism.

To explore this difference further, we can say in the first
place that political criticism, despite its frequent claims to the
contrary, moves entirely with the critical current of the present, which is emphatically an Age of Reading. Like many of
their critical contemporaries, political critics undertake to read
a text so as to make out, whatever it seems to say, what it
really means. They often, it is true, set themselves expressly

to counter the apolitical close-reading of New Critics, who analyzed a poem as an isolated and autonomous verbal construct, as well as what Paul de Man suggested was the still closer reading of apolitical deconstructive critics, who interpreted the text both as self-referential and as self-disseminative into an open set of undecidable meanings. In opposition to these precursors, New Political critics announce what seems to me a laudable intention to salvage a literary work as a determinably meaningful human product, rooted in the biographical circumstances of its author and the social particularities of its time and place, and consequential to us in our present circumstances. They do so, however, by appropriating the modes and devices of close reading that they undertake to displace, but adapting them to a "political"—which is primarily a neo-Marxist—way of reading. "Marxism," Irving Howe has ruefully noted, now "finds an old-age home in American universities."[2] We can add that political critics in the universities have modulated Marx's aim to change the world into changing the way we read poems.

Marjorie Levinson defines clearly the shift from earlier historical criticism, whether or not it was Marxist, to the kind she practices. "What [E. P.] Thompson and his fellow workers [she mentions Erdman and Woodring] could not, given their critical moment, address, were the subtler languages of politics in Wordsworth's poetry, and the way these languages inform and inflect the manifest doctrine of the poetry." Her own procedure is to use historical material expressly "for the purposes of textual intervention," in such a way as "to explain the poem's transformational grammar" and to produce "a closer reading of it"—a closer reading that discovers "new meanings" and, it turns out, typically "discredits" or "dismantles" a poem's "manifest statement," or "contradicts its expressed doctrine."[3] Political criticism is thus not only a mode of reading; it is also what I have elsewhere called a mode of "Newreading." That is, like the various critical "theories" of recent decades that it sets out to replace, political criticism is designed to subvert what a poet undertook to say, what his text seems to say, and what other readers have taken him to say, in order to convert manifest meanings into a mask, or displacement, or (another of Levinson's terms) an "alle-

gory" for the real meaning—in this case, a political meaning—
whose discovery has been reserved for the proponent of the
theory.

1

What, on analysis, turns out to be the logical structure of a
political theory and practice of reading literature? This
structure is both most clear and most rigorous in explicitly
principled critics like McGann and Levinson—who invoke
frequently both Marx and recent neo-Marxist theorists such
as Macherey, Eagleton, and Jameson—but it controls in varying degree the reading of other political critics as well.

(1) The basic premise, to cite Jerome McGann's version, is
that "poems are social and historical products"—products "at
the ideological level" of social functions, which he describes
as in complex interrelation with the "political" and the "economic" levels. That is, the ideology of a particular time and
place inescapably processes whatever authors undertake to
say into representations that McGann calls "concrete forms"
of ideology, or an "artistic reproduction" that "historicizes
the ideological materials, gives a local habitation and a name
to various kinds of abstractions." It follows "that the critical
study of such products must be grounded in a socio-historical analytic," and that all more "specialized studies"—such as
stylistic, rhetorical, formal—"must find their *raison d'être* in
the socio-historical ground." Like other current theories of
Newreading, then, a radically political criticism is a "must-
be," or necessitarian theory: it brings to the reading of any
literary work a predetermination of the kind of meaning—
in this instance, an ideological meaning—that the act of reading will necessarily discover.[4]

(2) Upon this must-be—that any literary work must be, and
must be treated as, a historicized and concretized ideology—
there follows another.

In my view ideology will necessarily be seen as false consciousness when observed from any *critical* vantage, and particularly
from the point of view of a materialist and historical criticism.

Since this book assumes that a critical vantage can and must
be taken toward its subject, the ideology represented through
Romantic works is *a fortiori* seen as a body of illusions.

In McGann's theory, as in that of most current Marxists, to
identify the deflection of an ideological literary product from
historical reality is complicated by the awareness that the
materialist critic has no option but to interpret that product
(as well as reality) through the ideology of the critic's own
historical moment. Nonetheless, McGann is able to carry out
his critical project with no lack of assurance. Of Wordsworth's "Intimations Ode," for example, he says: "The poem
generalizes—we now like to say mythologizes—all its conflicts, or rather resituates these conflicts out of a socio-historical context and into an ideological one."[5] Whatever the
epistemological problems posed by a radical historicist relativism, the political critic is reasonably confident that he possesses the key to all Romantic ideologies.

(3) In the practice of critical reading, it follows from these
linked premises that the first and essential task (whatever the
critic may in addition undertake) must be to identify and
expose the covert ideology implicated in a work's manifest or
ostensible meanings, and so to unravel, or penetrate through
the web of illusions generated by that ideology, which disguise, when they do not entirely displace, the economic, social,
and political realities of its time and place.

In applied political readings, we find an ever-recurrent
vocabulary of operative terms for undoing what a work
ostensibly signifies and transforming it into its historic meanings. These terms are the reciprocal, in a "critical" reading,
of what Levinson calls the "transformational grammar"
imposed on the writing of a work by its author's unconscious
ideology. Conspicuous in this transformative lexicon are
*suppression, sublimation, substitution, displacement, dislocation,
occlusion*. These of course are Freud's terms for the unconscious mechanisms that distort the latent, or true, meaning
of dreams; but as Levinson, echoing Jameson, remarks of the
procedures for uncovering the "ideological subtext" for
Wordsworth's poetic texts, "Freud worked out its psychic
economy and Marx produced its political logic." Other oper-

ative terms in political readings, such as *absence, elision, era-sure, effacement,* are mainly imported from deconstructive criticism. As Levinson says, with her usual awareness of her interpretive procedures: to determine in Wordsworth's "Peele Castle" what it is that "works with a cruel perseverance to discredit the manifest themes of the elegy," one "must read the poem closely and deconstructively," but only as prelimi-nary to "reconstructing the contemporary environment" in order that "one might explain the strangely redundant energy of the poem in terms of social contradiction and ideological necessity." To such a fusion of Derrida with Marx, Levinson applies the name "deconstructive materialism."[6]

Especially efficacious is a mechanism for transforming what a text does not say at all into what it most deeply means. As McGann puts it, citing Pierre Macherey on necessary silences in a text, "From Wordsworth's vantage, an ideology is born out of things which (literally) *cannot* be spoken of." And Lev-inson cites approvingly a long list of political theorists and critics who, "at once materialist and deconstructive, repre-sent the literary work as that which speaks of one thing because it cannot articulate another—presenting formally a sort of allegory by absence, where the signified is indicated by an identifiably absented signifier."[7] In the practice of a deter-mined political reader, it seems clear, a poet's silence can be made to speak louder than his words, and what that silence speaks, the critic knows in advance, must be an ideological necessity and a suppressed historical reality.

It seems to me that something like this set of assumptions and interpretive operations, if appropriately formulated and applied, can yield—in some critics, have yielded—credible political discoveries about a literary work. If, that is, the premises are formulated in terms of may-bes instead of must-bes—in other words, as a working hypothesis instead of a ruling hypothesis—and if they are applied in a way that per-mits the author's text some empirical possibility of counter-ing a proposed political reading so as to adjudge it probable, or forced, or even dead wrong. But the risk in an all-out, must-be theory and practice of political reading is obvious. The critic, bringing to any text an *a priori* knowledge of the kind of meaning that he or she must of necessity find, and possessed of a can't-fail set of devices for transforming any-thing whatever that a text says—or doesn't mention—into the predetermined subtext, will infallibly, given some biograph-ical and historical information and sufficient ingenuity, be able to produce a political reading. But such a reading is in effect self-confirming, because empirically incorrigible; it is the product of a discovery procedure that prepossesses the political meanings it triumphantly finds. The risk, in other words, is of a critical authoritarianism that brooks no oppo-sition, since no particulars of a text, no indications of what a poet undertook to say, and no appeal to able critics who read the text otherwise, can possibly resist conversion, by this apparatus, into an unconscious ideological cover-up, or dis-placement, or rationalization of political or social reality.[8] Nor have political Newreaders avoided the further risk of cancel-ing the imaginative delights that works of literature, in their diversity, have yielded to readers of all eras. For a rigorously political reading is not only a closed, monothematic reading; it is also joyless, casting a critical twilight in which all poems are gray.

2

Recent political readers of Wordsworth have concerned themselves not with his late conservative poems, but with his early, reputedly radical poems, especially the *Lyrical Ballads*. I shall comment only briefly on readings of Wordsworth's narrative ballads in order to focus on "Tintern Abbey," the longest and most notable of what Wordsworth in his title to *Lyrical Ballads* called "A Few Other Poems."

The many political treatments of the narrative ballads are mainly concerned to lay bare their covert evidences of Wordsworth's built-in social ideology, and especially of his upper-class consciousness. As Michael Friedman puts the critical assumption, Wordsworth's "adult consciousness of his class status"—for he was inescapably "a gentleman"—"cre-ated a gulf between him and the common folk he observed," although he was incapable of recognizing his assumptions of

superiority, because they are part of the "historical constraints that limit his consciousness, as they limit the consciousness of all those subject to history."[9] Revelations of
Wordsworth's unconscious social presuppositions and attitudes strike me as plausible to the degree that the political
point of view functions as a heuristic position rather than an
authoritarian imposition—to the degree, therefore, that what
Wordsworth wrote is given a fair chance to resist the interpretation. Roger Sales differs from other political critics in
his downright dismissal of the early narratives: "Wordsworth's travelling circus of freakish outcasts may appear to
offer a critique of the unacceptable face of rural society, yet
they merely endorse the same propagandist interpretation of
social change as 'Michael' tries to sell us."[10] What I find trou-
bling, however, in even qualified and empirical-minded
readings for ideology is that they derogate Wordsworth's ballads by ignoring their innovativeness and artistry and, in effect,
canceling their distinction from the flood of contemporary
magazine verses which, as Robert Mayo showed in a pioneer-
ing article more than three decades ago, dealt with similar
subjects and in similar ballad-meters.[11]

It is only when described in general terms, however, that
Wordsworth's ballads seem to approximate the popular narratives of the time. To put a Wordsworth ballad next to a
magazine poem it seems to resemble is to reveal sharp differences in idiom, artistry, and tone. The magazine verses con-
descend to their lowly subjects, are self-consciously simple in
manner, are cliché-ridden, and exploit a pathos in the plight
of the downtrodden and the social outcast that is tinged with
a complacent sense of the author's own upper-class moral
sensibility. In recent decades a number of excellent commentators have revealed the extent to which Wordsworth's seemingly simple ballads are in fact technically innovative; complex,
and sometimes self-ironic, in the control of tone (that is, in
the implicit expression of the social relations between narrator, subject, and reader); and reliant on implication and indi-
rection, instead of direct assertion, in making their social and
political as well as moral points. What I want to stress, in
addition, is that in these poems, as Wordsworth himself tells
us, he explicitly undertook to engage with, and to reform,

what we now call the "ideology" of the reading public of his time.

In a remarkable essay of 1825, William Hazlitt proposed a political interpretation of Wordsworth's "innovations" in the *Lyrical Ballads* and other early poems:

> It partakes of, and is carried along with, the revolutionary movement of our age: the political changes of the day were the model on which he formed and conducted his poetical experiments. His Muse . . . is a leveling one. It proceeds on a principle of equality, and strives to reduce all things to the same standard.[12]

What Hazlitt, I believe, had in mind was that, in his ballads and early narratives, and in the essays he wrote to explain and justify his poetic aims, Wordsworth had in effect subverted the official theory of poetry which had been dominant in European culture since the Renaissance and was still evident among conservative critics of the late-eighteenth century and early-nineteenth century. This theory had posited a hierarchy of poetic genres, modeled on the hierarchy of social classes, in which the ruling principle of decorum had fitted the social status of the protagonists, and the social level of the poetic language, to the rank of the genre. As Hazlitt says, Wordsworth's "popular style . . . gets rid of all the high places of poetry," while "the distinctions of rank, birth, wealth, power . . . are not to be found here." What Hazlitt recognized was that Wordsworth had leveled this built-in social hierarchy, and in doing so had translated the egalitarianism of French revolutionary politics into the egalitarianism of a revolutionary poetics.

But we can say more than this about the politics of Wordsworth's enterprise in *Lyrical Ballads*. In his "Advertisement" of 1798, he asserted that most of his poems were "experiments" that needed to overcome what he described, ironically, as "that most dreadful enemy to our pleasures, our own pre-established codes of decision." When he elaborated on this claim in his later Prefaces, he made it apparent that these "pre-established codes" are built-in determinants of what we now call "reading" but Wordsworth, in the critical parlance of his time, called "taste"; also that the reading-codes which his poems were designed to overcome consisted of a tacit upper-class consciousness, governing the way his contemporaries understood and responded to poetry, that, again in contemporary parlance, he called "pride." Wordsworth also indicated that in his view, the ways in which poetry is read and responded to are interdependent with revolutionary changes in the structure of society. He said in the *Preface* of 1800 that, to provide a "systematic defence of the theory" on which he had written poems "so materially different" from those now generally approved would necessitate "a full account of the present state of the public taste," which would in turn require "retracing the revolutions not of literature alone but likewise of society itself."[13] Fifteen years later, in the *Essay, Supplementary to the Preface* of 1815, Wordsworth returned to the subject of the social determinants of reading poetry, in dealing with the difficulty faced by himself, as an original poet, in "*creating* the taste by which he is to be enjoyed." There he raised the question of the extent to which that difficulty lies in "breaking the bonds of custom" and "overcoming the prejudices of false refinement," and especially, given the poetic object "which here and elsewhere I have proposed to myself," the extent to which it lies

> in divesting the Reader of the pride that induces him to dwell upon those points wherein Men differ from each other, to the exclusion of those in which all Men are alike, or the same; and in making him ashamed of the vanity that renders him insensible of the appropriate excellence which civil arrangements, less unjust than might appear, and Nature illimitable in her bounty, have conferred on Men who stand below him in the scale of society.[14]

Neither Wordsworth's qualification in this passage of his earlier radicalism, nor the critical idiom of his period, should conceal the fact that he viewed the prevailing mode of reading by the poetic public of his time as informed by upper-class social "codes" that constitute what political readers now call "ideology." Even in 1815, Wordsworth described his poetry as involving "emotions of the pathetic . . . that are complex and revolutionary," against which the heart of the reader "struggles with pride."[15] If political readers find that even Wordsworth's early poems, which he said were intended to revolutionize the built-in politics of his readers' sensibility, were by their present standards covertly conservative in their ideology, it seems an act of historical justice to recognize that in doing so, political readers apply to Wordsworth a theory of the class-determined writing and reading of poetry of which Wordsworth was himself a pre-Marxian innovator.

3

For an example of the radically transformative power of political readings, we need to turn from Wordsworth's spare narratives about the lowly and the down-and-out to that other poem in *Lyrical Ballads* that we conventionally call, by a convenient but misleading shorthand, "Tintern Abbey." To the uninitiate it might seem that a meditation in a natural setting on the course of the lyric speaker's life would be immune from a passage-by-passage political interpretation. From the ruling principle, however, that all Wordsworth's poems must be an ideological representation, it follows that the personal subject of "Tintern Abbey" must be an evasion of a political and public subject, and that its very silences bespeak what, by ideological necessity, it can neither know nor say, yet can't help revealing. As Marjorie Levinson sums up this way of reading the poem, "The primary poetic action is the suppression of the social. 'Tintern Abbey' achieves its fiercely private vision by directing a continuous energy toward the nonrepresentation of objects and points of view expressive of a public—we would say, ideological—dimension." Kenneth Johnston, in "The Politics of 'Tintern Abbey,' " is more guarded: "It may well be, in light of these interpretive possibilities, one of the most powerfully *de*politicized poems in the language—and, by that token, a uniquely political one."[16]

What makes such readings of "Tintern Abbey" especially interesting, and challenging, to an Oldreader like myself is that—unlike their procedure with other descriptive-meditative poems by Wordsworth—critics in this instance put forward an explicit textual ground for postulating an occluded political subtext. This ground, however, is not in "Tintern Abbey" but in William Gilpin's travel book *Tour of the Wye*, which had been published in 1771 and often reprinted. As early as 1957 Mary Moorman had remarked that, on their tour of the Wye valley during which the poem was composed, William and Dorothy Wordsworth "seem to have taken with them" Gilpin's book. Moorman pointed out that, by Gilpin's account, the ruined abbey itself "was a dwelling-place of beggars and the wretchedly poor," and that "the river was then full of shipping, carrying coal and timber from the Forest of Dean." In a footnote, she also cited a passage from Gilpin:

> Many of the furnaces, on the banks of the river, consume charcoal, which is manufactured on the spot; and the smoke, which is frequently seen issuing from the side of the hills, and spreading its thin veil over them, beautifully breaks their lines, and unites them with the sky.[17]

As Moorman suggests, this passage was probably echoed in the opening description in Wordsworth's poem, where the charcoal smoke is aestheticized, as in Gilpin, into "wreathes of smoke." It can be added that Wordsworth may also have mentioned the poor people in the vicinity of the abbey, although in the mode of a conjecture, in the lines that follow the reference to the smoke:

> wreathes of smoke
> Sent up, in silence, from among the trees,
> With some uncertain notice, as might seem,
> Of vagrant dwellers in the houseless woods. . . .

For a quarter-century this land mine remained buried in Moorman's *Wordsworth* until detonated by political readers, who added to Moorman's account the fact, mentioned by Gilpin and other travelers, that the iron-making furnaces along its lower banks made the river, however pristine in its upper reaches, "ouzy, and discolored" in the tidal section downstream from the abbey.[18] What these critics take to be Wordsworth's brief and unfeeling adversion to the wretched social realities in and near the ruined abbey seems to have made them especially severe in their reading of the poem as a whole. The stance at times verges on the prosecutorial, with the verdict "guilty as charged," though palliated by assertions that "Tintern Abbey" nonetheless remains, for reasons not clearly specified, a great poem.

Marjorie Levinson's analysis—paralleled by that of Jerome McGann—takes off from a detailed inquisition of what she calls its "snake of a title," whose length and particularity provide tacit evidence that it functions, although unconsciously, as an ideological cover-up for Wordsworth's true subject. (No matter, presumably, that such elaborate titles, specifying a locale, occasion, and even date—establishing, that is, the precise vantage point from which the poet views the prospect, and the time of the viewing—had long been standard in eighteenth-century local poems, the immediate precursors of "Tintern Abbey"; a convention that was continued by Coleridge and other writers of the extended Romantic lyric of description and meditation.)[19] In Levinson's view, that Wordsworth in his title should call attention to the abbey but "then studiously ignore it" indicates his suppression of the socio-economic facts of the miserably poor who populated the area. In the date of composition Wordsworth cites, July 13, 1798, what gets noted yet "overlooked" is its significance as marking "almost to the day the nine-year anniversary of the original Bastille Day, the eight-year anniversary of Wordsworth's first visit to France, and the five-year anniversary of the murder of Marat." By substituting "above Tintern Abbey" for "below Tintern Abbey," Wordsworth evades the fact that, downstream from the abbey, the river was polluted by effluents from the iron-furnaces.[20] She goes on through the text of the poem, intent always on exposing its "transformational grammar" and the ways in which its author "excludes from his field certain conflictual sights and meanings"—an "exclusion," she says, which "is, I believe, the poem's 'wherefore.' "[21]

These interpretive tactics and findings leave me unpersuaded; but also, I confess, somewhat nonplused. For radical political readers pre-empt the high ground, from which they can look down upon critical gainsayers as not only politically laggard and intellectually naive, but also as morally insensitive to social woes. According to Jerome McGann, for example, the "priests and clerics of Romanticism"—that is, scholars and critics who, like himself before his critical enlightenment, read Romantic poems for what they say, without exposing them as ideological "dramas of displacement and idealization"— serve to "perpetuate and maintain older ideas and attitudes," hence "typically serve only the most reactionary purposes of their societies"; although, he charitably adds, "they may not be aware of this."[22]

But I must risk confirming my status as a cleric of Romanticism, and at least inadvertently reactionary, by proposing, in place of the authoritarian must-bes of sternly political readers, some principles of a more open—in political terms, a liberal—way of reading poetry.

(1) First, as Coleridge in his radical youth wrote to his even more radical friend, "Citizen Thelwall": "Do not let us introduce an act of Uniformity against Poets."[23] Consequently, a poet is free to write a political poem, but also any kind of nonpolitical poem he or she may choose to write. As against the political version of the prevailing hermeneutics of suspicion, this principle entails that we respect a poet's chosen and manifest subject matter, without the theoretical predetermination that it must be an evasion or cover-up of socio-historic realities that the poet could not or would not confront. And as against a closed political monoreading, the principle requires that we keep our reading adaptive to the variousness of poetic possibilities, in subject as well as rendering; it is a reading open to surprises.

(2) Let us grant a poet also his *données*—that is, the conceptual frame of reference, or the belief system, that he may use to account for and to support, or may represent as following from, the modes of experience that the poem articulates. What traditional critics call Wordsworth's "philosophy," or "myth," of nature, as put forward in "Tintern Abbey," is entitled to the suspension of disbelief for the poetic moment that we yield to Homer, Dante, Milton, and the great preponderance of poets who write in accordance with postulates and beliefs

that we do not share. Wordsworth suggests, for example, that in trance states like the one induced in him by remembrance of the Wye valley, "We see into the life of things"; that he has felt in nature "a presence" that "rolls through all things"; and that the remembered scenes, and "nature and the language of the sense" in general, have profoundly influenced his moral life.[24] For the scholar and critic to expound such passages, and for any reader to yield to them a *pro tempore* imaginative consent, is not, as McGann proposes, to be seduced into accepting and propagating an outworn ideology. It is, instead, to make possible an adequate experience of the poem, part of whose value, in fact, is that it widens the limits of responsiveness imposed by our own beliefs.

The requisite for our imaginative consent to Wordsworth's myth of nature is the feature that he later proposed in order to justify his using, in the "Intimations Ode," the concept of the pre-existence of the soul. His subject in that poem, he says, is the experience of a lost "vividness and splendour" in the perceptions of a child to which "every one, I believe, if he would look back, could bear testimony." The sole requisite for employing the concept of pre-existence as a way of accounting for this general human experience is that it have "sufficient foundation in humanity for authorizing me to make for my purpose the best use of it I could as a Poet."[25] Furthermore, in "Tintern Abbey," if we attend to the syntax of the passages in question, it is notable how carefully Wordsworth distinguishes between the belief or creed he postulates and the actual experiences that the creed would serve to explain: "such, perhaps, / As may have had no trivial influence"; "Nor less, I trust, / To them I may have owed another gift"; and not "I have known," but "I have *felt* / A presence." Wordsworth's distinction between experiential fact and explanatory concept is especially obvious when, having proposed that in a trance state "We see into the life of things," he immediately qualifies the proposal as possibly mistaken— "If this / Be but a vain belief"—in order to reassert the experience itself:

> If this
> Be but a vain belief, yet, oh! how oft, . . .

How oft, in spirit, have I turned to thee
O sylvan Wye! Thou wanderer through the woods,
How often has my spirit turned to thee![26]

(3) A third principle of an open reading is that it take into account, and take delight in, the artistry of the poet in articulating and structuring the component parts of a poem, from its beginning to its end. When a strong political reader takes note of Wordsworth's artistry, it is by way of acknowledging his skill (albeit an unconscious skill) at deploying what Levinson calls "disarming discursive strategies," and McGann terms "a strategy of displacement," to disguise or evade the real political subject.[27]

When read in this open and adaptive way, and read in its entirety, "Tintern Abbey," I believe, is recognized to be about a subject that rigorous political readers, by their pre-established code of decision—that is, by imposing their critical ideology—have veiled, displaced, and in important aspects totally occluded. Put briefly, hence reductively: the poem that Wordsworth composed is a sustained lyric meditation, in a natural setting, about what it is to be mortally human, to grow older, and to grow up, through vicissitudes and disappointments, into the broader, sadder knowledge of maturity; about what in this temporal process is inevitably lost, but also what may be gained, and for another person as well as the lyric speaker himself.

In such a reading, the opening description of the natural scene is not interpreted as, of necessity, an elaborate evasion of painful social realities; on social injustices and the sufferings of the dispossessed—what in another of the *Lyrical Ballads* he decries as "What man has made of man"—Wordsworth had just written a number of other poems. In the course of the poem the setting functions in various ways, but an emphatic initiating function, since it is a scene revisited after a five-year absence, is to trigger in the lyric speaker a meditation, continued through all the poem, on the import of such a passage of time at a critical stage of his life and experience. "Five years have passed. . . ." The opening phrase, with its repetitions, announces the theme which resonates throughout, especially in the deployment of the adverbs *again* (again I hear . . . behold . . . repose . . . see), *when, while, still,* and above all in the recurrent opposition of *now* and *then,* with their shifting references. These are all temporal adverbs, and Wordsworth's manifest, reiterated, and sustained lyric subject is time—time present, past, and future. Not time, however, as an abstract concept, but (in a way that inaugurates a basic concern of Wordsworth's later poems, and also of much modern literature through Proust to the present) *erlebte Zeit*— concretely lived time and its significance to us, in whom time is of the human essence, and for whom time involves, for better or worse, change, on the way to the point at which our lived time must have its stop.

Our principles of reading, adaptive to the text the author chose to write, do not take the allusion to "Tintern Abbey" in the title to be an unconscious revelation of the true social subject of the poem. Instead they enable the recognition that the function of the reference, as in the titles of many local poems, is simply to locate the descriptive vantage point by reference to a recognizable landmark. And that point is "a few miles above Tintern Abbey" because, as the text makes clear, this is the precise place (line 10, "Here, under this dark sycamore") where the lyric speaker had been positioned five years before, and from which he "once again" sees (the text will soon reveal the functional importance of this fact) exactly the same objects, "these steep and lofty cliffs," "these plots," "these orchard-tufts," "these hedgerows." Our principles also grant the poet his representation of the scene again before his eyes as imbued with peace, harmony, and relationship— a relationship that incorporates the wild scene and quiet sky, woods and cottage grounds, and yes even the wreathes of smoke in line 18, whether or not the notice they seem to give is of vagrants who have not chosen their lot of being houseless. The observed landscape serves the speaker—as God, or the cosmic order, had served earlier poets—as an objectified norm for the connection and harmony he struggled to achieve in the disconnection and distresses of the experiences he goes on to describe.

Traditional scholars have their own critical predispositions, including a tendency to focus on the conceptual and philosophical elements of a work of literature. In the second verse-paragraph of "Tintern Abbey," scholarly interest in the creed of nature that Wordsworth puts forward has diverted attention from the no less compelling way in which he expresses his experiences of remembering the scene of the Wye amid the alien and anguished circumstances of the intervening five years. In a way without close precedent, Wordsworth represents his emotional states and feelings as modes of internal sensation, more than eight decades before William James propounded the theory that what we experience as moods and emotions is constituted by a complex of internal and organic sensations.[28] The lyric speaker has experienced

> In hours of weariness, sensations sweet,
> Felt in the blood, and felt along the heart;

and also

> that blessed mood,
> In which the burthen of the mystery,
> In which the heavy and the weary weight
> Of all this unintelligible world
> Is lighten'd;

as well as times

> when the fretful stir
> Unprofitable, and the fever of the world,
> Have hung upon the beatings of my heart.

In such passages Wordsworth does what only the great poets do: by transforming inherited descriptive categories, he makes us realize anew our shared, or sharable, human experiences.

"And now . . . / The picture of the mind revives again: / While here I stand." Both Levinson and McGann, having predetermined that the poem must be about an absented social subject, gloss "the picture of the mind" as a spiritual displacement for what Levinson calls "the picture of the place"—that is, the ruined abbey with its beggars and vagrants. What the lyric speaker asserts, however, is that now, as he stands at the precise spot on the upper Wye where he had stood five years before, the landscape he had pictured in his memory "revives again," in the landscape before his eyes.[29]

Wordsworth uses here a poetic tactic he had found in earlier local poems about a revisitation (including Gray's "Eton College Ode"), but in a way that he makes distinctively his own and will go on to exploit, with variants, in his later poems on the human significance of passing time, the "Intimations Ode" and "Peele Castle." The banks of the Wye, as the title announces, are revisited, and reposing once again "under this dark sycamore," he sees again the former prospect. This is the Wordsworthian *déjà vu;* the scene on the Wye is twice-seen. But as "the picture of the mind revives again," it is (line 61) with "somewhat of a sad perplexity." For while the scene as he remembers it and the scene now present are similar (there are "many recognitions dim and faint"), they nonetheless differ. And to account for, as well as to evaluate that difference, the speaker reviews the course of his life. For he recognizes that although the scene-as-now-perceived has changed, it is not because the visual givens have changed, but because the mind perceiving the scene has changed, as a result of its experiences during the intervening five years—"changed, no doubt, from what I was, when first / I came among these hills."

Wordsworth exploits here, as in later poems, his insight that an apparently integral perception involves what professional psychologists, decades later, were to call "apperception"; that is, *ad*-perception. What seems simply to be perceived is in fact apperceived—invested with aspects and a penumbra that are the product of prior experiences of the perceiving mind. Elsewhere Wordsworth often represents this alteration by the figure of the mind projecting light and color on the objects that it seemingly mirrors. At the end of the "Intimations Ode," for example, he represents the altered perception of a sunset that is effected by a matured mind in terms of a sober coloring projected on the visual radiance:

> The clouds that gather round the setting sun
> Do take a sober coloring from an eye
> That hath kept watch o'er man's mortality.

In a parallel way in "Tintern Abbey" the scene which, when first visited in his "thoughtless youth," had been perceived passionately, but without "any interest / Unborrowed from the eye," is now apperceived differently by a mind that has been matured by experience. In this passage, however, Wordsworth represents the change not in optical terms, but in the great alternative figure of a somber musical accompaniment to the visual phenomena:

> For I have learned
> To look on nature, not as in the hour
> Of thoughtless youth, but hearing oftentimes
> The still, sad music of humanity,
> Not harsh nor grating, though of ample power
> To chasten and subdue.

How the speaker, five years older, perceives the former prospect implicates his intervening experiences, summarized in the preceding two verse-paragraphs, of loneliness amid the din of towns and cities, of the heavy and weary weight of a world that has become unintelligible, and of the occasions, often, whether in darkness or joyless daylight, when the fret and fever of the world have hung upon the beatings of his heart.

Political readers ascribe a drastic evasiveness to these allusions to the formative five years, 1793–1798, between Wordsworth's first and second visit to the Wye. "We are not permitted," McGann says, "to remember 1793 and the turmoil of the French Revolution, neither its 1793 hopes nor— what is more to the point for Wordsworth—the subsequent ruin of those hopes." Kenneth Johnston, who recognizes, I think justly, the central function of the lines on "the still, sad music of humanity," asserts that Wordsworth represents therein his process of learning "as smooth, continuous, and unbroken" instead of "disruptive, violent, uncertain, or threatening," because "harsh, grating music" might "open up the gaps in the fabric of thought, or society, such as those that [Wordsworth] could only anticipate with dread." The critical assumption underlying such claims is made patent in James K. Chandler's comment on the "skewed treatment of the revolutionary period in 'Tintern Abbey.' " "The more," he says, "one looks at 'Tintern Abbey' as autobiography, the more the poem seems an evasion of what [Wordsworth] had actually stood for in 1793."[30] The assumption is that "Tintern Abbey" is not only a political poem, but a political autobiography as well, and as such commits the author to tell the truth, the explicit truth, and nothing but the truth about his political experiences. For their own knowledge of these experiences, political readers rely almost entirely on Wordsworth's expressly autobiographical poem *The Prelude*, parts of which he had already written in 1798, and in which, as completed seven years later, he details his inordinate revolutionary hopes, his disillusionment, and his consequent intellectual and emotional collapse. It seems an odd move, to use the political experiences that Wordsworth narrates in one poem as the ground for charging him with unconsciously evading or disguising those facts in another, earlier poem.

The main point, however, is that to an open and adaptive rather than a peremptory reading, the poem that Wordsworth undertook in "Tintern Abbey" is quite different from his narrative autobiography *The Prelude*, both in kind and in organizing principle. Its artistic intention is not to represent what is personal and unique about Wordsworth's experiences in France and with the Revolution, but to be a lyric meditation on what it generally is for a human being to grow older and, inevitably, to experience vicissitude, disappointment, and dismay. Consequently the "I" who utters the poem is recognizably Wordsworth, but Wordsworth in the literary agency that Coleridge called "the I-representative." To the lyric speaker, that is, the poet attributes experiences other men and women can be expected to share, of isolation and of fevered depression in a world that seems unintelligible; he trusted they might also share something of his speaker's consolation at achieving a mature identity that has been informed and tempered by exposure to what is recognizably the modern world of all of us.

The lyric speaker, of course, conducts his account, and accounting, of the changes effected by time in the elected terms of his changing relations to the natural world. "That time is past" (lines 84ff) of his youthful, passionately unreflective responses to nature, and that change is indubitably a loss. But the process of time has also brought a chastened maturity (signified by his hearing often the still, sad music of humanity), as well as the feeling of a pervasive "presence" that binds the mind of man with the enduring natural world. These constitute time's "other gifts . . . for such loss, I would believe, / Abundant recompense." This claim of abundant recompense in growing older is not an easy nor an unqualified optimism. "For such loss, I *would* believe" suggests a sought, or willed, belief; whatever the possible gain, time effects loss as we go our mortal way. Many readers of the poem have been sensitive to the elegiac tone in its seeming assurance. The sadness deepens in Wordsworth's later poems on what it means to grow older—the "Intimations Ode," and still later, after an experience of tragic loss, the "Elegiac Stanzas suggested by a Picture of Peele Castle."

A remarkably acute and sensitive contemporary, John Keats, did not read the wherefore of "Tintern Abbey" as an evasion of a harsh social reality or as the asseveration of a creed of nature, but as a meditation on growing up into the knowledge of a world of suffering. While nursing his dying younger brother in May 1818, Keats wrote, in a letter that repeatedly echoes the phrases of "Tintern Abbey," that "an extensive knowledge is needful to thinking people—it takes away the heat and fever; and helps, by widening speculation, to ease the Burden of the Mystery."[31] He went on to assert that "in his hintings at good and evil in the Paradise Lost," Milton "did not think into the human heart, as Wordsworth has done"; that is, Milton retained the religious creed of a heavenly recompense for earthly suffering, whereas Wordsworth proposes a rationale solely in terms of our temporal life in this world.[32] Keats sketches his own rationale, or "recompense," for suffering in what he calls a "simile of human life" as a "Mansion of Many Apartments," obviously modeled on the sequential stages of his life represented by Wordsworth in his fourth paragraph. From "the infant or thoughtless Chamber" (Wordsworth's "thoughtless youth," line 91), we move into "the second Chamber," where gradually we convince our nerves "that the World is full of Misery and Heartbreak, Pain, Sickness and oppression. . . ."

We see not the ballance of good and evil. . . . We feel the "burden of the Mystery." To this point was Wordsworth come, as far as I can conceive when he wrote "Tintern Abbey" and it seems to me that his Genius is explorative of those dark Passages.

Keats, I think, identified rightly the central concern of "Tintern Abbey," in its first four verse paragraphs.

But at this point we are not much more than two-thirds of the way through the poem. And at the beginning of the long last paragraph comes a lyric surprise. The speaker is not alone, "For thou art with me, here. . . ." Abruptly, what we had taken to be an interior monologue is revealed to have been overt speech addressed to an auditor, "My dear, dear Sister," who is not even, as the reference to hearing her voice in lines 117–18 shows, a silent auditor. And in this turn to his sister, the focus of the poem shifts from what it has meant for the speaker alone, to what it means to share with a loved other person, the experience of a life in time.

Political readers give remarkably short shrift to Dorothy and her role in the poem. "Dorothy," McGann declares, "is, of course, the reader's surrogate," which I take to be a laconic way of saying that she serves as a device for manipulating the reader into sharing with her the displacement of the actual abbey by "the abbey of the mind." Heather Glen reads the last section of the poem as affirming Wordsworth's "beleaguered subjective individualism." In his attempt to realize his own self "not in interaction with other men, but in isolation from them," any other person "can only be seen as a threat"—unless, that is, the other is "in some sense (as Dorothy is here) identified with the self" in a mode that Glen calls "an *égoisme-à-deux*." In a similar vein Marjorie Levinson, proposing that "the primary poetic action is the suppression of the social," or the "public," dimension so as to achieve a "fiercely private vision," says that while the role of Dorothy is to serve the poet as an audience, that "audience consists of one person, the poet's 'second self,' and even she is admitted into the process a third of the way through, a decidedly feeble gesture toward externality."[33]

Such readings demonstrate the potency of a political *parti-pris* to override all evidence to the contrary. Of course "Tintern Abbey" is "subjective" or "private" in its point of view; inescapably so, because the first-person lyric establishes the lyric speaker as its center of consciousness. But within this constraint of the genre, it is hard to imagine how Wordsworth could have made it more patent that, in the poem, Dorothy is both a real and crucially functional "other." He startles us into awareness of her presence, devotes the last fifty lines to her, and gives her the salient role of concluding the poem. He prefaces his address to her by asserting (lines 112–14) that, even if the course of his life hitherto had not provided the recompense he has described, the fact of her presence with him might in itself be enough to sustain his "genial spirits"—his vital strength of mind. He even risks seeming sacrilegious, in suggesting her importance to him by an echo from the best-known of the psalms, the twenty-third—"For thou art with me"—which, in the context of a meditation on a life in time, may carry with it some resonance of the sentence that precedes it: "Yea, though I walk through the valley of the shadow of death, I will fear no evil." Furthermore it is by the act of turning from himself to identify, in imagination, with the consciousness of the other person that the lyric speaker moves, with quiet artistry, from the present to the future, but a future that turns out to comprehend both the present and the past, until the discourse rounds back, in an echo of the lyric beginning, to an inclusive close.

I can only sketch briefly the flow of the speaker's memory and imagination—the human faculties that alone free us from the tyranny of time—as he identifies with the conjectured process of his younger sister's life, memory, and imagination. She is now, on her first visit to the Wye, at that stage of her life at which he had been on his first visit; for he detects in her voice and eyes the replication of his earlier responsiveness to the natural scene:

> in thy voice I catch
> The language of my former heart, and read
> My former pleasures in the shooting lights
> Of thy wild eyes. Oh! yet a little while

> May I behold in thee what I was once,
> My dear, dear sister!

His wish is that the procession of time might in her instance make a pause. But time and aging are inexorable, and he goes on at once to his sister's future life, in his elected terms of the interaction of her altering mind with the natural scene, whose normative stability and harmony will be able to counteract for her the experiences, inescapable even in a domestic life (lines 129–32), of evil tongues, rash judgments, selfish sneers, social hypocrisy, and the dreariness of the daily routine.

"Therefore let the moon / Shine on thee. . . ." In the traditional rhetorical cadence of a blessing by an older brother, he anticipates her "after years" when—in exact parallel with the change in him from the "dizzy raptures" of his youth to hearing "the still, sad music of humanity"—her "wild ecstasies shall be matured / Into a sober pleasure." "When . . . when . . . Oh! then. . . ." The temporal drama is managed by the adverbial shifters—the "whens" and "thens," which in the preceding paragraph had referred to his past visit, now refer to her conjectured future. "Oh! then, / If solitude, or fear, or pain, or grief, / Should be thy portion. . . ." But such sufferings, though expressed as conditional, are for all lives inescapable. And if then "I should be, where I no more can hear / Thy voice"—a suggestion, left inexplicit, that time is capable of removing him by more than physical distance. Her recourse then, like his now, will be to the memory of her earlier visit to the Wye; but with a crucial difference. What he now remembers is a visit when he had stood alone; what she will then remember, however, is that, at her first visit, "on the banks of this delightful stream / We stood together." And her remembrance will include also what he has been saying as they stand together—"me, / And these my exhortations."

"Nor wilt thou then forget. . . ." Thus, by way of her remembering in the future the discourse that constitutes the entire poem, the speaker rounds back to those aspects of the scene that he had described at the beginning; namely (lines 158–59),

        these steep woods and lofty cliffs
And this green pastoral landscape. . . .

But what she will then remember about these natural objects is what he now tells her, that they

                                    were to me
More dear, both for themselves, and for thy sake.

"For thy sake": more dear to him because now, on his second but her first visit, they stand on the banks of the Wye together.

    The effect of the lyric closure is only heightened by our awareness that this affirmation to another was uttered by the poet exemplifying what Keats, between admiration and exasperation, called "the wordsworthian or egotistical sublime." But as Keats recognized, the poet of the egotistical sublime had also thought "into the human heart."[34]

4

In presenting the course of life in terms of an interplay between nature and the observer's altering mind, in the way it conceptualizes that nature, and in its idiom and rhetoric, "Tintern Abbey" is not only distinctively Wordsworthian, but distinctly a poem of the Romantic age in England. Insofar, I agree with political readers who assert that the poem is, in Jerome McGann's terms, "time and place specific," although I disagree with the further claim that this specificity must be an ideological rationalization of the contemporary economic and social reality. And as so obviously a poem of its time and place, "Tintern Abbey" poses the cardinal critical question: "What's in it for us readers now?"

    Political critics, and New Historicists generally, are united in opposing the concept that literature and art can either represent or appeal to what Stephen Greenblatt calls "a timeless, cultureless, universal human essence."[35] "The idea that poetry deals with universal and transcendent human themes and subjects," McGann says, is itself "a culturally specific one."[36] The radical conclusion sometimes drawn from such claims is that the relevance and power of a literary work such as "Tintern Abbey" are confined to the form of consciousness specific to the poet and his moment, or to reactionary revivals of that ideology at a later time, or to a refashioning of the work in terms of the reader's own ideology. The only "trans-historical" value that McGann specifically recognizes is in fact trans-ideological: a critical determination of the ideology particular to an earlier work helps make us aware of the ideology particular to our own time and place.

> The importance of ancient or culturally removed works lies precisely in this fact: that they themselves, as culturally alienated products, confront present readers with ideological differentials that help to define the limits and special functions of those current ideological practices.[37]

In spite of such strictures, however, an open reader of "Tintern Abbey" finds that it speaks now, as it has spoken for almost two centuries, and will continue to speak in the future. Not because of transcendent and universal features (metaphysical essences of which I am no less wary than McGann), but for entirely empirical reasons. That is, the poem articulates and orders—although in time-and-place-specific ways that enhance its historical interest and invite imaginative participation beyond our parochial limits—modes of experience that we share with the poet, and that people will continue to share in any predictable future. Should the political and social conditions prophesied by Marx come to pass, it is beyond peradventure that even in a classless society men and women will continue to live a mortal life in time; will suffer, as Wordsworth put it (line 144), "solitude, or fear, or pain, or grief"; will as a result surely become sadder, but may also, provided they are both strong and fortunate, become more comprehensively and sensitively human; and will find support in the awareness that they are not alone, but share their lot with those they love. From such readers "Tintern Abbey" will continue to evoke a deep response because it speaks, in its innovative, ordered, and compelling way, to enduring constants amid the ever-changing conditions of what it is to be human.

Notes

Types and Orientations of Critical Theories

From *The Princeton Handbook of Poetic Terms,* ed. Alex Preminger (Princeton, 1986). Reprinted by permission of the publisher, Princeton University Press.

In *The Mirror and the Lamp* (1953), as a preliminary to differentiating Romantic criticism from previous criticism, Abrams proposed a way of classifying literary theories (as well as general theories of art) into four types, or "orientations." Three of these stress the relations of a work either to the external universe, or to the audience, or to the poet or artist; the fourth focuses on the work in isolation. The following diagram, now widely known, lays out these coordinates, and the four types of critical orientation:

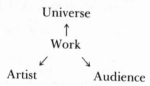

In the present essay, Abrams reformulates this classification (together with his associated analysis of the "constitutive metaphors" that characterize types of artistic theory), and applies the result to a comprehensive overview of the history of criticism, from Plato and Aristotle to current varieties of post-structural theory.

What's the Use of Theorizing about the Arts?

From *In Search of Literary Theory,* ed. Morton W. Bloomfield (Ithaca, N.Y., 1972), pp. 2–54. Reprinted by permission of the publisher, Cornell University Press. This essay anticipated the explosion of interest in theory that energizes current literary and humanistic studies.

1. William Elton, ed., *Aesthetics and Language* (New York, 1954).
2. Morris Weitz, "The Philosophy of Criticism," *Proceedings of the Third International Congress on Aesthetics* (Venice, Sept. 3–5, 1956), p. 207.
3. Morris Weitz, *Hamlet and the Philosophy of Literary Criticism* (Chicago and London, 1964), pp. ix–x, 213, 217, 285.
4. Ibid., chap. 14.
5. C. L. Stevenson, "Interpretation and Evaluation in Aesthetics," in *Philosophical Analysis,* ed. Max Black (Ithaca, N.Y., 1950), pp. 341–83.
6. Weitz, "The Philosophy of Criticism," pp. 207–16; idem, *Hamlet,* chap. 15.
7. See, e.g., Helen Knight, "The Use of 'Good' in Aesthetic Judgments," in Elton, *Aesthetics and Language;* Paul Ziff, "Reasons in Art Criticism," in *Philosophy Looks at the Arts,* ed. Joseph Margolis (New York, 1962); Morris Weitz, "Reasons in Criticism," *Journal of Aesthetics and Art Criticism* 20 (1962): 429–37; Weitz, *Hamlet,* chap. 16.
8. Weitz, "Reasons in Criticism," pp. 436–37; idem, *Hamlet,* pp. 276–84.
9. Ludwig Wittgenstein, *The Blue and Brown Books* (New York, 1965), p. 17; idem, *Philosophical Investigations,* trans. G. E. M. Anscombe (Oxford, 1953), secs. 65–67.
10. William E. Kennick, "Does Traditional Aesthetics Rest on a Mistake?" *Mind* 67 (1958): 318–19.
11. Morris Weitz, "The Role of Theory in Aesthetics," *Journal of Aesthetics and Art Criticism* 15 (1956): 27; idem, *Hamlet,* p. 286.
12. See, e.g., in addition to Weitz and Kennick: John Wisdom, "Things and Persons," in *Philosophy and Psychoanalysis* (New York, 1969), pp. 222–26; W. B. Gallie, "The Function of Philosophical Aesthetics," in Elton, *Aesthetics and Language;* Paul Ziff, "The Task of Defining a Work of Art," *Philosophical Review* 62 (1953): 57–78; Teddy Brunius, "The Uses of Works of Art," *Journal of Aesthetics and Art Criticism* 22 (1963): 123–33; Marshall Cohen, "Aesthetic Essence," in *Philosophy in America,* ed. Max Black (Ithaca, N.Y., 1965).
13. Weitz, "The Role of Theory," pp. 31–33; idem, *Hamlet,* pp. 307–8. Cf. Ziff, "The Task of Defining a Work of Art," pp. 67–71, and Brunius, "The Uses of Works of Art," p. 125.
14. Weitz, "The Role of Theory," pp. 27–28; idem, *Hamlet,* p. 311.
15. Weitz, "The Role of Theory," pp. 34–35; idem, *Hamlet,* pp. 309, 314–15; Kennick, "Does Traditional Aesthetics Rest on a Mistake?" pp. 323–25. See also Wisdom's brief but influential statement, *Philosophy and Psychoanalysis,* p. 225. On "persuasive definitions," see C. L. Stevenson, "Persuasive Definitions," in *Facts and Values* (New Haven and London, 1963), and "On 'What Is a Poem?'" *Philosophical Review* 66 (1957).

16. E.g., Wittgenstein, *Philosophical Investigations*, secs. 19–27, and pp. 223e–226e.

17. Wittgenstein, *Philosophical Investigations*, sec. 66.

18. Clive Bell, *What Is Art?* (London, 1928), pp. v, 7–8, 25, and *passim*.

19. Plato, *Laws*, vii, 817.

20. Recent and impressive examples of the expansion of the method and distinctions of Aristotle's *Poetics* to a variety of literary forms are the essays in R. S. Crane, ed., *Critics and Criticism* (Chicago, 1952).

21. Coleridge, *Biographia Literaria*, ed. John Shawcross, 2 vols. (Oxford, 1907), vol. 2, p. 64; vol. 1, p. 81.

22. Weitz, *Hamlet*, p. 166.

23. Coleridge, *Biographia Literaria*, vol. 2, p. 85; vol. 1, p. 14.

24. Ibid., vol. 2, p. 12.

25. Ibid., p. 65; T. M. Raysor, ed., *Coleridge's Shakespearean Criticism*, 2 vols. (Cambridge, Mass., 1930), vol. 1, p. 224.

26. Weitz, *Hamlet*, pp. 174, 187, 233.

27. Raysor, *Coleridge's Shakespearean Criticism*, vol. 1, p. 233; T. M. Raysor, ed., *Coleridge's Miscellaneous Criticism* (Cambridge, Mass., 1936), p. 89.

28. Wittgenstein, *Philosophical Investigations*, sec. 23.

29. Weitz, *Hamlet*, pp. 230, 238–39, 244.

30. Weitz, "The Philosophy of Criticism," pp. 207–9.

31. Coleridge, *The Table Talk and Omniana* (London, 1917), p. 165.

32. Kennick, "Does Traditional Aesthetics Rest on a Mistake?" p. 325, also p. 334; Weitz, *Hamlet*, p. 318; Stuart Hampshire, "Logic and Appreciation," in Elton, *Aesthetics and Language*, pp. 169, 165.

33. Matthew Arnold, in *Essays on Criticism, Second Series* (London, 1891), pp. 20, 32–33.

34. Hampshire, "Logic and Appreciation," pp. 161–67.

35. Kennick, "Does Traditional Aesthetics Rest on a Mistake?" pp. 331, 329; Paul Ziff, "Appreciation and Evaluation," in Margolis, *Philosophy Looks at the Arts*, p. 161.

36. Weitz, "The Philosophy of Criticism," pp. 215–16; see also idem, *Hamlet*, pp. 276–82.

37. T. E. Hulme, *Speculations*, ed. Herbert Read (London, 1936), p. 135.

38. For the emergence of the modern classification of "the fine arts" in the eighteenth century, see Paul Oskar Kristeller, "The Modern System of the Arts: A Study in the History of Aesthetics," *Journal of the History of Ideas* 12 (1951): 496–527, and 13 (1952): 17–46.

39. See Alexander Baumgarten, *Meditationes philosophicae* (1735), secs. 51–69, and *Aesthetica* (1750), secs. 14, 441, 511–18, 585; Karl Philipp Moritz, *Ueber die bildende Nachahmung des Schönen*, in *Deutsche Litteraturdenkmale des 18. und 19. Jahrhunderts* (1788), vol. 31, pp. 10–12, 16.

40. Shaftesbury, in *Characteristics*, ed. J. M. Robertson, 2 vols. (London, 1900), vol. 2, pp. 54–56. See Jerome Stolnitz, "On the Origins of 'Aesthetic Disinterestedness,'" *Journal of Aesthetics and Art Criticism* 20 (1961–62): 131–43.

41. Kant, *Critique of Aesthetic Judgement*, trans. J. C. Meredith (Oxford, 1911), pp. 48–50, 69.

42. For a critique of this view, see Maurice Mandelbaum, "Family Resemblances and Generalizations Concerning the Arts," *American Philosophical Quarterly* 2 (1965): 1–10.

43. E. D. Hirsch, Jr., "Value and Knowledge in the Humanities," in Mor-

ton W. Bloomfield, ed., *In Search of Literary Theory* (Ithaca, N.Y., 1972), pp. 57–89.

44. Wittgenstein, *Philosophical Investigations*, secs. 224e, 226e.
45. J. L. Austin, *Philosophical Papers* (Oxford, 1961), p. 100.
46. Wittgenstein, *Philosophical Investigations*, sec. 654.

A Note on Wittgenstein and Literary Criticism

From *ELH, A Journal of English Literary History* 41 (1974): 541–54. Reprinted by permission of the publisher, The Johns Hopkins University Press. Based on a paper for a colloquium, "Wittgenstein and the Philosophy of Literary Criticism," April 1974, at the University of Warwick, England. References are to two essays distributed in advance to participants in the colloquium: "What's the Use of Theorizing about the Arts?" (reprinted in the present volume); and J. R. Bambrough, "Literature and Philosophy," in *Wisdom: Twelve Essays*, ed. J. R. Bambrough (Oxford, 1974).

1. G. E. Moore, "Wittgenstein's Lectures in 1930–33," in *Philosophical Papers* (London, 1959); Cyril Barrett, ed., *Wittgenstein: Lectures and Conversations on Aesthetics, Psychology and Religious Belief* (Berkeley, 1967).
2. Wittgenstein, *The Blue and Brown Books*, ed. Rush Rhees (New York, 1965), pp. 6–7, 43; idem, *Philosophical Investigations*, trans. G. E. M. Anscombe (Oxford, 1953), sec. 111.

Belief and the Suspension of Disbelief

From *Literature and Belief*, ed. M. H. Abrams (New York, 1958). Reprinted by permission of the publisher, Columbia University Press. This essay originated as a paper presented to the English Institute Conference, 1957, on "Literature and Belief." The other speakers on the panel, mentioned by Abrams in the text, were Douglas Bush, Walter J. Ong, and Cleanth Brooks.

1. T. S. Eliot, *Selected Essays, 1917–1932* (London, 1932), p. 138.
2. J. S. Mill, "Bentham," in *Early Essays by John Stuart Mill*, ed. J. W. M. Gibbs (London, 1897), p. 208; Jeremy Bentham, *The Rationale of Reward*, in *Works*, ed. John Bowring (Edinburgh, 1843), vol. 2, pp. 253–54.
3. Gibbs, *Early Essays*, pp. 202, 208; H. S. R. Elliot, ed., *Letters of John Stuart Mill* (London, 1910), vol. 2, p. 358.
4. I. A. Richards, *Science and Poetry* (London, 1926), pp. 56–61.
5. Ibid., p. 82.
6. Richard Hurd, *Letters on Chivalry and Romance* (London, 1911), pp. 137–39.

7. Alexander Baumgarten, *Meditationes philosophicae* (1735), secs. 51–69, and *Aesthetica* (1750, 1758), secs. 14, 441, 511–18, 585. See also Karl Philipp Moritz, *Ueber die bildende Nachahmung des Schönen* (1788).

8. A. C. Bradley, *Oxford Lectures on Poetry* (London, 1909), pp. 4–6, 17.

9. Eliot, *Selected Essays*, p. 30, and *The Sacred Wood* (London, 1950), p. viii.

10. John Crowe Ransom, *The World's Body* (New York, 1938), p. 343.

11. Allen Tate, *On the Limits of Poetry* (New York, 1948), p. 48.

12. Bradley, *Oxford Lectures*, p. 6; John Crowe Ransom, *The New Criticism* (Norfolk, Conn., 1941), pp. 43, 281.

13. William K. Wimsatt, *The Verbal Icon* (Lexington, Ky., 1954), p. 241. E. M. Forster wrote, in *Anonymity* (London, 1925), p. 14, that in reading a poem, "we have entered a universe that only answers to its own laws, supports itself, internally coheres, and has a new standard of truth. Information is true if it is accurate. A poem is true if it hangs together." See also Philip Leon, "Aesthetic Knowledge," in *The Problems of Aesthetics*, ed. Eliseo Vivas and Murray Krieger (New York, 1953).

14. Tate, *On the Limits of Poetry*, p. 113.

15. Wimsatt, *Verbal Icon*, p. 87.

16. Middleton Murry, "Beauty Is Truth," *The Symposium* 1 (1930): 466–501.

17. I. A. Richards, *Practical Criticism* (London, 1930), pp. 187, 278–79; Eliot, *Selected Essays*, p. 256.

18. For another instance in which Keats uses *truth* as equivalent to *existence*, see *The Letters of John Keats*, ed. M. B. Forman (London, 1947), p. 67. I prefer attributing "That is all / Ye know on earth . . ." to the lyric speaker rather than to the Urn, because the former reading is at least as probable in the context and makes a richer poem. But even if we take the whole of the last two lines to be asserted by the Urn, the point holds that their significance is qualified by the nature imputed to the speaker.

19. Cleanth Brooks, *The Well Wrought Urn* (New York, 1947), pp. 141–42, 151–52.

20. Forman, *Letters of Keats*, pp. 72, 227–28.

21. E. de Selincourt and Helen Darbishire, eds., *The Poetical Works of William Wordsworth* (Oxford, 1940–49), vol. 4, pp. 463–64.

22. T. S. Eliot, "Poetry and Propaganda," in *Literary Opinion in America*, ed. Morton Dauwen Zabel (New York, 1951), p. 103.

23. William Blake, *Jerusalem*, I.10; Yeats, *A Vision* (New York, 1938), p. 8.

24. Coleridge, *Biographia Literaria*, ed. J. Shawcross, 2 vols. (Oxford, 1907), vol. 2, pp. 107, 111–13, 120–21.

25. I. A. Richards, *Coleridge on Imagination* (London, 1934), pp. 135–37.

26. Coleridge, *Biographia Literaria*, vol. 2, p. 6.

Rationality and Imagination in Cultural History

First published as "Rationality and Imagination in Cultural History: A Reply to Wayne Booth," *Critical Inquiry* 2 (1976): 447–64, then reprinted in Wayne C. Booth's *Critical Understanding: The Power and Limits of Pluralism* (Chicago, 1979), pp. 176–94. All page references in the text are to *Critical Understanding*. Reprinted by permission of the University of Chicago Press.

This essay was a response, invited by Wayne C. Booth, to Booth's treatment of Abrams's writings. In "M. H. Abrams: History as Criticism and the Plurality of Histories," published in *Critical Inquiry* (1976) and later included as a chapter in *Critical Understanding: The Power and Limits of Pluralism,* Booth discusses Abrams's methods and achievements, with special reference to his "pluralism." Booth situates pluralism between monism and relativism. Unlike extreme relativists, pluralists think that some critical views may be wrong; unlike monists, however, they claim that more than one critical view may be right. Booth's own pluralist viewpoint involves him in several problems, among them that of formulating criteria that will validate a diversity of critical views without holding all of them to a single, monistic standard. In exploring solutions to these problems, Booth turns to the writings of three self-described, though very different, pluralists: Kenneth Burke, R. S. Crane, and Abrams.

Noting that Abrams commits himself to the validity of—indeed, the need for—pluralism in literary criticism, in writings such as "What's the Use of Theorizing about the Arts?" and "A Note on Wittgenstein and Literary Criticism" [reprinted in this volume], Booth inquires whether Abrams's theoretical pluralism applies also to his books on critical, literary, and cultural history, *The Mirror and the Lamp* (1953) and especially *Natural Supernaturalism* (1971). After remarking that this was a question Abrams himself had not raised, Booth asks, "What kinds of knowledge can we hope for in humanistic inquiry? More specifically, what kinds of knowledge does Abrams provide?" (*Critical Understanding,* p. 141). He asserts that he is persuaded of the overall validity of Abrams's history in *Natural Supernaturalism,* but puts the question, "What right do I have to feel so thoroughly persuaded?" And also, "What alternative histories [of the same materials] could Abrams allow?" (p. 149).

The justifications Booth finds in the work for his right to feel persuaded of its historical validity are presented as especially problematic because the book evaluates in the course of describing the past, asserting not only that Wordsworth was a central Romantic poet and that he and his contemporaries produced great works in poetic and other genres, but also that the literary achievements of Romanticism remain highly relevant and valuable to us in our time. Booth contends that *Natural Supernaturalism* earns its description and assessment of Romantic achievements by such features as the range and pertinence of its historical references, its complex and adaptive organization, the cumulative effect of the multiplex historical connections it establishes, as well as the trust in the author's objectivity inspired by the quietness and "purity" of his style. What most surprises Booth is that *Natural Supernaturalism* seems to him to achieve what he, like many other critics, has thought impossible; that is, it employs "extrinsic" references to history to establish the high intrinsic value of the Romantic poetry it discusses. "Never before practiced in quite this form . . . it is finally a mode of criticism that proves a poem's greatness by discovering what kind of historical account you can give of it"; hence *Natural Supernaturalism* is "a great work of what might be called epideictic history, a history designed to show forth the greatness of the phenomena it explains" (pp. 159–61). But this assessment merely underlines the problem of pluralism: how to explain the possibility of "other legitimate histories of Abrams' subject, histories as imposing as his and yet contradicting him in many points, even important ones" (p. 168).

1. Coleridge, *Biographia Literaria*, ed. J. Shawcross, 2 vols. (Oxford, 1907), vol. 2, p. 64.
2. David Hume, *An Enquiry Concerning Human Understanding*, the concluding paragraph.
3. In *Critics and Criticism*, ed. R. S. Crane (Chicago, 1952), pp. 373–88; A. O. Lovejoy, *The Great Chain of Being* (Cambridge, Mass., 1936), chap. 10.
4. W. B. Gallie, "Essentially Contested Concepts," in *Philosophy and the Historical Understanding* (London, 1964), chap. 8. I don't mean to imply that contests about an essentially contested concept may not be profitable (though they are usually conducted in a very confusing way). My point is that arguments about the nature of "Romanticism" as such are on a different level from discussions about the accuracy and adequacy of a treatment of stipulated cultural phenomena within a stipulated period of time.
5. In my concluding paragraph (*Natural Supernaturalism*, p. 462), I add the judgment that the complex of ideas, motives, and values that I expound "has the best historical claim to be called the English Romantic tradition" on the ground that this complex was a central element in the burst of intellectual and imaginative creativity that many Romantic writers themselves recognized, related to the French Revolution, and specified as "the spirit of the age." See, for example, *Natural Supernaturalism*, pp. 11–12, 329–56, and 395–96.
6. Even Wayne Booth nods. He quotes on p. 156 the statement: "This region . . . is also *dimly remembered* in pagan myths. . . ." This indeed suggests a belief in a "Platonic" participation without historical causation; it is not, however, my own assertion, but what I cite Thomas Bur-

net as having asserted in *The Sacred Theory of the Earth* (*Natural Supernaturalism*, p. 100).

7. Spencer Hall, *Southern Humanities Review* 8 (1974): 246; E. D. Hirsch, *The Wordsworth Circle* 3 (1972): 19; and Morse Peckham, *Studies in Romanticism* 13 (1974): 364–65.

8. J. Hillis Miller, "Tradition and Difference," *Diacritics* 2 (1972): 11–12.

9. J. R. Bambrough, "Literature and Philosophy," in *Wisdom: Twelve Essays,* ed. J. R. Bambrough (Oxford, 1974).

10. In *Mill on Bentham and Coleridge,* ed. F. R. Leavis (London, 1950), pp. 99–100.

11. This partial circularity of humanistic demonstration (presuming between author and reader common grounds of consent in order to achieve consent) obtains also for the attempt by the poet to effect in his reader an understanding which involves imaginative consent to what his poem expresses. So Wordsworth suggests, in a passage that also bears on the question of his "optimism": "I am myself one of the happiest of men; and no man who does not partake of that happiness . . . can possibly comprehend the best of my poems" (cited from Henry Crabb Robinsons's *On Books and Their Writers,* ed. Edith J. Morley, 3 vols. [London, 1938], vol. 1, p. 73 [8 May 1812]).

Art-as-Such: The Sociology of Modern Aesthetics

From *Bulletin of the American Academy of Arts and Sciences* 38 (1985): 8–33. Reprinted by permission of the publisher. On April 10, 1985, Abrams was honored with the Academy of Arts and Sciences Humanistic Studies Award and delivered this lecture; an earlier version had been delivered to a Conference on the Enlightenment at Yale University in July 1975. Although the text reprinted here is that of the lecture at the American Academy, the author has added footnote references to the writings that it cites.

1. T. E. Hulme, *Speculations* (London, 1936), p. 136.

2. Iris Murdoch, *The Fire and the Sun: Why Plato Banished the Artists* (Oxford, 1977), pp. 76–77.

3. As James Hutton rightly stresses: "It must always be kept in mind that [Aristotle's] *Poetics* is not about poetry in some vague sense of the word but about the art of poetry; it is an 'art' or *techne* (how to compose successful poems)." Introduction to the *Poetics,* trans. and ed. James Hutton (New York, 1982), p. 9.

4. Kant *Critique of Aesthetic Judgement,* trans. James Creed Meredith (Oxford, 1911), p. 87. I have tried to translate more precisely than Meredith Kant's key phrases, and have inserted in brackets the original German.

5. Ibid., pp. 42–44, 48–49, 90, 69.

6. On the emergent concept in the eighteenth century of "the fine arts" as a distinctive class, see Paul Oskar Kristeller, "The Modern System of the Arts: A Study in the History of Aesthetics," *Journal of the History of Ideas* 12 (1951): 496–527, and 13 (1952): 17–46.

7. Henry Peacham, *The Complete Gentleman and Other Works,* ed. Virgil B. Heltzel (Ithaca, N.Y., 1962), p. 117.

8. "A Discourse on the Science of a Connoisseur," in *Works of Jonathan Richardson,* 3 vols. (London, 1773, 1792), vol. 3, pp. 241–44.

9. Ibid., pp. 266, 246, 338, 336. "The time will come when it shall be as dishonourable for a gentleman not to be a connoisseur, as now it is . . . not to see the beauties of a good author" (p. 337).

10. See Walter E. Houghton, Jr., "The English Virtuoso in the Seventeenth Century," *Journal of the History of Ideas* 3 (1942): 51–73, 190–219.

11. Alexandre Beljame, *Men of Letters and the English Public in the Eighteenth Century,* trans. E. O. Lorimer (London, 1948); Leslie Stephen, *English Literature and Society in the Eighteenth Century* (London, 1904); Arnold Hauser, *The Social History of Art,* 2 vols. (London, 1954), "The New Reading Public," vol. 2, pp. 534ff.; Ian Watt, *The Rise of the Novel* (Berkeley, Cal., 1957). In the sixteenth century and later, the English theater had been accessible, for pay, to a full spectrum of social classes. Insofar as it dealt with drama, however, poetic theory had concerned itself with published dramatic texts; it was not grounded on the viewpoint of a spectator during a stage presentation.

12. Cited in Percy M. Young, *The Concert Tradition from the Middle Ages to the Twentieth Century* (London, 1965), p. 77. On the development of public concerts in Europe and England, see also Henry Raynor, *A Social History of Music from the Middle Ages to Beethoven* (New York, 1972), and Stanley Sadie, "Concert Life in Eighteenth Century England," *Royal Musical Association Proceedings,* 9 Dec. 1958, pp. 17–30.

13. Ludwig Schudt, *Italienreisen im 17. und 18. Jahrhundert* (Vienna, 1959); Joseph Burke, "The Grand Tour and the Rule of Taste," *Studies in the Eighteenth Century* (1966), pp. 231–50; Hugh Trevor-Roper, *The Plunder of the Arts in the Seventeenth Century* (London, 1970).

14. Niels von Holst, *Creators, Collectors, and Connoisseurs* (London and New York, 1967); John Steegman, *The Rule of Taste from George I to George IV* (London, 1936); Frank Herrmann, ed., *The English as Collectors: A Documentary Chrestomathy* (London, 1972).

15. Von Holst, *Creators, Collectors, and Connoisseurs;* Alma S. Wittlin, *The Museum: Its History and Its Tasks in Education* (London, 1949); Elizabeth B. G. Holt, *The Triumph of Art for the Public* (Washington, D.C., 1979); Joseph Alsop, *The Rare Art Traditions* (New York, 1982).

16. Cited by Osbert Sitwell and Margaret Barton, "Taste," in *Johnson's England,* ed. A. S. Tuberville (Oxford, 1933), vol. 2, p. 38. Walpole lifted the pretentious mispronunciations of painters' names from Fielding's *Joseph Andrews* (1742), book 3, chap. 6.

17. Thomas Martyn, *The English Connoisseur* (Dublin, 1767), preface.

18. Esther Moir, *The Discovery of Britain: The English Tourists, 1540 to 1840* (London, 1964); John Harris, "English Country House Guides, 1740–1840," in *Concerning Architecture,* ed. John Summerson (London, 1968).

19. Harris, in Summerson, *Concerning Architecture,* pp. 59–60.

20. Most fully in "Kant and the Theology of Art," *Notre Dame English Journal* 13 (1981): 75–106; see also "From Addison to Kant: Modern Aesthetics and the Exemplary Art," in this volume.

21. Plato, *Symposium,* 210–12; *Philebus,* 59–60, 65, 67.

22. Plotinus, *Enneads*, trans. Stephen MacKenna, rev. by B. S. Page (London, 1956), pp. 380, 400–401, 619, 61–63, 409, 622–24.

23. *The Confessions of St. Augustine*, trans. F. J. Sheed (London and New York, 1944), X.xxxiv (pp. 196–97). The relevant terms and concepts cited in my text, repeated in a number of Augustine's writings, are collected in Anders Nygren, *Agape and Eros*, trans. Philip S. Watson (London, 1953), pp. 503–12, 532–48.

24. *Select Sermons of Dr. Whichcote* (London, 1698), p. 213; see also Shaftesbury's preface, and pp. 147, 151, 216, 409.

25. K. P. Moritz, "Versuch einer Vereinigung aller schönen Künste und Wissenschaften unter dem Begriff des in sich selbst Vollendeten," *Schriften zur Philosophie und Aesthetik*, ed. Fritz Bamberger (Tübingen, 1962), pp. 3–8. The emphases in my translation are Moritz's.

26. Wilhelm Heinrich Wackenroder, *Herzensergiessungen eines kunstliebenden Klosterbruders*, ed. Karl Detlev Jessen (Leipzig, 1904), pp. 100–103.

From Addison to Kant: Modern Aesthetics and the Exemplary Art.

From *Studies in Eighteenth-Century British Art and Aesthetics*, ed. Ralph Cohen (Berkeley, 1985). Reprinted by permission of the publisher, University of California Press. For expanded discussions of some of the matters treated here, see an essay by Abrams not included in this volume, "Kant and the Theology of Art," *Notre Dame English Journal* 13 (1981): 75–106.

1. See Paul Oskar Kristeller, "The Modern System of the Arts," *Journal of the History of Ideas* 12 (1951): 496–527; 13 (1952): 17–46.

2. Friedrich Schelling, *System des transcendentalen Idealismus, Sämtliche Werke* (Stuttgart und Augsburg, 1858), vol. 3, p. 349.

3. T. E. Hulme, *Speculations: Essays on Humanism and the Philosophy of Art*, ed. Herbert Read (London, 1924), p. 136.

4. Jerome Stolnitz, *Aesthetics and Philosophy of Art Criticism* (Cambridge, Mass., 1960), pp. 35, 209, 211. [For instances of the contemplation model in recent treatments of art by Stuart Hampshire and other "analytic philosophers," see, in this volume, "What's the Use of Theorizing about the Arts?" pp. 60–66. (Ed.)]

5. A. C. Bradley, "Poetry for Poetry's Sake," *Oxford Lectures on Poetry* (London, 1909), pp. 5–6.

6. E. M. Forster, "Anonymity: An Enquiry," *Two Cheers for Democracy* (New York, 1951), pp. 81–82.

7. See Jerome Stolnitz, "On the Significance of Lord Shaftesbury in Modern Aesthetic Theory," *Philosophical Quarterly* 2 (1961): 97–113; and "On the Origins of 'Aesthetic Disinterestedness,'" *Journal of Aesthetic and Art Criticism* 20 (1961–62): 131–43. For the history of the concepts of "contemplation" and "disinterestedness," before and after Shaftesbury, see M. H. Abrams, "Kant and the Theology of Art," *Notre Dame English Journal* (1981): 75–106.

8. K. P. Moritz, *Schriften zur Aesthetik und Poetik*, ed. Hans Joachim Schrimpf (Tübingen, 1962), p. 3. The emphases are Moritz's.

9. Ibid., pp. 6–8.

10. Ibid., p. 5. The emphasis on "love" is Moritz's.

11. Martha Woodmansee, "The Origin of the Doctrine of Literary Autonomy," paper delivered at the International Association for Philosophy and Literature, Orono, Maine, May 9, 1980. See the first chapter of Moritz's *Anton Reiser*.

12. *The Dialogues of Plato,* trans. B. Jowett, *Symposium,* 210–12; *Philebus,* 59–60, 67.

13. Plotinus, *Enneads,* trans. Stephen MacKenna, rev. by B. S. Page (London, 1956), pp. 380, 400–401, 619–20, 61–63, 409, 622–24.

14. See K. Svoboda, *L'Esthétique de St. Augustin et ses sources* (Brno, 1933), pp. 102ff. The relevant comments by Augustine on the distinction between love for use and love for enjoyment are conveniently collected in Anders Nygren, *Agape and Eros,* trans. Philip S. Watson (London, 1953), pp. 503–12, 532–48, footnotes. See also Abrams, "Kant and the Theology of Art."

    Jacques Maritain's theory of the fine arts is of interest because it reintegrates the contemplation of a work of art with the theological concept of the loving contemplation of God which earlier theorists had used as the model for developing a purely secular view of aesthetic experience. The work of art, says Maritain, "of its very nature and precisely as beautiful . . . stirs desire and produces love," in an ecstasy which the soul experiences in its fullness only "when it is absorbed . . . by the beauty of God." And on the express analogy of Scholastic views about contemplation of the divine wisdom, he declares that works of fine art are "disinterested, desired for themselves." A work is not made "in order that one may use it as a means, but in order that one may enjoy it as an end," and the "mode of being" of works of art "is contemplative . . . they aim at producing an intellectual delight, that is to say, a kind of contemplation" (*Art and Scholasticism and the Frontiers of Poetry,* trans. Joseph W. Evans [New York, 1962], pp. 23–37).

15. Kant *Critique of Aesthetic Judgement,* trans. James Creed Meredith (Oxford, 1911), pp. 43, 48–49, 69, 90; the emphases are Kant's. Where I have altered Meredith's translation, I have also inserted the German phrases.

16. Moritz, *Schriften zur Ästhetik und Poetik,* pp. 71, 73–74.

17. Kant, *Critique of Aesthetic Judgement,* p. 176.

18. In *Phaedrus* 250, for example, Plato says, in his account of the soul's journey to the realm of forms: "But of beauty, I repeat again that we saw her there shining in company with the celestial forms; and coming to earth we find her here too, shining in clearness through the clearest aperture of sense. For sight is the most piercing of our bodily senses. . . . This is the privilege of beauty, that being the loveliest she is also the most palpable to sight."

19. Clive Bell, *Art* (New York, 1958), pp. 54–55, 107.

20. On the sharp distinction between God's creation "out of nothing" and the poet's creation from pre-existing matter, see E. N. Tigerstedt, "The Poet as Creator: Origins of a Metaphor," *Comparative Literature Studies* 5 (1968): 455–88. Giovanni Capriano, in his *Della vera poetica* (1555), seems unique in his time by claiming that "the true poets must invent their poetry out of nothing" [*di nulla fingere la lor' poesia*]; he does not,

however, use the verb *creare*, which was a theological term reserved
uniquely for a power of God. Capriano is cited by Bernard Weinberg,
A History of Literary Criticism in the Italian Renaissance, 2 vols. (Chicago,
1963), vol. 2, p. 733.

Probably the earliest clear statement of the analogue between the
poet's activity and God's creativity is by Cristoforo Landino who, in the
"Proemio" to his *Commentary on Dante* (1481), said that the poet's feigning "is half-way between 'creating' [*creare*] which is proper only for God
. . . and 'making' [*fare*], which applies to men when they compose with
matter and form in any art [i.e., craft]. . . . Although the feigning [*fig-
mento*] of the poet is not entirely out of nothing, it nevertheless departs
from making and comes very near to creating." For similar passages
elsewhere in Landino, see Tigerstedt, pp. 458–59.

21. See Tigerstedt, "The Poet as Creator"; also M. H. Abrams, *The Mirror
and the Lamp* (New York, 1953), pp. 272–75, and notes, pp. 380–81.

22. Leonardo da Vinci in turn adapted to painting the parallel between
"the painter's mind" and "the divine mind"—with passing but unde-
veloped allusions to the painter as a "creator" and to aspects of his
work as "a creation"—in order to raise his own disparaged art over all
other arts, including poetry. See Martin Kemp, "From 'Mimesis' to
'Fantasia' . . . in the Visual Arts," *Viator* 8 (1970); 347–98.

23. Sir Philip Sidney, *An Apologie for Poetry*, in *Elizabethan Critical Essays*, ed.
G. Gregory Smith, 2 vols. (London, 1904), vol. 1, pp. 155–58. A parallel distinction between theoretical and laudatory aims is apparent in
J. C. Scaliger's influential *Poetices* (1561): "The basis of all poetry is
imitation," although imitation "is not the end of poetry, but is intermediate to the end" of giving "instruction in pleasurable form." It is
specifically in the attempt to elevate poetry over oratory and history
that Scaliger makes the later claim that it excels "those other arts" in
that while they "represent things just as they are . . . the poet depicts
another sort of nature," and thus "transforms himself almost into a
second God." For the poet, in making "images of things which are not"
as well as more beautiful images "of those things which are," exceeds
the historian and seems "like another God, to produce the things
themselves [*res ipsas . . . velut alter deus condere*]" (F. M. Padelford, *Select
Translations from J. C. Scaliger's Poetics* [New York, 1905], pp. 2, 7–8). I
have altered a few of Padelford's English phrases to bring them closer
to the Latin original.

24. Addison, *Spectator* 419. Addison had in mind the claims by empiricists
such as Thomas Hobbes that, since a poem is "an imitation of humane
life," the criterion of truth eliminates such elements as "impenetrable
Armors, Inchanted Castles . . . flying Horses." For, "the Resemblance
of truth is the utmost limit of Poeticall Liberty. . . . Beyond the actual
works of nature a Poet may now go; but beyond the conceived possibility of nature, never." Hobbes, "Answer to Davenant's Preface to
Gondibert" (1650), in *Critical Essays of the Seventeenth Century*, ed. J. E.
Spingarn, 3 vols. (Oxford, 1908), vol. 2, pp. 61–62. See Abrams, "Truth
and the Poetic Marvelous," in *The Mirror and the Lamp*, pp. 265–68.

25. *Spectator* 419 and 421. In lauding the poet as one who invents "another
nature," Sidney had already exemplified this power by reference to the
poet's ability to bring forth "formes such as never were in Nature, as
the Heroes, Demigods, Cyclops, Furies, and such like."

26. Baumgarten's *Reflections on Poetry*, trans. Karl Aschenbrenner and William B. Holther (Berkeley and Los Angeles, 1954), par. 115. In par. 116, Baumgarten goes on to apply the term *aesthetic* to "the science of perception" (which includes poetry in its scope), as distinguished from the noetic science of things that are "known by the superior faculty as the object of logic."

27. John Crowe Ransom, *The World's Body* (New York, 1938), pp. x, 205.

28. Ibid., pp. 206, 156–58, 130–33.

29. Ibid., pp. 44–45.

30. Leibniz to Arnaud, May 1686, in Leibniz, *Discourse on Metaphysics*, trans. George R. Montgomery (La Salle, Ill., 1947), pp. 108–09.

31. For Baumgarten's treatment in the *Aesthetica* of "heterocosmic fiction" as the creation of a "possible" new world, whose "heterocosmic truth" and "heterocosmic probability" are a matter of internal noncontradiction and coherence, see, e.g., pars. 441, 475, 511–38, 598–99.

   Georg Friedrich Meier, in his *Anfangsgründe aller schönen Wissenschaften* (1754), which is in large part an exposition of Baumgarten, declares that the "probability" of "heterocosmic fictions" such as fables is grounded "primarily on the fact that its inventor creates [*schaft*] a new world.... He draws the attention of his listener entirely to the coherence [*Zusammenhang*] that he has newly created. The listener so to speak forgets the present world ... and gets involved in an entirely new interconnection and order of things, and so must hold to be probable everything which is possible and grounded in the new order. These fictions are the ones in which a fine mind [*schöner Geist*] demonstrates his creative powers, or 'esprit créateur' ...." (part 1, par. 107).

32. Johann Jacob Breitinger, *Critische Dichtkunst* (1740), facsimile, ed. Wolfgang Bender, 2 vols. (Stuttgart, 1966), vol. 1, p. 273.

33. Johann Jacob Bodmer, *Critische Abhandlung von dem Wunderbaren in der Poesie* (1740), facsimile, ed. Wolfgang Bender (Stuttgart, 1966), pp. 165–66, 32.

34. Breitinger, *Critische Dichtkunst*, vol. 1, pp. 7, 54–57. It is noteworthy that in his "Formative Imitation of the Beautiful," written forty-five years later, Moritz also modeled his view of poetic creation on the creative power that God has delegated to a formative principle that operates within the natural world.

35. Bodmer, *Von dem Wunderbaren*, pp. 47, 49. See also pp. 144–45.

36. Breitinger, *Critische Dichtkunst*, vol. 1, pp. 425–26. See also pp. 270–78, 286–90. Breitinger explains that creative Nature, as Leibniz has shown, is constrained to bring into being the best of all possible worlds, and that since the concept of what is best entails the greatest possible diversity of existents, our world necessarily contains many degrees of imperfection. Relieved of God's constraint, however, the poet is able to bring over into being a world that is more perfect in its individual elements than our best of possible worlds (vol. 1, pp. 273–74).

37. Ibid., vol. 1, pp. 59–60. Breitinger repeats this assertion on p. 271.

38. Bodmer, *Critische Betrachtungen über die poetischen Gemälde der Dichter* (Zurich, 1741), p. 543.

39. Moritz, *Schriften zur Aesthetik*, pp. 73–75.

40. See, e.g., Breitinger's exposition of the poet's rendering of the nature that he imitates so as to enhance its moral qualities and effects: *Critische Dichtkunst*, vol. 1, pp. 282–90.

41. Moritz, *Schriften zur Aesthetik*, pp. 80, 83, 85–86. The emphases are Moritz's.

42. 18 May 1857, in Gustave Flaubert, *Correspondance* (Paris, 1926 ff.), vol. 4, p. 182.

43. 9 Dec. 1852, in *The Letters of Gustave Flaubert, 1830–1857*, trans. Francis Steegmuller (Cambridge, Mass., 1980), p. 173. See also 18 March 1857, p. 230: "The artist in his work must be like God in his creation—invisible and all-powerful: he must be everywhere felt but never seen."

   The basic text for this concept of God's relation to His created world is Paul's Epistle to the Romans, 1.20, which was the subject of endless comment and expansion by biblical commentators: "For the invisible things of Him from the creation of the world are clearly seen, being understood by the things that are made, even His eternal power and Godhead. . . ." In the 1790s, Friedrich Schlegel transferred this concept to the literary creator, as a ground for the mode of "Romantic irony": the literary artist, "visibly invisible," is both "objective" and "subjective" in his work; he establishes the illusion that his creation is a self-sufficient world, yet displays his own characteristics in that work, and is free to manifest his arbitrary power over that work. See Alfred Edwin Lussky, *Tieck's Romantic Irony* (Chapel Hill, N.C., 1932), chap. 2; and Abrams, *The Mirror and the Lamp*, pp. 237–41.

44. *Oeuvres complètes de Baudelaire*, ed. Y. G. Le Dantec and Claude Pichois (Bibliothèque de la Pléiade, 1963), pp. 637, 1037–38. The emphases are Baudelaire's.

45. "Notes nouvelles sur Edgar Poe," in *Oeuvres complètes de Charles Baudelaire*, ed F. F. Gautier and Y. G. Le Dantec (Paris, 1933), vol. 10, pp. 29–30.

   In Oscar Wilde's "The Critic as Artist," Ernest proposes that "it is the function of Literature to create, from the rough material of actual existence, a new world that will be more marvelous, more enduring, and more true than the world that common eyes look upon." If made by a great artist, "this new world . . . will be a thing so complete and perfect that there will be nothing left for the critic to do." To which Gilbert responds by adroitly transferring the creative analogue from the artist to the critic, and the concept of autonomy from the work of art to the work of criticism: "Criticism is, in fact, both creative and independent. . . . Nay, more, I would say that the highest Criticism . . . is in its way more creative than creation, as it . . . is, in fact, its own reason for existing, and, as the Greeks would put it, in itself, and to itself, an end." *The Artist as Critic: Critical Writings of Oscar Wilde*, ed. Richard Ellmann (New York, 1968–69), pp. 363–65.

46. *Oeuvres complètes de Stephane Mallarmé*, ed. Henri Mondor and G. Jean-Aubry (Bibliothèque de la Pléiade, 1961), pp. 400, 647.

47. Ibid., pp. 366–67, 372.

48. Vladimir Nabokov, *Lectures on Literature*, ed. Fredson Bowers (New York and London, 1980), p. 1.

49. Georg Lukács, *Writer and Critic and Other Essays*, trans. Arthur D. Kahn (New York, 1971), pp. 35–40.

50. Wassily Kandinsky, "Reminiscences," in *Modern Artists on Art*, ed. Robert L. Herbert (Englewood Cliffs, N.J., 1964), p. 35.

51. A. C. Bradley, *Oxford Lectures on Poetry* (London, 1909), pp. 4–5, 7.

52. Ibid., pp. 5, 17, 29.

53. Forster, *Two Cheers for Democracy*, pp. 82, 91–92, 85. R. G. Collingwood exemplifies the merging of the contemplative and heterocosmic models by a philosopher rather than a critic of art. "In art the mind has an object which it contemplates." But the object contemplated "is an imaginary object," created by the act of contemplation. "To imagine an object . . . is to be wholly indifferent to its reality," and the coherence of the imagined, hence simply contemplated, object "is a merely internal coherence . . . self-contained." Then, in a latter-day instance of the aesthetic application of a Leibnizian concept—this time, however, of Leibniz's concept of the monad:

> Every work of art as such, as an object of imagination, is a world wholly self-contained, a complete universe which has nothing outside it . . . [and is] imaginatively contemplated. . . . Every work of art is a monad, a windowless and self-contained universe which . . . indeed is nothing but a vision or perspective of the universe, and of a universe which is just itself. . . . Whatever is in it must have arisen from the creative act which constitutes it.

Outlines of a Philosophy of Art (London, 1925), pp. 10–24, 76.
54. Cleanth Brooks, "The Heresy of Paraphrase," in *The Well Wrought Urn* (New York, 1947), pp. 189, 194. Also Austin Warren, *Rage for Order* (Chicago, 1948), pp. v–vi: the poet's "final creation" is "a kind of world or cosmos; a concretely languaged, synoptically felt world, an ikon or image of the 'real world.' "
55. James Joyce, *A Portrait of the Artist as a Young Man*, in *The Portable James Joyce*, ed. Harry Levin (New York, 1947), pp. 481–82.

Five Types of Lycidas

This essay is based on a lecture given in 1957 at the Columbia Graduate Union and elsewhere. It first appeared in *Milton's Lycidas: The Tradition and the Poem*, ed. C. A. Patrides, foreword by M. H. Abrams (New York, 1961) and is reprinted from the revised edition (Columbia, Mo., 1983). Reprinted here by permission of the University of Missouri Press. The essay raises what has since become a central issue in critical theory: Does a poem have a decidable meaning?

1. Quotations without page references are from the following essays in *Milton's* Lycidas: *The Tradition and the Poem*, rev. ed.: E. M. W. Tillyard, "From *Milton*"; John Crowe Ransom, "A Poem Nearly Anonymous"; Richard P. Adams, "The Archetypal Pattern of Death and Rebirth in *Lycidas*"; Cleanth Brooks and John Edward Hardy, "Essays in Analysis: *Lycidas*"; and Northrop Frye, "Literature as Context: Milton's *Lycidas*."
2. See also Tillyard's analysis of *Lycidas* in *Poetry Direct and Oblique*, rev. ed. (London, 1948), pp. 81–84.
3. Cleanth Brooks and J. E. Hardy, eds., *Poems of Mr. John Milton* (New York, 1951), p. 259.

4. Ibid., pp. 256, 250.

5. I. A. Richards, *Science and Poetry* (London, 1926), pp. 47–48.

6. I have cited the original, extended form of this essay in *PMLA* 64 (1949): 183–88.

7. Northrop Frye, "Levels of Meaning in Literature," *Kenyon Review* 12 (1950): 258.

8. See J. M. French, "The Digressions in Milton's *Lycidas*," *Studies in Philology* 50 (1953): 486.

9. George Puttenham, *The Arte of English Poesie* (1589), in *Elizabethan Critical Essays*, ed. George G. Smith (New York, 1904), vol. 2, pp. 155, 27, 40.

10. Ibid., p. 156. In his epistle and gloss to Spenser's *Shepheardes Calender*, one of the chief models for *Lycidas*, E. K. has also emphasized the questions of stylistic decorum in the pastoral. He observed of the October Eclogue, which concerns poetry, that the style is properly "more loftye than the rest" and that at its inspired close Spenser's "verse groweth so big, that it seemeth he hath forgot the meanenesse of shepheards state and stile." (Ernest De Selincourt, ed., *Edmund Spenser: Minor Poems* [New York, 1910], pp. 101, 104.)

11. See R. S. Crane's analysis of critical interpretations as hypotheses for investigating the structures of poems, *The Languages of Criticism and the Structure of Poetry* (Toronto, 1953), pp. 164–83.

Postscript to "Five Types of Lycidas"

This essay appeared in *Milton's* Lycidas: *The Tradition and the Poem*, rev. ed., ed. C. A. Patrides (Columbia, Mo., 1983). It is reprinted by permission of the University of Missouri Press.

1. Two of these essays are referred to in the discussion that follows: Stanley E. Fish, "*Lycidas:* A Poem Finally Anonymous," and Isabel G. MacCaffrey, "*Lycidas:* The Poet in a Landscape."

2. Professor Fish has collected his theoretical essays, written over a span of ten years, in *Is There a Text in This Class?* (Cambridge, Mass., 1980). For his discussion of the evolution in his views during that period, see esp. the introduction, pp. 1–17.

Positivism and the Newer Criticism

This review of Philip Wheelwright's *The Burning Fountain: A Study in the Language of Symbolism* (Bloomington, Ind., 1954) appeared in *The Kenyon Review* 17 (Winter, 1955) under the title "The Newer Criticism: Prisoner of Logical Positivism?"—a title suggested by the journal's editor, John Crowe Ransom. It is reprinted by permission of *The Kenyon Review*.

Northrop Frye's Anatomy of Criticism

Abrams wrote this essay-review of *Anatomy of Criticism* (Princeton, 1957) at the request of the editors of the *University of Toronto Quarterly*. It appeared in *University of Toronto Quarterly* 28 (1959): 190–96. It is reprinted by permission of the publisher, University of Toronto Press.

The Deconstructive Angel

This essay appeared in *Critical Inquiry* 3 (1977): 423–38. Reprinted by permission of the University of Chicago Press. Abrams's first sustained response to deconstruction, "The Deconstructive Angel," was read at the MLA Convention in December 1976, at the initial session of the Division on Philosophical Approaches to Literature, chaired by the late Sheldon Sacks, editor of *Critical Inquiry*. The session also included papers by Wayne C. Booth and J. Hillis Miller; all three papers were published in the same issue of *Critical Inquiry*, under the general heading, "The Limits of Pluralism."

As Abrams explains, this session had been arranged by Sacks as a forum for discussing issues concerning Miller's mode of deconstructive criticism which had been raised by Booth and Abrams in a dialogue published in *Critical Inquiry* in 1976. (Abrams's contribution to this dialogue, "Rationality and Imagination in Cultural History," is reprinted in this volume.) Miller's review of *Natural Supernaturalism* ("Tradition and Difference," *Diacritics* 2 [1972]) had figured in both Abrams's and Booth's essays as an especially challenging treatment of the book. Citing *Natural Supernaturalism* as an instance of "the grand tradition of modern humanistic scholarship," Miller had adverted to Derrida, Nietzsche, and other writers in order to put to question Abrams's underlying assumptions, and above all the assumption that a literary or philosophical text has a determinate and determinable meaning.

1. "Rationality and Imagination in Cultural History: A Reply to Wayne Booth," *Critical Inquiry* 2 (1976): 456–60. (Reprinted in this volume.)
2. Miller, "Tradition and Difference," *Diacritics* 2 (1972): 6.
3. Ibid., pp. 10–11.
4. Ibid., pp. 8, 12.
5. Ibid.
6. Richard Rorty, ed., *The Linguistic Turn* (Chicago and London, 1967).

[Rorty points out, p. 9, that he has adopted the phrase "the linguistic turn" from the philosopher Gustav Bergman. (Ed.)]

7. Jacques Derrida, "La Double séance," in *La Dissémination* (Paris, 1972), p. 203.

8. Derrida, "La Mythologie blanche: la métaphore dans le texte philosophique," in *Marges de la philosophie* (Paris, 1972), p. 304. Translations throughout are my own.

9. Ferdinand de Saussure, *Course in General Linguistics,* trans. Wade Baskin (New York, 1959), pp. 117–21.

10. Derrida, "La Différance," in *Marges de la philosophie,* pp. 12–14, 25.

11. Ibid., pp. 23–24.

12. In the traditional or "classic" theory of signs, as Derrida describes the view that he dismantles, the sign is taken to be "a deferred presence . . . the circulation of signs defers the moment in which we will be able to encounter the thing itself, to get hold of it, consume or expend it, touch it, see it, have a present intuition of it" (ibid., p. 9). See also "Hors livre" in *La Dissémination,* pp. 10–11.

13. Derrida, "La Structure, le signe et le jeu dans le discours des sciences humaines," in *L'Écriture et la différence* (Paris, 1967), p. 411.

14. Ibid., p. 427. Derrida adds that this "interpretation of interpretation," which "affirms free-play . . . tries to pass beyond man and humanism. . . ." On the coming "monstrosity," see also *De la grammatologie* (Paris, 1967), p. 14.

15. Derrida, "La Structure, le signe," p. 428. "We possess no language . . . which is alien to this history; we cannot express a single destructive proposition which will not already have slipped into the form, the logic, and the implicit postulates of that very thing that it seeks to oppose." "Each limited borrowing drags along with it all of metaphysics" (pp. 412–13).

16. J. Hillis Miller, "Stevens' Rock and Criticism as Cure, II," *The Georgia Review* 30 (1976): 335–36.

17. Miller, "Walter Pater: A Partial Portrait," *Daedalus* 105 (1976): 107.

18. See, for example, his unfolding of the meanings of *cure* and *absurd* in "Stevens' Rock and Criticism as Cure," I, *The Georgia Review* 30 (1976): 6–11. For his analysis of significance in the altering shapes, through history, of the printed form of a word, see his exposition of *abyme,* ibid., p. 11; also his exposition of the letter *x* in "Ariadne's Thread: Repetition and the Narrative Line," *Critical Inquiry* 3 (1976): 75–76.

19. Miller, "Tradition and Difference," p. 12.

20. See, e.g., Miller, "Stevens' Rock," I, pp. 9–11; idem, "Walter Pater," p. 111.

21. Miller, "Walter Pater," p. 98; idem, "Stevens' Rock, II," p. 333.

22. Miller, "Ariadne's Thread," p. 66.

23. Miller, "Walter Pater," p. 112.

24. Miller, "Stevens' Rock, II," p. 341. See also "Walter Pater," p. 101, and "Adriadne's Thread," p. 74.

25. Miller, "Stevens' Rock," I, pp. 11–12. The unnameable abyss which Miller glimpses has its parallel in the unnameable and terrifying monstrosity which Derrida glimpses; see pp. 244–45 in this volume.

26. Miller, "Deconstructing the Deconstructors," *Diacritics* 5 (1975): 30.

27. "Steven's Rock, II," p. 337.

Behaviorism and Deconstruction

Written in response to Morse Peckham's "The Infinitude of Plu-ralism," *Critical Inquiry* 3 (1977): 803–16, this essay appeared in *Critical Inquiry* 4 (1977): 181–93. Reprinted by permission of the University of Chicago Press. All page references are to Peckham's essay.

"The Deconstructive Angel" (reprinted in this volume) evoked a number of responses, one of them by the distinguished Romantic scholar and literary critic Morse Peckham in "The Infinitude of Pluralism." Peckham is more severe than Abrams in rejecting the validity of J. Hillis Miller's deconstructive criticism, but he does so on the basis of his own behavioral theory of language—the view that the meaning of a spoken or written utterance is the appro-priate behavioral response to that utterance. Derrida and Miller, Peckham claims, don't deconstruct a text but only "an individual's ability to respond" to the text, in the same way that recourse to a mystic discipline, or to drugs, would disorder a reader's response. In fact, "were Miller consistent he would rapidly be reduced either to catatonia or to speaking in tongues."

  Peckham undertakes to show that his own behavioral paradigm for the meaning of an utterance is adequate to account for the valid interpretive procedures of cultural historians, and specifically for Abrams's "behavior" in composing *Natural Supernaturalism,* in which he disengages "the Fall-Redemption semiotic pattern" from a series of early texts, then shows how in the Romantic period it was given "a semiotic transformation," which Abrams calls the "seculariza-tion" of the Christian pattern. Peckham attributes to post-Romantic applications of this secularized redemptionism a large share of the responsibility for the "brutal and bloody authoritarianism" of our century, especially the horrors "perpetrated by Hitler and Stalin." In consequence, however invalid Peckham considers deconstruc-tion, he attributes to it the inadvertent virtue that, as part of a growing "analytic" movement in our time, it may help to destroy the Romantic ideology of secular redemptionism, together with the brutal authoritarianism which that ideology has effected in political practice.

1. J. Hillis Miller, "The Critic as Host," *Critical Inquiry* 3 (1977): 439.

How to Do Things with Texts

An expanded version of a paper read at the Lionel Trilling Seminar, Columbia University, February 23, 1978, this essay appeared in *Partisan Review* 46 (1979): 566–88. Reprinted by permission of the publisher.

Quotations from works that are not named in the text are from the following sources.

Michel Foucault: *Les Mots et les choses* (Paris, 1966); "What Is an Author?" *Partisan Review* (1975).

Edward Said: "*Abecedarium culturae:* structuralism, absence, writing," *TriQuarterly* (1971).

Jacques Derrida: *De la grammatologie* (Paris, 1967), trans. Gayatri Chakravorty Spivak (Baltimore, 1976); *La Structure, le signe et le jeu dans le discours des sciences humaines,* in *L'Écriture et la différence* (Paris, 1967); "Positions," Parts I and II, *Diacritics* (Winter, 1971 and Spring, 1973); "Différance," in *Speech and Phenomena and Other Essays on Husserl's Theory of Signs,* trans. David B. Allison (Evanston, Ill., 1973); "White Mythology: Metaphor in the Text of Philosophy," *New Literary History* 6 (1974); "Signature Event Context," *Glyph* 1 (1977); "Limited Inc abc . . . ," *Glyph* 2 (1978).

Stanley Fish: "Literature in the Reader: Affective Stylistics" (1970), reprinted in *Self-Consuming Artifacts* (Berkeley, 1972); "What Is Stylistics and Why Are They Saying Such Terrible Things about It?" in *Approaches to Poetics,* ed. Seymour Chatman (1973); "Facts and Fictions: A Reply to Ralph Rader," *Critical Inquiry* 1 (1975); "Interpreting the *Variorum,*" *Critical Inquiry* 2 (1976); "Interpreting Interpreting the *Variorum,*" *Critical Inquiry* 3 (1977).

Harold Bloom: *The Anxiety of Influence* (New York, 1973); *A Map of Misreading* (New York, 1975); *Kabbalah and Criticism* (New York, 1975); *Poetry and Repression* (New Haven, 1976).

Construing and Deconstructing

This essay, Abrams's fullest and most systematic analysis of deconstruction and its use in criticism, was given as a guest lecture in 1983, in a course at the University of New Mexico taught by Morris Eaves and Michael Fischer, who then published it in *Romanticism and Contemporary Criticism* (Ithaca, N.Y., 1986), which they edited. Reprinted by permission of Cornell University Press.

1. David Hume, *A Treatise of Human Nature*, ed. L. A. Selby-Bigge (Oxford, 1928), pp. 67, 73, 197, 265.

2. Jacques Derrida, "Structure, Sign, and Play in the Discourse of the Human Sciences," in *The Language of Criticism and the Sciences of Man*, ed. Richard Macksey and Eugenio Donato (Baltimore, 1970), pp. 272 ff., "Discussion."

3. Jacques Derrida, *Of Grammatology,* trans. Gayatri Spivak (Baltimore, 1976), p. 163; see also p. 158.

4. Derrida, "Structure, Sign, and Play," p. 249. See also Derrida, *Dissemination*, trans. Barbara Johnson (Chicago, 1981), p. 5.

5. Hume, *Treatise*, p. 264.

6. Ibid., pp. 265, 183, 269–70.

7. Derrida, "Signature Event Context," *Glyph* 1 (1977): 195.

8. Derrida, "Structure, Sign, and Play," pp. 264–65.

9. See, for example, in Derrida's "Structure, Sign, and Play," "Discussion," pp. 270–71; "Signature Event Context," pp. 174, 193; *Dissemination*, pp. 43–44.

10. "Différance," in Derrida, *Speech and Phenomena*, trans. David B. Allison (Evanston, Ill., 1973), p. 156.

11. Derrida, "Signature Event Context," pp. 174, 192. See also Derrida, "Living On: Border Lines," in *Deconstruction and Criticism*, ed. Geoffrey Hartman (New York, 1979), p. 78: "Hence no context is saturable any more. . . . No meaning can be fixed or decided upon." And p. 81: "No meaning can be determined out of context, but no context permits saturation."

12. Derrida, "Signature Event Context," pp. 172, 186, 191.

13. Ibid., pp. 174, 193, 195.

14. Derrida, "Living On: Border Lines," pp. 83, 142.

15. Ibid., pp. 83–84.

16. E.g., *Of Grammatology*, p. 243: Rousseau's "declared intention is not annulled . . . but rather *inscribed* within a system which it no longer dominates." "Signature Event Context," p. 192: In "a differential typology of forms of iteration . . . the category of intention will not disappear; it will have its place, but from that place it will no longer be able to govern the entire scene and system of utterance."

17. *Of Grammatology*, p. 158. Derrida adds (pp. 158–59) that obedience to the exigencies of standard interpretive commentary, though it is an "indispensable guardrail," "has always only *protected*, it has never *opened* a reading." A critical reading, however, that recognizes that, in the inescapable lack of a "natural presence," a text "has never been anything but writing"—that is, "substitutive significations which could only come forth in a chain of differential references"—"opens" meaning and language, as he puts it, "to infinity."

18. Hume, *Treatise*, pp. 182, 186–87, 267. Hume's idiom for describing his dilemmas at times converges with that favored by Derrida. For example, he declares in the *Treatise* that in reconsidering his section on the self, or personal identity, he finds himself "involv'd in such a labyrinth, that . . . I neither know how to correct my former opinions, nor how to render them consistent," and ends in the undecidability of what Derrida calls the "double bind" of an "aporia": "In short there are two principles, which I cannot render consistent; nor is it in my power to renounce either of them" (appendix, pp. 633, 636).

19. Ibid., pp. 270, 273.
20. Derrida, *Of Grammatology*, pp. 24, 314, 164; also "Structure, Sign, and Play," pp. 250–51: "We have no language—no syntax and no lexicon—which is alien to this history [of metaphysics]; we cannot utter a single deconstructive proposition which has not already slipped in the form, the logic, and the implicit postulations of precisely what it seeks to contest. . . . Every particular borrowing drags along with it the whole of metaphysics."
21. Derrida, *Of Grammatology*, p. 14; idem, "Structure, Sign, and Play," p. 264; "Différance," p. 159.
22. Derrida, in "Structure, Sign, and Play," "Discussion," p. 271.
23. Derrida: "White Mythology: Metaphor in the Text of Philosophy," *New Literary History* 6 (1974): 48–49; "Living On," p. 91; *Dissemination*, pp. 25–26. See also "Signature Event Context," pp. 173, 181, 188, 195.
24. Paul de Man, introduction to the special issue entitled "The Rhetoric of Romanticism," *Studies in Romanticism* 28 (1979): 498.
25. J. Hillis Miller, "On Edge: The Crossways of Contemporary Criticism," in *Romanticism and Contemporary Criticism*, ed. Morris Eaves and Michael Fischer (Ithaca, N.Y., 1986), p. 110. Subsequent references are inserted in the text.
26. Miller identifies the "she" referred to in the poem as "Lucy" on the standard ground that we have convincing reasons to believe that Wordsworth intended "A Slumber" to be one of a group of five short lyrics—what Miller calls "the Lucy poems as a group" (p. 106). In the other four poems, the girl is named as "Lucy," and as one of the poems puts it, "she is in her grave, and, oh, / The difference to me!"
27. The disagreement about "A Slumber" between Cleanth Brooks and F. W. Bateson (which E. D. Hirsch has publicized and made a notable interpretive crux) has to do solely with this issue. (See E. D. Hirsch, Jr., *Validity in Interpretation* [New Haven, 1967], pp. 227–30.) Both readers construe the text as signifying that a girl who was alive in stanza 1 is dead in stanza 2; their disagreement is about what we are to infer about the speaker's state of mind from the terms in which he represents the circumstances of her death. Brooks says that the closing lines "suggest . . . [his] agonized shock at the loved one's present lack of motion . . . her utter and horrible inertness"; Bateson claims that his "mood" mounts to "the pantheistic magnificence of the last two lines. . . . Lucy is actually more alive now that she is dead, because she is now a part of the life of Nature, and not just a human 'thing.'" Miller's description of the lyric speaker's state of mind seems to me much better attuned to what the speaker says than either of these extreme versions.

Almost all of the many critics who have written about "A Slumber" agree with Miller's construal of the basic situation—a lyric speaker confronting the fact that a girl who seemed invulnerable to aging and death is now dead; they differ mainly in their explication of the overtones and significance of the presented facts. The one drastic divergence I know of is that proposed by Hugh Sykes Davies, in "Another New Poem by Wordsworth," *Essays in Criticism* 15 (1965): 135–61. Davies argues against the evidence that Wordsworth intended "A Slumber" to be one of the Lucy group and suggests that Wordsworth intended the "she" in the third line to refer back to "spirit" in the first line; hence that the text is to be construed as a poem about a trance state of the speaker's own spirit. Such a reading seems to me to be not impossible, but extremely unlikely. What Davies's essay does serve to indicate is that no construal of a poem can, by reference to an infallible criterion, be absolutely certain; it is a matter of adequate assurance, as confirmed by the consensus of other competent readers.

28. Paul de Man, "The Rhetoric of Temporality," in *Interpretation: Theory and Practice*, ed. Charles S. Singleton (Baltimore, 1969), pp. 205–6.
29. Paul de Man, *Allegories of Reading* (New Haven, Conn., 1979), p. 205; see also p. 131.
30. As Miller puts it, the poem instances the way in which, in any "given work of literature . . . metaphysical assumptions are both present and at the same time undermined by the text itself" ("On Edge," p. 101).
31. From *The Abelard Folk Song Book*, ed. Abner Graboff (New York and London, 1958).
32. Derrida, "White Mythology," p. 74.

A Colloquy on Recent Critical Theories

Following Abrams's lecture "Construing and Deconstructing" at the University of New Mexico (reprinted in this volume), there was a question-and-answer session with the audience which was edited and printed as a postscript to the lecture by Morris Eaves and Michael Fischer in *Romanticism and Contemporary Criticism* (1986). The colloquy is reprinted here as a separate item because, in addition to enlarging upon Abrams's engagement with deconstruction over the preceding decade, it ranges widely over the New Criticism, Frye's comprehensive system of literature, Stanley Fish's theory of interpretive communities, and poststructuralist views of writing and reading as a mode of *Machtpolitik*, and deals also with theoretical issues raised by Abrams's own writings on literature and on criticism.

On Political Readings of Lyrical Ballads

This was a lecture given between the fall of 1987 and the spring of 1988 at the New York Public Library and elsewhere, in association with the traveling exhibition "William Wordsworth and the Age of English Romanticism."

1. Stephen Greenblatt, ed., *Representing the English Renaissance* (Berkeley, 1988), introduction, p. viii.
2. Irving Howe, *Politics and the Novel* (New York, 1987), p. 253.

3. Marjorie Levinson, *Wordsworth's Great Period Poems* (Cambridge, England, 1986), pp. 6, 18, 2, 101, 107, 113.

4. Jerome McGann, *The Romantic Ideology: A Critical Investigation* (Chicago, 1983), pp. 3, 11.

5. Ibid., pp. 12, 89; see also p. 134.

6. Levinson, *Wordsworth's Great Period Poems*, pp. 130, 103, 10.

7. McGann, *The Romantic Ideology*, p. 91; Levinson, *Wordsworth's Great Period Poems*, pp. 8–9.

8. The impossibility of countering a predetermined political reading is exemplified on a small scale by McGann's treatment (pp. 68–9) of Wordsworth's eight-line poem, "A Slumber Did My Spirit Seal," and by Levinson's divergent interpretation of the same poem, p. 125.

9. Michael H. Friedman, *The Making of a Tory Humanist* (New York, 1979), pp. 191–92.

10. Roger Sales, *English Literature in History, 1780–1830: Pastoral and Politics* (New York, 1983), p. 63. Even Heather Glen, who illuminates what was distinctive in Wordsworth's ballads in their time, nonetheless finds, in contrast to Blake's *Songs of Innocence,* "an implicit affirmation of the primacy of the polite point of view." Wordsworth's portrayal of Simon Lee, for example, is "never entirely free of condescension"; and the blow of the mattock with which the narrator severs the root at which the old man has been vainly hacking—which, Glen remarks, "in its violence seems almost like castration"—"completes that belittlement of him which has been implicitly present in the tone throughout," and so serves as an "image for the unwitting ease of the paternalistic 'pity' which diminishes that which is to the suffering other impossible" (*Vision and Disenchantment: Blake's "Songs" and Wordsworth's "Lyrical Ballads"* [Cambridge, England, 1983], pp. 236–37).

11. Robert Mayo, "The Contemporaneity of the *Lyrical Ballads,*" *PMLA* 69 (1954): 486–522.

12. "Mr. Wordsworth," in *The Spirit of the Age; The Complete Works of William Hazlitt,* ed. P. P. Howe (London, 1932), vol. 11, p. 87. Although Hazlitt couldn't have known it, his political analysis of Wordsworth's early poetry paralleled what Wordsworth himself had asserted in *The Prelude* of 1805—that he had discovered that his vocation as an original poet lay in a shift of his revolutionary and democratic creed from the realm of politics into that of poetry. See *The Prelude* (1805), Book XII, lines 45–312.

13. Paul M. Zall, ed., *Literary Criticism of William Wordsworth* (Lincoln, Nebraska, 1966), pp. 10, 16–17.

14. Ibid., pp. 182–83. In this passage and its context, both Wordsworth's argument and his syntax are tortuous. He poses the question, "Where lies the real difficulty of creating the taste by which a truly original Poet is to be relished?" then proceeds to answer it by a series of rhetorical questions, each of which proposes a difficulty in altering his readers' taste, although not "the *real*" (that is, the supreme, most demanding) difficulty. Wordsworth then asserts the principle that a reader's taste for poetry is not simply a passive responsiveness to proffered knowledge; hence, the supreme difficulty for a writer is to evoke an active cooperation, or "power," on the part of a reader, adapted to the originality of his poetry: "Therefore to create taste is to call forth and bestow

power, of which knowledge is the effect; and *there* lies the true difficulty" (p. 184).

15. Ibid., p. 185.

16. Levinson, *Wordsworth's Great Period Poems,* pp. 37–38; Kenneth R.
Johnston, "The Politics of 'Tintern Abbey,'" *The Wordsworth Circle* 14
(1983): 13. In reading Wordsworth, Johnston does not apply the neo-
Marxist hypothesis that all Wordsworth's poems are ideological representations; instead, he applies to Wordsworth's early nature poems the
hypothesis that they are troubled attempts "to satisfactorily establish
the connection between landscape viewing and social responsibility" (p.
9; see also p. 7).

17. Mary Moorman, *William Wordsworth: A Biography,* vol. 1 (Oxford, 1957),
pp. 402–3.

18. See the quotations in Levinson, *Wordsworth's Great Period Poems,* pp.
29–32.

19. A few examples of eighteenth-century titles of prospect-poems: Lady
Mary Wortley Montagu, "Verses written in the Chiask at Pera, over-
looking Constantinople, December 26, 1718"; Thomas Gibbons, "A View
from Hay-Cliff near Dover, June, 1749"; Henry James Pye, "Ode,
Written at Eaglehurst, which commands a View of Spithead, October
10, 1790." For the continuation of such titular specifications in the
Romantic era, see M. H. Abrams, "Structure and Style in the Greater
Romantic Lyric," in *The Correspondent Breeze: Essays on English Romanticism* (New York, 1984), pp. 83–89.

20. Levinson, *Wordsworth's Great Period Poems,* pp. 15–16, 55. Kenneth
Johnston, giving reasons for conjecturing that Wordsworth might have
completed the poem one day later than the title specifies, proposes that
Wordsworth may have "turned its clock back twenty-four hours, to
avoid setting off the powerful buried charges that would be exploded,"
if the poem had been dated July 14, the *quatorze juillet* ("The Politics of
'Tintern Abbey,'" p. 13).

21. Levinson, *Wordsworth's Great Period Poems,* pp. 18, 25. David Simpson's
political reading of "Tintern Abbey" as an "example of displacement
rather than of the Wordsworthian affirmation of nature and imaginative memory" parallels that of Levinson and McGann. See his *Wordsworth's Historical Imagination: The Poetry of Displacement* (New York and
London, 1987), pp. 109–13.

22. McGann, *The Romantic Ideology,* pp. 1–2; see also p. 13.

23. Coleridge to John Thelwall, 17 December 1796, *Collected Letters,* ed.
E. L. Griggs (Oxford, 1956), vol. 1, p. 279. On 13 May of that year
Coleridge had written to Thelwall, "Why pass an act of *Uniformity* against
Poets?—I received a letter from a very sensible friend abusing Love-
verses—another blaming the introduction of Politics. . . . *Some for each—*
is my Motto. That Poetry pleases which interests" (p. 215).

24. Lines 36–50, 94–103, 31–36, and 108–12. I cite throughout the text
of "Tintern Abbey" as Wordsworth published it in *Lyrical Ballads,* 1798.
The passage on the "presence . . . that rolls through all things," by the
way, if it is a Romantic ideological representation, nonetheless echoes
the description of the *spiritus mundi* in Wordsworth's revered predecessor Virgil, in *Aeneid* VI, pp. 724 ff.

25. Wordsworth to Isabella Fenwick, in *The Poetical Works,* ed. E. de Selincourt and Helen Darbishire (Oxford, 1947), vol. 4, pp. 463–64.

26. Lines 50–58. In accord with his ruling political hypothesis, McGann (p. 88) reads "If this be a vain belief" not as a reference to the immediately preceding assertion that "We see into the life of things," but as one of the moves whereby Wordsworth "displaces" unpleasant socio-economic facts and his ruined political hopes "into a spiritual economy where disaster is self-consciously transformed into the threat of disaster."

27. Levinson, *Wordsworth's Great Period Poems*, p. 41; McGann, *The Romantic Ideology*, p. 90. Both these readers apparently attribute the artistic greatness of "Tintern Abbey" to the intricacy and efficacy of its tactics of displacement and evasion. As McGann says, p. 88, with reference to the process by which Wordsworth "displaces" political disaster first into a threat and then a hope, and also converts political loss into seeming spiritual gain: "The greatness of this great poem lies in the clarity and candor with which it dramatizes not merely this event, but the structure of this event." And Levinson, p. 56: the poem's "identity, or peculiar virtue, in Pater's sense, resides in its particular patterns of displacement."

28. William James, *Principles of Psychology*, 2 vols. (New York, 1890), vol. 2, chap. 25.

29. Levinson, *Wordsworth's Great Period Poems*, pp. 5–6, 24–25. McGann, *The Romantic Ideology*, p. 87, comments on "The picture of the mind revives again": "The abbey associated with 1793 fades . . . and in its disappearing outlines we begin to discern not a material reality" but, by an act of "spiritual displacement," the "landscape of Wordsworth's emotional needs."

30. McGann, *The Romantic Ideology*, p. 88; Johnston, "The Politics of 'Tintern Abbey,' " p. 12 (see also p. 7); James K. Chandler, *Wordsworth's Second Nature: A Study of the Poetry and Politics* (Chicago, 1984), pp. 8–9.

31. To J. H. Reynolds, 3 May 1818, *The Letters of John Keats*, ed. Hyder Edward Rollins, 2 vols. (Cambridge, Mass., 1958), vol. 1, pp. 277–82.

32. Keats's comparison of Wordsworth to Milton, in their treatment of human suffering, is clarified in his later letter of 15 April 1819; see *Letters*, vol. 2, pp. 101–3. In that letter Keats replaced the simile of life as a sequence of chambers by the simile of the world as "The vale of Soul-Making," and (still in parallel with Wordsworth's theme in "Tintern Abbey,") justified the human experience of "a World of Pains and Troubles" as "necessary . . . to school an Intelligence and make it a Soul," and thus to give it "the sense of Identity."

33. McGann, *The Romantic Ideology*, pp. 87–88; Heather Glen, *Vision and Disenchantment*, pp. 257–58; Levinson, *Wordsworth's Great Period Poems*, pp. 37–38. And see pp. 45–46: "the turn to Dorothy, then, is a move toward otherness, or toward a social reality," by making her "a kind of alienated *tabula rasa*"; and p. 49. Also Simpson, *Wordsworth's Historical Imagination*, p. 110: the poem acknowledges "access to a community. . . . But it is a self-reflecting community, for what he sees in Dorothy is an image of his former self"; and p. 113: his final turn is toward "the desperately limited version of the social world represented by Dorothy."

34. Rollins, *The Letters of John Keats*, vol. 1, pp. 387, 282.

35. Stephen Greenblatt, *Renaissance Self-Fashioning: From More to Shakespeare* (Chicago, 1980), p. 4.
36. McGann, *The Romantic Ideology*, p. 71; see also pp. 69, 134.
37. Jerome J. McGann, *The Beauty of Inflections: Literary Investigations in Historical Method and Theory* (Oxford, 1985), p. 158; see also his *The Romantic Ideology*, p. 13. Similarly Levinson, *Wordsworth's Great Period Poems*, p. 57, voices the need for an "enabling, alienated purchase on the poems we study," and on p. 129 says: "It is precisely the contradictions and the formal ruptures . . . beneath that smooth surface that endear ['Peele Castle'] to readers who thereby know it *as* a work, a work profoundly of its time, and one which therefore and thereby, criticizes our work and our time."

Index